BUILDING BLOCKS
for
Social-Emotional
Learning

Creating Safe, Secure, and Successful Elementary Schools

TRACEY A. HULEN &
ANN-BAILEY LIPSETT

Foreword by Claudia M. Gold

Solution Tree | Press

a division of
Solution Tree

555 North Morton Street
Bloomington, IN 47404
800.733.6786 (toll free) / 812.336.7700
FAX: 812.336.7790
email: info@SolutionTree.com

SolutionTree.com

Visit **go.SolutionTree.com/instruction** to download the free reproducibles in this book.

Printed in the United States of America

Library of Congress Cataloging-in-Publication Data

Names: Hulen, Tracey A., author. | Lipsett, Ann-Bailey, author.
Title: Building blocks for social-emotional learning : creating safe,
    secure, and successful elementary schools / Tracey A. Hulen, Ann-Bailey
    Lipsett.
Description: Bloomington, IN : Solution Tree Press, 2021. | Includes
    bibliographical references and index.
Identifiers: LCCN 2021044107 (print) | LCCN 2021044108 (ebook) | ISBN
    9781952812477 (paperback) | ISBN 9781952812484 (ebook)
Subjects: LCSH: Affective education. | Social learning--Study and teaching
    (Elementary) | Emotional intelligence. | Cognition in children. |
    Education, Elementary--Aims and objectives.
Classification: LCC LB1072 .H85 2021 (print) | LCC LB1072 (ebook) | DDC
    370.15/34--dc23
LC record available at https://lccn.loc.gov/2021044107
LC ebook record available at https://lccn.loc.gov/2021044108

Solution Tree
Jeffrey C. Jones, CEO
Edmund M. Ackerman, President

Solution Tree Press
President and Publisher: Douglas M. Rife
Associate Publisher: Sarah Payne-Mills
Managing Production Editor: Kendra Slayton
Editorial Director: Todd Brakke
Art Director: Rian Anderson
Copy Chief: Jessi Finn
Production Editor: Alissa Voss
Content Development Specialist: Amy Rubenstein
Acquisitions Editor: Sarah Jubar
Proofreader: Jessi Finn
Text and Cover Designer: Kelsey Hergül
Editorial Assistants: Charlotte Jones, Sarah Ludwig, and Elijah Oates

Acknowledgments

My learning journey started when I was a student at The Pennsylvania State University, where I had the opportunity to engage in a full year of student teaching with my outstanding mentor, Brenda Khayat. During that year working alongside her in a fifth-grade classroom, I was able to see and experience effective relationship building with students, their families, and colleagues. I was awestruck by the seamless skills she had crafted over her teaching career and for her establishment of a supportive, healthy classroom environment. This experience was not only the catalyst for my own learning, but it also ignited a lifelong passion for how to support effective healthy learning environments in all settings and for all children.

To my supportive and loving parents and family, especially my encouraging husband, thank you for your partnership on this journey and your openness and willingness to learn new ideas, try new things, and put forth immense efforts into our exceptional little family.

I also owe so much to my three beautiful children (TJ, Nate, and Kyle). You have been my motivation for learning and inspiring my passion for social-emotional learning (SEL). Watching you learn and grow as individuals with the support of strong relationships with family, friends, and your peers has been a true gift.

To the countless educators and students who have helped me grow and learn throughout my educational career, every collaborative experience has helped shape me personally and professionally. You have helped me reach beyond my expectations and played a vital role in getting these critical ideas out to schools across the world.

Finally, to my friend and colleague Ann-Bailey Lipsett, working with you truly has been life changing. I am forever grateful for your expertise and support, and I'm excited to continue learning alongside you and countless others on this new, incredible journey.

—Tracey Hulen

Writing a book on social-emotional learning is a humbling one, as I found myself often relying on the very strategies here in this book. I am so thankful to my parents for their support, and to my husband, Peter, and my children, Lilly Bell and Harper, for being there to remind me to use my calm-down strategies and growth mindset as well as being there to help me coregulate when it all felt like a bit too much. This would not have been possible without Team Lipsett behind me (and, of course, the Alden family for providing adventures and entertainment during a global pandemic).

To my co-fellows and faculty in the Infant-Parent Mental Health Fellowship at University of Massachusetts–Boston, thank you for allowing me to use our small-group discussions to reflect as I grappled with how to apply what we were learning in class to this book. You each influenced my thinking and this work in a significant way. A particular thank you to faculty members Dr. Alexandra Harrison for taking time to provide specific feedback and Silvia Juarez-Marazzo for our discussions on the immigrant experience regarding SEL.

To all the school counselors I have worked with at Annandale Terrace, Mason Crest, Carlin Springs Central, and Kings Park elementary schools, thank you for always being willing to collaborate with me, whether I was in the role of general education teacher, special education teacher, inclusion specialist, or parent. I learned so much about SEL from working with each of you.

Finally, to my coauthor, Tracey. Since we began working together in the early days of Mason Crest, you have pushed me to think beyond traditional practices and look at the possibilities. I am a stronger educator thanks to you. Thank you for your wisdom, collaboration, and friendship.

—ANN-BAILEY LIPSETT

Solution Tree Press would like to thank the following reviewers:

Heather Bell-Williams
Principal, Milltown Elementary School
Anglophone South School District—
South
St. Stephen, New Brunswick

Katie McCluskey
Assistant Superintendent of Teaching,
Learning, and Accountability
Glen Ellyn School District 41
Glen Ellyn, Illinois

Robert Hanrahan
Principal
Ivy Hall Elementary School
Buffalo Grove, Illinois

Alyssa McCool
Teacher & SEL Coordinator
Washington Woods Elementary
Westfield, Indiana

Marty Huitt

Aisha Thomas
Principal
Zach Elementary
Fort Collins, Colorado

Table of Contents

CHAPTER 2

Establishing Culture, Climate, and the Learning Environment for SEL in Elementary Schools

CHAPTER 3

Building a Schoolwide Foundation for SEL in Elementary Schools

CHAPTER 4

Effective SEL Teaching Practices and Strategies in Elementary Schools

CHAPTER 5

Effective SEL Lesson Planning

CHAPTER 6
Monitoring Student Learning of SEL

About the Authors

 **Tracey A. Hulen,** an education consultant and elementary and middle school mathematics specialist, has been part of the leadership team at two model professional learning communities (PLCs) in Fairfax County, Virginia. She specializes in mathematics and social-emotional learning and has a wide range of experience collaborating about data-driven instruction. She served as a mathematics specialist at Mason Crest Elementary School in Annandale, Virginia, the first model PLC to receive Solution Tree's annual DuFour Award in 2016. While serving in this role, Tracey worked with preK–6 teams of teachers and was instrumental in helping build and support the school's innovative mathematics program. Under her leadership, Mason Crest consistently achieved outstanding results in mathematics on the Standards of Learning for Virginia Public Schools. Her work also included supporting early childhood teams with integrating social-emotional learning with academic learning.

In addition to her work at Mason Crest, Tracey worked with the mathematics team in the Fairfax County Public Schools (FCPS) Instructional Services Department for four years, which serves 141 elementary schools. During that time, she supported the development of FCPS's rigorous mathematics curriculum, assessments, and instructional programs. Tracey's work included creating and facilitating FCPS's mathematics professional development for administrators, instructional coaches, and elementary teachers. In addition, she provided more individualized support to schools in planning, creating assessments, discussing data, supporting lesson study, differentiating instruction, and utilizing best practices in mathematics.

In 2006, Tracey was a Title I mathematics coach who passionately led other mathematics specialists and resources teachers in Fairfax County's Title I schools. Tracey previously served as a member of the National Council of Teachers of Mathematics Educational Materials Committee, advising board members on matters related to the council's publications, as well as proposing, reviewing, and approving manuscripts for publication. She is a coauthor of *What About Us?: The PLC at Work® Process for Grades PreK–2 Teams* and has been published in *AllThingsPLC Magazine* and *The Journal of Mathematics and Science: Collaborative Explorations* from the Virginia Mathematics and Science Coalition.

Tracey earned a bachelor of science in education from Pennsylvania State University; a master's in education (mathematics specialist) from the University of Virginia; and, most recently, a specialization in The Teacher and Social-Emotional Learning (SEL) from the University of Colorado–Boulder.

To learn more about Tracey's work, visit www.theducationalsolutions.com or follow @traceyhulen on Twitter.

Ann-Bailey Lipsett is a special education consultant with eighteen years of experience working with children, families, and schools. She founded her educational consulting company, Lipsett Learning Connection, in 2016 to develop positive social-emotional learning experiences for all children, regardless of their abilities and backgrounds. She works with schools, foundations, and individual families in one-on-one, virtual, and group settings.

Many of Ann-Bailey's beliefs in education formed during her six-year tenure at Mason Crest Elementary School in Fairfax County, Virginia— the first school to win the DuFour Award. It was here that she truly came to understand that *all* means *all* and how to set high expectations while providing students with the help they need through the power of a collaborative team.

As an education writer, Ann-Bailey has blogged for the Council for Exceptional Children's *Reality 101* blog in 2014 as well as for Joey's Foundation. In this latter endeavor, she followed the growth of one child with cerebral palsy learning to use an augmentative and alternative communication device. She is the coauthor of *PREVENT Problem Behaviors: Seven Contemplative Discipline Steps*, and she authored the article "Supporting Emotional Regulation in Elementary School: Brain-Based Strategies and Classroom Interventions to Promote Self-Regulation," published in *Learning Landscapes*. Ann-Bailey has presented her work on increasing engagement in students with disabilities at the state, national, and international levels.

Ann-Bailey is a fellow in the Infant-Parent Mental Health Program at the University of Massachusetts–Boston. She earned her bachelor's degree from Washington and Lee University in Lexington, Virginia, and her master's in special education from the University of Virginia. She has advanced her understanding of neurodevelopmental practices through her coursework through the Interdisciplinary

Council on Development and Learning (ICDL). She is also certified as a Circle of Security facilitator.

To learn more about Ann-Bailey's work, visit her website at Lipsett Learning Connection (lipsettlearningconnection.com).

To book Tracey A. Hulen or Ann-Bailey Lipsett for professional development, contact pd@SolutionTree.com.

Foreword

By Claudia M. Gold, MD

What a joy and privilege it is to write the foreword for this paradigm-shifting book. Why, you may ask, is a pediatrician writing a foreword to a book about education? Authors Ann-Bailey Lipsett and Tracey A. Hulen and I share a great respect for the process of child development. In fact, this book's writing coincided with author Ann-Bailey Lipsett's participation in the University of Massachusetts–Boston's fellowship program, where I am a faculty member. Learning from luminaries in the field variously referred to as infant mental health, infant-parent mental health, or more recently early relational health, Lipsett and Hulen integrated the concepts of child development into this book in real time.

Decades of research has revealed that our physical and emotional health emerges in moment-to-moment interactions in our social world, beginning in infancy and continuing through the lifespan. The meanings we make of ourselves as hopeful and capable of empathy—or, in contrast, as hopeless, fearful, and closed off—evolve in a developmental process in relationships with people close to us. The authors draw on this contemporary science to create a practical approach to supporting successful learning in the classroom. While social-emotional learning is the subject, the research they present reveals the relevance of developmental and relational context to education as a whole.

Opening with the primacy of a sense of safety in the learning environment, they introduce neuroscience research not typically included in literature on social-emotional learning. They draw on a model of brain development to demonstrate the importance of bringing in the body to promote behavioral and emotional regulation, with rhythmic regulating activities that educators can intentionally integrate into daily classroom activities. They call the reader's attention to the inevitably messy nature of relationships, identifying the imperfections themselves as necessary for promoting growth and facilitating learning. They apply these concepts to a model for listening to people from the full spectrum of different cultures.

The book's organizing graphic directly draws on infant research that informs our understanding of the development of self-regulation, which begins at birth in co-regulation with primary caregivers. The notion that *I exist* forms as caregivers give shape to their child's emerging sense of self. By naming *sense of self* as the foundational building block, the authors bring this lesson learned from infants to create a frame that teachers can use to organize their approach to the full range of issues in the classroom.

Self-regulation and co-regulation continue to emerge as children learn to put words to feelings. In preschoolers and school-aged children, in addition to emotional and body regulation, self-regulation encompasses attention, flexible thinking, and impulse control that are central to social interaction and learning.

The authors draw on the value of careful observation of infant behavior and apply it to their work as teachers. Babies enter the world with a capacity for complex communication, well before the parts of the brain responsible for thinking in words come online. Applying this developmental frame to the classroom, they reveal how careful observation of behavioral cues can help teachers identify a child's subtle communication of changes in state, which may foreshadow a loss of the capacity for emotional or behavioral regulation. Being fully present in the moment to support connection serves to create an environment that promotes learning.

The authors show a profound empathy for teacher and student alike. They identify the basic human need to feel heard in order to be open to listening to others. They bring the concept of reflective supervision—a parallel process of listening to clinicians to promote listening to parents, which in turn promotes listening to children—to the world of education. Especially in the time of COVID-19, teachers often feel overwhelmed by demands on their time and attention. To best listen to students, teachers themselves need to feel understood.

Vast areas of research in developmental science have historically been siloed from fields to which they have gre at relevance. In *Building Blocks for Social-Emotional Learning*, Lipsett and Hulen succeed in breaking down barriers of knowledge in this masterful work of integration. I hope the book is both widely read and widely used.

Why Teach Social-Emotional Learning to All?

"I did then what I knew how to do. Now that I know better, I do better."

—Maya Angelou

Vignette: Why Teach SEL?

Daniel stood in front of his classroom, his hands shaking. He looked as though he was about to either run from the room or throw the chair in front of him, but his teacher, Ms. Maria Smith, couldn't be sure. Everyone in the classroom stood silently, waiting for six-year-old Daniel to make his next move. Finally, the teacher took a breath, centered herself, and put her hand out. "You look so frustrated, Daniel. That's a big feeling to have. Can you walk with me and tell me about it?"

Daniel looked confused by the word "frustrated," but he put out his hand and walked with the teacher to the water fountain.

"That was lucky," the teacher found herself thinking. "Why did that work? What will I do next time when he doesn't come with me? What if my co-teacher was not in the classroom and I was not able to take him for a walk? More important, how can I help Daniel so that we don't get to that moment again? I am an expert at teaching first graders to read, write, and do mathematics. But students like Daniel, who seem to explode so easily, end up spending more time in the office than with me. How can I teach him if he isn't even in my room? How can we stop this pattern so we can actually keep him in the classroom so he can access instruction and learn?"

Why Is SEL Needed?

In 2016, the Center for American Progress noted that an average of 250 preschool students were suspended and expelled daily (Malik, 2017). The long-term outcome for preschool students facing suspension and expulsion is heartbreaking—these children are ten times more likely to drop out of high school, be incarcerated, have failing grades, be retained, or have negative attitudes towards school (Hamre & Pianta, 2001). And this is not just true for preschool students. A working paper from the National Bureau of Economic Research addresses the broader public issue, finding that "students assigned to a school that has a one standard deviation higher suspension rate are 15 to 20 percent more likely to be arrested and incarcerated as adults" (Bacher-Hicks et al., 2019). Students who attend schools that rely on punitive discipline practices are more likely to report they do not experience high levels of support, safety, and trust (Skiba et al., 2014). The unfortunate reality is that when we do not understand our students, we are not just impacting their current school year—we are failing to provide them with what they need to be successful throughout their school careers and later on in life.

Therefore, we can and *must* do better.

Children are not born with social skills; rather, they are born with the ability to *acquire* these skills as they develop, learn, and grow. From the time a child is born until they enter a formal school setting, parents, caregivers, and family members play a primary role in developing these social competencies in children. In fact, research shows that early relationships between child, parent, and caregiver help to form a child's social-emotional foundation (Lillas, 2014; Lillas & Turnbull, 2009; Tronick, 2014). In a nurturing environment, where parents and caregivers are attuned to the children's needs and form deep connections with them, children have a great deal of opportunities to build these necessary and important social-emotional foundations. When students take that giant leap from the home learning environment to a formal school setting, social-emotional learning (SEL) and deep relationship building should not stop. We cannot assume, even with that strong foundation, that children will enter kindergarten having built *all* the social-emotional skills they need to thrive in their relationships and be successful in school and later in life. Additionally, we know that children develop at different rates and enter school having had varied experiences and many may even enter with weak social-emotional foundations. In fact, Megan M. McClelland, Shauna L. Tominey, Sara A. Schmitt, and Robert Duncan (2017) share that teachers report numerous students enter school without social-emotional skills, which impacts their learning.

For many, the time spent between children and primary caregivers significantly shifts when students enter elementary school. On average, teachers spend about seven hours a day with young learners. Elementary school is a critical time in a child's life, and these years set the stage for how these children will view the world, and themselves, throughout their lives. We now know that as humans, we continue to learn and develop our social-emotional skills over time (Aspen Institute, 2018), and that a strong relationship with an adult can support those children who may come to school with weak foundations (Osher, Cantor, Berg, Steyer, & Rose, 2020). We also know from Maslow's hierarchy of needs that many children cannot access the academic content until their basic physical and emotional needs are met (Huitt, 2007), while others can learn the content easily but struggle to apply it meaningfully due to a lack of social and emotional skills. If teachers' sole learning goals only involve academics, what happens to students' social-emotional learning and development? Our teaching goals should not be a choice between the false dichotomy of either academics or social-emotional learning. Rather, it should be a question of how we support students' development of social-emotional *and* academic learning.

In the end, if we fail to teach SEL in a meaningful way, we are failing our neediest children, leaving promising students without essential 21st century skills, and adding undue stress to our school communities. We can and must do better, and our pathway for change is the PLC at Work process.

The Powerful Impact of SEL

Fortunately, intentionally teaching, supporting, and emphasizing SEL concepts and skills can change our children's futures. A meta-analysis published in 2011 (Durlak, Weissberg, Dymnicki, Taylor, & Schellinger, 2011) and updated in 2017 (Taylor, Oberle, Durlak, & Weissberg, 2017) found that SEL programs showed a statistically significant positive improvement on student behavior, attitudes, academic performance, and SEL skills in general (see also Hanover Research, 2019). Research continues to show that strong social-emotional and executive functioning skills are correlated with long-term achievement. Students with these skills are more likely to graduate from high school, attend and graduate from college, hold a job, and have positive relationships with their family (Jones & Kahn, 2017), and are less likely to use or abuse drugs (Klapp et al., 2017). In addition, schools that take time to teach, model, and practice SEL skills show positive increases in school climate and overall student behavior, and a decrease in teacher burnout rates (Jones & Kahn, 2017). McClelland and colleagues (2017) also reference research that children's engagement in SEL interventions has the potential to not only enhance behavior but possibly even change brain structure and function. The overall outcomes of establishing SEL in school are positive for both students and teachers. Yet, to avoid potential pitfalls which could lead to negative consequences, we must get this right. We must mindfully consider the important factors of effectively establishing SEL in our schools.

Key Factors When Establishing SEL

A 2018 National Commission on Social, Emotional, and Academic Development report finds that a high percentage of parents, students, teachers, administrators, and employers all agree that the development of social-emotional learning should be a focus for schools (Aspen Institute, 2018). However, we often see that school approaches and methods vary drastically. Some schools engaged in teaching SEL may use a preset curriculum or framework that focuses on specific skills development (possibly even in just one particular domain—either cognitive, social, or emotional—or in a particular focal area relating to mindset, motivation, or values). Other programs encourage teachers to focus primarily on the classroom environment, using specific routines, procedures, and language in their classrooms. These programs may be either student or adult focused, target student or teacher competencies, or (ideally) both. Most target the classroom setting, while some also focus on the larger school setting as well as parent support and training (Jones, Barnes, Bailey, & Doolittle, 2017).

Regardless of the approach to SEL, to be successful, schools must prioritize relationships and create a psychologically and physically safe environment for learning (Aspen Institute, 2018). They must also address, teach, and support social and emotional learning starting in preschool and continuing throughout students' educational careers, as we know that SEL skills are developmental and build over time.

Schools need a collaborative approach and the important work of a PLC to effectively implement SEL and meet the needs of all learners. This requires a shared purpose and collective responsibility by *all* (DuFour, DuFour, Eaker, Many, & Mattos, 2016). Whether you are new to the ideas of creating a PLC or already function as a PLC, building a strong, solid foundation is the very first step. Professional learning communities are built on the four pillars—(1) mission, (2) vision, (3) values, and (4) goals—and answer the following associated questions (DuFour et al., 2016).

- Why do we exist?
- What must we become in order to accomplish our fundamental purpose?
- How must we behave to create the school that will achieve our purpose?
- How will we know if all of this is making a difference?

More often than not, schools answer these questions primarily by focusing on ideas around academic learning and leave out key elements of student and adult well-being. However, to implement and sustain school communities that provide the best learning environments for *all* students, schools must address SEL alongside academics through the careful focused work of the PLC. The PLC's shared mission, vision, values (collective commitments), and goals should be at the center of all discussions and actions across the school's settings, and the targeted focus of the PLC should be on learning, a collaborative culture and collective responsibility, and results (DuFour et al., 2016). In our experience, unfortunately, we have seen many schools that do not see SEL as part of their collective responsibility.

Richard DuFour and colleagues (2016) state that a PLC "is an ongoing process in which educators work collaboratively in recurring cycles of collective inquiry and action research to achieve better results for the students they serve" (p. 10). Therefore, in doing this work, collaborative teams must commit to taking time to assess current practices and determine the needs of their school community. Dena Simmons (2021), a researcher of social-emotional learning, writes that we must "find the time to take inventory of our curricula, pedagogy, and policies to ensure they prioritize student safety and belonging" (p. 34). This work is best done through the work of a PLC, where collaborative teams commit to thoughtfully learning and growing in their understanding of what their students need and make commitments to building their own competencies that promote SEL and effective, more equitable teaching approaches. In doing this work, schools must first recognize the unique community they serve and realize the SEL strategies that may be successful at one school may not meet the needs of their current community. Therefore, discussions should reach beyond the school walls and include voices from local community members as well as leading experts. Collaborative teams should consider current research in multiple fields beyond SEL, such as the fields of mental health, child development, trauma-informed care, and equity in education, to inform their teaching practices and support their learning environments.

Although school approaches to SEL may vary in order to reflect the communities they serve, schools must put the essential aspects of SEL systematically in place through the work of the PLC and include everyone in the school community. As a part of the systematic process, the school's collaborative teams need to first do the work around examining their current practices, mindsets, and assumptions to begin to ensure that they are offering inclusive practices and a message of belonging to *all* students (Buckley, 2020). This work should also include everyone who works in the school, including the bus drivers, office staff, and cafeteria workers. Without this first step, the SEL will not effectively reach all students. The Collaborative for Academic, Social, and Emotional Learning (CASEL, n.d.g) states that:

> Systemic implementation of SEL both fosters and depends upon an equitable learning environment, where all students and adults feel respected, valued and affirmed in their individual interests, talents, social identities, cultural values, and backgrounds. While SEL alone will not solve longstanding and deep-seated inequities in the education system, it can help school districts promote understanding, examine biases, reflect on and address the impact of racism, build cross-cultural relationships, and cultivate adult and student practices that close opportunity gaps and create more inclusive school communities. In doing so, districts can promote high-quality educational opportunities and outcomes for all students, irrespective of race, socioeconomic status, gender, sexual orientation, and other differences.

We believe the keystones to successfully answering the question of SEL reside in the child's *relationships* and their *learning environment* (Aspen Institute, 2018).

This learning environment includes the setup of the physical and cultural larger school and classroom settings as well as the quality of the instruction used for both social-emotional and academic development. For students to learn new academic content, we must teach them and support their developmental growth. The same is true for social-emotional learning (Coelho, Cadima, Pinto, & Guimarães, 2018). The path toward establishing effective SEL instruction for *all* students within a school community requires collaborative teams to focus on the four critical questions of the PLC process (DuFour et al., 2016):

1. What do we want all students to know and be able to do?
2. How will we know if they learn it?
3. How will we respond if they do not learn?
4. How will we extend the learning of those who are already proficient?

As we engage in this work together, functioning as a PLC, we must determine how we can weave social-emotional support and learning into our academics. Research shows that when this occurs, students show a higher level of engagement, motivation, and a deeper understanding of the topic (Aspen Institute, 2018). When we provide students with high expectations and challenging material, we can include guided support in SEL that will help our students understand how to tackle the challenges. This is where effective, meaningful instruction occurs no matter the content being learned (either academic or social-emotional). The quality of the learning environment, the teaching approaches, and tools we use play a large role in students' learning outcomes (Blomeke, Olsen, & Suhl, 2016). When we engage in the work of a PLC by participating in collaborative collective practices and put our focus on the development of the whole child while working at building relationships with parents, students, and our colleagues, we have a better shot at reaching these quality educational experiences and outcomes for *all*.

To achieve effective and sustainable SEL, schools working as a PLC must (1) commit to both academic and SEL instruction; (2) build a strong schoolwide collaborative culture and climate; (3) find ways to create and foster an effective, supportive environment for both adults and students; and (4) develop systems as a means for continuous school improvement and supporting student needs. To support elementary schools on their journey of providing quality SEL, we have created an SEL pyramid, which includes these core essential elements (see figure I.1). We maintain that all four elements need to be in place for SEL to be successful.

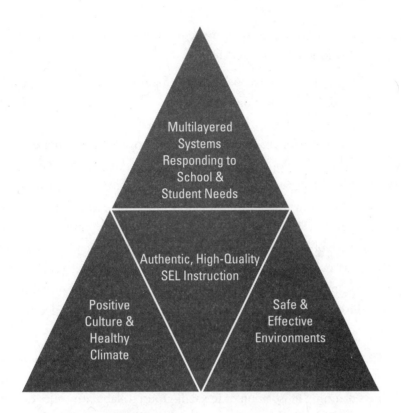

Figure I.1: SEL schoolwide pyramid.

*Visit **go.SolutionTree.com/instruction** for a free reproducible version of this figure.*

Overcoming Potential Challenges of Teaching SEL

According to a research brief created by the Pennsylvania State University with support from the Robert Wood Johnson Foundation (Greenberg, Brown, & Abenavoli, 2016), teaching is one of the most stressful occupations in the United States. Despite the amount of stress the job already entails, teachers cite the need for dedicated time for SEL in schools. In fact, 93 percent of teachers want schools to focus on SEL (Bridgeland, Bruce, & Hariharan, 2013), yet they state that few training opportunities are provided for them (Greenberg, Brown, & Abenavoli, 2016). As a result, SEL at the basic level may be frequently taught through vocabulary lessons associated with sporadic read-alouds or in monthly lessons from a school counselor. In some schools, teachers devote specific time to SEL by using a scripted program that may fail to provide teachers with the decision-making capabilities and insight to support meaningful change in their students. Learning vocabulary is only the first step in successfully using SEL skills, yet most of our schools stop there. Stephanie M. Jones, Sophie P. Barnes, Rebecca Bailey, and Emily J. Doolittle (2017) share how many SEL frameworks leave out cognitive skills relating to executive functions and typically don't address relationship building or make room for teachers to focus on building their own social-emotional competencies.

Effective SEL programs, on the other hand, focus on increasing cooperative play skills, language and communication skills, emotional knowledge and regulation, and social and interpersonal problem solving and control of aggression (Lillas & Turnbull, 2009). In addition, effective programs focus on inclusive learning environments with a positive climate; provide opportunities for *all* students to learn as well as to practice social and emotional competencies; integrate SEL with academic learning; promote relationship building between students, teachers, and parents; and build teachers' own SEL competencies (CASEL, 2020). We argue that one stand-alone curriculum, program, or framework often does not encompass all aspects of a school's SEL needs, and thus students may not generalize and apply the skills taught in isolated SEL lessons. Therefore, a PLC must carefully evaluate its current needs based on all community members (both the adults and students) and seek the resources needed to effectively establish SEL across the school setting and throughout the school day.

Without a collaborative lens in understanding, planning, teaching, and assessing SEL, schools are only able to scratch the surface of providing students with what they need. Teachers planning in isolation or in small-group collaborative silos disconnected from the rest of the school are unable to tackle the difficult questions that come when looking to understand what *all* students within the school community may need.

Some of these difficult topics that must be approached within the PLC are the issues of poverty, social justice, and the real-world issues students live with. Beyond feeling unprepared for teaching specific SEL skills, teachers are hesitant to address the broader real-life issues that impact student lives—the very issues that we want our students to use their social-emotional learning to handle (Collado et al., 2021; Simmons, 2019). So often these more complex issues of poverty and social justice are overlooked or minimized. As schools dive into SEL, they must remember that SEL alone is not enough to address the larger issues their communities face on a daily basis. As Simmons (2019) states, "Simply put, to be effective equity centered educators, we cannot be emotionally intelligent without being culturally responsive." Therefore, we cannot teach SEL as though our selected program is the only way for people to be successful in the world. Instead, we must integrate culturally and contextually responsive practices throughout our school day and prioritize partnership with the community to ensure equity, justice, and humanity in our work with students (Simmons, 2021).

Social-Emotional Components: The Building Blocks of SEL Skills

The Collaborative for Academic, Social, and Emotional Learning (CASEL) is a leading trusted source for embedding social-emotional learning in schools. CASEL presents SEL in five core competencies that include self-awareness, self-management, responsible decision making, relationship skills, and social awareness (CASEL, n.d.f). Based on research and practice, the EASEL Lab at Harvard University, another trusted source in the field of SEL, identifies six domains: cognitive, emotion, social, identity, values, and perspective (Jones, Brush, Ramirez et al., 2021). Our SEL framework, which we refer to as *building blocks*, integrates the work of CASEL and the EASEL Lab (see figure A.1, page 316) while also incorporating the work from the fields of mental health and child development. Specifically, we apply the essential work of Dr. Stephen Porges on the importance of sensing safety in our environment, Dr. Bruce Perry's investigations into the power of relationships, and the critical research and work of Dr. Stanley Greenspan regarding functional and emotional developmental capacities.

Our SEL framework represents the integrated work of leading experts in various fields, and the building blocks metaphor reminds us that human development builds on itself. For secure social-emotional development, we want a strong foundation in those early competencies for the other components to build on.

Why Our SEL Building Block Model?

In this book, we moved toward representing human development in a building block image to remind ourselves of the developmental nature of social-emotional and cognitive processing skills. Too often in education we overlook the factors of development and the role it plays in the behaviors we see in the classroom. To do this, we integrated CASEL's five competencies and the EASEL Lab's six SEL domains within each of the social-emotional building blocks (see figure I.2, page 10). If your state or district uses these approaches or another SEL framework as an avenue for teaching SEL, we recommend you continue on this path of learning. However, we encourage you to see how our developmental social-emotional building block components fit with the SEL framework or curriculum you are using. How could this developmental approach strengthen your own understanding of SEL? Keep in mind, you will not be able to draw a one-to-one correlation between their categories and ours, as elements of their competencies or domains are interspersed within the building block model to reflect the developmental nature of SEL learning.

Logical and Responsible Decision Making

Considerations:

- Can I see the whole picture?
- Can I make logical connections between ideas?
- Can I take perspective and include the perspective of others in my decisions?

Social-Emotional Regulation

Considerations:

- How do I stay calm and regulated?
- How do I maintain attention on targeted goals?
- How do I set goals and create plans?

Social Awareness

Considerations:

- Do I understand I am separate from others?
- Do I understand I have different opinions?
- Do I recognize and understand prosocial behaviors?

Reciprocal Engagement

Considerations:

- Do I relate and engage with others?
- Do I maintain two-way communication with others?
- Do I recognize and understand social cues?
- Can I respond to and initiate communication with others?

Sense of Self

Considerations:

- Who am I?
- Where do I belong?
- What do I like?
- What makes me happy or sad?

Source: Adapted from Collaborative for Academic, Social, and Emotional Learning, 2020; Greenspan, 2006; Interdisciplinary Council on Development and Learning, 2020; Jones et al., 2021; Perry, 2014, 2020; Porges, 2004, 2017.

Figure I.2: Building blocks of social-emotional learning.

Visit **go.SolutionTree.com/instruction** *for a free reproducible version of this figure.*

The building block image itself (figure I.2) reminds us that the growth in these areas is developmental and builds on itself. Growth is also significantly impacted by the supports in the child's environment, particularly by strong, secure relationships with a trusted adult (Nelson, Parker, & Siegel, 2014). We dig deeper into the importance of relationships and how they support the building blocks in chapter 1 (page 23).

When we view human development as though we are building a tower, we recognize that each new block added to the tower relies on the security and strength of the blocks below. Susanne A. Denham (2018), professor of psychology at George Mason University, writes:

> Developmental tasks underlie *all* components of SEL promotion: frameworks, assessments, standards, and practice. None of these

components of SEL can succeed without a developmental task perspective; ignoring the developmental tasks makes them less useful, rendering them incomplete or out of sync with what is happening with children and youth as they grow. Further, the SEL components are dynamically related via the developmental perspective. (p. 4)

As humans, we move through our neurological development in a sequence, beginning with our ability to regulate our body's needs, and progressing through until we begin to develop our prefrontal cortex and the executive functioning skills that come with it (Greenspan, 2006; Lillas, 2014; Perry, 2014). Because our development happens from the bottom up, each layer is built on the layer below it. In order to increase our students' executive functioning skills that will allow them to set goals and make responsible decisions, we need to ensure that there is a strong foundation in the underlying components of a sense of self, reciprocal engagement, and social awareness.

Building Block 1: Sense of Self

The very first block we develop is our *sense of self*, or *self-concept*. We begin developing this capacity from birth, in our interactions with our caregivers. Our sense of self is our general understanding of who we are, our likes, and our dislikes. This develops along with our ability to engage in reciprocal engagement as we learn where our self ends and another begins (Gold, 2017; Nelson et al., 2014). In this building block, students explore who they are and identify what makes them unique, what they are proud of in themselves, and what their weaknesses are. This is where students learn to identify specific emotions and apply those emotions to themselves. They go beyond knowing the concept of what it means for someone to be happy or sad, and begin to understand what their body feels like when they experience emotions (Lillas & Turnbull, 2009) and to recognize the events in their lives that can lead to these emotional responses.

This foundational stage is also when a child begins to develop their perspective (an EASEL Lab domain) on the world and whether they interpret their experiences through a positive or negative lens. The nature of how a child interprets the experiences as either positive or negative will have a longer-term impact on the child than the child's emotions themselves. While emotions can change quickly, the positive or negative meaning a child associates with events in their life will not change as quickly and will make it more difficult for a child to engage, absorb new information, and explore (Lillas & Turnbull, 2009).

The sense of self is also where children recognize their place in the world and build a sense of safety. It becomes the social narrative that can remind these children that they belong and are safe, loved, and unique. Unfortunately, children can develop a negative individual narrative that leads them to believe they do not belong, do not have strengths, or are not worthy (Lillas & Turnbull, 2009). A negative sense of self, or a sense of self not grounded in a true understanding of one's personal emotional responses, will create disruption or insecurity in the development of later building blocks. Imagine playing the popular children's block game, Jenga®. As long as the block tower continues to have a strong foundation the top of the tower will be secure. However, if pieces from the bottom of the tower are removed (or were never there in the first place) the tower is far more susceptible to the slightest wrong move (see figure I.3). The sense of self building block is found in these lower blocks on the Jenga tower. Children will have a difficult time regulating their own emotions, setting goals, and controlling their impulses if they have a negative self-narrative or are unable to recognize their emotional responses. This can also lead children to experience inconsistent boundaries in their social awareness development and make ill-advised, disconnected decisions.

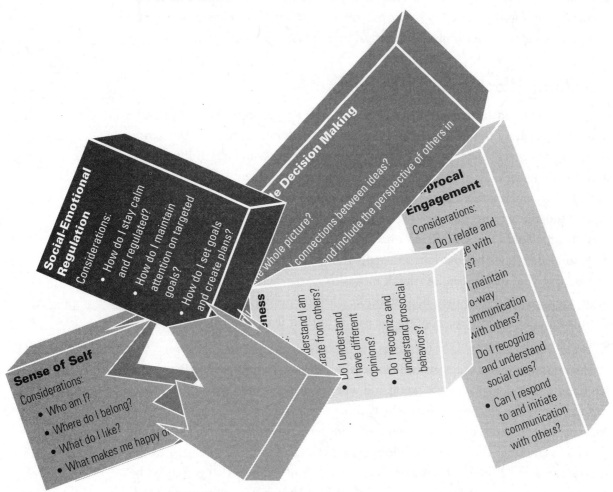

Figure I.3: Effects of a broken *sense of self* building block.

I (Ann-Bailey) once worked with a child whose sense of self was so negative that any sort of praise from an adult made him angry and uncomfortable. He did not view himself as the rest of the world saw him and believed that if someone praised him that they were lying. This interfered with his ability to build positive relationships with school staff until his team developed ways to work with him that did not involve praise or challenging his sense of self.

We should not think of this component solely in terms of our students. It is critical for *all* humans, including educators. Before beginning to be able to help others understand, accept, and regulate themselves, we must be secure in our own understandings of ourselves. As child development researcher and author Arthur T. Jersild (1955) states, "The self is the citadel of one's own being and worth and the stronghold from which one moves out to others" (p. 135). As educators, do we have self-acceptance and compassion for ourselves so we can be genuine in our relationships with students and coworkers? Or do we just go through the motions and not allow true connections to form? Do we understand our own emotions and have a sense for the ebb and flow in the rhythms of our day? A sense of self allows us to have a lesson go poorly in front of our principal and recover because we know we are quality educators who make mistakes. This sense allows us to recognize our strengths and weaknesses without feeling threatened or competitive with our teammates. A secure sense of self is what allows us to take risks without a deep worry of failure, to connect with those around us.

Building Block 2: Reciprocal Engagement

Our earliest interactions with others come from nonverbal *reciprocal engagements* (Gold, 2017; Greenspan, 2009; Nelson et al., 2014). Reciprocal engagement begins when an infant cries for food and a caregiver responds, or when a caregiver tickles a baby's foot and the baby giggles and puts their foot out, hoping for the caregiver to tickle it again. At only three months, an infant may learn that if they smile, their caregiver will smile back (Greenspan, 2006). This cause-and-effect relationship is the very beginning of reciprocal engagement and is also the base upon which a sense of self and a sense of others is built (Gold, 2017). When we are babies, our reciprocal engagement building block develops at about the same time as the sense of self block. These two blocks make up the bottom of our tower (see figure I.2, page 10). Although these components fall into separate blocks on the graphic, they depend on one another for concurrent development and growth.

Reciprocal interactions, called *circles of engagement* (Greenspan, 2006) or *serve-and-return responses* (Harvard Center on the Developing Child, n.d.c)—where a communicator "serves" the conversation ball and their partner returns it to them like in a game of tennis—strengthen the child's sense of self, social awareness, and ability to self-regulate. The ability to engage in sustained back-and-forth interactions can act as neural exercises strengthening how we interact, how we *up regulate* or increase our energy level to meet our environment, how we *down regulate* and decrease our energy based on our surroundings, and how we problem solve with others (Harvard Center on the Developing Child, n.d.c).

When we get older, our reciprocal engagement is our ability to have long conversations with another person, begin a conversation with someone, or respond when someone tries to get our attention. These interactions can be through words or gestures.

People with strong reciprocal engagement skills can maintain a conversation with others on one topic, without changing the subject or walking away.

Children who are still developing this capacity may stop interactions when they become bored or when the interaction becomes too challenging. They may not be open and comfortable interacting with others (EASEL Lab, n.d.; Jones et al., 2021), which leads to restrictions in this building block. Children's development of this area can also be impacted by difficulties reading nonverbal social cues, or by sensory systems that make it difficult to comfortably engage with someone else.

In schools, reciprocal engagement can play out in a variety of ways. Can students sustain conversation with one another or an adult for up to twenty back-and-forth exchanges? Can they play a nonverbal "follow the leader" game where they see what another does, follow it, and add an action to it? Are they able to sustain discussion on a single topic, even when it becomes uncomfortable or they become bored? Can they take turns with one another both in structured partner games and in unstructured playground time? Reciprocal engagement requires students to respond, initiate, and sustain communication with others. These prosocial and cooperative behaviors will be essential in the coming developmental stages.

Reciprocal engagement is an area where adults can also monitor their own behaviors. Although this component began developing in each of us when we were babies, it is a capacity we may have but don't often practice. As society's use of technology and smartphones increases, we as educators are less likely to model sustained back-and-forth communication. It is important to remember that many students don't even experience longer exchanges with parents at home without a text message or phone alert interrupting them. These interruptions disrupt the flow of the interactions and weaken the exchanges. This interference over time can potentially create weaknesses in the building block itself. When we teach, model, and support SEL skills in the school setting, it is important to honor the need for reciprocal engagement. We need to give our students the opportunities to interact in this space, even in the older grades, when we may assume it is already part of a child's secure foundation.

Building Block 3: Social Awareness

As a child develops a sense of self (building block 1) along with the ability to interact with others in a back-and-forth, meaningful pattern (building block 2), the child begins to develop a sense of *social awareness*. In the early years, this is when a child begins to realize that their thoughts are different than other people's thoughts and that they may have beliefs others do not have (Thompson, 2017; Tomasello, 2019). Children at this stage become aware that others may have different favorite colors, preferences, and family lives. As they get older, children begin to understand further differences in social awareness—recognizing and appreciating different cultures, political views, religions, and socio-economic statuses.

Social awareness encompasses when children begin to recognize others' emotions and develop a sense of empathy. They can see that someone is sad or angry and can identify ways they can help that person. As they continue to grow in their social awareness, they can identify how their own actions may have negative or positive impacts on those around them and can cause others to become happy or sad. This is when their ability to take the perspectives of others develops.

In the classroom, students will be able to recognize that their peers may have different likes and dislikes, may hold different religious or political beliefs, or may be having a good day even though another student is having a rough day. I (Ann-Bailey) once had a first-grade student become angry because he did not understand that I could be happy when he was feeling sad and tired. As his awareness of our emotional differences grew, he began using tricks to help himself, such as drawing pictures of my emotions and his. He was still developing his social awareness but was approaching the problem as logically as he could.

For adults, our sense of social awareness can play a significant role in whether we have positive or negative interactions with others. Taking time to consider our team members' perspectives or realize that we may not hold the same values as the families we serve will allow us to make deeper connections with those around us.

Building Block 4: Social-Emotional Regulation

The next building block to add to the tower is *social-emotional regulation*. In this block, we begin to develop an ability to recognize our own emotions and respond appropriately. This is when we recognize we are angry and are able to regulate ourselves so that our emotions do not overtake our actions. This is where we develop flexibility, control of our attention, and the ability to pause before acting, or *inhibitory control* (cognitive-executive functioning skills).

These executive functioning skills are ones children will rely heavily on to be successful later in life (Harvard Center on the Developing Child, n.d.a). For example, children need to develop the ability to set a goal and create a plan that will help them reach that goal, as well as recognize ways to be flexible and resilient if the original plan does not go as desired. This is when students begin to develop a growth mindset. In chapter 1 (page 23), we will go into further detail about how we learn to regulate our emotions through interacting with others, as well as how to support social-emotional regulation.

Although social-emotional regulation is often the area of social-emotional development we target the most in schools, it is important to remember that this block depends on the *sense of self* and *reciprocal engagement* blocks. Children cannot develop a capacity for *social-emotional regulation* until they have a secure development in both their sense of self (building block 1) and their ability to engage in reciprocal interactions (building block 2). Humans learn to regulate emotions through playful interactions with others (Porges, 2017; Tronick, 2014). Children are able to understand their own emotions as their sense of self develops through the support of trusted caregivers. As children strengthen their reciprocal engagement capacities, they are able to interact with adults when they are distressed so the adult can soothe them. This co-regulation through responsive, back-and-forth exchanges is where a child first learns that it is possible to manage uncomfortable emotions. As development continues, children learn how to regulate themselves and recognize strategies they can use to change their emotional states.

It is important to remember that because we develop our social-emotional capacity in relation to those around us, the skills developed within this capacity are cultural. When we consider teaching, supporting, and assessing skills within the social-emotional regulation capacity, we must take a student's culture into consideration.

Often, when emotional outbursts occur in the classroom, educators provide students with specific strategies to use yet forget to return to the base of the tower (see figure I.2, page 10). Is that student able to identify their emotions appropriately? What is that student's sense of self, and where do they feel they belong? Is that child able to sustain back-and-forth engagement that can help them learn to regulate themself? If not, the teacher will need to start with the lower building blocks to secure the foundation before moving forward with additional regulating strategies. The key to supporting this building block is to prompt students to use their strategies or to accept help from a trusted adult before they become too upset. We will go into more detail about this in chapter 1 (page 23).

One year I (Ann-Bailey) was working hard with a group of fourth-grade students to recognize when they were upset and to use their self-calming strategies. We created lists of strategies and tested which worked and which did not for each individual child. A teacher later told me that one of the students had not had any outbursts all week and that she was very excited by this. But she also noted she was confused. Multiple times a day, she noticed him leaning back in his desk with his arms folded and breathing with his eyes closed. She thought this was rude behavior but had let it go because there had not been any outbursts that week. Together we realized that this behavior was his unique self-calming strategy and that her student was actually catching himself becoming upset and calming himself down before an outburst.

As with the sense-of-self building block, it is essential that educators apply social-emotional regulation to themselves and not just their students. Educators must become reflective in the moment and monitor their own emotional reactions within their classroom. When adults become dysregulated yet are unaware of their emotional reactions, they can disrupt their connections with students. Research finds that "dysregulated emotions can inhibit healthy relationships—between teachers and their students, between teachers and their students' families, and between family members. If we do not manage our emotions effectively, we will not be available to teach, learn, or parent" (Cipriano, Rappolt-Schlichtmann, & Brackett, 2020). Educators must apply self-reflection and understanding of their emotional reactions to their unconscious bias. We will discuss unconscious bias in more detail in chapter 1 (page 29) and chapter 2 (page 88).

Building Block 5: Logical and Responsible Decision Making

The fifth component, *logical and responsible decision making*, builds on the abilities the student has developed in the lower building blocks, such as a strong sense of *social awareness* (building block 3), and the ability to self-regulate and use executive functioning skills (building block 4). Within the *logical and responsible decision making* building block, students are ready to merge two ideas together and draw their own conclusions (Interdisciplinary Council on Development and Learning, n.d.). They can take in multiple pieces of information, make a decision, and act on it. They can revise their own opinions and decisions based on new information. These cognitive skills are known as *cognitive flexibility* and *critical thinking*. In older grades, discussions about current events can become meaningful debates, pushing students to think beyond themselves. In this stage, students' values will form based on their experiences earlier in development and how they interpret the world. A child's sense of purpose continues to develop here as well (EASEL Lab, n.d.; Jones et al., 2021).

I (Ann-Bailey) was recently working with a group of upper elementary students engaged in an "escape room" scenario. This game-like situation allowed us to watch each student process the different pieces of information, put them together, consider someone else's perspective, and develop a plan based on that information. One student in particular stood out. Instead of just focusing on the main goal of escaping the room, she also took into account the overall goal of having fun with her friends and making sure everyone was able to participate. She processed not just the elements of the game but also the abilities and needs of her peers. With this strong moment within logical and responsible decision making, she was able to not just help the team win the game but ensure everyone had a good time doing so.

As responsible adults, whenever we make a decision, we are unconsciously influenced by our underlying emotional response to the situation, our ability to socially interpret the situation, and our ability to analyze the situation using our executive functioning skills. Our students also rely on those emotional, cognitive, and social skills as well as their belief systems relating to identity, values, and perspective (EASEL Lab, n.d.; Jones et al., 2021) contained within the lower building blocks when they are working in this building block.

Students can often appear competent with many of the skills in these higher building blocks and yet somehow still seem to be lacking the nuances that would make them successful. At these times, it is important to return to the base of the blocks (see figure I.2, page 10). Students may believe they are making responsible decisions, but because of limitations in engaging in reciprocal engagement, they are unable to fully sustain attention to another and thus cannot truly understand another's perspective. Their daily rhythm may be such that they move too quickly to fully connect with others, leaving weaker blocks in this area of development.

When you imagine this developmental block tower, return to the image of playing the popular game, Jenga. Think of each individual Jenga block as being made up of various combinations of social, emotional, and cognitive skills and one's beliefs (identity, perspective, and values). The goal in Jenga is to remove blocks from the tower itself to make the tower higher without it falling down. If you have played Jenga once or twice, you know that to avoid knocking down the tower you try to resist removing too many pieces from the base of the tower. Once these pieces are removed, your tower is more likely to fall. No matter how neatly and precisely you place a block on the top of the tower, it is far more likely to fall if there are gaps in the foundation below. The same is true for social-emotional development and learning. Keep the block tower in mind as you work with students. When it seems a student can perform the skills and shows the abilities in one of the higher building blocks but is still having trouble, consider what might be missing from the tower. Which block is not fully developed?

> In reflecting on Daniel's abilities and needs, his teacher realized that he is still developing a strong sense of self. Daniel is not yet able to identify what makes him happy, sad, or frustrated, although he knows the vocabulary words. Before Maria can expect him to stay calm in her classroom, she recognizes that she will first need to help him understand when he is getting frustrated without getting overly frustrated herself. "How am I ever going to have time to give Daniel those skills on top of everything else I must do?" she wondered. "There must be a better way to reach Daniel and all the other students."

The Goals and Design of the Book

Educators are asking for resources, training, and support in reaching all of their students (Tatter, 2019). Therefore, we have written this book with elementary principals, school psychologists, school counselors, teacher teams, and individual classroom teachers in mind. This book offers ideas for how to build and establish a schoolwide foundation for SEL in elementary schools to benefit *all* members of the school community with a focus on how the PLC process supports SEL. In addition, this book is designed to provide educators with an understanding of SEL skills and how they impact behavior, specific SEL teaching practices, and strategies and equip collaborative teacher teams with the tools necessary to plan, teach, and support these skills in an organized, meaningful, and culturally responsive way. We also offer planning templates to support teaching SEL, so students can develop and practice these skills throughout the school day and so teachers are not attempting to carve out additional time from an already busy schedule.

By the end of this book, collaborative school teams will feel confident in their ability to plan and guide SEL within their classrooms throughout the day and across school settings. The school staff will understand the importance of SEL and what it is, how neurological development can play a role in the need for differing approaches, and how these elements reveal themselves through the behaviors educators see in the classroom and across school settings. Educators will learn how to create safe and effective physical and cultural learning environments to enhance 21st century learning. We also share ideas for how to monitor students' growth of SEL through the use of developmentally appropriate assessments and tools used to inform instruction.

The primary goal of this book is to provide educators with the research, tools, and overall guidance regarding how to build meaningful, effective, and manageable social-emotional learning across school settings. Schools will learn how the PLC process can support, strengthen, and sustain SEL and help the school staff collectively build common understandings, knowledge, language, and practices around SEL. Collaborative teams will enjoy rich discussion around applying the neurological need for SEL supports to their own students and determining the best way to approach their unique communities.

In chapter 1 (page 23), we provide the reader with background information and research about children's neurological development and its impact on student behavior. We take time to truly understand what we mean by a *sense of safety* as we apply Stephen Porges and Bruce Perry's work to the education field. This chapter is perhaps the most important because it lays the foundation for the rest of the book. Without understanding the background, it is easy for educators to go through the motions of SEL without truly providing that safe and secure learning environment. In chapter 2 (page 45), we lay the groundwork for establishing a positive culture and healthy climate as well as safe and effective physical and cultural learning environments within a 21st century classroom. Chapter 3 (page 93) explains how the work of a PLC best supports a school's efforts in building a strong foundation for SEL. The chapter provides schools with ideas and tools for how to implement SEL across the school setting and build a communitywide common understanding of SEL among students, teachers, school counselors, administrators, the entire school staff, and families.

Chapters 4 (page 157), 5 (page 223), and 6 (page 293) break down the specific work of collaborative teacher teams in regard to instructional practices, planning, and assessment. Chapter 4 discusses teaching practices and strategies for effectively teaching SEL in elementary school, focusing on ten instructional practices teachers can use to integrate SEL into academics and daily routines throughout the day. Next, chapter 5 provides readers with an abundance of resources and steps for effective SEL lesson planning. It considers how teacher teams can plan for differentiation and provides multiple planning tools and templates for direct SEL instruction. While it can be tempting to solely rely on these chapters, these chapters are not where the deep work is. The deeper work comes in the understanding and reflections of part one of the book (the introduction through to chapter 3), and then the careful considerations as to how one can apply this knowledge to what chapters 4, 5, and 6 discuss.

We agonized over writing chapter 6, which focuses on assessment, because we are mindful that it is difficult to create nonbiased SEL assessments. In chapter 6, we will ask you to reflect more on your own practices than those of the students as you create, administer, and analyze assessments. Before forming a support or intervention group, we will direct you and your team to look at the students who fall into the intervention category. Are they of a similar culture or socioeconomic background? Are they all younger than their peers? We will ask your team to consider what these similarities tell you about your common formative assessments and ask you to reflect on your expectations—are they culturally unbiased and developmentally appropriate?

As you read this book, you will notice that we start each chapter with a vignette that shares students' and teachers' classroom journeys. We end each chapter with a tips chart for administrators, classroom teachers, and support staff. We encourage you to reflect on your own students, classrooms, and current SEL practices. While you read and learn, collaborate with your grade-level teams to ensure high levels of social-emotional learning for *all* students. No matter where you are with your current SEL practices, continuous learning and growing is a huge part of the teaching profession and the work of a highly effective PLC. When we discover our students' current needs, uncover the answers behind the *why*, and learn about the *how*, then it becomes our moral obligation to roll up our sleeves, dig in, and improve on our practices in the best interest of our students.

As you read, consider the students with similar behaviors and needs to Daniel's—those who are currently in your classroom and those who you have taught in the past. Think about how you could use the tools and structures this book provides to support *all* the students in your school or classroom while specifically providing Daniel with what he needs to develop SEL skills and be successful in school. The goal of this book is not to give you specific steps to take to teach SEL effectively so that your students behave appropriately in your classroom. Instead, we ask you to read this book with an open mind. Consider your current practices and how they reflect your students' needs. Honestly assess your school's historical routines and procedures and determine if they are truly effective at creating safe, meaningful learning environments or if they simply encourage some students to comply with the school social norms for the convenience and comfort of the adults. Watch what happens to the students who do not comply in your current structures. Who are the students who are most often in trouble? What changes can you make? As you try out ideas, be an objective observer. What works for your students? What can you improve? Where do you see your students shine, and where do they struggle? Reach out to families and involve them in discussions about how to best meet their children's goals and needs. The goal is not to just teach specific

SEL skills and concepts; rather, the primary focus and this book's overarching goal is to help you connect with students and provide them with safe and secure environments where they can become the best versions of themselves.

Although we dedicate a large portion of time discussing how to support our students' learning of social-emotional skills, time and time again you'll notice how we advocate for the critical work of the individual teachers, collaborative school teams, and the larger school community in building the adults' social-emotional skills and competencies. This requires internal personal work and reflection from each individual educator as well as dedicated time for teacher teams to learn and grow together.

Final Thoughts

We began this book six months before the COVID-19 pandemic changed our school landscapes. Sitting in a coffee shop in September 2019, we reflected on our own teaching experiences that we had encountered working together and separately, outlined what we wanted our own children's teachers to know and understand about the research, and excitedly dug in. We had no idea that our own children would not finish out the year in the school building or that a full year later we would be rereading what we wrote to remind ourselves of how to give our children a sense of safety and security within the walls of our unexpected homeschool environment. In our schools, we watched the gaps widen between those with middle- to upper-class resources and those without, as well as between resilient students and those students who needed additional time and support to develop resiliency.

Beyond differences in class resources and resiliency, our entire population has experienced a great trauma of having our daily routines disappear overnight and our relationships with those outside our houses change and, in some cases, vanish. For children who relied on those relationships and the security of the daily structure of school, the COVID-19 quarantine, as necessary as it was, was that much more jarring to their systems. These students may be more resistant to building trusting relationships with adults outside their homes in fear of having to lose those relationships again. They may be more alert and vigilant to their surroundings, not able to settle into a trusting emotional state where they are open to learning. This book, which was always a passion project, became even more vital. After everything that has happened since the pandemic began, our students need to re-enter school buildings or virtually connect with educators who are committed to collaboratively doing the work of fully understanding social-emotional learning and embedding it into the school day. Understanding the *whys* behind the need for relationships, connections, safe learning environments, and reflective teaching will allow us as educators to truly create the schools our children need going forward. For those continuing to teach in a virtual format, it is vital to understand these *whys* so that you can apply them over the computer to create safe virtual learning spaces. You can use the same ideas to connect with students and help them thrive even virtually.

As we wrote, we watched our country confront racism. We knew, from our own experiences within schools, how unintended discrimination can interfere with an individual student's abilities to meet their potential. Our own actions as educators are where we need to start to make change. Where does SEL fall into the conversation about race and the unconscious assumptions we make? Beyond the area of race, how does it apply to any of the conversations we have as educators about different groups of students—those from different cultures or socioeconomic statuses, or with special education labels? Dena Simmons describes in her 2019 article for *Equity in Action*, when SEL is done poorly it creates more harm than good. Unfortunately, she notes, educators use SEL in schools to teach compliance and to give the school and teacher control. This is not true social-emotional learning. This type of "SEL" teaches specific skills, which educators can use to punish students who do not demonstrate these skills. Often, these specific skills are taught in a way that is familiar and practiced by the dominant culture of the school, therefore creating a sense of "good kids" who use these skills and "bad kids" who do not. These isolated skills are not truly supporting a student's social-emotional learning.

Our hope with this book is not to provide you with a specific roadmap for how to teach and monitor students for specific skills, but rather to share several ideas and provide many examples for how you can go about doing this important work collaboratively with your school community and grade-level teammates as well as inside your individual classroom with and alongside your students and their families. In fact, if you take away nothing else, we want you to understand that SEL is not just about the observable skills but rather about providing students with a safe place to learn, where they feel connected and have meaningful relationships with others.

We know that we are far from being experts in this field of unconscious bias and equity in education. In fact, as we reflect on our early careers, we cringe at examples of when we unknowingly let our own bias interfere with our classroom's sense of safety, or when we disguised classroom management and behavior modification with social-emotional learning. Yet we believe strongly in the words attributed to Maya Angelou: "Now that you know better, you do better" (Winfrey, 2011), and we are committed to continuing to learn so we can do better. We ask you to join us in this journey of reflection and relationship building as we all work to find the best ways to implement inclusive communities and provide equitable SEL to make our schools better for *all* students.

CHAPTER 1

What Is Social-Emotional Learning?

> ### Vignette: The Story of Daniel
>
> Maria Smith, Daniel's teacher, sat alone in her classroom after school, reflecting on her day. She wondered how she was supposed to meet Daniel's needs while also teaching him reading, writing, and mathematics and keeping the other students safe. Rightly so, she wondered how she could be proactive in changing his behaviors so that she was not left in near-dangerous situations.
>
> To begin changing Daniel's behaviors, Maria needs to look at his actions as more than simply behaviors but instead as clues into Daniel's unique, individual profile. She needs to identify what skills he may be missing to comfortably access learning. *Why can't Daniel lose a game without melting down? Why does independent work make him so angry, yet he can complete the same work if he is sitting next to the teacher? Why can he appear to be perfectly happy and then suddenly erupt with anger and violence? Why can't Daniel sit still during focus lessons, remember to raise his hand when he has a question, and wait in line without bumping into the person in front of him?*
>
> What's going on with Daniel and other students like him who seem to have something keeping them from moving forward?

Every student that enters a school has social and emotional needs, regardless of their socioeconomic, cultural, or linguistic background. For individuals to meet their full capacity, they need to feel that they are physically and emotionally safe, have a sense of belonging, and know they are loved (Huitt, 2007). While some students may enter the school building without needing more than a high five from the teacher, others require more to fulfill this basic human need of safety and belonging. These individual differences may come from a student's background outside school or a student's unique neurological factors within the regulatory and sensory systems. These systems create individual processing differences that influence the student's social and emotional development as well as their executive functioning skills.

Before we begin to teach social-emotional learning skills, we must first understand how those skills relate to a student's individual differences. Throughout this chapter, we use the example of our fictitious student named Daniel and his teacher Maria to help you define what SEL is, understand the importance of teaching it, learn how to support students' emotional regulation, teach emotional regulation strategies, and discover students' neurological development and its relationship to behaviors. The chapter will conclude with tips for administrators, teachers, and support staff based on the content of the chapter.

Defining Social-Emotional Learning

While there are no easy answers to this work, diving into social and emotional learning will help Maria and educators like her understand what skills students need to develop. The Collaborative for Academic, Social, and Emotional Learning (CASEL; https://casel.org) is a nonprofit organization based in Chicago, Illinois, that identifies SEL as essential for moving students forward. CASEL (n.d.f; see also Niemi, 2020) defines SEL as:

> an integral part of education and human development. SEL is the process through which all young people and adults acquire and apply the knowledge, skills and attitudes to develop healthy identities, manage emotions and achieve personal and collective goals, feel and show empathy for others, establish and maintain supportive relationships, and make responsible and caring decisions.

This complex definition encompasses multiple essential competencies needed for both students' and adults' success.

SEL is not teaching students different character traits. It is not reading a book like *How Do Dinosaurs Stay Safe?* (Yolen, 2014) and labeling the positive and negative actions its characters demonstrate. It is not assigning worksheets that ask students to identify good and bad choices. Most importantly, it is not a system for managing student behavior.

Although SEL is defined in a variety of ways throughout the field of education, for the purposes of this book, when we refer to SEL we use the SEL pyramid (see figure I.1, page 7) to describe the four essential elements that a school needs to put in place and continuously monitor. However, we will discuss SEL skill development through the lens of our developmental building blocks (figure I.2, page 10). These building blocks closely interrelate and correspond with CASEL's five core competencies and EASEL's six SEL domains (cognitive, emotion, social, identity, perspective, and values; see figure A.1, page 316, in the appendix for a visual integration of these three frameworks). The social, emotion, and cognitive domains involve a set of skills and competencies students are able to learn, whereas the identity, values, and perspective domains are associated with students' beliefs, values, attitudes, mindsets, and motivations that play a role in guiding students' behaviors (EASEL Lab, n.d.; Jones et al., 2021).

There are observable behaviors associated with each of these six SEL learning domains that teachers witness in their classes. When we mention *behaviors* in this book, we are only labeling what is observable through a student's actions. The answers to why a student is or is not demonstrating a certain behavior are often more complicated than what educators can observe. As you read, keep in mind that this is not a behavior management book but rather one on social-emotional learning. Our focus is to support the student's development and skills in each of the building blocks. As we stated in the introduction (page 1), the nature of human development leads to abilities and skills developing in relation to one another (Jones, Barnes et al., 2017; Jones et al., 2021), with people needing a strong foundation in the building blocks to continue to build strong skills. When considering teaching SEL, it is important to remember this developmental nature.

Throughout the school day, we as teachers engage students in various learning experiences (working independently on a learning task, playing a game with a partner, working on a group project, engaging in play, and so on) that require a range of simple to more complex skills within multiple domains (social, emotional, cognitive, physical, language, academic, and so on) that are often interdependent of one another (see figure 1.1).

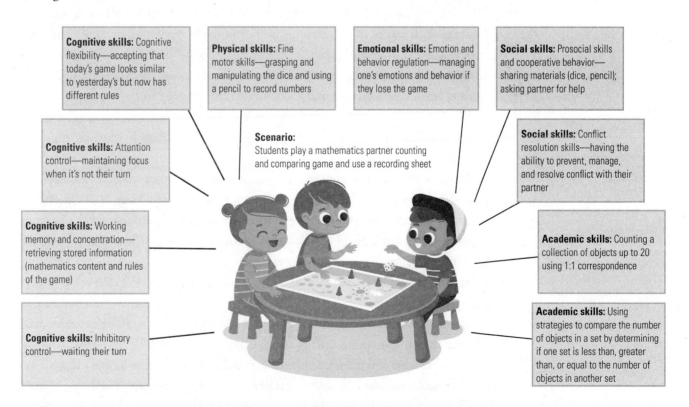

Cognitive skills: Cognitive flexibility—accepting that today's game looks similar to yesterday's but now has different rules

Physical skills: Fine motor skills—grasping and manipulating the dice and using a pencil to record numbers

Emotional skills: Emotion and behavior regulation—managing one's emotions and behavior if they lose the game

Social skills: Prosocial skills and cooperative behavior—sharing materials (dice, pencil); asking partner for help

Cognitive skills: Attention control—maintaining focus when it's not their turn

Scenario: Students play a mathematics partner counting and comparing game and use a recording sheet

Social skills: Conflict resolution skills—having the ability to prevent, manage, and resolve conflict with their partner

Cognitive skills: Working memory and concentration—retrieving stored information (mathematics content and rules of the game)

Academic skills: Counting a collection of objects up to 20 using 1:1 correspondence

Cognitive skills: Inhibitory control—waiting their turn

Academic skills: Using strategies to compare the number of objects in a set by determining if one set is less than, greater than, or equal to the number of objects in another set

Figure 1.1: Common classroom multi-skill activity example.

In our encounters, many educators often have the underlying assumption that students either come to school already having a strong foundation of these cognitive, emotional, and social competencies and belief systems (perspective, values, and identity), or are unaware that they actually need them to access the academic learning. Yet, this is simply not the case. The underlying system required for a student to be successful in a school environment in all three domains (cognitive, social, and emotional) is a student's executive functioning skills (Hamilton, Doss, & Steiner, 2019).

Executive functioning skills (EFS) are often referred to as the "air traffic control" for our brains and bodies as they play a large role in a student's ability to demonstrate a range of academic, social, and emotional skills. According to the Center on the Developing Child at Harvard University (2012), these skills include working memory, self-control, and mental flexibility; and the prefrontal cortex of our brain controls them. This is the last area of our brains to develop. While aspects of our executive functioning development begin in infancy, this development continues into adulthood (McCloskey, Perkins, & Van Divner, 2009). As educators we often forget that the children we are working with do not have access to the same executive functioning skills that we, as adults with fully developed brains, are able to use. Our students, who are still developing these skills, may have difficulty ending one task (or even topic!) and moving to another because they have not yet fully developed their mental flexibility. Students may not fully remember multistep directions like an adult would because their working memory is still developing.

When considering executive functioning skills, it is also important to keep in mind how these skills can be impacted by a child's emotional regulation or emotional competency skills in any given moment (Delahooke, 2019; Lillas & Turnbull, 2009). Both conscious and unconscious emotions can play a role in the development of knowledge and learning; in fact, conscious emotions can be used to harness learning and shape future behaviors (Lillas, 2014). As students begin to feel emotional signals—for example, feelings of happiness when a teacher recognizes their hard work, nervousness before raising their hand to speak in class, or fear of an adult's outburst—their emotions can then serve as guides in the decision-making process of how students can utilize this learned knowledge in new situations (Immordino-Yang & Faeth, 2010). Students who remember their feeling of fear after an adult's outburst may be hesitant to approach that adult again or may feel a small sense of fear whenever they go near that adult. Alternatively, a child who experiences being nervous about participating in class but then feels joy for sharing a successful answer may feel that sense of nervousness the next time they go to participate. Remembering that the uncomfortable feeling of nervousness will not last long and can be replaced with pride or joy will move the child toward participating again. Figure 1.2 shows skills' and belief systems' interconnectedness and interdependency. As educators, we can no longer just be masters of the academic learning domain. Rather, we must extend our knowledge beyond academics and become competent in teaching social-emotional learning and in understanding how executive functioning skills play a vital role in all aspects of learning.

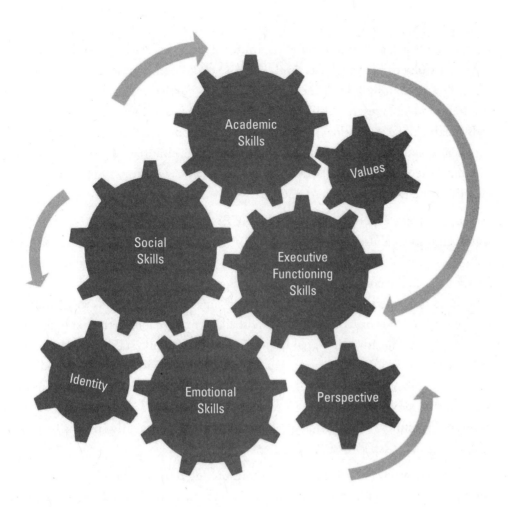

Figure 1.2: Interdependent skills and beliefs model.

CASEL's (2020) definition describes SEL as a process (see also Niemi, 2020). This is not because there is so much to teach, but rather because SEL connects to the developmental process that occurs within each individual (Denham, 2018). Before we can teach SEL skills, we must first understand that developmental process. While a teacher can teach specific skills, a student's actual SEL processing cannot change without practice, support, and a safe environment. Students cannot simply be told to manage emotions, feel empathy, be kind, or be responsible. They must specifically explore these individual yet interconnecting skills in ways that will allow the students to have true and meaningful ownership over their skills. Only then will the behavior teachers see begin to change.

Understanding ACEs and What They Mean for Educators

In 1995, Kaiser Permanente conducted what turned out to be a groundbreaking study on adverse childhood experiences and the impact these early experiences have on an individual's lifespan (Centers for Disease Control and Prevention, n.d.). Although it began as a study around the causes of obesity, the researchers discovered that their study participants had similar adverse childhood experiences (ACEs) that seemed to profoundly impact the person's lifespan. Further investigation led to the researchers identifying ten childhood experiences that can cause toxic stress in an individual. Unlike the normal stress we each deal with over the course of a day, these experiences cause a physiological reaction that impacts children's developing brains, immune systems, cardiovascular systems, and metabolic regulatory systems (Harvard Center on the Developing Child, n.d.b).

The ten adverse experiences identified as ACEs fall into three categories—(1) physical or emotional abuse, (2) neglect, and (3) household challenges such as a parent going to jail, witnessing violence in the house, parent separation or abuse, or substance abuse in the household. Although children may experience one or two of these events and not experience a profound negative impact, the study finds that children who experience four or more ACEs are more likely to have long-term consequences in their physical health, emotional well-being, and economic stability. People who experience four or more ACEs are significantly more likely to achieve lower education and income levels, more likely to have depression or to commit suicide, more likely to have problems with substance abuse, and even more likely to have broken bones and fractures. The physiological impact of significant, early stress is lifelong and reaches every aspect of a person's life.

As teachers we often feel that the world is looking to us to find all social justice solutions. Learning about studies like ACEs can make us feel overwhelmed and helpless. We can only control what happens to the students within our school walls. As much as we want to, we are unable to visit each student's house and protect them from experiences that may cause toxic stress.

So, what can we control?

We can understand the toxic stress our students may be experiencing in their lives and acknowledge that there may be unknown toxic stressors in their environments that interfere with their ability to sit calmly in a classroom and engage with an adult (Morsy & Rothstein, 2019). Once we understand the neurological implications of toxic stress and how it can lead to behaviors in our classrooms, we can begin to *design environments that promote a sense of safety*. In addition, we must remember that all children—from upper-, middle-, and lower-class households—can face toxic stress. We cannot assume we must first know about a child's history before deciding to treat them with more understanding and care than others. Instead, we must accept that we will never know everything about our students' lives but can create environments and communities where all students are safe. It is not our job to know the details of each child's traumatic past. It *is* our job to give each child a safe place where they can succeed.

As educators we also must *monitor our own unconscious biases* and beliefs about certain students in our classrooms. We cannot make assumptions about a student's toxic stress history simply because of what we know about the student's socioeconomic status, race, or special education label. It can be tempting to assume that, because a child comes from a certain neighborhood or culture, they do not have enough to eat, live in a dangerous situation, or do not have strong, nurturing relationships. When we make these assumptions, we are influenced by our unconscious bias, and it can cause more harm than good (Collado et al., 2021). Our students and families can sense our assumptions through our words and body language and will recognize that we do not truly see who they are. Parents can end up feeling judged, which may lead to a lack of trust, and students will begin to see that we have different beliefs about their lives than we do for other students. When thinking about a child's background, ask yourself what you know to be facts and what are the assumptions you are drawing based on those facts. Sometimes what we initially believe to be facts are actually assumptions based on our previous experiences and what we may have seen in the media.

In addition to understanding that our students may have unknown stressors in their lives, and working to create a safe environment for them, as educators we must also *build strong relationships* with our students. Harvard's Center on the Developing Child (n.d.a) notes three developmental principles to improve child outcomes.

1. Reduce toxic stress for children

2. Strengthen students' core life skills

3. Support responsive relationships

Within our school walls, we must work to reduce sources of toxic stress for our students, strengthen students' core life skills, and actively support responsive relationships if we are to adequately teach and support SEL. Although the Harvard Center on the Developing Child's work focuses on early childhood, an insightful teacher and the support and collaborative work of teacher teams (armed with the templates and plans in this book!) can strengthen each principle within the elementary school classroom.

Reduce Toxic Stress for Children

There are several sources of potential toxic stress in a student's life, and many of those sources are not within the teacher or school's control. However, schools that create positive learning environments, support SEL, and build strong relationships between the students and adults in the building can reduce the potential of school being a cause of toxic stress in a student's life (Morsy & Rothstein, 2019). Alternatively, schools that do not address these aspects can contribute to a student's toxic stress levels. Chapters 2 (page 45) and 3 (page 93) further address reducing sources of toxic stress and building responsive relationships.

Strengthen Students' Core Life Skills

We must strengthen their core life skills, or teach SEL, to build resilience in students. Yet, as we stated previously, we cannot just teach specific skills and assume the student will use them. Instead, we must first understand the student's developmental capabilities and physiological states and use the building blocks the introduction (page 10) discusses to determine how best to intervene and support our students. Take a moment to think about how to strengthen the core skills with the components of social-emotional learning building blocks. A sense of safety acts as the glue holding the blocks in the tower together (see figure 1.3). While each is an individual component, all the blocks are essential in the developmental sequence; and each block must be secure to ensure that the blocks above are stable. A student without a strong sense of self will have difficulty understanding social awareness. It is difficult to have empathy for others if you do not first understand who you are, what your feelings are, and your own likes and dislikes. While the individual blocks represent the components of the child's development (see figure 1.3), the people and hands on the outside show how the tower itself is supported by secure relationships with trusted adults. The interactions within these relationships are what will begin the child's developmental process from birth and will continue to influence the child's continued development of social, emotional, and cognitive processes (Gold, 2017; Lillas, 2014). Later on, in chapters 4 (page 157) and 5 (page 223), we will provide examples of how to plan, teach, and support these essential components throughout the school day.

Support Responsive Relationships

Before we can begin teaching and supporting our students in developing SEL skills, we must first address their neurophysiological states and whether they feel safe (Delahooke, 2019). To understand the world around us, our bodies first take in information through our sensory system. This information is then relayed to the neural circuits in our brain (Porges, 2004). These neural circuits process the information they receive from the sensory system and evaluate it for cues of safety or danger. Stephen Porges (2004), founding director of the Kinsey Institute Traumatic Stress Research Consortium (https://kinseyinstitute.org/research/traumatic-stress.php), coined the term *neuroception* to describe this ability to process one's environment for safety or danger and respond accordingly. When working correctly, neuroception is what allows us to change our behavior based on different settings, be wary of strangers but open with trusted friends, and be able to quickly escape from threats. Without a threat, we can engage in social communication or social engagement. But when our neural circuits perceive a threat, we are either sent into a defensive mobilization state (fight or flight) or a state of life threat or immobilization (freezing; Gold, 2017; Porges, 2004, 2017). This entire process occurs before a person is cognitively aware of their response.

Not everyone's neuroception works identically, though, and individuals perceive sensory information in different ways. This may be due to past traumas or

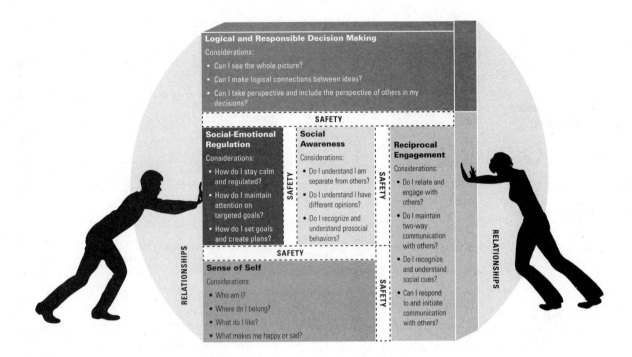

Source: Adapted from Collaborative for Academic, Social, and Emotional Learning, n.d.f; Greenspan, 2006; Interdisciplinary Council on Development and Learning, 2020; Jones & Bouffard, 2012; Perry, 2020; Porges, 2017.

Figure 1.3: The building block components of social-emotional learning.

experiences, or just from a neurological difference in how the body processes the sensory input. Porges (2004) refers to this misinterpretation of sensory input as *faulty neuroception*. When our students experience faulty neuroception, they react to environmental stimulus as though it is a threat, causing them to move into the neurophysiological defensive states of fight, flight, or freeze. Unfortunately, the behaviors that students demonstrate when in these defensive states are often what our schools consider problem or antisocial behaviors. It is important to keep in mind that students with faulty neuroception are not *choosing to* respond to a stimulus as a threat; instead, their bodies are automatically working to protect them without their conscious awareness. To change a student's behaviors that occur from faulty neuroception, we must first send signals of safety to the student. As we learn about these three neurophysiological states (see figure 1.4, page 32), keep in mind that we may not know what is causing an individual to perceive a threat. It could be past experiences, or it could be a learner's unique sensory processing that turns the sound of the air conditioner into a threat.

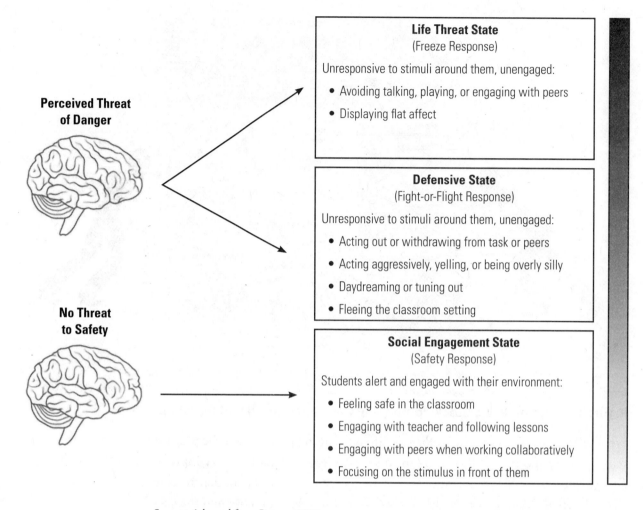

Source: Adapted from Porges, 2017.

Figure 1.4: The perception of safety.

Students enter our schools in various neurophysiological states. Some enter in the social engagement state—alert and engaged with their environment. They do not perceive threats to their safety, and the natural stress of a school day is met as "good stress" that challenges them just the right amount to help them grow. Students in this state feel safe in the classroom. They can engage with their teacher and follow the lesson. Their bodies allow them to focus on the stimulus in front of them.

Other students enter our schools in a defensive state. As a response to their life experiences, their bodies adapted to a state of constantly being on the lookout for danger. They are hyperaware of their environment—or to specific threats to their environment—while tuning out other stimuli around them. Their bodies provide an adaptive response to the threat of danger. Unfortunately, these adapted responses do not always fit well in school environments. As educators, we do not always recognize the threats these students' bodies are defending against, and it can often be hard for us to logically understand why the student in front of us is behaving a certain way. To the outside eye, it can appear that the student is acting willfully against our rules. In fact, the student's body is holding them hostage in this defensive state.

The other neurophysiological state our students may experience is the life threat, or freeze, response. This is another adaptive response that allows our bodies to reserve as much energy as possible for warding off the threat. Students in this state appear unresponsive to stimuli around them, or unengaged. They may not talk, play, or engage with peers, and may have a flat affect. Just like in the defensive state, the student is not making an active choice to be in this stage; rather, the body is again holding the student hostage as a way to protect them from a perceived threat.

Unfortunately, simply telling a student that an environment is safe and supportive is not enough to help the student transition to a physiological state appropriate for learning. Instead, we must provide students with that sense of safety. Once a student feels safe, regulated, and in the appropriate neurophysiological state, we as educators can then begin to address the additional building blocks that teach core life skills.

Supporting Students' Emotional Regulation

Vignette: The Power of Co-Regulation

Let's take a moment to think back to the student Daniel in the vignette at the beginning of the chapter (page 23). How does Daniel's neuroception impact his overall health and well-being in addition to his ability to learn?

Later that day, Maria saw Daniel display his telltale signs of getting ready to have a behavior explosion. His fists were shaking, and his face grew red. He held his scissors in one hand and a ripped art project in the other. Oh no, thought Maria, a ripped project. Daniel wants everything to be perfect—and he has such a hard time recovering from a mistake. What is he going to do with those scissors? I need to act fast.

Careful and slowly, Maria stood up. "Daniel," she said in a calm voice. "It looks like that didn't work like you wanted it to. How frustrating. Let's see if we can fix it."

Daniel's eyes shifted to hers and his body visibly relaxed. He put down the scissors and brought his project to her. Yelling about his scissors and his friend bumping into him, he explained what happened. The yelling disrupted the class, but Maria kept her voice even. She slowed down the pace of her words, giving longer pauses in between her phrases while keeping her attention on him. In those slow, measured movements, Maria was giving Daniel's faulty neuroception a sense of safety. These safe signals helped Daniel de-escalate and move from being in a defensive state to a more socially engaged one. It would take time—that rush of cortisol to his body would take about twenty minutes to leave his system.

What if Maria had spoken sharply to Daniel, yelled, or simply told him, "Your paper is fine! Put those scissors down"? Daniel would not have received any signals that he was safe and that Maria was there with him. Instead, he would have sensed that he was unsafe, misunderstood, and—once again—had done something wrong. Instead of putting down the scissors and getting help, his body could have reacted in a much more serious manner while he was holding the scissors.

While Daniel needs to work on his ability to handle frustration, Maria was not going to achieve that in a moment when Daniel was so dysregulated. Instead, Maria gave him a sense of safety and helped regulate and redirect him. Once Daniel was calm, Maria could begin teaching skills to handle frustration.

Notice how the teacher Maria's action steps in the vignette directly affected the student, Daniel, who needs individual support (see figure 1.5). However, Maria's actions also indirectly affected the entire class. Her carefully crafted actions de-escalate a situation rather than escalate it, which potentially has a bigger impact on the whole classroom.

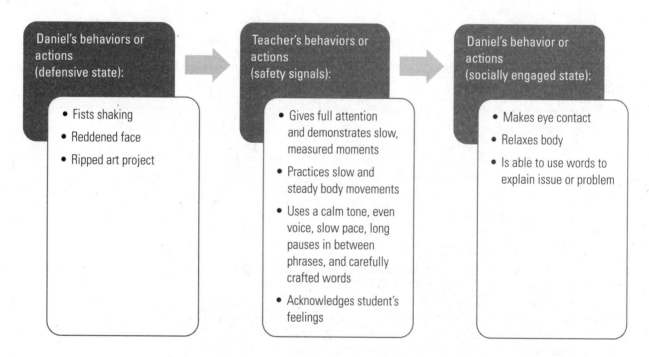

Figure 1.5: Behavior responses to safety signals.

Maria observed Daniel's significant outward cues of dysregulation—his shaking fists and his reddening face. However, students show many other subtle disengagement cues that also provide input to teachers and caregivers about the students' emotional responses to the task and the environment. Teachers who notice these subtle cues can intervene to provide safety cues and support before the behavioral cues escalate. Students also show a variety of engagement cues that let caregivers and teachers know when they are engaged and ready to learn. Figure 1.6 contains a list of some of the cues adapted from the Nursing Child Assessment Satellite Training (NCAST) Parent-Child Relationship Program at the University of Washington's Barnard Center (Oxford & Findlay, 2019). NCAST breaks down both the engagement and disengagement cues into the categories of subtle and potent, with *potent* being the cues we are most likely to recognize, and *subtle* listing cues we may not easily observe.

Examples of Potent Disengagement Cues	
Cue	**Description**
Maximal lateral gaze aversion (head turn)	Student turns their head away from the stimulation as far as it will go (almost over their shoulder).
Halt hand	Student puts hand up with the fingers spread out as though they are stopping traffic. The hand gesture is between the student and the stimulation or object.
Walking away	The student walks away from the stimulation.
Coughing	The student coughs suddenly and noisily without needing to do so.
Pushing away	The student touches the object or teacher they are intended to engage with and then extends their arm as though to push the object away.
Examples of Subtle Disengagement Cues	
Cue	**Description**
Straightening arms down the side of the body	Student may stand with a rigid stance holding arms close to the side of their body.
Displaying a dull expression on face and in eyes (low affect)	Student may look uninterested or unengaged. This may be particularly noticeable when other students are animated.
Eye blinking or clinching	Student blinks eyes rapidly or clinches eyes shut for a moment.
Facial grimacing	Student scrunches facial muscles for a moment and then releases them.
Fast breathing	Student takes quick breaths unrelated to physical activity.
Frowning with the brow lowering	Student's frown is reflected in the brow area as well as on the mouth.
Averting gaze	Student looks away from the activity, peer, or adult stimulus before looking back. Student avoids eye contact for a moment.
Touching hands to eye, ear, or stomach	Student touches their eye, ear, or stomach to self-calm or self-soothe.
Lowering head	Student lowers head for a moment during a task or activity. This is more noticeable when it is not an activity that requires the head to lower (such as writing or working at a desk).

Figure 1.6: Subtle disengagement cues.

continued →

Cue	Description
Increasing foot or leg movements	Student may rapidly move their foot or swing their legs. Small foot movements may also signal that the student is attempting to self-regulate themself or maintain attention to the task.
Compressing lips together or grimacing	Student brings lips together in a straight, flat line. This may only be for a moment.
Wrinkling forehead	Student scrunches forehead for a moment while concentrating or working.
Yawning	Student yawns to self-regulate and attend to task.
Turning head away	Student momentarily turns head away from the activity, assignment, or stimulus.

Source: Adapted from Oxford & Findlay, 2019.

*Visit **go.SolutionTree.com/instruction** for a free reproducible version of this figure.*

Obvious disengagement or cues of dysregulation include a student saying "no," walking away, putting up a "halt" hand, whining, withdrawing, pushing away from the table, pounding the table, or demonstrating overhand beating movements such as waving a hand downward in the air but not necessarily hitting anything. These are cues we usually observe and react to (Oxford & Findlay, 2019).

The more subtle disengagement or dysregulated cues can be harder to spot in a busy or virtual classroom and yet can be an excellent source of information on a child like Daniel who may need additional signals from an adult that he is safe and connected to the adult in the classroom, as well as further opportunities to co-regulate (see figure 1.7). As teachers observe subtle cues in students, they will be able to monitor the pace and expectations of tasks and provide support to the child before a student becomes overly dysregulated.

Support Strategy	How to Use It
Increase your wait time	Give the child additional space, both literally and figuratively to answer the question or comply with the task. Take a step back, bend down on the child's level, soften your gaze, and wait. When a child is entering a distressed period it will be more difficult for them to find their words.
Offer the child a break	When you observe a subtle disengagement cue offer the child a break based on what you know about the child's profile. Some children need more movement or a change of scenery, so they can be asked to run an errand for a teacher or take a note to another classroom. Some children need to lift heavy objects and can be asked to take a box of books or a ream of printer paper to another location. Other children may need a quiet place to write or draw.
Connection with an adult	Some children need a connection by an adult quietly putting a hand on their shoulder, giving them a high five. Others may benefit from a silent thumbs-up from across the room. The adult and child can even create a secret "I see you" signal that the adult can share with the student during these moments of early disengagement.

Figure 1.7: Sample strategies to support a child showing subtle disengagement cues.

It is important to note that when we talk about providing students with a sense of safety, we are not talking about making their lives 100 percent stress free. If we did, we would not give students a chance to learn, grow, and build resilience. Instead, we want to make sure students know they are in a place where they are safe enough to take risks and handle uncomfortable situations (Delahooke, 2019). When you have a strong relationship with your students, they know you are there to help them with uncomfortable stress. In fact, having a strong relationship with your students allows you to handle mismatch and repair—for example, when you are tired and snap at them unexpectedly (as we all do, even though we wish we did not). The strong, healthy relationship you build with them will allow for students to recover and grow from these moments of imperfect interactions (Tronick & Gold, 2020). It may not be pleasant, but they can become confident in their ability to sit with an unpleasant and uncomfortable situation and to use the self-regulation strategies they learn because they are otherwise safe and secure. In chapter 2 (page 45), we discuss the proactive measures teachers like Maria can take to provide a safe learning environment and specific measures that support relationship building between teachers and students and among student peers.

Teaching Students Emotional Regulation Strategies

Many social-emotional programs, such as *Conscious Discipline*, *Social Thinking*, *Emotional Intelligence*, and *Unstuck and On Target*, specifically teach students emotional regulation strategies. These strategies often include taking a deep breath, engaging in mindful breathing, getting a drink of water, taking a break, or going for a walk. These are all ways to let an individual gain control over their dysregulation and engage in rhythmic, regulating activities that will allow more oxygen to enter the brain (Perry, 2020). As we discuss in chapter 5 (page 223), you should teach and practice these strategies when students are calm and in a social engagement neuropsychological state. Telling a student to take a deep breath when they are in a fight, flight, or freeze state is not going to send the appropriate safety cues if the student is not already familiar with this strategy, has not practiced it, or has not seen others use the strategy. The student must recognize it as a helpful and normal tool and be comfortable using it. I often have students share with me that they hate when teachers tell them to take a deep breath because it just makes them more upset. They share they feel they are always "doing it [taking the breath] wrong." They have not had enough time to practice taking belly breaths, and the instructions to "calm down" or "take a deep breath" feel like another requirement they must jump through in order to make those around them comfortable.

Keep in mind that teaching these specific emotional regulation skills is similar to teaching isolated academic skills. When a student is learning to read, they may take a while to remember all their sight words. Every time they see the word *come*, students may need a moment to recognize that it is not the word *came*. Sometimes they may read the word correctly on the first try, and other times they may blurt out *came* without pausing to check to see if they are right. They may be able to read the word *come* correctly from a flash card in their reading group, but they become stumped when they see it in a book. While eventually recognizing this word becomes automatic, it can take practice, time, and repetition. We cannot simply teach students to take deep breaths and then expect them to take deep breaths every time they are upset. Just like with learning to read, students need support, practice, and time to generalize the skill to other contexts.

With practice, students can make these emotional regulation strategies their own and use them automatically in many situations. Yet there will be times that students will be in such a defensive neuropsychological state that they will not automatically use their calm-down tools. They may need an adult to help them co-regulate—modeling taking deep breaths, taking them for a walk, or sitting silently with them while their neuroception picks up on the adult's cues of safety (Perry, 2020). Others may benefit from an adult using a familiar script, such as, "What calm-down strategy can you use?" or "Plan A didn't work. Can you try Plan B?" (Cannon, Kenworthy, Alexander, Werner, & Anthony, 2014). These familiar phrases or scripts can act as safety cues when a trusting adult delivers them in a calm and safe tone. Scripts allow the students to shift their focus from the upsetting stimuli to the broader world around them. Students are then available to process safety cues.

When we expect students to use the social-emotional regulation skills we teach them, we must remember that their ability to demonstrate these tools depends on their understanding, practice, and familiarity with the tools as well as their neuropsychological state. When students show difficulty regulating themselves, even if we have previously taught specific strategies, we must offer cues of safety and support to help them co-regulate.

Understanding How Neurological Development Relates to Behaviors

While neurological development follows a similar sequence in everyone, the timing of this development is not always the same (Shonkoff & Phillips, 2000). Each of us has a unique developmental sequence due to biological, environmental, and cultural factors and how the factors interacts with each other. Yet our schools were originally created in an industrial-style model, with a sequence of learning and needs designed as though each student develops at the same rate. As we learned more about human development and the nature of learning, we have come to an exciting precipice as educators where we can begin to change the structures of our more institutional learning environments. Recognizing the differences in each student's development and understanding how to maintain high expectations for all learners, while simultaneously offering a learning environment that allows for the difference in neurological development, will allow our students to flourish in both school and life.

A variety of factors can lead to differences in neurological development, and a deeper dive into these factors is beyond this book's scope. It is not possible for every teacher to become an expert on each and every aspect of a student's developmental profile. Instead, teachers can create supportive environments and look deeper into misbehavior when it occurs. Instead of responding to specific behaviors with negative consequences, teachers can investigate what SEL skills the students are missing and what possible delays in neurological development may be making it difficult for the student to develop the needed skill.

What we address in this book is the importance of teachers understanding that the difference in developmental rates can lead to students reacting to their environmental expectations in different ways. Some ways students react to their developmental differences are acceptable within the school setting, while others tend to lead to adults labeling a student as a problem. For example, consider two students with visual-spatial planning delays. Both students' delays may cause them to frequently but accidently bump into peers, step on people's feet, or sit on top of people when coming to the carpet. One student may react to this difficulty by refusing to participate in whole-class transitions or simply by transitioning after the rest of the class to actively avoid bumping into peers. While it would appear slightly noncompliant, this behavior would not be particularly disruptive to a classroom. However, frequent bumping may embarrass another student with a visual-spatial planning delay, and they may decide to take ownership of it. Instead of avoiding being around groups of people, this student may act as though the bumps were intentional, appearing to the outside world as aggressive. For both students, the teacher can provide a safe environment for physical transitions in the classroom. Depending on the student's needs, the teacher may allow them to transition before or after the rest of the class, give the student a specific path or destination, or even ask them to orally plan their route with the teacher before starting the transition.

In schools we often get caught up in discussing students' negative behaviors. In truth, when many school teams talk about teaching SEL, they incorrectly believe they are teaching students how to behave. When schools simply address *behaviors*, they often miss the larger picture of a student's needs. Instead of considering how they can fix or manage behaviors, teams need to consider what the behaviors are telling us about the student's neurophysiological processes. We need to identify which of the student's SEL building blocks we need to strengthen to make the rest of the tower secure.

The following section briefly presents individual and developmental differences that may impact a student's behaviors in the classroom.

Executive Functioning and SEL Cultural Environment

Earlier in the chapter, we defined executive functioning skills as those cognitive skills (attention and inhibitory control, working memory and planning, self-control, and mental flexibility) needed to access other important and often complex skills (academic, social, and emotional). Individuals develop certain aspects of executive functioning at different rates and with different intensities. Although there is a common developmental sequence that occurs, each person's rate of development varies. Because of this varied development, it is important to remember that some students in our classrooms may not neurologically have the capacity to demonstrate the strong executive functioning skills some of their peers display. This does not mean that they *will not* demonstrate them, or that they have a deficit in executive functioning abilities. It simply means that their brain is still developing. We must be mindful of what we ask students to do and whether the task is developmentally appropriate for their neurological makeup at this time.

Many of our higher-level social-emotional skills require strong executive functioning (see figure 1.8). These two critical areas are interdependent. A child must be able to first recognize his impulses and then stop those impulses. Often that also requires the additional step of recognizing the social need to resist the impulse. Is the child able to understand the consequences of their impulsive actions? Most children who have difficulty controlling their impulses do not intend to harm those around them. They often feel terrible once they realize the consequence of their actions, and yet they are unable to "fast forward" in their heads to predict what the consequences of their action may be in that moment.

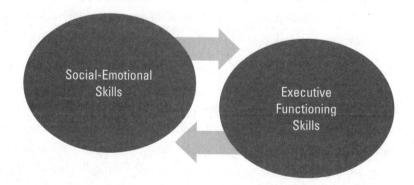

Figure 1.8: Interdependency model.

Throughout the school day, our students are asked to follow two- or three-step directions, problem solve, adapt to changes, and manage disappointment (all higher-order SEL skills). However, many of our students do not have the tools to demonstrate these skills independently. This leads to frustration, behavioral outbursts, and teachers feeling that the child just wants to escape from work. When a teacher asks everyone to put their work away and join the class on the carpet, the teacher is requiring those students to cognitively shift from focusing on their work to focusing on moving around the room. For some students, this hard stop is difficult—not because the students are choosing to ignore the teacher, but because their brains have not adapted to the new task. The students are still processing the last task of assigned work! Coming to the carpet is another cognitive task that can be difficult for some children. This simple direction requires the students to navigate around a large group of peers without bumping into anyone and find a spot on the rug. Students with visual-spatial processing delays, motor and coordination delays, vestibular dysfunctions, or weak executive functioning skills may have a difficult time identifying how to move through the room without bumping into anyone. This can look like reckless behavior, but instead it is the result of either difficulty processing space or a lack of planning how to walk through a room. While to adults this seems to be an easy task, some students struggle to identify a clear path in the room and how to change direction when someone is in their way.

While teachers can support a child's development and provide direct instruction in how a child can mentally plan to cross a room, this is a skill that will require some patience from the teacher as the child develops over time. Instead, teachers can be aware of these delays and adapt their instructions, room setup, and the flow of the day to meet all students' needs (see chapter 2, page 45). When teachers proactively plan for these developmental needs, they create smoother school days and waste less time redirecting negative behavior. Students in these supportive environments are more likely to develop a positive sense of self, which leads to a positive attitude towards school, teachers, and learning. Students' difficulty with impulse control should not make them feel that they are not a part of a classroom, that they are unable to learn, or that the teacher dislikes them. Yet so often, this is what happens to our developing learners.

Discovering the Underlying Reasons Behind Observable Behaviors

It is important to note that teachers can provide direct instruction, guided practice, and support on the missing skills, but if the root of the behavior is a developmental delay, the teacher will also need to create a supportive environment to meet the needs. Figure 1.9 (page 42) presents examples of observable behaviors you may see in your classroom and offers potential reasons behind the behaviors. The reason behind behaviors may stem from a variety of reasons, including specific skills the student is missing, difficulties with processing information, a developmental delay, and so on. For the difficulties in either column, it is essential to remember that the child is not making a conscious choice to be "bad" or "naughty," but instead is working within their own abilities and skills. To learn more about factors that may contribute to behaviors in the classroom, refer to Mona Delahooke's book *Beyond Behaviors* (2019). We also encourage you to consult with your school's occupational, physical, and speech therapists.

Behavior	Possible Skills That May be Missing	Possible Neurological Factors
Bumping into others when moving around the classroom	Skills: • Understanding of when to use socially appropriate phrases like "Excuse me" • Knowing how to get peers' attention • Recognizing when to wait one's turn during non-structured routines	Factors: • Difficulty with motor planning, visual-spatial processing, or sensory processing, or other delays that make it difficult for the child to navigate the room and anticipate how to maintain a social distance from others • Delays in understanding others' perspectives and that peers may not want to be bumped into
Frequently becoming angry by losing a game	• Identifying own emotions • Recognizing self-regulatory strategies to stay calm when frustrated • Recognizing emotions in peers • Knowing socially acceptable phrases to use when losing a game	• Processing delays that may limit the child's ability to succeed in the game. This leads to frustration • Delays in the child's executive functioning ability to not act impulsively
Calling out	• Self-management, or the ability to control impulses • Recognizing social cues of others and how frustrated they become with frequent call-outs	• Executive functioning delay • Delays in processing the affect of others
Ignoring teacher directions	• Self-management of stopping one task and transitioning to another • Motor planning of identifying next steps • Not identifying problem-solving steps of how to follow the direction	• Prefrontal cortex delays in executive functioning skills • Not remembering the second or third step in a direction
Frequent movement	• Self-management strategies of how to maintain attention to task • Self-awareness in recognizing one's need and how to appropriately respond	• Weak core that makes it difficult to sit still • Difficulty in maintaining focus for a prolonged period of time • Difficulties with vestibular processing; unable to sit still or sustain attention without moving
Arguing with peers	• Self-awareness in recognizing when one is frustrated • Self-management in recognizing how to remain calm when frustrated • Social awareness and relationship skills in recognizing how to take a peer's perspective and interact with the peer appropriately • Responsible decision making in anticipating what may happen if one does or does not argue	• Delays in recognizing emotions of others • Delays in perspective taking
Avoiding work	• Self-management with understanding how to get started on tasks • Relationship skills of understanding how and when to ask for help	• Executive functioning skills of identifying the steps needed to reach a goal and holding that main goal in one's head in order to meet the goal

Figure 1.9: Observable behaviors and possible reasons behind them.

*Visit **go.SolutionTree.com/instruction** for a free reproducible version of this figure.*

As we dive into the *whys* and *hows* of social-emotional learning, it is important to recognize what an essential piece each individual teacher plays. The relationships students create with their teachers, the teachers' own understanding of social-emotional development and learning, and the teachers' ability to regulate themselves all play a role in providing the right learning environment for students to learn both academics and social-emotional skills (Jennings, 2011).

Conclusion

Now that you have a foundational understanding of how students' neuropsychological states, their individual development, and their executive functioning skills all impact students' behaviors (figure 1.10), you are ready to begin setting up a learning environment that will support *all* children, regardless of developmental differences or neuroceptions. Remember that throughout all these steps, the individual teachers themselves play the greatest roles. Teachers make it possible for students to co-regulate, feel safe, and experience the proper environment to take risks and learn. Social-emotional learning cannot be done through computer games or solely through reading books aloud. The seemingly small decisions teachers make every day in regard to their interactions with both their colleagues and students play a large role in creating these safe learning environments. Chapter 2 (page 45) discusses the key factors educators need to design a safe and effective environment for learning.

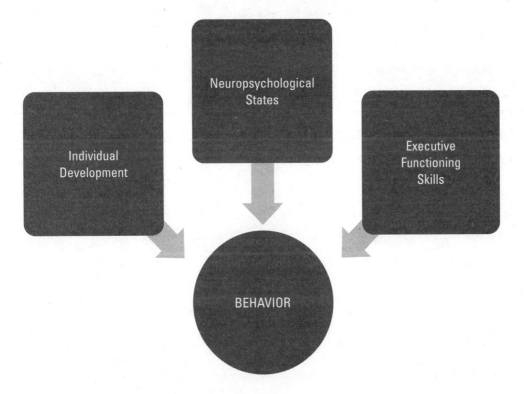

Figure 1.10: Factors influencing behavior.

Tips for Administrators, Teachers, and Support Staff

Figure 1.11 contains tips and reflection questions relating to the contents of this chapter. As you consider these questions and next steps, reflect on your current practices in your own classroom and school.

Administrators	Teachers	Support Staff
• Consider how your interactions with teachers, students, and families support social engagement and neuropsychological safety within your building. • Reflect on your discipline practices. When students need redirection, are the emotional regulation strategies taught in the classrooms supported throughout the building? • Ask: Has your staff built common knowledge, understandings, and language around neuroception, safety cues, and executive functioning skills? • Ask: Does your school have structures in place that allow teachers to come together to brainstorm the best way to support students like Daniel?	• Provide direct instruction, guided practice, and support on the missing SEL and EF skills. (If the root of the behavior is a developmental delay, create a supportive environment to meet your students' needs.) • Work with your colleagues to become SEL competent. Does your team understand the role executive functioning skills play throughout the school day? Build a common understanding of what SEL is and what it is not. • Keep in mind, it is not your job as teachers to diagnose students with developmental delays, but to support students where you see a need. • Teach and practice emotional regulation strategies when students are calm and in the social engagement neuropsychological state.	• During co-teaching, help classroom teachers by observing students' subtle cues. Either provide safety cues and support before the students' behavioral cues escalate or notify the classroom teacher so the teacher can provide the needed support to the student. • Be sure you understand the purpose behind the supportive environment in each classroom you work with. If unsure, ask to set up a time with the classroom teacher to discuss the environment and reflect on how it is working.

Figure 1.11: Tips for administrators, teachers, and support staff from chapter 1.

CHAPTER 2

Establishing Culture, Climate, and the Learning Environment for SEL in Elementary Schools

Vignette: A Tale of Two Schools

After the last bus pulled away from the school, Maria headed to the office to look at Daniel's school file. He had joined her classroom a few months ago after transferring from a school in a nearby district. Maria wanted to get a better idea of what his behavior had been like at his old school and if there was anything that school had found that worked well to keep Daniel calm, engaged, and learning. Peering through the file, she found stacks of office referrals, notes on his report card about his inability to stay calm in the classroom, and a letter to his mother noting that "despite Daniel's daily participation in our schoolwide social-emotional curriculum, Daniel continues to display disrespectful and irresponsible behavior throughout his school day."

Wow, thought Maria. *No wonder his mother doesn't return my phone calls. I wouldn't want to talk to a school either if they were going to write about my son like that. I'd better get in touch with his old teacher to get the full story of what was going on. This file seems to reflect the worst of Daniel—there had to be something positive happening.*

Maria was able to schedule a phone call with Daniel's former teacher for the next day. She soon got an earful from his teacher and filled pages with notes about Daniel's difficulties earlier in the year. From what she learned, Daniel's whole school did a social-emotional lesson every morning that taught self-regulation strategies and helped students identify their feelings. Daniel was often late to school, so he missed some of these lessons. Yet, his teacher said when he was there, he did participate, so he knew how to use strategies like taking a belly breath and asking to take a break and could identify his feelings. He just didn't do any of those things when he was upset. The former teacher stated, "I would tell him, 'I don't want to put up with another outburst; use your calm-down strategies. You're too old to act like this.' Then I'd send him to the back of the room or out to the hall to calm down. Usually, he just kicked things, so then he'd go to the office. I did not have time for that behavior."

His teacher also complained that she had no support or help with Daniel's outbursts from anyone in the school. Unless a student was already in a special education program, there was no available support. She brought him up to various student support committees to talk about his academics, but everyone agreed that his behavior needed to be fixed first. And yet, there were no committees to look into student behavior.

Another issue that became clear to Maria was that Daniel had a positive relationship with the music teacher he'd known since kindergarten. Unfortunately, the music teacher was always stopping by Daniel's classroom to give him mints. They were buddies, the music teacher explained to the classroom teacher in the beginning of the year, and she did not know why his teacher was having so much trouble with him. "He never acts like that for me," she reportedly told his teacher. This clearly bothered the classroom teacher, who was working hard and feeling isolated. Yet the way the school operated, she felt she had nowhere to go but her teammates, whom she often texted after a run-in with the music teacher. "My team agrees that the music teacher is crazy, just like Daniel," she shared. It became clear to Maria that much of this conversation was not about Daniel himself but instead about the school culture and the discomfort the classroom teacher felt with the music teacher. Daniel's former teacher ended the call with, "Sorry you are stuck with him. Good luck."

Maria put down the phone feeling discouraged and heartbroken. Although his old school had an elaborate social-emotional learning program in place, it almost seemed to work against Daniel. It sounded as though it made his teachers resentful of Daniel's behavior since they were teaching everyone to calm down. More than anything, though, Maria was struck by the discord among the staff. It sounded as though the teachers did not respect each other, did not actively work to get on the same page when working with a student like Daniel, and, when tensions ran high, formed cliques to complain instead of addressing the real issues.

What if the school had formed a small team to discuss Daniel? Maria thought. *A team that brought the music teacher, the classroom teacher, and the school counselor together to create a plan so that everyone would be on the same page? I'm sure Daniel picked up on the fact that his classroom teacher disliked the one adult in the building who was nice to him. What message did that send him? What if it was reversed? What if he saw that his trusted adult was a team with his classroom teacher?*

When Maria brought up her thoughts to her grade-level team, she discovered that her colleagues shared her belief that Daniel can learn at high levels. In fact, they were all committed to Daniel's learning and believed it was their collective responsibility to ensure he learned along with all students at that grade level. It was also part of the school's culture to presume positive intentions of all colleagues and honor the collective commitments they had made to each other. You see, Maria and Daniel's school operates as a professional learning community (PLC), where teachers work in collaborative teams deeply engaged in doing the necessary and important but hard work of ensuring all students learn and at high levels.

One main factor of *ensuring learning for all*, as mentioned in the introductory vignette, is careful consideration of the learning environments within schools. For students to have access to learning, they must feel safe and secure, and be a part of their learning environment. We often find this is a missing link for many schools. When schools take time to make these critical elements a focus, they see overall improvement in academic achievement and the social-emotional well-being of the adults and students. In this chapter, we will provide background information regarding positive culture, healthy climate, and safe and effective learning environments, which we consider the foundation of SEL within a school (see figure 2.1, page 48). We will discuss how to establish a deep-rooted positive culture that persists over time to enable effective SEL learning, and how to maintain a healthy school climate. We will then move on to the subject of creating safe, effective, and meaningful physical and cultural learning environments for students. This chapter will conclude with tips for administrators, teachers, and support staff.

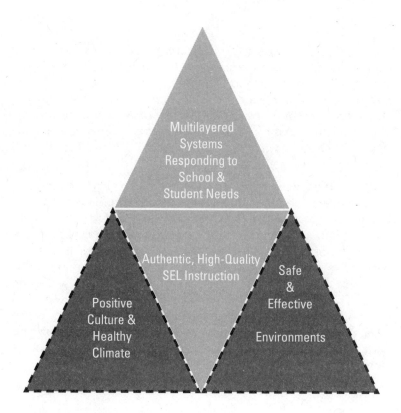

Figure 2.1: SEL schoolwide pyramid.

Establishing a Deep-Rooted Positive Culture and Maintaining a Healthy Climate

When referring to schools, you may often hear people using the terms *climate* and *culture* interchangeably. Yet, school culture and climate are not the same, though they both can have a significant impact on the staff, students, and families. In fact, school culture experts Terrence E. Deal and Kent D. Peterson (1998) state that *culture* involves the norms, values, beliefs, traditions, rituals, and behaviors that build up over time. The beliefs and values of the school faculty have the potential to have a ripple effect on the beliefs and values of students and families. For example, if administrators and teachers have the shared common belief that "all students can and will learn," and students consistently hear language that fosters a growth mindset (for example, "I can do hard things"), it is likely that students will begin to internalize and hold onto these same beliefs. Teachers' collective thoughts, language, and actions can either negatively or positively shape a school's culture. According to Anthony Muhammad (2009), *culture* can be defined as the way we do things and behave, whereas *climate* is how we feel. All things considered, culture takes deep root whereas climate can fluctuate based on people's individual experiences and feelings.

Let's take a moment to consider the analogy of a flower and its root system, as seen in figure 2.2, to help us better understand the differences between culture and climate as well as their close-knit connection. With the proper amount of daily sun and water, a flower can form a solid foundation for itself with its root system deeply embedded into rich, healthy soil. The intricate infrastructure of the flower's root system is a critical component needed for the flower to grow, thrive, and eventually blossom. The root system serves as the flower's foundation, just as culture serves as a school's foundation. Culture shapes how the school's community members think, act, and feel, and it also has the power to affect the overall climate of the school.

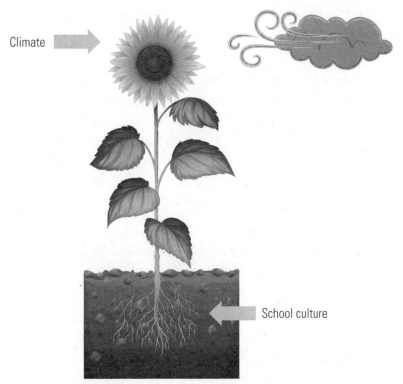

Deeply rooted culture with a strong foundation

Figure 2.2: Visual illustration of school culture versus school climate.

School climate is the part of the flower we see above the ground. While the ever-changing elements (wind, animals, hail, and so on) don't easily affect the flower roots, the stem or petals (climate) have a better chance of being damaged. Although the individual petals may have difficulty weathering a storm, a flower with deep roots will continue to survive. As humans, we are all unique and our feelings can widely differ. Therefore, the attitude or action from one colleague having a bad day has the potential to affect other team members. Likewise, it may be possible for a school's climate to slightly shift or change due to an unforeseen event, such as the death of a colleague or the retirement of a beloved staff member. Yet, if the school has a deeply rooted healthy culture, the temporary climate will not dramatically affect or change the school's built structures, values, or belief systems. A secure culture with deep roots allows for times of discord and provides the security for relationships to repair themselves and resolve conflict (Tronick & Gold, 2020).

Now let's take a moment to think about what might happen if that flower does not get its needed sunlight and water, or if that flower encounters gradual pollution over time. Just as pollution over time can put that flower's root system in jeopardy, so can the consistent negative attitudes and behaviors of a school's community members. Therefore, how can we maintain a positive healthy climate and avoid any cracks that may begin to seep into the foundation—cracks that have the possibility of negatively shifting a school's culture? If we build a strong culture as our foundation (the school's values, beliefs, and behaviors), then when those outside, unexpected events or bad days occur, it will be our strong cultural foundation that holds us up and keeps us moving forward. If we have effective systems in place to consistently monitor the climate, then we can proactively avoid the cracks from even forming.

Creating and maintaining a positive school culture and healthy climate is not just about implementing one particular schoolwide program or behavior plan. In fact, it requires the collective effort of all school community members, including caregivers or families. In a strategy brief, Elisabeth Kane, Natalie Hoff, Ana Cathcart, Allie Heifner, Shir Palmon, and Reece L. Peterson (2016) share Albert Bandura's (2001) social-cognitive theory:

> While teachers and students share the same school environment, they have very different roles in the school, which leads to different perceptions of the same experience. Although parents and families are not consistently in the schools, their perceptions are also important because they often dictate their children's attitudes about school, where they send their children to school, and the degree to which their family engages or participates with the school (Schueler, Capotosto, Bahena, McIntyre, & Gehlbach, 2014). (p. 6)

A strong positive culture is built with a community; therefore, it takes the work of all faculty and staff members (administrators, office and cafeteria staff, bus drivers, teachers, and so on), students, and families to build a supportive, positive, and effective schoolwide culture. Additionally, it is critical that schools also find ways to promote a positive and healthy climate for all school community members. The feelings surrounding our safety and our relationships can affect school climate. Tim Walker (2016) shares, from a review of Ruth Berkowitz, Hadass Moore, Ron Avi Astor, and Rami Benbenishty's (2016) educational research, that:

> Many educators, for example, instinctively tie school climate to school safety. But a positive school climate can also depend on how connected or engaged a student feels in school, the strength of relationships with school staff, and the state of parental involvement.

When a student walks into a building or a parent enters a school's office, are they welcomed with smiles, a positive tone, and kind words? Are teachers facilitating relationship building with and between students? The Centers for Disease Control and Prevention (CDC, 2009) describe *school connectedness* as "the belief by students that adults and peers in the school care about their learning as well as about them as individuals" (p. 3). That connectedness and sense of community comes from students' daily experiences and the strong relationships they build over time. When relationships (staff/student, staff/staff, or student/student) are built on mutual trust and respect and these relationships are perceived as safe (psychologically, socially, or emotionally), it readily lays the foundation for both student and adult learning to occur (Niehaus et al., 2012). Shared collaborative learning experiences between adults and students can help cultivate a growth mindset and build community. When students see teachers embrace their own errors, make mistakes, or model productive struggle, they are nurturing a growth mindset and actively modeling persistence. As a result, if community members feel psychologically safe in their relationships, they are more likely to take responsible risks and be transparent and open to learning from others. SEL is not about asking the students to change but rather asking every member of the school to become a part of this growth mindset community.

Administrators and school leaders play a vital role in helping a school build a positive healthy culture and climate. In fact, building a healthy school culture requires more than a set of policies and procedures school administrators dictate. Some of this critical work involves setting expectations, supporting collective responsibility and accountability, and encouraging transparency and relationship building, amongst many other important facets (see figure 2.3).

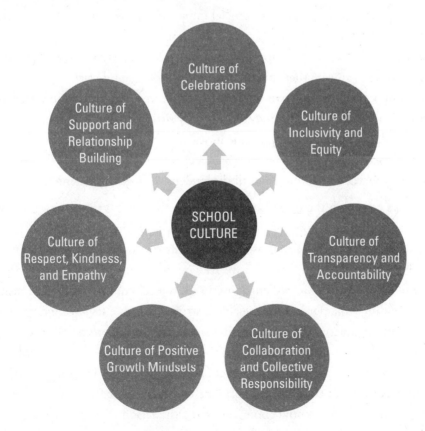

Figure 2.3: Facets of school culture.

All things considered, culture is built through our shared experiences, and to establish a community of learners, all its members must provide input, have a voice, and be actively engaged in the decision-making process. Therefore, we suggest that a school's community members invest time into collaboratively building the culture and developing systems for closely monitoring the climate.

To learn more about how to build the collaborative culture of a professional learning community, refer to SolutionTree.com, and to specifically learn about transforming a school's culture, refer to Anthony Muhammad's (2009) book *Transforming School Culture: How to Overcome Staff Division*. We focus in greater detail on the work of a school establishing a positive schoolwide culture and maintaining a healthy climate in chapter 3 (page 93).

Creating Effective and Meaningful Physical and Cultural Environments in Elementary School

The learning environment for both adults and students is equally important and intertwined with school culture and climate. In fact, Strong-Wilson and Ellis (2007) state that "because children's experiences are limited by their surroundings, the environment we provide for them has a crucial impact on the way the child's brain develops" (p. 43). In the 21st century, we expect that when students leave their school experiences and enter the workforce, they will have the skills to collaborate and work on teams, communicate their ideas, and use technology and critical thinking skills to problem solve. But how can students learn to work on a team in a traditional classroom model if they spend most of their day sitting quietly in rows at a desk and working independently? How can students learn how to communicate their ideas and learn how to agree or disagree with peers in a classroom when most of the instruction consists of the teacher telling while all the students just sit and listen?

Teachers can teach these 21st century skills by integrating them with the instruction of core academic content areas (mathematics, science, language arts, social studies, and so on) as well as those content areas relating to fine arts and physical education and health, and SEL. But we ask you, how can students become rigorous problem solvers if they are not engaging in high-level-cognitive-demand tasks but rather spending large portions of valuable instructional time reviewing homework or solving thirty mathematics problems using algorithms that they don't have conceptual understanding of? A teacher's pedagogy, the learning environment, the relationships teachers have with their students, instructional practices, and how they facilitate and structure learning all connect and correlate to one another (figure 2.4). Therefore, teachers not only must know about the best instructional practices used to teach concepts but must also think about the learning environment and how it supports children's varied learning profiles as well as necessary 21st century skills (for example, problem solving, communication, critical thinking, and so on).

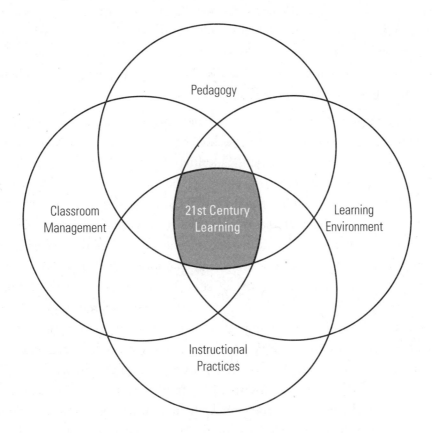

Figure 2.4: Interconnections of the 21st century classroom.

In the following sections, we explore how various schools' physical and cultural environments are key elements in students' social-emotional learning. While it can be tempting to use a specific curriculum to teach SEL skills, or to teach SEL as though it is a separate subject area, it is important to keep in mind that students' ability to learn, use, and make a developmental process hinges not just on our specific lessons but on the broader learning environment. Therefore, we must carefully consider the different features of both the physical and cultural environment to ensure strong SEL and development.

Have you ever walked into a space and immediately felt a sense of calm, warmth, or welcoming? Was the space light or dark? Did it contain objects or walls with warm or cool colors? Was it quiet, loud, or was there gentle music playing? Pamela Woolner, Elaine Hall, Steve Higgins, Caroline McCaughey, and Kate Wall (2007) share that, "Physical features of learning spaces can stimulate emotions, create a sense of security, and prepare the students to learn" (p. 70). If twenty-five third graders walk into a classroom, will they all have the same emotions or feelings? We have been in many classrooms over twenty years of teaching, and we have noticed similar trends that occur in many classroom environments. One trend is teachers dimming the lights and playing soft music after students come in from recess. For many, this experience could create a feeling of calm, but for some students that music, although quiet and slow paced, might be overstimulating. Too many visual stimuli or a disorganized classroom can create overstimulation for some. Did you ever think that what might seem appealing to you or some of your students might actually be overwhelming or dysregulating for others? It's important to consider what the current research says about the physical environment and how we can create environments throughout the school that are supportive to *all* learners.

Think about the various environments a child shifts between each day after leaving their home environment each morning (school bus, gymnasium, classroom, cafeteria, playground, and so on) and the potential positive or negative impacts of each of these environments on the student's psychological and physical safety. If a child's neuroception of safety, as discussed in chapter 1 (page 23), has the potential to affect student learning, then it is vital that all members of the school community have time to learn together about how to provide safe and secure spaces in each of these environments. Although a great deal of academic and social-emotional learning occurs within the classroom settings, we must remember that considerable social-emotional learning and skill practicing also occurs in the nonacademic environmental settings (for example, the cafeteria, playground, or school bus). Therefore, careful consideration regarding all these learning environments is necessary and important. In chapter 3 (page 93), we share useful tools that highlight important features of both the physical and cultural environment that can support teams in shifting from being reactive to more proactive and encourage schools to work collaboratively in creating highly effective environments across the school setting and within the learning environments of classrooms.

You will notice that in figure 2.5 we outline some key features of both the physical and cultural environments of the school. Within the physical environment, we discuss learning spaces, sensory features, and storage and materials. Within the cultural environment, we discuss classroom expectations and organization; relationship building; mindset, motivation, and engagement; and learning experiences. In the following sections, we will touch on these key components of both the physical and cultural environments and provide you with many examples of how you can adapt these to create an environment optimal for all learning.

Schoolwide Environments

SAFETY

Physical Environment			Cultural Environment			
Learning Spaces	Sensory Features	Storage & Materials	Schoolwide & Classroom Expectations & Organization	Relationship Building	Mindset, Motivation, and Engagement	Learning Experiences

Physical Environment

Learning Spaces

Schoolwide Spaces (including playground, gym, cafeteria, hallways, and classrooms):
- Safe and organized
- Interactive, well organized, and visually appealing wall space

Classroom Furniture Arrangements and Physical Spaces:
- Designated large-group, small-group, and individual learning spaces
- Designated areas where students can calm down and use self-regulation strategies
- Content-specific spaces (for example, independent reading area with classroom library)
- Storage for student belongings
- Outdoor learning spaces

Sensory Features

Schoolwide and Classroom Sensory Features:
- Lighting that is not harsh and does not make distracting sounds (effective suggestions include use of natural light or LED lighting)
- Good acoustics in all parts of the room as well as positive acoustical strategies
- Comfortable temperature
- Accessible, clear visuals
- Flexible seating to allow students to participate by sitting, standing, or accessing adapted seating options (such as stools, wobble chairs, or exercise balls)

Storage & Materials

Learning Materials and Tools:
- Materials are organized and easy access for teachers and students
- Students have choices of provided learning materials
- Learning tools promote engagement, exploration, and experimentation
- Learning tools showcase diversity and reflect students' cultural backgrounds in read-alouds, bulletin boards, interactive visuals, and other areas

Cultural Environment

Schoolwide & Classroom Expectations & Organization

Procedures and Routines:
- Efficient and clear instructions
- Responsive and flexible daily schedule
- Transitions maximize instructional time

Behavioral Expectations:
- Community created and clearly defined
- Clearly understood and commonly used across school settings

Student-Centered Problem Solving:
- Opportunities for both students and staff to brainstorm solutions
- Encourage collaborative discussions.

Staff Self-Reflection and Self-Regulation:
- Scheduled time for staff reflection
- Staff learning opportunities on the importance of monitoring their own emotional responses

Relationship Building

Intentionally Fostering Positive Relationships Between:
- School community
- Classroom community
- Teachers and students
- Students and other students
- School staff
- Families and school staff

Mindset, Motivation, and Engagement

Positive Atmosphere:
- Positive language and actions of school staff (administrators, teachers, office staff, and so on) and students

Growth Mindset:
- Teacher classroom practices and behaviors

Respect and Values:
- Involve the ideas and learning of all community members
- Reflect diversity and inclusion

Student Voice and Agency:
- Student-centered learning
- Student choice and responsibility in learning
- Opportunities for students to give constructive feedback to teachers and peers
- Class and individual student goal setting

Engagement and Motivation:
- Effective teacher practices
- Measuring and monitoring levels of student engagement

Learning Experiences

Learning Activities:
- Differentiated and accessible to all students
- Reflect values and cultures of all learners
- Promote diversity
- Are rigorous, engaging, and foster critical thinking skills

Rich Classroom Discourse:
- Students engage in productive struggle and practice skills of reasoning and justifying, agreeing and disagreeing, and so on within the classroom community.

Teacher-Guided Learning Structures:
- Whole- and small-group guided instruction (for example, workshop model)
- Guided play

Student Learning Structures:
- Individual independent learning
- Cooperative learning (working with a partner or in a group)
- Student-directed activities (student choice, play)

Figure 2.5: Physical and cultural environmental qualities for effective and meaningful environments.

Visit go.SolutionTree.com/instruction for a free reproducible version of this figure.

The Physical Environment

Many teachers already have their physical environment ready to go before students even enter the classroom on day one. So much hard work goes into the process of setting up the classroom learning environment. In fact, many of the visual displays will become interactive teaching tools, and the systems put into place early on will allow for easy access of tools for both teachers and students. Yet, think about the message we send to students if there is a list of rules posted on the wall and everything is already set up for them, including their names neatly written on a laminated name tag taped onto the top of students' desks. Now consider what it might look like for both teachers and students to have shared input into the physical and cultural aspects of the learning environment. Take a moment to think if those rules were created during the first week of school, with student contributions through guided facilitation, and if students had some choice in seating as well as an opportunity to create their own name tags. These little tasks may seem trivial, yet they can be very meaningful and often set the tone for a shared learning space. As a matter of fact, Marzita Puteh, Che Nidzam Che Ahmad, Noraini Mohamed Noh, Mazlini Adnan, and Mohd Hairy Ibrahim (2015) share evidence of a significantly positive relationship between the physical environment and the comfort level of both teachers and learners. Often how we structure the physical environment can set the tone for the cultural environment.

Some physical environmental features may be out of a teacher's control, such as the ability to regulate the temperature, the noise of a loud heater, or those bright fluorescent lights that flicker throughout the school day. But believe it or not, the cold room and bright fluorescent lights of a classroom can affect a student's ability to learn. Schneider (2002) reviewed literature on the physical aspects of the classroom and their effect on student outcomes. As expected, he concluded that structuring a classroom with attention to the physical elements of furnishings, technology, air quality, temperature, light, and acoustic conditions, as well as comfortable and safe learning environments, is important to a student's performance. The physical environment of the school includes the indoor spaces (classrooms, gym, lunchroom, and so on) as well as the outdoor spaces (the playground and outdoor learning areas), and how we arrange these spaces for students' physical health, safety, and security is an important and influential task for the school and all its community members.

The following sections will discuss how to create an effective physical learning environment by considering (1) sensory features, and (2) learning spaces, storage, and materials.

Sensory Features

There is great power in being aware of the sensory features within school spaces and how they might have an effect on your students' learning. Often there are simple solutions to these issues. For instance, if the temperature of the room is cold, encourage students to bring in sweatshirts, or if the noise of a heater might bother a particular student, consider providing that student with earplugs, noise-canceling headphones, or an alternative place to work away from the noise.

Light

Shishegar and Boubekri (2016) state that studies show while many factors can influence the school environment and student performance, light has been found to be one of the biggest influencers. Not only does light have visual influences on people by creating glare or causing headaches but it also has nonvisual effects on people. Natural light can impact students physically, mentally, behaviorally, and academically. In fact, these studies show that natural light can improve a person's mood, attention, cognitive performance, sleep, and overall alertness. One study by the Heschong Mahone Group (1999) showed that students learning in classrooms with more natural light rather than artificial light perform better on assessments. Some schools that have fluorescent lights, which can be harsh and make loud buzzing noises, have now begun to purchase filter light covers, which can reduce the harsh glare of the light. Some schools are shifting to using LED lighting and providing more access to natural light. Although natural light has proven to be a benefit to students, careful considerations of its influence in classroom spaces should be well planned and thought out when designing learning spaces within the larger school and classroom settings. In fact, the *National Best Practices Manual for Building High Performance Schools* from the Department of Energy (2007) recommends designing classroom spaces to avoid sunlight penetrating into sensitive teaching spaces and creating a glare. It also recommends providing uniform and gentle lighting throughout learning spaces, controlling the natural light source with the use of blinds, and planning the layout of school spaces to take advantage of daylight conditions.

Additionally, Anthes (2009) shares that brain research may assist people in creating spaces that could help people relax or be more alert. This specifically states that while bright light has the potential to boost cognition, on the other hand it may also affect one's actual current need for relaxation. As we mentioned earlier, some teachers seem aware of this as they often dim lights after recess, seeing that it has a relaxing effect on some students. I (Tracey) will admit that although I may have made small decisions about light usage within my classroom, such as moving a whiteboard or closing the blinds to avoid the sun's glare, when initially designing the layout and setting up the learning spaces for myself and students, I never specifically considered the positive or negative impacts of light. It was not until later in my career that I learned how the light within and outside my classroom may impact students with sensory issues. Had I known some of these influential factors previously, I would have made different decisions about my classroom setup. Now I know to take light into consideration when deciding where to place the mobile whiteboard and the technology stations, and when to use light as a tool for recharging or boosting cognition. Additionally, I know it is worth advocating to change the flickering fluorescent lights and taking time to modify the environment for sensory-sensitive students.

Sound

In addition to considerations regarding the light features of our classrooms, the acoustics within a classroom setting can affect student learning as well. According to the American Speech-Language-Hearing Association (ASHA, n.d.), part of the learning process takes into account hearing as well as understanding. A variety of ambient noises from inside the classroom (such as elevated levels of talking or background noises) can create conditions that can make it more difficult for learning. This can be true in different spaces within one classroom as well. I (Ann-Bailey) once had a student who complained that he could not hear his teacher because of the loud air conditioner. When he asked his teacher to repeat herself, she thought he was being difficult on purpose and would reprimand him. He stopped asking for repetition and felt disconnected from the classroom. He assumed the teacher did not like him and stopped turning in his work. When I went to observe in the classroom, I discovered that while most of the classroom could hear the teacher, for some reason, there was a small pocket in the room, near my student's desk, where it was nearly impossible to hear the teacher over the air conditioner. Once I brought this to the teacher's attention and she experienced it herself, she was able to change the environment and begin to make repairs in her relationship with the student.

Recommendations from ASHA for improving classroom acoustics include the following (American Speech-Language-Hearing Association, n.d.):

- Place rugs or carpet in the room.
- Hang curtains or blinds in the windows.
- Hang soft materials such as felt or corkboard on the walls.
- Place tables at an angle around the room instead of in rows.
- Turn off noisy equipment when it is not in use.
- Replace noisy light fixtures.
- Show students how hard it can be to hear when many children talk at the same time.
- Place soft tips on the bottom of chairs and tables.

Schools may also consider using sound field systems, which can help students focus on their teachers' voice over background noises (da Cruz et al., 2016). Often these systems require the teacher to wear a wireless microphone and place speakers throughout the room to dispense sound throughout the classroom for students. These systems differ from traditional speakers as they evenly distribute the sound across the room instead of simply making the sound louder. The goal is not to increase the volume of the teacher's voice but to make it easiest to hear above the ambient noise in the room. Teachers who misunderstand this concept believe they can amplify their own voice by just speaking louder or using microphones to increase their volume. This can backfire as it creates additional stress in the environment. Gail Gegg Rosenberg and colleagues (1999) share research that "students in amplified classrooms demonstrated significant improvement in listening and learning behaviors and skills, and progressed at a faster rate than their grade-alike peers in unamplified classrooms" (p. 8). In surveying my first-grade class in 2007, the speech pathologist and I (Ann-Bailey) found that students self-reported being able to pay better attention and feeling less frustration when the sound field system was in use. In addition, we found that the first-grade students learning English showed a better use of suffixes in their writing than those in classrooms that did not use the sound system. We believed the students were better able to tune in, hear the ends of their teachers' words, and apply that to their writing.

Teachers should also be mindful of the general noise levels during certain times of the day and with certain subject areas. During these known high-noise periods, they can implement specific management strategies when needed, as well as making modifications for students with sensitivity to noises or those with learning disabilities.

Seating

In addition to considering the importance of the lighting and acoustics in the classroom, teachers should also consider where their students are sitting and working in the classroom. A newer trend is providing flexible seating options for students. Eric Jensen (2005) shares that there is strong evidence regarding learning and movement. He states:

> When we keep students active, we keep their energy levels up and provide their brains with the oxygen-rich blood needed for highest performance. Teachers who insist that students remain seated during the entire class period are not promoting optimal conditions for learning. (p. 66)

Jensen (2005) shares evidence that exercise and even moderate movement improves cognition. Unlike traditional desks and chairs, flexible seating options, such as standing at a table or desk, sitting on a stool (possibly one that requires a student to use their core strength to stay balanced), or even using an exercise ball as a seat, all allow students to have some level of movement. In fact, in one study, Denise Lynn Schilling and Ilene S. Schwartz (2004) showed that improvements in engagement and in-seat behavior were seen when students with autism spectrum disorders were able to use therapy balls as seating. In addition, Judy Willis (2010) shares that curiosity and change can support student engagement. So take a moment to envision a classroom with various seating options, where students have some level of choice in the seating that works for them in varied learning situations through their day. The term *flexible* implies that students are not just assigned to one seating option for the day, week, or month; rather, they may start off sitting in a chair but know that it is acceptable and encouraged for them to take breaks, stand, and stretch during writing time, or at independent reading time they can find a comfortable spot in the classroom to read, which may be at the carpet or near the window to access more natural light. Or, think about those students who may struggle to stay seated at the carpet for a read-aloud and consider offering them a wobble stool or exercise ball to sit on at the edge of the carpet during this time. Although this might at first seem overwhelming, the use of flexible seating can be effective when paired with a clear set of routines and procedures understood by students and closely monitored by the teacher.

As the field of neuroscience brings us more information about how children and adults maintain a regulated and alert state of awareness to best process, store, and retrieve information, we can continue to make improvements to our classroom environments. School teams should stay open to new research providing insight into how best to create learning environments for all students.

Learning Spaces, Storage, and Materials

Schoolwide beliefs and values will influence many of the physical features of the classroom. For example, if we want students to be able to easily communicate and process ideas with each other, having a designated space in one area for students to gather, such as a carpet in the front of the classroom or a group of chairs moved closer together, can be very meaningful. When we offer things such as choice in the learning environment, it is important to carefully and thoughtfully plan out the learning spaces where students can exert their independence and have easy access to the needed learning materials. In making these decisions, it is important for the teacher to think about not only how the learning materials should be organized but also the necessary procedures and policies required to limit transition and off-task time. These materials should be engaging, invoke a sense of curiosity and exploration, and serve as a catalyst for student learning. Beyond the aesthetics of the carpet or the newest technology being used, carefully considered learning spaces (whole- or small-group, student focused, or independent) and materials should be something that teachers proactively plan for and reflect on in an ongoing basis.

We know that all learners are individuals and what might work for some may not work for others. Therefore, we can start by establishing an effective learning environment that supports all students and tailoring that environment to meet the needs of individual students. Getting to know your students and their needs is important and should start from day one and continue throughout the entire school year. In chapter 5 (page 223), we will share a planning tool to help teachers in adapting the learning environment and building in additional support for students (see table 5.2, page 259).

Informal surveying during your morning meetings and messages can be a constant way to get to know some of your students and their individual needs or preferences. Also, think about using a more formal type of survey that you could administer to students in school or send home to parents regarding possible aversions to sound, light, temperature, or a student's need for frequent movement during learning. At the start of the year, questionnaires sent home to parents to gather student information are typically open ended or generic. Questions may include the following.

- Share some important information about your child.

- What are your child's strengths or challenges?

However, think about the power of specifically asking questions about students' preferences regarding the physical features of the learning environments. For example,

- Describe your child when they are focused and intently working on a task they enjoy (for example, building a Lego set). Do they move their feet or sway with their body? Do they prefer to stand, sit, or lie down?

- Does your child remain quiet when focused on a challenging but enjoyable task, or do they like to share their ideas with someone nearby?

- What type of distractions are likely to frustrate your child? For example, are they frustrated by noises like a vacuum cleaner or lots of talking? By pictures or other items they can see? By different smells?

The learning environments within the school setting should be flexible, and environmental shifts throughout the year should be based primarily on the needs of the students.

Ultimately, we need to start asking ourselves the following questions.

- Do we expect students to conform to the environment of the adults' needs, or should the environment be created to meet the needs of all community members?

- What action steps will be taken to learn about students' specific environmental needs, preferences, or supports?

- Are there any environmental features that could potentially interfere with student learning, and if so, can anything be done to modify the physical environment or can additional supports be used to meet student needs?

Taking proactive measures early on in the school year has the potential to thwart some significant behavioral issues, which may have been challenging and possibly difficult to interpret. Consider having the knowledge, early on in the year, that one of your students struggles with loud noises. In this situation, you have the opportunity not only to support the student within your classroom but also to proactively accommodate other potentially challenging settings for that student, such as the lunch room, music class, physical education environment, outdoor recess spaces, fire drills, and so on. Living through the COVID-19 pandemic makes us all consider how our physical health and safety significantly impact our psychological safety, and how careful considerations about the physical aspects of the school setting can support both student and adult physical and emotional well-being.

We can see how much goes into learning, and as we continue to discover more about the brain and navigate 21st century influential factors, it's important to continuously learn, adapt, and improve on our practices. All aspects of the school environment should be safe and supportive, and the physical and cultural learning spaces should be teacher directed and student empowered.

The Cultural Environment

Just as we must devote time to structuring the physical environment of our classrooms, we must equally dedicate time to the cultural aspects of both the larger school and classroom settings.

If you walk into a classroom where all students are sitting quietly at the carpet listening to the teacher talk, it may feel as though this teacher is doing everything right. But quiet students do not necessarily indicate that learning is occurring. Some students may be learning, while others may have learned to sit quietly and nod along with the teacher so as not to give a clue that they do not understand the material. No matter how the classroom environment appears to outsiders—no matter how new the technology is or how beautifully organized the classroom is—students may not be learning due to factors such as attention and focus difficulties or other disorders that have the potential to impede a student's learning. Alternatively, it could just be that students might not feel psychologically safe and may be too worried to ask questions, may resist taking responsible risks, or may not allow themselves to become immersed in the material because they are worried about psychological threats in the environment. Although some factors may be out of our control, many are actually within it, and how we build the cultural environment is paramount to student learning and achievement.

We have begun to paint the picture that there is more to learning than just structuring the physical environment and using effective curriculum tools. In fact, teaching and student learning requires a multifaceted approach. According to Robert J. Marzano, Jana S. Marzano, and Debra J. Pickering (2003), student learning is impacted by the results of effective teachers who have a well-managed classroom, employ effective instructional practices and a well-designed curriculum, and use effective classroom management techniques. Rules and procedures, disciplinary interventions, teacher-student relationship building, mental set, and student responsibilities are five distinct areas that Marzano's team identifies as essential to overall classroom management. Building off of this work, we have broken down the cultural aspects of the environment into four distinct areas: (1) classroom expectations and organization; (2) relationship building; (3) mindsets, motivation, and engagement; and (4) learning experiences (see figure 2.5, page 55). As you read each section, take time to reflect on the cultural environment of your own school and classroom and consider what is well-established and which areas you may want to strengthen.

Schoolwide and Classroom Expectations and Organization

Any first-year teacher can relate to the notion that one's ability to manage a classroom full of multiple personalities is key to a teacher's survival. Although it can be tempting to attempt to create an intricate system that keeps all negative behaviors away and encourages perfect student actions, it is important to keep in mind that our management systems play a large role in creating our classroom environment and contributing to a student's sense of safety, belonging, and connection. Systems such as using a public behavior chart that shows a student is on a red, yellow, or green color (a stoplight system) can interfere with a child's ability to learn self-regulation skills, reflect on behavior, and build a positive relationship with the adult in the classroom (Jung & Smith, 2018). We must keep in mind that the word *discipline* stems from the Latin word *discipulus*, which means "knowledge" or "to learn." Discipline should be about teaching and supporting our students, not simply providing consequences for misbehaviors.

I (Ann-Bailey) once attended a conference where they asked each of us to submit our name and the phone number of a loved one. After each of us had completed this task, they collected our responses and introduced us to our new behavior system. If we were talking or getting up too much during the lecture, our name would be written on the board. If we did it again, we would receive a check mark. After two checks, our loved one would be called. The room went silent as 200 adults contemplated what it felt like to be treated in this manner. Although we quickly realized they were using this exercise to make a point, we still had an initial visceral reaction. Though we responded in different ways—some felt insulted, some were stressed, some wanted to please, and others immediately decided not to please and to act up on purpose—a few people walked out. These systems do not create community or the positive learning environment needed to provide safety and positive relationships. In fact, they do the opposite. And while these behavior management systems may create the illusion of a quiet, well-behaved set of students that administrators may write up positively or earn their teacher a reputation of running a tight ship, they can undermine the very environment needed for true and authentic learning.

Instead of creating reactive classroom management systems that focus on noting or tracking a student's misbehavior, the focus of classroom management should be on proactively providing students with a structured learning environment where they know the routines, have positive relationships with their teachers and other students, and are able to reflect and reframe behavior (Rimm-Kaufman & Chiu, 2007). Misbehavior should be met through a student-teacher problem-solving approach (Greene, 2008). Classroom management should be intricately tied into your SEL program so that students understand how their behaviors stem from their own emotions. So, if we shift our mindset from the teacher as a classroom manager to a classroom facilitator—one who organizes, designs, and coordinates many of the functions to support learning—we encourage shared responsibility on the parts of both the teacher and the students.

In the following sections, we will address six aspects of classroom expectations and organization.

- Planned and structured procedures and routines
- Timing and transitions
- Responsive routines

- Behavioral expectations
- Student-focused problem solving
- Self-reflection and self-regulation

Planned and Structured Procedures and Routines

An essential aspect of a classroom management system is that students clearly know and understand the expectations within the space. At the beginning of the year, as well as after longer breaks from school, teachers should devote time to teaching and practicing the classroom routines such as how to enter the classroom, put away backpacks, turn in work, or come to the group gathering space. Practicing these routines and using positive language to reinforce, remind, and redirect students of the expected behaviors within the routines will serve to both give students the procedural memories of physically participating in the routines and send the message that the teachers believe the students are capable of following the expectations (Crowe, 2009).

Teachers should clearly teach every routine—from how to calmly enter the classroom in the morning, to how to line up for lunch—and these should be practiced and understood by all students. Students should have a clear understanding of classroom procedures such as how to turn in homework, how to ask to go to the bathroom, and how to ask for help when needed. Procedures should be simple, easy to understand and remember. To support all students, the individual steps of the routine should be posted in a picture schedule. This will help students who may have difficulty organizing themselves when given multistep directions, students who are easily distracted, students who have difficulty remembering verbal directions, and students with strong visual memories. Proactively providing a picture support for the steps of the routine will support all learners, not just those with identified disabilities. Teachers can use stock pictures or take pictures of their students following the routine and post those in the classroom. Some schools post visuals to reinforce whole-school routines in the common areas, such as the gym, hallways, bathrooms, and cafeteria.

Ideally, these familiar and practiced procedures should be consistent from classroom to classroom, including the music, art, and physical education rooms. This allows all students to put their cognitive energy into learning their academic work instead of trying to remember the expectations of each teacher and individual environment. Simplicity and familiarity with procedures is key for students with anxiety and ADHD, as well as those learning English. It can be difficult to remember the English words to ask to go to the bathroom, let alone to remember the key terminology each teacher requests. Some schools use a consistent sign language gesture for students to request to use the bathroom. The consistency in this routine across a school allows students to feel comfortable knowing they can get their needs met.

Another procedure that schools and classrooms should consider in maintaining a proactive learning environment is to provide students with an area in the room where they feel comfortable going to help themselves calm down, regroup, or take a break.

This can be an area where students choose to go on their own, or where a teacher asks them to go to take a break if needed. Both the Responsive Classroom program and the Conscious Discipline program share examples of such classroom spaces (Bailey, 2015; Castelli, 2017). Students should be proactively taught how to use these spaces and allowed to practice removing themselves and going to the area. Teachers can leave a sand timer in the space along with clear visual explanations of the appropriate behaviors in the spot. This area should be visible to the teacher and allow the student to still see instruction so that they do not miss out on the learning in the lesson from this spot. The design of these spaces is not to punish students but to give them an opportunity to self-regulate and use calming strategies. This should not be seen as a negative consequence but instead a more factual "I need some space right now to calm down. I know where I can go." In fact, teachers can model using the space themselves when they are feeling overwhelmed and need regulating themselves. To support students who utilize the safe place or calm-down area often, proactively talk with them about how they can use those same strategies at times when these spaces are not available to them. Develop a plan with that student for what to do if another student is in the calm-down spot, or if they are in the cafeteria, playground, or gym where a calm-down area is not designated. Come up with alternative plans so that the students will feel empowered and able to use these strategies no matter the location.

Timing and Transitions

Misbehavior or off-task activities can occur during transitions when students are moving from one area of the classroom to another or from one activity to another. These more open-ended moments of whole-class activity lend themselves to students becoming distracted or even overwhelmed with a noisy environment or the visual stimulation of lots of movement. Students with motor-planning difficulties may worry about navigating their way from one place in the classroom to another in the midst of all the movement.

Tight transitions keep students engaged and on task, and decrease anxiety. And yet, well-timed transitions are difficult for teachers to manage effectively. We provide more tips about engaging transitions connected to learning content and skills in chapters 4 (page 157) and 5 (page 223).

Transitions are another aspect of the classroom that students should practice throughout the year. Teachers should provide a set amount of time so that students know how much time they have to transition, which often includes multistep directions of putting items away, moving to a new place in the classroom, and getting out a new set of materials. A visual timer placed where all students can see it will assist with this process and allow students to make decisions about their time management. Another way to provide positive support during a transition is to play a familiar song. Use the same song every time so the students know exactly how much time they have to transition as they become familiar with the rhythm of the song. As a kindergarten and first-grade teacher, I (Ann-Bailey) used to signal students to transition by beginning to sing *Five Little Ducks Went Out to Play*. The students joined in with me—singing students cannot talk to each other, so they were immediately less off-task—and they knew that everyone needed to be sitting down by the time all five ducks were back. Another favorite song from my first graders was the "Everybody have a seat" song, which let us sing exactly what the expectation was: "Everybody have a seat, have a seat, have a seat, everybody have a seat on the floor. Not on the ceiling, not on the door! Everybody have a seat on the floor!"

Responsive Routines

A key to providing students with predictability is to provide a set daily schedule for the class. You should post this daily schedule in a common area so that all students can view it, and include pictures as well as words to support students who may still be learning to read. Review the schedule each morning so that students know what to expect and what is occurring each day. Some children may benefit from individual schedules at their desks and individual morning check-ins with an adult in the building who can further discuss the schedule and any changes that may develop. Daily schedules should also allow for flexibility and responsiveness to change. Using a pocket chart, a magnetic board, or a Velcro board with schedule icons you can move will allow you to create a schedule you can change to reflect the needs of each day.

While each classroom needs clear routines and procedures, these routines must also provide flexibility for when teachers are called to respond to the needs of the students. There are times when lessons need to go longer or should be shortened, or when there is a need for a class meeting because of strong emotions of students. During college, I (Ann-Bailey) was taking a computer science class when September 11 occurred. While every other professor cancelled class that day, our professor did not feel the need to do so. I remember staring at my computer in the lab, not processing the assignment. I wanted to complete it, but I had no idea where to start. The professor's inability to respond to our class needs left many of us with additional anxiety and a belief that we could not do computer science, when in fact many of us could complete the same lab the day before or a week later—we only failed to do it on the afternoon of September 11. Alternatively, if students are not understanding the content being taught and you begin to notice more off-task behavior, it may be a clear signal that you need to modify the lesson you had originally planned to meet the needs of students in the moment in real time.

Another factor to consider when thinking about our routines and schedules is to acknowledge the importance of being consistent and predictable in our relationships with students. Bruce Perry (2016) states that,

> Safety is created by predictability, and predictability is created by consistent behaviors. And the consistency that leads to predictability does not come from rigidity in the timing of activities it comes from the consistency of interaction from the teacher. If a schedule

is consistent, but the teacher is not, there is no predictability for the child. Predictability in time means less to a young child than predictability in people.

Therefore, we can't just dedicate time to establishing well-structured and consistent procedures and routines within our classrooms; we must also ensure that our interactions with our students are predictable as well as genuine, helping our students to feel safe in their learning environments. This sense of safety is what students truly need for student learning and growth!

Behavioral Expectations

Along with teaching routines and procedures in the beginning of the year, teachers must also clearly state their behavioral expectations. These expectations should be simple, clear, and positive. A long list of rules or expectations makes it difficult for students to remember all the rules. It can also take students' cognitive attention away from academics while they try to remember all the rules. Long lists of rules can create anxiety in some students, while in others they create a sense of hopelessness: "Why try to follow any of them? I can't even remember them!"

Instead, identify clear and simple expectations that are easy to remember and cover a wide range of settings and behaviors. Turn "No running in the hallways" into "Treat our environment with respect." (See table 2.1 for additional examples.) Take time to discuss what treating an environment with respect looks like, sounds like, and feels like. Help students to recognize how they will treat their hallways with respect (walking, hands to sides, quiet whispers if they need to talk). Walk your students through the hallways to have them practice these expectations and use positive language to reinforce their behavior. The program Conscious Discipline recommends only two expectations—*Be Safe* and *Be Helpful*—noting that every student action can fall under either category. Some teachers use one rule—*Take care of yourself, your classmates, and your environment*. Expectations should be stated as what a student will do, not what behavior they will not do. Notice that these statements can be applied anywhere in the school building as they are not specific to a location, subject, or teacher.

Table 2.1: Restating Expected Behaviors

Negative Statement	Restated With Expected Behavior
No running.	Use walking feet.
No hitting.	Keep hands and feet to yourself.
Do not call out.	Raise your hand to speak.

Source: Adapted from Bechtel, Clayton, & Denton, 2003.

Students can often orally tell us the "right" way to behave but do not always follow through in the moment. They may have difficulty understanding the meaning behind the words, or they may have difficulty stopping their impulses. To support students in following through, asking them to physically practice is important.

In addition, ask students to practice changing their behaviors. Introduce a signal to students that will let them know you are asking them to pause and shift. It may be using phrases like "Remind me how to walk in the hallways," or "Show me how to use your seat as a tool, not a toy"—or something even simpler such as a gesture, or a call-and-response to get students' attention. A teacher may say "Ready to rock?" signaling the class to respond, "Ready to roll!" As the class chorally responds with the familiar phrase, their eyes are expected to go to the teacher. Some teachers ring a bell or use a calming chime (Bechtel, Clayton, & Denton, 2003). These signals should be practiced as a class. Ask the students to "pretend" to be silly on the carpet or talk too loudly, and then stop when they hear your given phrase or signal. When introducing new mathematics tools with students, I (Tracey) would explain that they could explore and play with the new material, but when I rang the chime they were to immediately stop touching the mathematics tools and be ready to actively listen for directions. I would let them play for one minute and then ring the chime. I would repeat this routine several times and make positive comments about how quickly students removed their hands from the tools and were ready to engage in active listening practices. Each time students would become quicker and more mindful of removing their hands from the tools and ready to listen to directions. For younger students a chant would accompany this routine, whereby I would ring the chime and say "paws up" and the students would follow with "tigers ready" (our school's mascot was a tiger). When teaching the mathematics unit using these same tools, at any point in time if I rang the chime, my students would take their hands off the tools and be ready to listen. Prior to doing this routine, it took me a long time to get my students to stop playing with the tools and listen to directions or focus in on the daily lesson. The more you practice these signals, the more likely it is that your students will respond appropriately when you need them to. This teaching, followed by guided practice, should occur throughout the school building—in the cafeteria, on the playground, and in various parts of the building where students are expected to react in a specific way to meet a behavior expectation.

Student-Focused Problem Solving

As we shift our thoughts from extinguishing "negative" behaviors and turn toward asking "What is behind the behaviors?" we start to develop proactive systems that maintain a student's sense of safety and meet the child's individual needs. In doing so, we can consider our SEL building blocks again. When we see behaviors or even subtle disengagement cues, we can begin to consider which building block needs to be addressed (see figure I.2, page 10).

Our first stop in determining the cause of misbehavior is in observing and thinking critically about the behavior. What do we observe? Where does it occur? What might the student be thinking and feeling in these moments? Using the building blocks as a reference, we can work with our team (described in more detail in chapters 3, page 93, and 6, page 293) to determine where a child's needs may be. Does the child feel a sense of belonging in our classroom? Do they understand who they are, and can they recognize their emotions? Do they have difficulty engaging with others or recognizing that their opinions are not the same as their peers'? Are they able to self-regulate when upset? Identifying these areas of difficulty will help you begin to recognize where to target an intervention, and when to put positive, proactive supports in place.

Our next step is to talk to the child. As Dr. Ross Greene recommends in his collaborative problem-solving approach, begin by stating to the child, "I've noticed . . . [state the problem behavior here]. What's up?" Allow the child to share their perspective with you (Greene, 2008). After listening to the child's perspective, teachers can begin to consider the child's missing skills or unmet need. Tables 2.2 to 2.6 (pages 69–73) provide possible needs, what the behaviors may look like in the classroom, and potential interventions.

Table 2.2: Supporting a Sense of Self

Building Block: Sense of Self Belonging and Connection	Examples
What you may observe	Frequent calling out, arguing with the teacher, withdrawing from the class, intentionally picking fights with other students, attempting to gain the teacher's attention in either a positive or negative manner.
What the student may be communicating	*"I need to connect with others! I need to feel as though I belong in this space!"* The student may not feel connected to the teacher and other students. The student may not feel recognized in any environment (at home or at school) or may subconsciously feel that they may be forgotten if they are not drawing attention to themselves. The student needs to feel as though they belong in the classroom.
Possible interventions	• Find opportunities for the child to connect with the teacher early in the school day. • Provide the child with specific jobs that help the teacher and the class. This provides a sense of importance and belonging in the class community. • Establish specific times of the day when the student and teachers can connect. The student should know when they are able to tell the teacher something so their needs to interrupt diminish. • Develop a secret sign to communicate with the student as a nonverbal check-in. This is a way for the teacher to say, "I see you and appreciate you," even from across the room or when working with another student.

*Visit **go.SolutionTree.com/instruction** for a free reproducible version of this table.*

Table 2.3: Supporting Social-Emotional Regulation

Building Block: Social-Emotional Regulation	Examples
What you may observe	Frequent fidgeting; getting up during lessons to wander around the room, get water, or go to the bathroom. The student may touch other students, play with objects, or rock back and forth.
What the student may be communicating	The student may be using the frequent moving to attempt to regulate and refocus themself. The student may have difficulty focusing on the work or maintaining attention to the lesson.
Possible interventions	Examples of interventions: • Keep in mind that the student is likely getting up not to avoid the work but to attempt to continue to be regulated. Students (and adults) can often maintain a focus on a task while walking or fidgeting. Students figure out that they listen better when moving or fidgeting and often subconsciously attempt to continue this to maintain focus. • Provide a structured, teacher-approved way to take a silent movement break. • Give the child an area in the classroom where it is acceptable to stand or pace and listen. • Offer seating opportunities so the child may choose a seat that allows them to regulate themselves with movement without distracting others in the class. • Establish a way for a student to let the teacher know they need a break. Provide the student with a pre-created "break" pass to give to the teacher, or another less obvious school tool such as a paperclip or a mathematics manipulative. • Keep a nearby box of "jobs for teacher" so a child who needs movement can, for example, reshelve books quietly while still listening and participating in the lesson.

Visit **go.SolutionTree.com/instruction** *for a free reproducible version of this table.*

Table 2.4: Supporting Social Awareness, Reciprocal Engagement, and Self-Regulation

Building Blocks: Self-Regulation, Reciprocal Engagement, and Social Awareness Help Refocusing and Cognitively Shifting From One Task to Another	Examples
What you may observe	Staying on one topic for an extended period of time or frequently interrupting lessons for an off-topic response. Asking the same question repeatedly. Continuing to bring up losing a game or a disagreement at recess. Showing disengagement or dysregulation cues.
What the student may be communicating	The student may be having difficulty shifting cognitive focus from one activity to another. It is important to keep in mind that this behavior is not a choice but a moment where the child feels "stuck." Think about a time you were waiting on important health news—either good or bad. Were you able to focus on a conversation that did not pertain to you directly? Could you carry on a conversation about American history? As much as you wanted to shift your focus, it was difficult to maintain your full thought on the conversation. Our students experience this often for a variety of reasons. They may be neurologically more inclined to hyper-focus on one subject, may not have a clear concept for the passage of time, or may have experienced trauma or a one-time bad experience. Regardless of the reason, the child is telling you that they need help staying in the moment.
Possible interventions	• Provide warnings of upcoming transitions so the child can wrap up their thoughts and task before moving on. • Use a visual timer during assignments so that students can monitor their own time and understand how time is moving during a given assignment. • Provide visuals that signal the given topic, such as a sign for mathematics, reading, or writing. • Remind students who bring up off-topic ideas of when they can talk about that with you. "Right now, our topic is mathematics. You can tell me about recess at _____." (Be sure to follow through on this! You can let the child quickly write you a note to remind you to check in with them.) • Offer a safe and quiet space in the classroom where students can go to use their self-regulation strategies if they are having difficulty shifting from an emotional topic. • Refrain from judgement in your redirection. Use simple, direct phrases. • Use a special phrase, gesture, or visual to signal to students that they are off topic. This will save them from the embarrassment of you constantly reminding them in front of everyone, will begin to help them self-regulate by using a visual cue to shift their behavior (that can eventually be done independently), and will build your relationship.

*Visit **go.SolutionTree.com/instruction** for a free reproducible version of this table.*

Table 2.5: Supporting Reciprocal Engagement and Social Awareness in Friendships

Building Blocks: Reciprocal Engagement and Social Awareness Support Making and Maintaining Friendships	Examples
What you may observe	Making negative comments to peers or greeting peers in a way that is not socially appropriate (for example, bathroom humor, comments on blood and gore, discussing topics other students are not interested in). Beginning conversations with other students without waiting for the other students to acknowledge them or choosing the same conversation topic each time they interact.
What the student may be communicating0	I want friends but I do not know how to appropriately make them, or I do not want to be hurt by others, so I am keeping students away by being mean.
Possible interventions	• Teach the student how to engage with peers appropriately when away from other peers. Practice those specific skills with the intervening adult or supportive peer models. Then ask the student to practice those skills in an unstructured environment, such as at recess or lunch, with the supporting adult nearby to coach if needed. • These techniques can include teaching the student to move the appropriate distance to the peer (not too close, not too far away) and ways to appropriately get the person's attention before initiating a conversation. • Support students in choosing topics that peers may be interested in. Coach the student in looking at peers' faces and noticing signs that they may not be interested (looking away, walking away, not looking up at the speaker).

*Visit **go.SolutionTree.com/instruction** for a free reproducible version of this table.*

Table 2.6: Supporting Logical and Responsible Decision Making

Building Block: Logical and Responsible Decision Making	Examples
What you may observe	Having difficulty getting started on a multistep task or project; starting a project but becoming so focused on a small aspect of the project that they do not finish in time; displaying difficulty identifying the steps within a project in order to reach a final goal; having difficulty identifying how their actions impacted those around them or explaining how they are going to achieve a task.
What the student may be communicating	I need help connecting the steps of the project in a way that makes sense to me. My brain jumps from where I am to the broad goal without helping me see the individual steps and ways to get there. I know what I did and understand that someone is upset, but I have trouble seeing what part of my actions hurt my friend. I need help seeing the steps that caused the problem.

Building Block: Logical and Responsible Decision Making	Examples
Possible interventions	• Provide the student with visual steps in order to help them see the individual steps needed to achieve a goal. • Conference with the student in a calm manner. Help the student explore what happened from their point of view. Do not tell the student what happened but ask questions that can lead to the student making the connections. • Draw steps out for the student to see the concrete connections between each step.

*Visit **go.SolutionTree.com/instruction** for a free reproducible version of this table.*

Self-Reflection and Self-Regulation

Successful schoolwide social-emotional learning starts with the educator's ability to understand, model, and practice the strategies themselves (Peeters, De Backer, Reina, Kindekens, Buffel, & Lombaerts, 2013). Students learn SEL skills from observation as well as from direct instruction. They must see their teachers using and modeling these strategies throughout the day to see the strategies as viable options to use. This begins with a school culture that encourages teachers to use self-regulation throughout the day, reflect on how their lessons and interactions with students went, and problem solve based on those reflections.

Importantly, teachers experience taxing situations throughout the school day where there are many opportunities for stress to build up (Peeters et al., 2013). As schools ask teachers to work with students who show difficult-to-manage behaviors, like Daniel, it is vital that they are aware of their own visceral and emotional reactions in the moment. For teachers to stand back, avoid engaging in a power struggle, or gain broader insight about a behavior in the moment, teachers need to be able to engage in the exact social-emotional regulation strategies they teach the students. Teachers set the climate for their individual classrooms, and a teacher who is able to self-regulate and reflect will create a learning environment where learners feel safe, as opposed to a teacher who ignores their own emotions and is unaware that their tone and actions are not sending safety signals.

The school climate and culture are important not just for the students but for teachers as well. For teachers to feel comfortable and safe enough to be able to self-reflect, they must work in an environment that allows for open dialogue, reflection, and group decision making. School culture should encourage reflective practices that enable teachers to review their work with others in a safe way and connect their own emotional reactions to their actions.

Adult actions can directly influence students' feelings and actions. Bandura (2001) states that:

> Monitoring one's pattern of behavior and the cognitive and environmental conditions under which it occurs is the first step toward

doing something to affect it. Actions give rise to self-reactive influence through performance comparison with personal goals and standards. (p. 8)

While research shows that to help students regulate their own emotions it is vital for teachers to be self-aware of their own emotions (Peeters et al., 2013), we also know that this is not always easy. In a busy classroom, teachers are often acting as the air-traffic controller for twenty-five or more students. Teachers simultaneously keep everyone on pace and on task, while managing behaviors that arise and differentiating for each lesson. In more intense classroom moments, being self-aware and self-regulated as a teacher is not a simple task. In fact, in our personal experience, it can feel better to be less self-aware. If we fully stepped back and realized our gut emotional reaction to all the ins and outs of any moment in a school classroom, we may want to crawl under a table and not come back out. Our jobs are not easy. This is why it is even more essential for teams to establish a culture and climate that allows them to reflect on their emotions and reactions to what is occurring in the classroom and to be aware of their internal thoughts (Perry, 2020).

Teachers who can reflect, both in the moment and outside the moment, are able to work with students' behaviors in a calmer, more structured way (Greene, 2008). Dysregulated teachers are more likely to cause students' behaviors to escalate. Teachers need to be aware of their internal reactions to power struggles with students. Language, whether it be verbal or through our gestures and expressions, is how we communicate and provide signals that students could perceive as safe or a possible threat.

Relationship Building

Building relationships within a school community is essential to students' social and emotional learning. As teachers we can instruct students on how to manage their emotions, be good citizens, and take turns, but if we are not actively modeling those actions through the relationships we have with *everyone* in our building, our lessons will not truly resonate with our students. We must intentionally take time to build relationships within the classroom community itself (teacher to student and teacher to teacher) and support how students build relationships with one another (student to student). We must also make space to build relationships with our students' families as well as school staff. We discuss these relationships in greater detail in chapter 3 (page 93) as well as the following sections.

Relationships Between Teachers and Students

Students are more likely to be open to learning, taking risks, and persevering through difficult tasks when they believe the adults working with them care about them (Decker, Dona, & Christenson, 2007; Macklem, 2008). Positive relationships with teachers can reduce students' risky behaviors and increase their prosocial behaviors (Rudasill, Reio, Stipanovic, & Taylor, 2010). Our relationships with students are vital to their academic and SEL success. For students experiencing adverse childhood experiences (ACEs), positive relationships with adults can provide the resiliency and support needed to allow the child to process the experience (Perry, 2020). Keep in mind that these relationships do not need to only be between the classroom teacher and the students. Many different adults in the school building can take a role in building relationships with students. I (Ann-Bailey) have seen office staff and custodians play meaningful roles in a student's life simply by being there with a high five and a smile each morning.

Although providing twenty-something students with a meaningful relationship can feel daunting, it is important for teachers to remember that they can build positive and meaningful relationships with students in simple ways. Greeting students at the door each morning with a smile, appearing genuinely glad to see them, asking how they are, and sharing a positive comment or observation will start off a student's day with a positive connection. These small, positive connections help the child feel welcomed in the classroom community and remind them that they belong. Small, positive interactions throughout the day maintain this positive sense of connection and belonging. High fives, silent thumbs-up, smiles, and quiet moments of providing encouragement and motivation support this sense.

One way to foster positive relationships with your individual students is to watch their individual cues during group and independent work (Cooper, Hoffman, & Powell, 2017). Notice when they look toward you—are their eyes bright and smiling, looking for you to take pride in their work and to celebrate or connect? In these moments, despite being in a busy classroom, you can lock eyes with them, smile, and use a gesture to signal your pride in their work, and then move on. Or are their eyes more concerned? Are they looking to you for help and support with their work (Circle of Security, 2020)? In these moments, even if you are busy, you can again take a moment to connect with the concerned student. Make eye contact back, signal that you will check in soon, or recommend that they get a drink of water or use the calm-down strategies you have taught them. When you can check in, move your body so that you are on the same level as the child. Use open-ended questions to determine what is going on—for example, "You look stuck. What's up?" (Greene, 2016). Often, listening to their concerns over work and providing reassurance ("You've got this!") will go a long way in letting them know they can handle the feelings that come with difficult work. Students avoid work that is too hard not because of the work itself but because of the feelings that come up when they are doing hard work.

As teachers, it is our job to help those students hold those feelings and sit with the uncomfortableness. As we hold our students' feelings in these moments, we are doing the true work of teaching social-emotional learning. Students learn to self-regulate through co-regulation (Tronick, 2014), and in these moments we are saying, "We know this is hard, but we also know you can handle it. Let me sit with you with that hard feeling. It's not such a bad and scary feeling" (Lillas & Turnbull, 2009). These moments of sitting with our students' feelings are what allow them to handle those emotions on their own, and to process the social-emotional information we teach.

Throughout the school day, take a moment to pause and scan your classroom. Watch your students' body language. Who is looking to connect with you in a moment of pride? Who is looking for a connection to be reassured? Who is exploring (either academically or behaviorally) and may not appear to want a connection, but may need strong but kind guiding support (Cooper et al., 2017)? Observing your students for these cues and then responding briefly but appropriately will allow them to experience a positive relationship with you. This relationship will ground them in experiencing the social-emotional skills we want them to take on independently.

In order to maintain a positive relationship, teachers are also encouraged to monitor the language they use with the whole class as well as individual students (Denton, 2007). Redirecting student misbehavior with simple, to-the-point directions instead of lecturing shows the child that the teacher believes they can achieve the desired behavior expectations, as well as that the teacher understands that sometimes everyone makes mistakes. When a teacher comes down harshly on one student, it can damage the teacher's relationship not just with the student in question but also with other students in the class. Quieter students may assume the teacher is only friendly with them because they are "good" and that if they were to make a mistake with their behavior the teacher will no longer maintain the same positive relationship with them. This can limit these students' ability to take risks and feel safe in the classroom. Figure 2.6 provides examples of turning negative statements into positive ones that contain the same desired message.

Instead of This . . .	Try This . . .
Don't run.	Show me how we walk in the hallway. (Shows the expected, positive behavior and communicates you know the child can demonstrate the behavior.)
How many times do I have to tell you to raise your hand?	We raise our hands. (Direct and refrains from judgement.)
I don't care what you do at your house; here we don't interrupt each other.	Remind me how we wait our turns to speak. (Refrains from judging the student's family.)
I like the way Josie is sitting.	I am looking for classmates sitting on their bottoms, with their eyes on me, and their hands in their laps. (Uses specific language about the expected behavior.)
I'm tired of looking at the back of your head during my lessons.	I notice that when I am teaching you often turn around and I cannot see your eyes. Can you tell me more about what's going on? (Invites collaboration without judgement to solve the problem.)
It should not take so long to come to our gathering space! We waste so much time—why do I say this every day?	I'm noticing that we have a hard time cleaning up and gathering quickly. I'm wondering how we can help each other make that time go faster. (Invites collaboration without judgement to solve the problem.)

Figure 2.6: Positive versus reactive language.

Relationships Between Teacher and Teacher

When it comes to our school climate and culture, the relationships we form with one another, teacher to teacher and staff to staff, are just as important as the relationships we form with our students. To collaboratively provide a safe and academically rigorous learning environment for our students, teachers must be able to professionally and cooperatively work together to both plan and co-teach.

Co-teaching, or when two teachers are paired together to plan, deliver, assess, and implement strategies for a shared set of students (Trites, 2017), is most effective when the two teachers plan and differentiate instruction together (Van Heck, 2017). Although providing time for teachers to co-plan is often an administrator's responsibility, the willingness and openness of the teachers is what will drive the meat of the co-planning meetings. These relationships between teachers, instructional coaches, and support staff are essential for the best practices of co-teaching to take place. The positive relationships co-teachers have in the classroom can be felt by the students. Classroom teachers can work to include their co-teachers and aides in their classroom community by signing both teachers' names at the bottom of a morning message, referring to their classroom as belonging to all the teachers and not just the general classroom teacher, and encouraging students to refer to any of the teachers in the room for help and support. Being intentional about how co-teachers work together will improve the effect of co-teaching for students while also supporting a positive school climate for students and staff (Friend, 2007).

One aspect to consider when thinking about creating strong teacher-to-teacher relationships is to examine the strength and welcoming nature of grade-level teams. While it is clear that the members of these teams include the classroom teachers at this grade level, those members must also remember to welcome and include the additional staff they work with on a daily basis. The special education teachers, English as a second language teachers, aides and classroom assistants, and instructional coaches should be recognized as a part of the grade-level team. These additional teachers who often provide the co-teaching support should be included in social celebrations, planning meetings, and general well-being check-ins. When teachers feel welcomed into the social community of the grade-level team, they are more likely to contribute ideas and perspectives in team planning meetings, which leads to improved collaboration for students. Although these individuals may serve on multiple teams, it is important that grade-level teams work to include them both socially and academically in their team community.

Student-to-Student Relationships

While our teacher-to-student relationships are essential to providing students with a safe environment for learning, student-to-student relationships are equally important, yet often overlooked. Positive student-to-student relationships can support individual students' resilience, buffer them from life stress, and facilitate an inclusive environment by promoting peer acceptance (Mantz & Bear, 2020). Students need to feel safe not just with the adults in the classroom but also with the other students.

Teachers can support these relationships by being responsive to the social dynamics in the room, supporting peer assistance and collaborative projects during the school day, and providing student-centered practices. Teachers can also be mindful of how they interact with individual students and whether they unconsciously treat particular students differently than others. One aspect of this is how teachers redirect and respond to particular students' misbehavior. Without being aware, some teachers can respond more harshly or publicly reprimand particular students in the classroom. Students pick up on the difference in treatment, and it is reflected in their acceptance of peers. When educators make class placement decisions, they should consider the bonds students form with one another and the micro-communities within a classroom.

Mindset, Motivation, and Engagement

The 21st century classroom has gone beyond the idea of the "sage on the stage," where the teacher puts information into the minds of the students sitting in front of the teacher and it is up to the students if they learn or not. Jennifer A. Fredricks (2014) states that engagement is one of the biggest challenges that teachers encounter and is more than just on-task behavior and compliance. She shares that students' relationships (with teachers and peers) and the type of tasks assigned to students can affect a level of student engagement. Students are more engaged when tasks are motivational and require a higher level of cognitive demand, and when teachers provide support to students academically and interpersonally. As educators, we now know that all students can learn and that we can adapt and change our lessons, activities, tasks, delivery methods, and the environment to enhance the learning of all students.

In the following sections, we will consider how to create an optimal cultural learning environment by focusing on three areas: (1) engagement and motivation, (2) mindset, and (3) student voice and agency.

Engagement and Motivation

Engagement and motivation, although closely related and tied together, are two different things. Motivation is a person's drive or will to do something, whereas engagement happens while we are doing that something. For example, a student may be motivated to participate in project-based learning, but while participating in the project they may not actually be engaged. So, how do we motivate our students to want to learn and then keep them focused on the learning?

Early on in my (Tracey's) career, I remember learning about ideas regarding intrinsic motivation versus extrinsic motivation. *Intrinsic motivation* involved a student's drive to do something for internal satisfaction (for example, "Wow, I'm so proud of myself for working through that tough problem!"), whereas *extrinsic motivation* involved completing a task and being rewarded for it (for example, "I stayed in my seat during read-aloud, so I get a sticker on my chart that goes home to my parents"). If we were to describe a student as being "motivated," would that mean motivated to get good grades or perform well on assessments; motivated to behave; or motivated to learn new ideas or concepts? If you were to survey a large set of teachers, we imagine the answers would vary widely, including answers beyond this short list. We have to remember that even though our students may be motivated to learn, it does not necessarily mean they will be engaged in the learning. Therefore, we first have the uphill battle of motivating our students to learn, then the challenge of keeping our students engaged in the learning.

In reviewing research that measures student engagement, Jennifer A. Fredricks, Phyllis C. Blumenfeld, and Alison H. Paris (2004) break students' overall engagement down into three observable and measurable categories: (1) behavioral, (2) emotional, and (3) cognitive (see table 2.7). They describe how environmental changes and contextual features can influence student engagement. Jordan et al. (2014) state that engagement is the foundation of learning in the classroom and that academic success hinges on the interdependence of all three areas of engagement to avoid disengagement, which can then hinder learning.

Table 2.7: Types of Student Engagement

Engagement		
Behavioral	**Emotional**	**Cognitive**
• Compliance with rules and procedures • Level of involvement and effort in the learning	• Emotional reactions to the school environments and people (peers, teachers, counselors, administrators, and so on) and sense of belonging • Perceptions of the learning as valuable	• Willingness to exert effort and use learned skills (metacognitive skills, such as persistence; executive skills, such as self-regulation; and previously learned content skills) with strategy to understand or form new knowledge

Source: Adapted from Fredricks et al., 2014.

Behavioral Engagement

Behavioral engagement can often be defined as compliance with rules and procedures, use of prosocial behaviors, and an overall level of involvement and effort in the learning. Research suggests that behavioral engagement in learning is a key factor for predicting student achievement (Downer, Rimm-Kaufman, & Pianta, 2007). Students may use prosocial behaviors during a lesson, raise their hands without calling out, and listen to what the teacher says; however, they may not necessarily be emotionally or cognitively engaged in learning and may not be taking in the information and applying it. Keep in mind that behavioral engagement does not mean students sitting perfectly still in an identical fashion. For students who may have difficulty with classroom behavior expectations or who are easily distracted, consider ways to heighten their involvement and participation in activities.

- **Preteach your rules and routines in your classroom and set clear behavior expectation.** Before expecting students to follow the rules or routines, state them clearly and then ask students to practice the routines and rules while you provide feedback.

- **Modify the learning environment.** Monitor your classroom space to ensure it supports behavioral engagement and participation by reducing distraction. Also, determine if specific tools can be used to support behavior engagement (for example, using a wobble chair at the carpet or having a talkative student sit next to you at the carpet for close proximity).

- **Increase opportunities for whole-class responses to a question.** Provide time for students to answer a question posed to the whole class by telling their neighbor in a turn-and-talk opportunity. You can also provide opportunities for students to respond nonverbally (for example, "If you think the answer is X, stand on one leg. If you think the answer is Y, hop up and down").

- **Provide students with *think time*.** Before accepting an answer, tell the students everyone will have thirty seconds to think about the answer. If the students know they have time to think of the answer before you accept a response, they are more likely to think about the answer than simply wait for another student to answer quickly.

- **Use anticipation strategies.** Create engagement with students who may have difficulty with behavioral expectations. As human beings, we are uniquely positioned to become engaged in the unknown—what is inside the present? Who will win the game? What will happen at a gambling table in Vegas? Toy companies have used this theory in recent years and have entire toy lines built around the concept that when the child buys the product, they will not know what is inside. Place something that tangibly represents the lesson (for example, mathematics manipulatives, a copy of an artifact, a book, or even class materials) into a bag. Use your voice, tone, and body language to build excitement or wonder. At the right time, reveal what is inside the bag.

Emotional Engagement

Emotional engagement involves students' emotional reactions (bored, excited, sad, nervous, and so on) to their school environments and people (for example, peers, teachers, counselors, administrators) and sense of belonging. Emotional engagement also includes students' perceptions of the learning or tasks they are engaged in as either valuable or unimportant. A student who is emotionally engaged may be excited about the lesson and want to listen to every word the teacher says, but without the self-regulator ability to show behavioral engagement, may not be able to focus on the lesson enough to learn.

I (Tracey) remember working with a school where a teacher gave thirty mathematics problems as homework. The problems required students to use procedures without connections (a traditional multiplication algorithm). Several students didn't complete their homework or only completed some problems, arguing why they had to complete so many. After talking to the teacher, I suggested only giving five or ten problems to practice and possibly a rich task which required them to use the same skills in a problem-solving setting. The teacher noticed that more students completed the homework, and when reviewing the homework together as a class, the students were able to have rich discussions regarding the mathematics in the story problem. Originally, the number of required problems along with the lack of meaning in the straight traditional algorithms caused the students to react emotionally, perceiving the task as too difficult and meaningless. Once the task was altered to seem manageable and engaging, the students were able to approach and complete the homework and, in turn, had a more active and productive learning experience. I also encouraged the teacher to give the students mathematics tasks that reflected their backgrounds, culture, and interests.

Strategies to build emotional engagement include the following:

- **Build relationships with students.** Consider using a voice and body language that promotes a sense of openness and connection with the students. When we support relationship building and students feel as though they are accepted and belong, they tend to be more behaviorally engaged (Jordan et al., 2014). You can also be responsive to your students' moods and perceptions of the lesson and acknowledge their emotional reaction to tasks. In addition, when beginning a lesson, be sure to link what you are teaching to the students' lives or previously learned material. As a special education teacher, engaging the students with meaningful work connected to their lives was essential to engagement. I (Ann-Bailey) learned the hard way one day when I sat down to read a book about children going on a walk in the woods with a young boy in a wheelchair. He refused to read the book and threw it on the floor. This was surprising behavior for him, but as I thought about it, I realized I had chosen a book he had no connection or experience with. He could not go walking through the woods. I chose another book to teach the same concepts and he became his highly engaged self again.

- **Provide choice.** Allow students choice in what they learn, how they learn, and the materials they can use for learning. When teaching problem solving in mathematics, I (Tracey) would give students a mathematics toolbox with an assortment of mathematics tools and let them choose the tool that made sense and had meaning to their own learning, rather than giving them a tool and telling them to solve the problem using the tool of my choice. I consistently observed that when students had choice in the tools they used for problem solving, they were more engaged in learning and they were able to make more connections and build deeper understandings.

Cognitive Engagement

Cognitive engagement involves looking at students' abilities and willingness to exert effort and use learned skills (metacognitive skills, such as persistence and growth mindset; executive functioning skills, such as self-regulation and flexibility in thinking during problem solving; and previously learned content skills) with strategy to understand or form new knowledge (Fredricks, Blumenfeld, & Paris, 2004). A student with strong critical thinking skills and cognitive engagement may not be emotionally invested in the work or have the behavioral engagement necessary to learn and complete the task.

- **Use open-ended tasks and questions.** Find unique ways to stimulate all students' curiosity, and use tasks and materials that match students' zones of proximal development, pique their interest, and push their thinking without creating negative stress or anxiety. Consider beginning your lessons with open-ended challenges for students to set a goal related to the task or solve a problem using the information students will learn during the lesson. Again, be mindful of your students' developmental abilities, as placing cognitive demands beyond their abilities will decrease engagement and lead to frustration.

  As a first-grade teacher, I (Ann-Bailey) introduced the question "What is a problem solver?" at the beginning of the school year. We spent the entire school year answering this one question. We discussed what it meant to be a problem solver in reading, where we learned to decode words; a problem solver in science, where we learned facts about our world and applied them to experiments; a problem solver in mathematics as we solved word problems; and a problem solver in the world, where we learned about famous problem solvers in history. Each new concept we learned tied back to our yearlong question, which provided the students an additional layer of cognitive engagement. It helped them organize the information we were learning and apply it with a purpose. Project-based learning is another great method for engaging students in open-ended tasks.

- **Differentiate the learning.** Differentiate learning through the use of varied questioning techniques and tasks that are accessible to all learners. Consider ways to scaffold the learning and determine needed supports or extensions. (See the following section on "Differentiated Lessons That Are Accessible to All Students," page 86, and chapter 5, page 223.)

- **Support ideas around growth mindset.** Embed growth mindset concepts into lessons or model them by thinking aloud with students. Having a growth mindset when engaging in a problem-solving situation will allow students to grapple with challenging ideas and engage in persistence. (See also the following section on "Mindset.")

Nguyen, Cannata, and Miller (2016) share research which suggests that "student engagement varies by the environment created by the school and teacher, and by the learning opportunities teachers create in their classrooms" (see also Boaler & Staples, 2008; Kelly & Turner, 2009; Nasir, Jones, & McLaughlin, 2011; Walker & Greene, 2009; Watanabe, 2008). Therefore, one way for teachers to ensure higher engagement levels for all students is to participate in collaborative practices and plan for engagement. Teams should engage in rich discussions about the learning experiences, tasks, and materials they will use to engage learners and determine ways to modify aspects of the physical or cultural environment as a means of increasing academic engagement and minimizing off-task or disruptive behaviors. Additionally, it is also the team's role to determine how it will measure student engagement. This requires that teachers determine when students are or are not engaged (for example, engaged students contribute to discussions by asking and answering questions or model thinking and understanding using tools, models, or written products) and then collect and analyze data to assist teachers in modifying their practices or the environment. (See chapter 5, page 223, for planning tools on adapting the learning environment.)

Mindset

As people we have many thoughts and beliefs, but when those beliefs become patterns of habitual thoughts, they begin to form mental attitudes. Sometimes we go about our daily lives and engage in actions or behaviors that almost seem automatic or happen from a subconscious level, but when we engage in reflective practices, we become mindful of our ideas and beliefs and their positive or negative consequences and how they might affect ourselves or others. Those who have a growth mindset believe that their abilities can be developed with effort and are not fixed and defined by nature (Dweck, 2006). Craig Wacker and Lynn Olson (2019) share research from the University of Chicago Consortium, which identifies four aspects of positive student mindsets:

1. Students' perception that they belong in the school

2. Students' perception that they can succeed

3. Students' perception that, with effort, their ability can grow

4. Students' perception that the work they are doing is personally valuable

The Teaching and Learning Lab staff who work closely with MIT (MIT Teaching+Learning Lab, n.d.) refer to research (Park, Gunderson, Tsukayama, Levine, & Beilock, 2016; Rattan, Good, & Dweck, 2012) regarding the impact teachers' own mindsets have on student behaviors; subsequently, they share the need for teachers to embed growth mindset in their classroom practices and behaviors. Therefore, it is important that we take time to monitor our own attitudes and language (verbal or nonverbal) toward ourselves, students, and colleagues; use a growth mindset with positive expectations; and continuously look for ways to promote a growth mindset into all aspects of the various schoolwide environments. I (Tracey) remember working with my four-year-old child on wooden puzzles. At the time, puzzles were challenging for my child, and I caught myself subconsciously and consistently fixing the pieces for him. I soon realized that I was using a fixed mindset in that I didn't think he could complete the puzzle without my support, and instead of letting my child grapple with it and persist on his own, I was swooping in and nonverbally sending the message "You can't do it." From that point on, I made sure that *he* was doing the puzzle and I was using appropriate scaffolds and growth mindset language to support him. To learn more about growth mindset refer to the book *Mindset: The New Psychology of Success* by Carol S. Dweck (2006).

Student Voice and Agency

Student engagement and motivation can increase when students have an opportunity to take an active role in their own learning. When students have opportunities to make choices about their learning and engage in the process of setting learning goals for themselves, they can become empowered to take control of their own learning. A report by Eric Toshalis and Michael J. Nakkula (2012) states:

> When students feel like they can do what is being asked of them with some level of facility (competence), when they feel like they have some control over how an activity is conducted (autonomy), and when they feel meaningfully connected to those around them while doing it (relatedness), students are understood to be self-determined. The more often these self-determining experiences occur, the higher and more durable the motivation tends to be. (p. 9)

In this student-centered approach to learning, the teacher acts as a facilitator of the students' learning, and that role requires strong teacher-student relationships built on respect, trust, and shared growth mindsets. Therefore, to truly create inclusive school environments, *all* students (including students with disabilities and students whose first language is not English) must have choice in the learning activities as well as the schoolwide and classroom procedures, policies, and systems. Not only does this pave a path for student buy-in, but it also has the potential to create strong communities that reflect their members' beliefs, values, languages, and backgrounds.

As a young teacher early in my career, I (Tracey) was so proud of myself for using differentiation strategies. I had three different color-coded papers. One was purple, and it had problems that were challenging; one was yellow, comprising grade-level word problems; and one was blue, and it had problems that consisted of a combination of below-grade-level and grade-level word problems (scaffolded activity). Yet, my students immediately came to know which problem types they were getting. I soon realized the message I was sending to my students and knew I needed to make a change. Thereafter, I decided to have story problems that all students would get on one paper but with three sets of numbers for students to choose from (supportive to challenging). I began to support students by telling them to start off with the numbers that were just right for them and then to move on to more challenging numbers when ready. When doing this, my students were able to see their growth, and *all* students were given the opportunity to challenge themselves.

Edwin A. Locke and Gary P. Latham (2006) share evidence regarding the relationship between goal setting and academic achievement. When students have opportunities to have ownership in their own learning and take time to set goals, they are engaging in reflective practices that can be beneficial lifelong skills. Instead of looking to the teacher as the one who has all the power and holds all the knowledge and answers, teachers can help students foster the mindset that they have control over their own learning, and they can direct their own learning path. In addition to academic learning, the Midwest Comprehensive Center at American Institutes for Research shares research that:

> goal setting has also shown links with a range of outcomes associated with the deeper learning intrapersonal domain, such as self-regulated learning (Ames & Archer, 1988; Pajares, Britner, & Valiante, 2000), self-efficacy (Bandura & Schunk, 1981; Schunk & Rice, 1993), intrinsic motivation (Murayama & Elliot, 2009), and cognitive engagement (Meece, Blumenfeld, & Hoyle, 1988). (p. 3)

In chapter 4 (page 157), we will discuss more about how student goal setting can be an avenue for SEL.

Learning Experiences

The way students encounter learning in their schoolwide experiences or in their individual classrooms plays a large role in supporting the culture and climate as well as the child's individual level of engagement. In his book *Why Don't Students Like School?* cognitive scientist Daniel Willingham (2009) notes that students often become disconnected in school due to the type of instruction provided. As discussed in the "Engagement and Motivation" section (page 78), to engage students enough for them to learn and remember information, teachers and school teams must think critically about what information they are teaching as well as how they deliver the instruction, respond to students' thinking, and provide feedback. A student who comes to school willingly and is ready to learn is our ideal student—so how do we foster that within our lessons? No matter how strong our social-emotional learning curriculum is, it will not overcome disengaging academic instruction. Teaching students to think positively and use calm-down strategies when upset will not magically engage them in tedious lessons. Instead, we must provide students with learning experiences where they will feel safe enough to take academic risks and engaged enough to recognize their own social-emotional experiences while learning.

In the following sections, we will examine four aspects of learning experiences that help build an effective cultural environment for SEL.

1. Differentiated lessons that are accessible to all

2. The need to reflect diversity and provide culturally responsive lessons

3. Rich classroom discourse

4. Teacher- and student-guided learning structures

Differentiated Lessons That Are Accessible to All Students

So how do we create a safe, meaningful, and rigorous learning experience for students? We start with ensuring that our lessons are intended for the students in our classroom—not our ideal students or the students we had last year. In teams, teachers focus on the critical questions of learning (DuFour, DuFour, Eaker, Many, & Mattos, 2016):

- What do we want our students to learn?

- How will we know our students have learned?

- How will we respond when some students do not learn?

- How will we extend the learning for those students who are already proficient?

We then use data to support instruction. This data-driven learning cycle is critical because it guarantees that we are focused on the students in our classroom and are creating lessons that will respond to the needs of all learners. Imagine being in a classroom where it is clear everything being taught is intended not for you but for the other students. For you, the teachers have decided the work is too hard and you are simply pulled off to the side of the classroom or moved to another room to work on something else. Your experience of that classroom community becomes that you are not a part of the main group—you are welcome to sit and enjoy, but the main focus of the community (learning) is not for you. Alternatively, imagine sitting in a classroom where everything comes easily for you. Again, you experience your classroom community in a different way. You recognize that you are not a part of the main group—and although you see yourself as a part of the broader community, you know that the main lesson is not intended for you. Shelley Moore, a Canadian inclusion advocate and writer, produced a video comparing teaching to bowling (Moore, 2016). In this video, she notes the similarities between teaching the students at the margins of the group and knocking over the hardest-to-hit bowling pins—the 7–10 split. If you aim your ball (or your lesson) down the middle of the aisle, you will hit *most* of your pins (or students) but not those on the outside. You can get a fine score never hitting those two outside pins, but what if you hit all of them? Moore recommends planning your lessons intentionally to hit those hard-to-reach pins, noting that when teachers do so, everyone in the middle benefits as well. To provide positive learning experiences for all, we must intentionally plan how we will engage the students who already know what we are teaching, and how we will reach students who may not learn what we are teaching the first time.

In planning for differentiation, work with your teammates to determine the essential knowledge for each lesson and maintain high expectations for all students while carefully supporting the needs of all students using supports, scaffolds, or extensions.

The Need to Reflect Diversity and Provide Culturally Responsive Lessons

In addition to ensuring we are providing differentiated lessons that reach the needs of all learners, we must also consider if we are providing instruction that promotes diversity with teachers engaging in culturally responsive and inclusive practices. When educators discuss being culturally responsive they are referring to the need to carefully consider the cultural nuances (religion, race, ethnicity, socioeconomics, gender, and so on) that may interfere with the educator's ability to form a meaningful relationship with their student (Rucker, 2019). Mariana Souto-Manning (n.d.) writes that "Teachers who engage in these practices understand the importance of culture to teaching, learning, growing and developing—what Rogoff (2003) called the cultural nature of human development." And yet, despite our best intentions, we often fall short in this area. At the Council for Exceptional Children conference in 2020 (Campbell, Hagan-Burke, & Burke, 2020), researcher Aaron Campbell from the department of educational psychology at Texas A&M shared that through her research on social-emotional learning she continued to have students tell her, "Only white kids have bad days, and it gets better the next day" (in response to *Alexander and the Terrible, Horrible, No Good, Very Bad Day*), and "Only white kids use calm-down strategies." She notes, through the eyes of the students she met in her research, that a significant amount of the social-emotional literature we share with our students is based on white characters with middle-class problems. This sends the unintended message to our students that our SEL lessons are not intended for them. As teachers shy away from addressing larger topics around poverty, race, and discrimination, they continue to send the message that while SEL skills may be appropriate for in-school expectations, they are not skills or strategies to be applied to larger problems (Simmons, 2019). In short, when we do not present culturally responsive SEL materials and frameworks, we will not be effective for all students, regardless of how strong our content is otherwise.

One of the first steps to providing a culturally responsive and diverse learning experience is to examine the learning materials being used and determine if they reflect the racial, ethnic, and cultural diversity of students. These learning materials include the books in the classroom library, the posters on the walls, and the visuals and content in tasks and various projects, among others (Collado et al., 2021). Can your students see themselves in the books you read to them? Are they able to find and read books about students that share similarities with them?

Another important step to consider is whether your lessons include the historical contributions from underrepresented cultural groups (IRIS Center, 2021). In teaching about Thanksgiving, are you including the story and perspective of the Wampanoag Native American Tribe?

Cultural responsiveness is not a standalone curriculum; rather, it is a way of being. In fact, this understanding should be embedded and integrated into all aspects of learning. We also must not confuse multicultural teaching with cultural responsiveness. In fact, Louis Volante, Christopher DeLuca, and Don A. Klinger (2019) share that:

> Such training needs to extend beyond traditional multicultural education approaches, or what has been called a 'tourist' curriculum characterized by occasional or 'highlight' additions. Instead, training for teachers must model a multi-dimensional approach that includes integrating content from diverse cultures and experiences, and critically examining how cultural identity impacts learning.

Together we can use our collective strengths, values, and backgrounds to build a strong community of learners. Perhaps more important than any of these other actions is for the teacher teams themselves to monitor their own immediate reactions to student behavior and be aware of any biases they may have. As Washington Collado and his co-authors write in their 2021 book *Beyond Conversations About Race*, "Bias is any conclusion we draw that depends inappropriately on some information and excludes other, more relevant information" (Collado et al., 2021, p. 53). This bias is often not intentional but is unconscious or implicit. The term *implicit* indicates this is not a bias we are conscious of, which means it takes reflection and work to realize where we may display our own bias. When we are not aware of our own biases, we as educators may punish some students for one behavior while ignoring other students for the same behavior (Riddle & Sinclair, 2019). Studies find that Black boys are often punished for behaviors ignored or found cute when done by White boys (Little & Tolbert, 2018). Though the term *implicit bias* is most often used in discussions about race, it includes any bias one has that they are unaware of, which could include assumptions or reactions to students from different socioeconomic statuses or students with special education labels as well as other factors that make a student different. To even begin recognizing these biases, schools must start by providing the adults in the building a safe space to discuss and reflect (Collado et al., 2021). They can then become aware of how these unconscious biases may play out by taking their own data on which students are being referred to the office or encouraged to take a break with a counselor. Many schools are often surprised to see their data reflects bias they were unaware they had. Once the schools are aware, they can begin the work of recognizing their bias and making the school a safe and welcoming environment for *all* students.

Rich Classroom Discourse

Classroom discourse, or the academic conversations students and a teacher have around a topic, can support students in experiencing a safe learning environment, enhancing engagement, and establishing student voice and agency. Rich classroom discourse occurs in classrooms where teachers foster students' inquisitive questions and encourage them to think critically, listen to one another, and respectfully engage with each other. These discussions also build safe relationships between students where they feel comfortable navigating disagreements with one another (Collado et al., 2021; Simmons, 2019).

Students can learn to use *quality talk* positive statements to participate in these discussions (Quality Talk, n.d.). Introduce the statements in figure 2.7 to the class and practice using them in a mock discussion. You can have fun encouraging students to participate in a mock debate using these quality talk markers, such as arguing whether the sky is blue. Once students are comfortable with these statements, you can facilitate academic conversations. Quality talk not only benefits the students' ability to feel safe to contribute and take risks with classmates during the discussion but also promotes students to think more critically about the subject. When the teacher acts as a facilitator of the learning, students begin to pose questions and foster conversations with each other rather than expecting the teacher to be the one to pose all the questions or lead the conversation. In classrooms with rich discourse, students begin to restate the ideas of others, reason and justify thinking, agree and disagree, or build on peers' ideas (Ferris, 2014).

Quality Talk Sentence Stems
I agree with _____ because _____.
I respectfully disagree because _____.
I would like to add on to _____'s statement because _____.
What I heard _____ say was _____.

Source: Adapted from Quality Talk Project, 2020.

Figure 2.7: Quality talk sentence stem examples.

*Visit **go.SolutionTree.com/instruction** for a free blank reproducible version of this figure.*

Teacher- and Student-Guided Learning Structures

Providing students with multiple opportunities to learn from each other and interact with the material is another way to increase engagement and learning. These guided learning structures include a workshop model, where teachers provide a short focus lesson and then set the students to work independently or in small groups on differentiated activities while a teacher meets with other students in a small, guided instructional group. These groups, often called *guided reading or guided mathematics*, allow the teacher to meet with students in their zone of proximal development, supporting them in work that is above where the students could access independently and allowing them to grapple with ideas, make connections, and build new knowledge. Teachers carefully plan these learning experiences to help them connect the lesson they provided in direct instruction to the child's individual skills and needs.

Students who require additional interventions, such as support from a special education teacher or an English language teacher, can get support during this time (Mattos, 2016). It is essential that students do not miss the focus lesson. This short lesson typically covers the grade-level content. If students are pulled out of these short lessons to work on remedial skills, they will never learn their grade-level skills. Missing the focus lesson also signals to the student that they are not a part of the larger classroom community. Keeping students from accessing grade-level instruction and separating them from their community to receive remedial work interferes with the development of their social-emotional building blocks by signaling to them that they do not belong. Instead, teachers should rely on their grade-level teams to plan short focus lessons that will engage all students, incorporating the special education supports, the English language supports, and the advanced academic supports into those ten to fifteen minutes of whole-group instruction.

When students are working independently, with a partner, or in a small group without the direct support of the teacher, peer partnerships may be either homogeneous or heterogeneous depending on the content area and goals of the tasks or the needs of the students. Both have their benefits as well as their drawbacks, so it's important to know your students and learning targets when making these important instructional decisions. It is critical to use a balance of teacher and student choice when determining students' learning experiences. At times, you may find it appropriate to choose the learning tasks and materials students will use, but it is also important to allow students to have choices in what they learn and the materials they use to learn these ideas, concepts, and skills. The workshop model lends itself to incorporating "play," which we will discuss in more detail in chapters 4 (page 157) and 5 (page 223), and learning by means of student-directed projects. Both play and project learning can either be teacher- or student-directed—again we recommend both—and each requires careful strategic planning in a supportive learning environment.

Conclusion

We have shared a multitude of considerations for creating a strong schoolwide positive culture and a healthy climate, as well as effective safe and meaningful learning environments that include both physical and cultural features. A school's positive culture and healthy climate are essential to providing strong social-emotional learning, and without them the lessons taught during direct instruction of social-emotional learning will not be practiced and applied. It can feel overwhelming to consider all the factors that contribute to a positive and safe learning environment in the 21st century. It is important to remember that creating this environment is not the responsibility of one individual teacher but rather the responsibility of the whole school community. It is a collaborative task that requires buy-in and support from teachers, students, families, and the administration. When schools engage in collaborative practices and put in the proactive work to create these learning environments across the building and in individual classrooms, students will benefit, not just in their SEL skills but in academic areas as well. Chapter 3 (page 93) provides a framework and tools for building a schoolwide foundation for SEL in elementary schools and the necessary steps needed to turn many of these ideas into actions.

Tips for Administrators, Teachers, and Support Staff

Figure 2.8 contains tips and reflection questions relating to the contents of this chapter. As you consider these questions and next steps, reflect on your current practices in your own classroom and school.

Administrators	Teachers	Support Staff
• Remember the difference between culture and climate and monitor both within the school. Ensure the language used throughout the school reflects this understanding. • Reflect on both the physical and cultural environment throughout the school. Do students feel safe? Are all adults actively forming relationships with students? • Does your staff understand the importance of recognizing their unconscious bias? Do they feel comfortable discussing it with one another and reflecting on it openly? Do staff members have a safe place for this reflection?	• Maintain a classroom environment that reflects 21st century learning. Consider sensory features and student choice. Be ready to adapt to the students' needs! • Be deliberate with the language you use with both colleagues and students. Intentionally use words and phrases that promote a growth mindset and reflect a safe environment with high expectations. • Model self-regulation strategies naturally throughout the day so that students understand these are meaningful tools that adults use. • Above all, work to build and maintain relationships with students.	• Talk with your teams about how you can help support all students during whole-group focus lessons. How can you repeat, rephrase, or enhance the instruction so that all students can meaningfully participate? • Understand the responsible routines and behavior expectations the classroom teachers have in place. As you work with classes, be sure to support these intentional routines so that students feel secure in these expectations.

Figure 2.8: Tips for administrators, teachers, and support staff from chapter 2.

CHAPTER 3

Building a Schoolwide Foundation for SEL in Elementary Schools

Vignette: Implementing Learning Environment Norms

Maria sat with her teammates to reflect on what they had just observed. That year, their school had made the commitment to create a positive learning environment for all students—a commitment that began with the school and the teams determining their norms for the learning environment. These positive, collective norms would allow students to feel safe in each setting throughout the school because they would know what to expect in each classroom.

While Maria liked this in theory, she also had a hard time giving up some of the elements she felt made her classroom "hers." She knew other people on the team felt this way as well. Carol, who had been teaching for twenty-three years, had a structured behavior system that kept everyone in her classroom quiet and on task. It was a stoplight system, where students moved their names throughout the day depending on their behavior. The rest of the team avoided that system. When team members' students went to Carol for reading or mathematics groups, they had difficulty with the different system and often came back to their home rooms complaining. It was frequently a source of tension on the team.

Maria, on the other hand, loved art, and her classroom reflected it. Decorations hung from the ceiling, and former and current students' colorful art projects lined every inch of the walls. Her organization wasn't great, she knew, and her students were never quite as independent as Carol's because she didn't have easily accessible materials. So she came to this group discussion knowing that she and her teammates were each going to have to be open and make changes. Even if it was what was best for the students, Maria felt a bit judged and vulnerable when she arrived at the meeting. Yet, as her principal said, it was time to get comfortable being uncomfortable. They had a strong team, and she knew that although she felt vulnerable, her team would not judge her or gossip about the meeting later, as no post-meeting complaining sessions was a schoolwide norm that everyone honored.

The team had just observed another teacher in the building and was gathering back together to discuss what elements of the teacher's positive classroom environment it would designate as norms at their grade level. Maria thought of what she had just seen. The classroom was clean and organized so that students could access materials they needed easily and independently. Unlike her own classroom, there was not much on the walls, yet the classroom still felt warm and inviting. The teacher used a calm voice, played soothing music to signal transitions, and allowed students to find places to sit and work where they would feel comfortable. When a student needed to be redirected, Maria noticed that the teacher did not call out across the room but slowly walked over to the student, bent down to their eye level, and gave a positive redirection. Just being in the classroom was such a calm experience that the team did not want to end the observation.

Maria felt as though it would be a learning curve to implement this calm style and would make her feel as though she was a first-year teacher again (hadn't she come farther than that feeling?). And yet, when she thought of Daniel, she knew she needed to make changes. Determined to not let her ego get in the way, she was the first to open the discussion with her team. "I loved how simple her room was," she found herself saying.

In chapter 2 (page 45), we took time to dig into the common and differential features of a school's culture, climate, and environments. In this chapter, we will describe how schools might use school climate standards and implement CASEL's recommendations to improve SEL through schoolwide tasks that are both effective and sustainable. If we want our students to develop academic and social-emotional skills, knowledge, and dispositions, we must first begin by forming a deeply rooted schoolwide culture of collaboration and collective responsibility (one of the three big ideas of a PLC; DuFour et al., 2016). We also must establish and maintain a positive schoolwide culture and healthy climate and create safe and effective learning environments (the foundational work of a school in establishing effective and sustainable SEL; see figure 3.1).

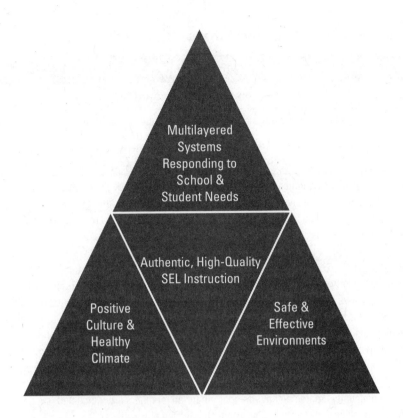

Figure 3.1: SEL schoolwide pyramid.

This chapter will discuss how the work of a PLC supports schools in effectively establishing schoolwide social-emotional learning in elementary schools. It also includes helpful tools elementary schools can use when developing schoolwide action plans focused on SEL and for evaluating current SEL practices. As always, the chapter will conclude with tips for administrators, teachers, and support staff based on this chapter's contents.

Establishing Schoolwide Social-Emotional Learning in Elementary Schools

In 2009, the National School Climate Council (NSCC) developed a set of national school climate standards (see table 3.1, page 96). The NSCC recognizes that the terms *culture*, *climate*, and *environment* are often used interchangeably in education and note that it in fact has used these terms interchangeably within the standards seen in table 3.1.

Table 3.1: National School Climate Standards

National School Climate Standards
School Climate Standard 1
The school community has a shared vision and plan for promoting, enhancing, and sustaining a positive school climate.
School Climate Standard 2
The school community sets policies specifically promoting (a) the development and sustainability of social, emotional, ethical, civic, and intellectual skills, knowledge, and dispositions, and (b) a comprehensive system to address barriers to learning and teaching and reengage students who have become disengaged.
School Climate Standard 3
The school community's practices are identified, prioritized, and supported to (a) promote the learning and positive social, emotional, ethical, and civic development of students; (b) enhance engagement in teaching, learning, and schoolwide activities; (c) address barriers to learning and teaching and reengage those who have become disengaged; and (d) develop and sustain an appropriate operational infrastructure and capacity-building mechanisms for meeting this standard.
School Climate Standard 4
The school community creates an environment where all members are welcomed, supported, and feel safe in school: socially, emotionally, intellectually, and physically.
School Climate Standard 5
The school community develops meaningful and engaging practices, activities, and norms that promote social and civic responsibilities and a commitment to social justice.

Source for standards: The National School Climate Council, 2009.

Additionally, the Collaborative for Academic, Social, and Emotional Learning (CASEL) has developed a wealth of tools to support schools in establishing SEL (see CASEL.org). In fact, CASEL recommends that schools focus on four areas to improve SEL (see table 3.2).

Table 3.2: CASEL's Four Focus Areas

CASEL Four Focus Areas
1. Building a foundation of support by establishing an SEL team to support SEL implementation within a school, which would include helping to develop the school's vision for SEL and developing specific schoolwide action plans.
2. Strengthening the adults' learning of SEL through ongoing professional development regarding instructional best practices and strategies and establishing supportive and equitable learning environments.
3. Developing a collaborative and common approach for supporting students' social and emotional learning across the school setting and building parent and community partnerships.
4. Establishing a system for monitoring schoolwide progress and improvement.

Source: CASEL, n.d.c.

In a professional learning community (PLC), "the first step educators take when making decisions is to learn together" (DuFour et al., 2016, p. 113). The school's culture, climate, and learning environment should support the learning of both academic and social-emotional skills and content. In fact, "a rich body of recent neuroscience research has demonstrated the interrelatedness of emotions and cognition and the importance of emotion in rational thought" (Immordino-Yang & Faeth, 2010, p. 82). If emotion and cognition are neurologically interrelated, then, we argue, so should be our approaches of implementing academic and SEL learning. Schools should establish one system for learning (both academic and social-emotional) to prohibit isolating SEL from academics and to avoid teams operating in academic and SEL silos. Therefore, the process of how a school goes about establishing both academic and social-emotional learning should be the same.

A school must focus on the three big ideas that drive the work of a PLC. These ideas include a focus on learning, a collaborative culture and collective responsibility, and results (evidence of student learning; DuFour et al., 2016, pp. 11–12). You can also see how these ideas are embedded in CASEL's four focus areas of SEL (see table 3.2). We believe there is great benefit in having shared values, knowledge, language, and commitments around both academic and social-emotional learning. We have seen schools that are strongly committed to either the academic or social-emotional learning of students and have strongly aligned their priorities to either one or the other. We believe this is not an either-or situation. Rather, the entire school community should make strong commitments to both academic *and* social-emotional learning, in partnership with families.

As a result, in this chapter, we hope to marry the mission of a PLC with many of the ideas from CASEL and the National School Climate Council regarding SEL. Our main focus will be on the work of a school in developing collective commitments that relate to a school's culture, climate, environments, and commitments that are specifically geared toward SEL instruction. Visit **go.SolutionTree.com /PLCbooks** to learn more about the deeply embedded work of a professional learning community. Solution Tree provides a plethora of resources that can support a school in determining those necessary collective commitments that target specific aspects of academic learning and can also help in the process of transforming schools into strong PLCs.

In the following sections, we share a set of tools schools can utilize as they take a schoolwide approach to forming a strong foundation for social-emotional learning—where the adults and students work collaboratively to build a positive culture and healthy climate and form strong relationships in safe and effective learning environments. Schools must also consider their instructional approach to SEL by determining what essential SEL standards their students need to learn. Teams must then determine how students' learning will be monitored for growth over time. When a school takes time to form common language and works together to build common understandings, the school teams learn new ideas from one another, gain deeper overall understandings of the content, and ensure equitable educational experiences for their students. In education, equity is driven by the common instructional practices used but also grounded in the overall systems we put into place for *all* students. Therefore, we will also share how schools can develop a multilayered system to support the needs of *all* learners.

Creating a Mission, a Vision, Shared Collective Commitments, and Goals That Support and Promote SEL

The PLC process relies on the collaborative work of the whole school and not just the ideas of one individual such as a principal or teacher leader, or the work of one individual team within the school. Take a moment to look at figure 3.2, which refers to a school's important schoolwide work when considering how to implement SEL. As we describe each task, take time to think about what your school has already put into place and what areas you could strengthen or implement. Let's begin by asking an important question: *Is social and emotional growth valued as much as academic growth, and what specific policies, structures, and action plans has our school established to support SEL?*

Intentions are great, but it takes a shared mission, vision, collective commitments, and goals by the staff and students to maintain the intended positive culture and healthy climate that will pave the path for students' academic success and their social-emotional well-being. Whether you are a principal, a classroom teacher, the school counselor, or any other staff member, you have the power to invoke change and share ideas regarding the value of collaboration and effective social-emotional learning.

The PLC process has a direct impact on the culture of the school and its community members' values and practices. The foundation of a PLC consists of the school's mission, vision, values, and goals (DuFour et al., 2016). The mission of a school answers the question of why the school organization exists. The vision helps the school determine what it strives to become by stating the values and goals the school team shares. To achieve the school's mission and vision, the school community must make a set of collective commitments to each other around their shared values and beliefs. It is important that these rich discussions don't remain stagnant conversations; rather, once the school identifies these collective commitments, it is time to dig in and act. Some of these collective commitments can require the development of goals to achieve the desired results and a clear set of action plans with established timelines.

Schoolwide Tasks for Establishing Social-Emotional Learning	
Build Mission Statement	Create a schoolwide mission statement, which should include and answer the question of why the school exists or state the purpose of the school.
Create Vision Statement	Create a schoolwide vision statement, which includes a description of what the school wants to become and accomplish, both in academic and social-emotional learning and while taking into account teacher and student wellbeing.
Create Collective Commitments	Determine how you will behave to achieve your school's vision by creating a set of schoolwide collective commitments and team norms that include a focus on social-emotional learning as well as the wellbeing of the staff and students. These should include the following critical SEL elements: ☐ Positive culture and healthy climate ☐ Safe and effective learning environments ☐ Authentic, high-quality SEL instruction ☐ Multilayered systems responding to the school and students' needs
Develop Goals and Schoolwide Action Plans	Create goals for determining SEL progress and implement schoolwide action plans.

Source: Adapted from DuFour et al., 2016.

Figure 3.2: Schoolwide tasks for establishing social-emotional learning.

*Visit **go.SolutionTree.com/instruction** for a free blank reproducible version of this figure.*

For example, if part of a school's vision is to have a positive schoolwide culture and healthy climate, then a school operating as a PLC will first commit to establishing a positive schoolwide culture and climate and then collaborate and determine the necessary action steps they need to take to make that vision a reality. Table 3.3 (page 100) highlights a few sample schoolwide mission and vision statements, and table 3.4 (page 100) lists a set of sample collective commitments framed around SEL critical elements, which were derived from CASEL's focus areas, the National School Climate Council's standards, and Mariale M. Hardiman's (2003) brain-targeted teaching model. It is important to note that safety is a critical SEL element and is equally as important. It is embedded into the four SEL categories (positive culture and healthy climate, safe and effective learning environments, authentic, high-quality SEL instruction, and a multilayered system responding to school and student needs).

Table 3.3: Elementary School Vision Statement Examples

Elementary School	Mission	Vision
Rose Hill Elementary School, Fairfax County Public Schools, Alexandria, Virginia	We seek to build a supportive community among staff, students, and parents where we work together and celebrate social and academic growth. As a community, we will maintain honest, respectful relationships and be responsible to one another to ensure student success.	Rose Hill Elementary: Where *all* community members have pride, passion, and high expectations for student success.
Richland Community School Unit, District Number 1, Olney, Illinois	The mission of Richland School District, in partnership with families and the community, is to create a safe and effective learning environment that provides our students with opportunities to prepare them for academic success, career readiness, lifelong learning, citizenship, and global awareness.	We are a learning community that prepares our students for success by meeting the individual needs of each and every student.
Hialeah Gardens Elementary School, Miami-Dade School District, Hialeah Gardens, Florida	To promote academic excellence in an environment where all students and adults feel welcome, respected, trusted, and an important part of the school. We will foster a school community which values diversity and nurtures self-esteem.	Empower future leaders in a safe environment where they are valued for their individuality and diverse capabilities.

Table 3.4: SEL Collective Commitments Examples

Positive Culture and Healthy Climate
• Maintain a positive culture and climate.
• Monitor the schoolwide climate from the perspective of the staff, students, and families.
• Monitor our individual emotions and be mindful of the role our own behaviors play in the overall climate.
Safe and Effective Learning Environments
• Establish learning environment norms by identifying collective common factors of the physical and cultural learning environments of the school (larger school setting and classroom settings).
Authentic, High-Quality SEL Instruction
• Learn together, build communitywide common understandings about SEL, and use common SEL language across the school.
• Use a guaranteed and viable SEL curriculum and identify essential SEL standards at each grade level.
Multilayered Systems Responding to School and Student Needs
• Implement a social-emotional support system.
• Monitor students' social-emotional growth.
• Establish a home-school partnership.

Developing Schoolwide Action Plans and Setting Goals

This work should not just fall on one person, nor should it be separate from discussions around academic learning. It is also not realistic to have all the work monitored only by the administration. Therefore, it is important for schools to create a *guiding coalition* (DuFour et al., 2016) to lead the school in the direction of carrying out its mission and vision. To obtain schoolwide buy-in, it takes getting the right group of stakeholders together, assembling individuals with varied experiences, expertise, and perspectives to support the school in carrying out the school's mission and vision.

A pivotal role of the guiding coalition is to guide the school in creating or revisiting collective commitments during a staff meeting at the start of each school year. Once the staff forms collective commitments, the next step is to begin the process of developing schoolwide SEL goals and action plans. Missions, visions, and collective commitments remain just good ideas unless schools take action and make detailed plans, which include the process of creating timelines, setting goals, and designating people who are responsible for monitoring and evaluating them. It is important that schools take a collaborative approach to generate, implement, and monitor these schoolwide action plans. The administration may monitor some plans, while the guiding coalition or possibly a designated vertical team of staff members (for example, an SEL or equity team) will monitor others. We will go into more detail about how these teams can specifically support efforts in SEL when we share the importance of schools using a multilayered system to respond to school and student needs (page 138).

Schools must determine how all their efforts will make a difference; establish goals that are consistent with the mission, vision, and collective commitments; and have systems in place for monitoring the effectiveness of the school's action plan. Schools can develop SMART goals (Conzemius & O'Neill, 2014) regarding what it is they want to achieve. These goals are strategic, measurable, attainable, results-oriented, and time-bound as a means for identifying progress. The following are two samples of SMART goals specifically related to SEL.

- All teachers will implement SEL practices (calendar routines, morning meetings, reading comprehension strategies, and so on) and growth mindset habits into daily instruction in 100 percent of classrooms as indicated in lesson plans by June 2022.

- All teachers will support student goal setting in 100 percent of classrooms, as documented by a timeline, team plans, and student work on the school's shared server in the goal-setting folder by June 2022.

To learn more about establishing SMART goals in a professional learning community, visit **go.SolutionTree.com/PLCbooks**.

If a school creates a plan and finds it is not working, they may need to modify or change it at some point in the year. It is in the best interest of all community members to modify plans and make all necessary shifts, but what they should not change are the collective commitments and established goals themselves. For instance, as teachers, we plan our lessons with the best intentions. Yet, teaching does not always lead to learning, so if students did not learn the skills and knowledge the first time, we must be reflective about our approaches and go back to the drawing board to make a new plan for reteaching. In this example, the teacher's learning goals never changed; rather, it was the teacher's approach, plans, and practices that changed. Sometimes schools or collaborative teams initially create plans and stick with them even if they are not very effective. These schoolwide action plans can be thought of as living, breathing documents that are continuously monitored and evaluated. It can also be tempting for schools to consistently change commitments to fit school plans. However, being transparent as well as responsive to the needs of the school and its community members reflects a healthy school that embraces a growth mindset.

When schools begin the process of establishing SEL it truly becomes a process, one that builds over time and from year to year. It is important that schools revise collective commitments yearly and that the staff reflects on these commitments as well as the systems and policies that are put into place on an ongoing yearly basis. Taking a reflective and responsive approach helps to establish SEL more effectively than a set of disconnected procedures, policies, and ineffective systems.

As we begin to explore what collective commitments might look like and how schools can use these commitments to create productive action plans, think about your own individual role and what it would take from your perspective to honor these commitments and the various contributions needed on the part of yourself and your teammates.

The following sections introduce tools and examples for creating collective commitments and schoolwide action plans for the four critical SEL elements: (1) positive culture and healthy climate, (2) safe and effective learning environments, (3) authentic, high-quality SEL instruction, and (4) multilayered systems responding to the school and student needs. As you explore these sections, you will start to see what it can look like when schools turn these collective commitments into actions. We have provided just a few ideas under each of the four critical SEL elements. As you read, begin to think about the effective SEL procedures and policies you may already have in place, and consider where they might fit under one of these four critical SEL elements. You will notice that some of these plans take more time than others, yet none of them are completed by teachers in isolation. In fact, these plans come from those collective commitments made by the staff using a schoolwide team approach.

In each section, we have embedded a set of tools for schools to consider using when developing their collective commitments and specific schoolwide action plans. Notice how each tool includes a set of indicators relating to each of the SEL critical elements and encourages the staff to use those indicators, look-fors, examples, and nonexamples to generate their collective commitments and schoolwide action plans specifically related to SEL. Often, when schools engage in the process of creating collective commitments, they generate statements with consensus but sometimes not with the full clarity of all community members. Therefore, this process can help the school community begin to develop quality plans that match the school's mission, vision, collective commitments, and goals, as well as help the school and its staff in building common understandings around these critical SEL elements.

Positive Culture and Healthy Climate

As discussed in chapter 2 (page 45), school culture and climate can have a significant impact on staff, students, and families. To maintain and fulfill a positive school culture and healthy climate, staff members must understand the nuances between the two terms and be committed to maintaining both. Chapter 2 presented the analogy of a flower, with culture being the deep roots of the plant and climate being the flower (stem and petals) exposed to elements such as weather and pollution. To maintain the school's desired positive culture and healthy climate that allow for the best growth, each member of the team must understand its own individual role in contributing to both the roots and the blossom. How each school staff member interacts with students, coworkers, and families will impact this critical SEL element.

Indicators of a positive culture and healthy school climate include all members of the school feeling a sense of community and a sense of safety. Students and staff should feel safe in their school environment, and this feeling of safety should include both physical and psychological safety. In addition, school members should use positive and respectful language, demonstrate a growth mindset, and maintain strong positive relationships between staff and students. This positive relationship must include being culturally responsive to the families the school serves (EdTrust, 2020). Tables 3.5 (page 104), 3.6 (page 107), and 3.7 (page 108) share a few action plan examples focused on different methods of building a positive school culture and maintaining a healthy school climate.

Table 3.5: Example Collective Commitments—Positive Culture and Healthy Climate (Example 1)

Collective Commitments Focused on SEL	Schoolwide Action Plan Examples
Maintain a positive culture and healthy climate: • Staff members model positive growth mindset language and presume positive intentions with students and with one another. Staff members reflect on their unconscious biases and seek to create culturally responsive interactions with families and students.	• **Greeting Students:** All members of the staff (including secretaries, cafeteria workers, and custodians) greet students with eye contact and warmth throughout the school day. Administrators walk the halls during student arrival to greet students and teachers. Teachers stand at the doors of classrooms to greet students. • **Greeting Families:** All members of the staff greet parents and families, use positive growth mindset language during conversations, and create culturally responsive interactions with parents and family members. • **Model Learning on Bias:** School leaders model being learners in the area of race and implicit bias within schools (Boudreau, 2020). Teams work together to identify stumbling blocks that prevent them from having deeper conversations. • **Model Growth Mindset:** Administrators find ways to model growth mindset with staff and students (for example, at the beginning of the school year administrators join in on morning meetings and team meetings and share a growth mindset moment with staff and students). Teachers participate in a book study with families to learn about using growth mindset. • **Celebrate:** Create opportunities to celebrate one another, student growth, successes, and show gratitude (for example, designate celebration time during team meetings, have a celebration staff section in the weekly staff newsletter, create gratitude boards throughout the school building and within classrooms).

While it is easy for school communities to say they commit to building a positive culture and healthy school climate, there are small yet essential day-to-day actions staff must commit to in order to meet this goal. These small acts entrench themselves into the hearts and minds of the school community. One example is having every adult in the building—principals, teachers, custodians, and secretaries—commit to greeting students with eye contact and a smile. A school can develop a morning routine of teachers standing in their doorways to positively welcome students each morning, while support staff and the principals can commit to walking the halls during arrival time each day to greet both teachers and students.

Just as the expectation would be to greet students in a welcoming manner each day, school staff should also commit to being as welcoming to our students' families. When staff members communicate with families, it is important to facilitate engagement that is welcoming and respectful.

Encouraging both staff and students to create gratitude or kindness boards is another way to maintain a positive school climate (Conscious Discipline, n.d.; Froh & Bono, 2012). Teachers can dedicate an area of their classroom wall for students to add a note of something they are grateful for, share something kind about a classmate, or write a celebration. Schools can dedicate a bulletin board near their entrance for this as well, so that students can share these grateful thoughts with the entire school. This encourages students and staff to focus on what they are grateful for as well as allowing them to positively support one another. These gratitude practices build a sense of community and positive relationships while encouraging students and staff to develop habits of thankfulness that can lead to a stronger sense of optimism and less negative emotions (Froh & Bono, 2012).

Providing time for staff to share small celebrations throughout the week is another example of a staff committing to maintaining a strong culture and a positive and healthy climate. Team meetings can begin with teachers sharing small celebrations from the week before the team gets into the more serious business of planning and data analysis. These moments to celebrate small teacher wins—nailing a lesson, watching a student take a risk and raise their hand for the first time—connect us as a team and remind us of why we gather to do the hard work together. Celebrations can also include moments of celebrating a personal growth experience or the success of a colleague. Being self-aware of one's own accomplishments or small wins, or those of a teammate, can support relationship building between team members and help staff reflect on the SEL skills they are helping the students build. Just as we work to increase our students' SEL competencies, we also work to support our own. In fact, these celebrations can build our own SEL building block of self-awareness. For example, you can honor how you used a new practice or strategy you tried with your students or acknowledge something positive or effective you noticed your colleague do with students in the hallway that week.

These celebration moments do not need to last more than five minutes (at the most!) and can bring the team's focus to the individual students. While a child may not have scored well on the assessment the team is about to discuss, this celebration moment is a chance to discuss what the student accomplished that week. As a special education teacher, I (Ann-Bailey) often saw these discussions as a way to bring all students into the focus of the team. After leaving a positive, student-focused school, I found myself teaching at a school with a different culture. When we sat down to discuss what was going well and I shared a celebration I had for the students in the self-contained autism class, the room fell silent. Not knowing what to say about the small victories I had just shared, the discussion moved on. It soon became clear that this school did not embody the belief that all students belong to all teachers, or that all students can learn at high levels. That was my first inkling that this school was different from my former PLC school, although I continued to see evidence of the different culture in how the students greeted one another, how teachers interacted with students, and how teachers interacted with each other.

Although this section lists some small actions schools can take to promote a positive culture and healthy climate, there are deeper, most significant tasks schools must attend to. One task is fully examining how unconscious bias impacts the school's community. This is not an easy task, nor one that can be fully accomplished within a year. However, we strongly recommend that your school dedicate a deep dive into this work. How we unconsciously judge, decide, or act based on our unrecognized reactions to a person can significantly impact classroom communities and the ability of all students to feel safe, and welcome (Beachum & Gullo, 2020). These unconscious judgements we make can form because of a student's race, culture, gender, or even special education label or medical diagnosis. These judgements end up having an impact on student achievement, student discipline, and student access to opportunities (Collado et al., 2021). School leadership is the key to addressing this unconscious reaction. Creating a culture of openness and vulnerability; being a humble, lifelong learner; and demonstrating a willingness to sit with discomfort can go a long way in addressing this issue (Bourdeau, 2020). In addition, school teams can identify stumbling blocks that prevent them from having honest conversations about the underlying assumptions they make that may inform their practice. Once they are able to have these conversations, they can then work on moving past those blocks. We recommend reading further on this topic from experts in the field. *Unconscious Bias in Schools* (Benson & Fiarman, 2020) from Harvard Education Press provides additional resources and information on this topic. Another excellent source for support in implementing this work is *Beyond Conversations About Race: A Guide for Discussions With Students, Teachers, and Communities* from Solution Tree (Collado et al., 2021).

The second sample schoolwide collective commitment we share involves monitoring the schoolwide climate from the perspective of the staff, students, and families (see table 3.6). To do so, a school needs to develop a system to monitor its climate and provide opportunities for connection, reflection, and support when it discovers that the climate needs a boost. Thinking back to the image of the flower in chapter 2 (page 45), with the culture being the roots and the climate being the blossom, we must remember that *every flower will get rained on*. Every school will have moments when their climate is tested while their culture remains strong. Being able to recognize when this occurs and help one another find an umbrella will go a long way in supporting the school's mission and vision.

Table 3.6: Example Collective Commitments—Positive Culture and Healthy Climate (Example 2)

Collective Commitments Focused on SEL	Schoolwide Action Plan Examples
Monitor the schoolwide climate from the perspective of the staff, students, and families: • Establish a system for staff and families to share ideas and constructive criticism. • Plan opportunities for staff and students to connect with each other as a way to support co-regulation and connection. • Allow for flexibility when students or staff are showing signs of a tense climate.	• Regularly survey the entire school community and designate a team to evaluate the results using a growth mindset. Work collaboratively to learn about research-based best practices and policy or develop inquiry-based practices that can support the schoolwide climate. • Implement a high-five buddy system for students. • Host a multicultural night. • Plan schoolwide celebrations with families. • Have specialist teachers (art, music, PE, library, and so on) invite classroom teachers to attend classes to see students shine in nonacademic subjects. • Implement reading buddies. • Implement secret pals and genuine recognition for staff.

Schools can implement a system for teachers, parents, and students to provide feedback or insights spontaneously as well as through surveys provided throughout the year. This can be as simple as sending out short quarterly electronic surveys, sending home short paper surveys for families to return to school, placing a feedback box in the office where families are encouraged to share their insights, or having quarterly family gatherings where family members are given a safe place to share their perspectives. When the climate is starting to get rainy, schools should look for opportunities to bring students and staff together for reflection and connection. One example is to implement a "High-Five Buddy System," in which every student is paired with an adult in the school. The adult makes a point to make sure to connect with their buddies at least once a week, with either a high five, fist bump, elbow bump, or wave. This will provide students with another connection outside of the student's familiar teachers.

School communities can also look for ways to offer student and teacher connections throughout the school day. Music, art, library, and physical education teachers can invite the classroom teachers into their rooms to watch the final product of a unit. This allows the specialist and the classroom teacher to connect and gives the classroom teacher insight into aspects of the school outside the classroom. Alternatively, classroom teachers can invite the specialists into their classrooms to participate in morning meetings or to observe a class project or end-of-unit celebration.

Schools can proactively plan for connection opportunities as well, particularly ones that allow for families to participate at the school. Family picnics, multicultural nights, food-truck Fridays at the playground, or simple academic celebrations that invite family members to visit during the day offer unique opportunities for connections between families, teachers, and students (Collado et al., 2021).

The final collective commitment relating to culture and climate relates to the regulation of our own behaviors as community members (see table 3.7). Some schools employ instructional coaches whom they designate to support teachers in both instructional techniques and reflective practices. These resources can be invaluable in maintaining a positive school climate by creating coaching routines and practices that build on reflection. These practices encourage teachers to openly reflect on their own emotional reactions, thoughts, and decisions throughout the school day. These reflective coaching experiences can allow teachers to identify their emotions and reflect on them in the same manner we hope students will do when working with a teacher. It is important to note that many schools do not have these types of positions; therefore, it may be a team member or the administration who will be the ones to play an active role in supporting teachers and teams in reflective practices.

Table 3.7: Example Collective Commitments—Positive Culture and Healthy Climate (Example 3)

Collective Commitments Focused on SEL	Schoolwide Action Plan Examples
Monitor our individual emotions and be mindful of the role our own behaviors play in the group climate	• Staff have opportunities to work with one another in a reflective capacity, where they can listen to one another and discuss their emotional reactions to events. This may occur during meetings with the whole team or in individual one-on-one conversations before or after the school day.

In addition to providing space for instructional coaches, mentor teachers, or administrators to sit in reflection with teachers, school teams can also be aware and thoughtful of their work together. In thinking about the individual members of any team, it is important to keep personalities, tone, and learning styles in mind. A team with varied personalities and ideas can produce great accomplishments for students as long as they learn to assume positive intentions with one another's tone and conversation style. Often, teams hit roadblocks when members begin to read negative emotions and intentions behind tone, body language, and comments. Appreciating that each team member may interact and contribute to the team in their own individual style will allow the members of the team to accept differences and mismatches in conversation. Instead of dwelling on a conversation that felt disrespectful or frustrating, members can remind themselves of their shared goal—being present for the students—and intentionally assume positive intentions of the team members. This intentionality will go a long way to maintaining a positive school climate. We often remind ourselves that we need to provide students with five positive comments for every negative comment we give. This is true not just for children but for adults as well. The most effective teams are ones that maintain an 8:1 ratio of positive comments to criticism (Zenger & Folkman, 2013).

Although we only shared three examples of collective commitments focused around positive school culture and climate, there are countless actions that can support schools in building a positive culture and maintaining a healthy schoolwide climate. Anthony Muhammad shares invaluable information in his book *Transforming School Culture: How to Overcome Staff Division* (2009). Additionally, there is a great deal more that goes into building a strong collaborative school culture beyond the few examples we shared with you here regarding the work of building a positive culture and healthy school climate. For instance, for teachers to have the time to collaborate with one another around this important work, the school's master schedule must be crafted in a way that provides teams with common planning time, and teams must then commit to working together. Also, leadership needs to determine which elements need to be tight (top-down leadership) and loose (bottom-up leadership) within the professional learning community. For instance, administrators may be tight on the fact that all teams will engage in weekly team planning meetings; therefore, this would not be optional. But, administrators from that same school might be loose on what that time looks like and allow each team to form their own team meeting agendas. Again, we encourage you to seek out additional PLC resources (for example, at www.allthingsPLC.info) for a full scope of what it takes to build a strong schoolwide collaborative culture.

The content discussed in tables 3.5–3.7 involves school staff's collective commitments. While it is easy to say a school is committed to maintaining a positive culture and healthy climate, it is more difficult to ensure that each member of the staff understands what that means and what their role is in supporting the commitment. Taking the time to write out the collective commitment and break it down into concrete and observable elements that are needed to support the overall commitment will better ensure that the school will meet the commitment. Sometimes it will be important to designate who is committing to work on specific tasks by labeling them as the administration's specific commitments to staff or of teachers' commitments to one another, students, or families. Some commitments may not require an elaborate plan, while others may need one. Figure 3.3 (page 110) presents a tool that can help schools turn their collective commitments into schoolwide action plans while building common understandings and language around a positive school culture and a healthy school climate. (A blank reproducible version of this SEL Schoolwide Action Plan Tool can be found online at **go.SolutionTree.com/instruction**.) Notice how the tool begins with a set of look-fors as well as schoolwide and classroom examples and nonexamples. The tool also includes several sections for recording collective commitments and developing common schoolwide specific action plans associated with them (namely, what is the plan, who will implement and monitor the plan, what is the timeline, how do we document the process, and what are the next steps). The tool itself is not what is most important; rather, it is the work done by teams (grade-level teams, SEL teams, the equity team, the guiding coalition, and so on). In addition to the tools we share with you (see figures 3.3–3.9, 3.12, and 3.13), CASEL has a set of their own tools that can be used to support schools in establishing SEL schoolwide. You may also consider developing your own tool when doing this important work.

Critical SEL Element: **Positive Culture and Healthy Climate**—Schoolwide policies and procedures are collaborative and equitable; and practices promote schoolwide safety, building trusting relationships and a strong community.

Indicators

Safety:

- Physical safety
- Psychological safety, including safety for both students and teachers to take risks, maintain a growth mindset, and make choices (agency), as well as the safety within teacher teams to disagree without judgement and retaliation
- Social safety
- Emotional safety

Trusting Relationships (positive, supportive, collaborative, and open):

- Staff/student relationships
- Staff/staff relationships
- Student/student relationships
- Staff/family relationships

Sense of Community:

- Positive language
- Collaboration
- Celebrations (of adult and student accomplishments as well as cultural and community celebrations)
- Respect
- Empathy and kindness
- Collective efficacy
- Shared leadership, values, beliefs, norms, and behaviors

Schoolwide:

What it looks like, sounds like, feels like

Safety

- Students feel psychologically safe, as evident through feeling comfortable advocating for their academic and social-emotional needs, demonstrating a growth mindset, and feeling comfortable making choices about their learning in multiple settings throughout the school
- All learning environments are physically safe, and procedures and policies are in place for adults and students in daily routines throughout the building
- Staff post expectations for students visually throughout the school building (lunchroom, playground, hallways, classrooms)
- Adults use positive language and actions to promote and model a growth mindset
- Schoolwide discipline is student centered
- Staff support one another in learning about and recognizing unconscious bias

Classroom:

What it looks like, sounds like, feels like

Safety

- Students feel psychologically safe in both academic and social interactions
- The classroom learning environment is physically safe and easy to navigate around, with the teacher able to see all areas of the room
- Students are given voice and choice in how they learn, in their culture, and in their physical learning environments
- Students feel comfortable advocating for their academic and social-emotional needs
- Students understand the expectations within the classroom and feel ownership of their classroom and these expectations
- The student expectations are visually posted in the classroom
- Discipline is student centered

Schoolwide: What it looks like, sounds like, feels like	**Classroom:** What it looks like, sounds like, feels like
Trusting Relationships • Students use respectful words and actions with adults and peers • Adults model prosocial skills • As a step towards supporting teacher wellness, staff have opportunities to work with one another in a reflective capacity, where they can listen to one another and discuss emotional reactions to events. This may occur during meetings with the whole team or in individual ones on conversations before or after the school day. • Adults model and support the use of calm-down strategies and self-regulation tools. This is genuinely supported by the school with an understanding of the importance of teacher wellness. • Staff dedicates time to relationship building • Staff works positively with one another and assumes positive intentions of one another's actions • Adults support the facilitation of peer-mediated conflict and students use conflict resolution strategies **Sense of Community** • School staff throughout the building use common language when discussing children's learning, development, and behaviors • Students respect differences of other students • The school contains visual displays that promote positive mindsets, kindness, and gratitude • Staff builds collective efficacy around high expectations for students • There is schoolwide collaboration (teachers work together in vertical and grade-level teams) • Teachers are transparent and coordinate efforts across the grade level • Families understand SEL in the school • Families feel welcomed and part of the school community, and the school builds in opportunities for family engagement throughout the school (multicultural nights, parent coffees, and so on)	**Trusting Relationships** • Teachers facilitate relationship building with students and between students • In classrooms, teachers and students use growth mindset language with one another and when they share their academic work • Teachers communicate high expectations and belief in students' ability to learn and achieve to the students • Teachers maintain an 8:1 ratio for positive interactions to every negative redirection • Students understand how to solve conflicts with peers and recognize when it is appropriate to seek adult support • The teacher models and supports conflict resolution strategies among the students within the classroom • Co-teaching relationships model positive adult interaction and collaboration for students **Sense of Community** • There is a sense of community and belonging among students within the classroom • Classmates respect differences in their peers • Visual displays promote a positive mindset, a belief all children belong and can achieve • Students are encouraged to interact with visual displays in the classroom to honor moments of kindness or gratitude • Families know that teachers care about their child individually and will respond in a reasonable timeframe with any concerns the parent has • Teachers communicate a partnership relationship with families • Families are welcome to observe and participate in classroom learning • Families understand what SEL components and standards are being taught at any given time and how to support those skills in the home environment

continued →

Figure 3.3: SEL schoolwide action plan tool—positive culture and healthy climate example.

Classroom Examples:

- Teachers and students together build a class community where the teacher acts as a facilitator of the learning and strong teacher and peer relationships exist. Students have rich conversations and work collaboratively. Students are engaged in rigorous and differentiated learning tasks that meet the needs of all learners.
- Students feel comfortable taking responsible risks in their learning, asking questions of their teacher and peers, and receiving constructive feedback. Students have the mindset that they can do hard things and they can learn at high levels with hard work and effort.
- Classroom management is community based, and students use conflict resolution strategies with peers and seek adult help when needed. Students use kind words and show respect to their teachers and peers. Each student is valued by the others in the classroom, representing the community's inclusive nature. Teachers implement brain-based discipline policies based on individual student needs and non-punitive natural consequences. The classroom has a place for students to go when they need self-time, and students can use learned strategies to self-regulate. Teachers engage in frequent communication with families.

Classroom Nonexamples:

- The classroom features authoritarian teaching where the learning tasks are mostly paper based and students mostly work quietly and independently at their assigned desks. The school pulls students receiving special education from the classroom environment and engages them in learning that is below grade-level expectations.
- Students do not feel fully safe and secure in their classrooms because they are not always aware of what the teacher expects of them. Rules and expectations change based on the teacher's mood and tolerance level for that day. Teachers use ineffective, reactive, and public procedures such as stoplight systems or clip charts to ensure "good" behavior in the classroom. Family communication is at a minimum, and teachers typically use it to communicate about students' negative behaviors.

Schoolwide Examples:

- From the time students enter the bus to when they leave at the end of the day, students interact positively with adults throughout the school building. Adult staff greet students and make eye contact and use positive language to reinforce and remind students of behavior expectations. The entire school staff has the shared belief that all students can learn at high levels, and their collaborative efforts can have a positive impact on student achievement. This belief translates to a strong inclusive community. Staff feels respected within the school and knows the school truly cares about their wellbeing. Positive discipline approaches are used in a consistent manner and throughout the school.
- Families feel welcomed into the building and know that if they have a concern teachers will listen and respond. Families and students feel physically and psychologically safe within the school environment. The school staff clearly communicates growth mindset ideas with students and families and understands that effort and growth are valued. Teachers check in with one another, share ideas, collaborate, and use self-regulation strategies with their students and peers. Families are greeted upon entering the school building and are viewed as contributing partners in students' education and learning.

Schoolwide Nonexamples:

- Students enter the building while adults yell behavior corrections. The school lists an excessive number of rules, which students have difficulty remembering and following. Adults speak to students to correct behavior before they greet them or smile.
- Teachers work in isolation. Teachers develop their own sets of rules and procedures, and students do not have consistent expectations throughout the building. Access to learning opportunities and positive learning environments is not equitable across the building.
- Teachers complain to one another about students' behavior. Teachers and students operate with a fixed mindset approach, where students see mistakes not as learning opportunities but rather as failures. Teachers do not model mistakes as opportunities for growth. School staff downplay bullying. Gossiping occurs frequently between staff members. Decisions made as a team are later undermined by a small group of teachers that decide to go against the decision. Leadership is limited to administration and not dispersed throughout the building.

Climate and Culture Collective Commitments	Culture & Climate Schoolwide Action Plan(s)	What Possible Resources are Needed to Carry Out the Plan(s)?	Who is Responsible for Carrying Out the Action Plan(s)?	Who is Responsible for Monitoring and Evaluating the Plan(s)?	What is the Timeline for the Action Plan(s)?	Indicators of Progress and Success	Next Steps
Maintain a positive culture and climate.	**Greeting Students:** • All members of the staff (including secretaries, cafeteria workers, and custodians) greet students with eye contact and warmth throughout the school day. Administrators walk the halls during student arrival to greet students and teachers. (Administrators block off this time in their schedules. No meetings occur during arrival.) Teachers stand at the door to greet students. • Administrators find ways to model growth mindset with staff and students (for example, at the beginning of the school year, administrators join in on morning meetings and share a growth mindset moment with staff and students). Teachers participate in a book study with families to learn about using growth mindset.	• Books and resources on growth mindset for staff and students • Individual copies of growth mindset professional books for a staff book study • Specifically assigned bulletin boards and materials	• Administrators, school counselors, and teachers maintain mindset culture. • Administrators are responsible for maintaining greeting culture and mindset culture. Also, administrators manage the celebrations section of the school newsletter, by asking staff to submit small gratitudes and holding staff member celebrations. • SEL team facilitates the mindset book study and oversees bulletin boards. • Individual teams ensure opportunities for celebration in agendas at team meetings.	• Administrators are responsible for monitoring the greeting culture. • Administrators, school counselors, and guiding coalition model and provide professional development on mindset. • Administrators, instructional coaches, and team meeting facilitators monitor opportunities for celebration and sharing.	• Greeting begins when school starts. Administrators immediately clear schedule for arrival. • Teachers commit to a five-week growth mindset book study in October–November. • Introduce gratitude boards in November and maintain throughout the year. Revisit in February around Valentine's Day. • Evidence of celebrations embedded in all meetings beginning with the initial team meetings at the start of school.	• Principals' calendars reflect a dedicated time to greeting students each day. Meetings are scheduled at other times. • Mindset book club met on 10/05–11/15. Teachers shared their revelations and classroom successes at the December staff meeting. • Gratitude boards were overflowing in November. • Teachers are sharing more celebrations at both whole-school and team meetings during quarter 1 and 2.	• Maintain morning greeting practice throughout year, even during testing months. • Offer the mindset book club again in the winter for teachers and families who were not able to participate the first time. • Remind teachers of gratitude boards and revisit as a whole school in February. • In the staff newsletter, remind teams to leave time in the agendas for celebrations.

continued ↑

Climate and Culture Collective Commitments	Culture & Climate Schoolwide Action Plan(s)	What Possible Resources are Needed to Carry Out the Plan(s)?	Who is Responsible for Carrying Out the Action Plan(s)?	Who is Responsible for Monitoring and Evaluating the Plan(s)?	What is the Timeline for the Action Plan(s)?	Indicators of Progress and Success	Next Steps
	• Opportunities are created to celebrate one another and student growth and successes and show gratitude (for example, designate celebration time during team meetings, have a celebration section in the weekly staff newsletter, create gratitude boards throughout the school building and within classrooms).						

Goal	Action Steps	Resources	Person(s) Responsible	Timeline	Monitoring	Status	Next Steps
Monitor the schoolwide climate from the perspective of the staff, students, and families.	• Regularly survey the entire school community and designate a team to evaluate the results using a growth mindset. Work collaboratively to learn about research-based best practices and policy or develop inquiry-based practices that can support the schoolwide climate. • Implement a high-five buddy system for students. • Hold schoolwide celebrations with families. • Have specialist teachers invite classroom teachers to attend classes to see students shine in additional areas.	• Technology to administer a climate survey • Materials and art supplies for multicultural crafts • Multicultural night: Paper and poster boards (flyers, student passports)	• Guiding coalition creates and sends out surveys • Multicultural night: Ten parent and teacher volunteers • Specialist teachers (PE, music, art, or library) will invite (email) grade-level teacher teams and administrators to attend brief, culminating student projects, presentations, or special class events • SEL team develops the high-five buddy system	• Surveys given at the end of each quarter. • High-five buddies with staff will begin September the following school year. • Multicultural night: November • Specialists will invite teacher teams and administrators to brief student celebrations (at least once a quarter).	• Guiding coalition analyzes the survey results, communicates its results with administrators, and uses the data to modify existing schoolwide action plans or develop new plans if needed. • Administration will monitor the multicultural night plans and event. • To monitor the plan and support the school's culture and climate, administrators receiving emails from specialists about grade-level celebrations will try to attend one celebration at every grade level during each quarter. • SEL team will evaluate and monitor the high-five buddy system.	• Survey sent November 2nd (end of first quarter). • Schoolwide celebration of learning kick-off was held September 29th with 75% of families in attendance. • Multicultural night is scheduled for January 5th. • Administrators attended one student celebration from every grade level during the first quarter, and teachers provided pictures of student celebrations in the weekly newsletters in October and November.	• Share results of survey with whole school during December staff meeting. • The SEL team will meet by April 5th to make a plan for next year's high-five buddy system. • Reach out to families who did not make the celebration to touch base about their child's successes this quarter. • Specialist teachers will make plans for inviting families to student celebrations during the third and fourth quarters.
Monitor our individual emotions and be mindful of the role our own behaviors play in the group climate.	• Staff have opportunities to work with one another in a reflective capacity, where they can listen to one another and discuss the emotional reactions to events. This may occur during meetings with the whole team or in individual one-on-one conversations before or after the school day.	• None at this time	• All staff members	• Throughout the entire school year on an ongoing basis.	• Administration	• Team agendas reflect time for reflective discussions. • Academic coaches have designated time in their schedule and an online sign-up sheet for teachers to request reflective coaching.	• Continue to uphold the expectation of including reflective discussions. • Check in with teachers who are not accessing reflective coaching to find out what is keeping them from scheduling a session. Talk with teachers who are using it to see what they find beneficial and what could be improved.

Source: Adapted from CASEL, 2017; The National School Climate Council, 2007.

Visit go.SolutionTree.com/instruction for a free blank reproducible version of this figure.

Take some time to reflect on your own school and classroom and consider where you and your school are at in the process of building a positive culture and maintaining a healthy climate. This work does not happen overnight, and it takes time and a great deal of effort. Just taking time to have conversations about culture and climate is a great first start. Collaboration is the key to this important work and proficiency doesn't necessarily mean mastery. Just like with relationship building, maintaining a strong and positive school culture and healthy climate takes time and effort; in fact the process never ends. Figure 3.4 is an SEL evaluation rubric to help schools determine where they are at in the process and where they want to go. This is just a guide, and it may not fit your school's exact situation, but it gives the administrators, school, teams, or individual teachers ideas for improving and growing.

Safe and Effective Learning Environments

In chapter 2 (page 45), we discussed in detail the value of establishing a safe and effective learning environment that supports *all* students. We also shared the importance of teachers modifying their classroom learning environment to support individual student needs. While each classroom should support the individual needs of the students within it, classrooms should also reflect the established collective commitments and norms of the school. Physical and cultural environments are often visual reflections of community members' beliefs and values. If you were to walk the school hallways, enter several classrooms, and allow your senses to process what you are seeing and hearing, you would most definitely get a feel (school climate) for the school's belief system. Every classroom should reflect cultural responsiveness, clearly defined classroom routines and procedures, well-organized and sensory-sensitive learning spaces, and student-centered discipline. Safe and effective learning environments will also include opportunities for community building among students as well as teacher-directed and student-empowered learning.

CASEL (n.d.g) stresses the need to establish equitable learning environments across settings of classrooms, schools, families, and communities to strengthen students' academic and social-emotional learning. Therefore, we must ask ourselves not only what our students need to learn but also what the conditions are in which our students will learn, and whether we are providing equitable opportunities for all learners to feel safe, secure, and have opportunities to take ownership of their own learning. It should not be an option for only some students to gain opportunities to learn within an environment where flexible seating is available and students are given choice in their learning. Grade-level teams should set aside time to share ideas around safe and effective learning environments so they may learn from each other just as they do when sharing effective academic instructional practices. Table 3.8 (page 118) shares a set of action plan examples focused around maintaining safe and effective learning environments we feel are vital to the important work of elementary schools.

Social-Emotional Learning Rubric: Positive Culture and Healthy Climate

Criteria	Level 1 Not Yet Observed	Level 2 Beginning	Level 3 Emerging	Level 4 Implementing	Level 5 Developing	Level 6 Proficient
Mission and Vision	A mission and vision do not exist.	A mission and vision statement exist, but they are primarily focused on academic learning.	The mission and vision statement include student social-emotional learning.	The mission and vision statement include student and adult social-emotional learning and well-being.	The mission and vision statement include student and adult social-emotional learning, well-being, and a focus on safety.	Schoolwide procedures and policies reflect the mission and vision, which include student and adult social-emotional learning, well-being, and a focus on all aspects of safety.
Safety: Physical, Psychological, Emotional, and Social	Student safety is not discussed. There is not an expectation that teachers will self-reflect on their own emotional reactions.	Discussions on safety focus only on physical aspects. There is not an expectation that teachers will self-reflect on their emotions. The school is not addressing teacher wellness.	Teams begin to discuss the existence of psychological safety but only consider it for at-risk students or students with known trauma. There are developing conversations around teacher reflection and teacher wellness.	Both physical and psychological safety are discussed, but only in terms of students, and not applied to how teachers interact with each other. Small groups of teachers are beginning to promote using self-regulating techniques for themselves in the classroom. Teacher wellness is not a whole-school priority.	All aspects of safety are considered in making schoolwide decisions and on some individual teams. Individual teams are encouraging members to use self-regulating strategies. Reflective teacher conversations are beginning to occur on certain teams. Teams are beginning to address teacher wellness.	Procedures are in place for teams, individual classrooms, and schoolwide decisions to take all aspects of safety into consideration when making decisions. Whole-school systems are in place to promote teachers to use self-regulating strategies and to practice reflective teaching. Teacher wellness is a schoolwide priority.
Relationships and Community	The importance of relationships and community is not discussed. Families of students are not considered part of the school community.	Relationship building and the importance of community are not a school focus. Inconsistent relationship practices exist across the school. Families are not included in discussion around school community.	Individual relationships exist but there is not a schoolwide focus; often cliques form within the school and among parents and families. There is not a schoolwide sense of community. Families are not included in discussion around school community.	Relationship building is a focus throughout the school but primarily exists between teachers and students and among teachers on grade-level teams. Small efforts are being made to create a whole-school community though no systems are in place yet. Families are included in minimal discussions around school community.	Relationship building among all parties—administrators, teachers, support staff, students, and families—is a primary focus across the school setting. Structures are in place for fostering whole-school community, which includes families. These systems do not yet offer opportunities for school staff and families to reflect and offer feedback.	Relationship building is a focus, and all school staff works at developing strong relationships with students, families, and colleagues. Systems are in place for monitoring the climate of the whole school community, including families. This includes opportunities for members of the community to offer feedback and collaborative ideas.

Figure 3.4: Social-emotional learning evaluation rubric—Positive culture and healthy climate.

Visit go.SolutionTree.com/instruction for a free reproducible version of this figure.

Table 3.8: Example Collective Commitments—Safe and Effective Learning Environments

Collective Commitments Focused on SEL	Schoolwide Action Plan Examples
Determine common key factors of the physical and cultural learning environments (schoolwide settings within the school building and within the classrooms).	• The staff works together to establish a set of physical and cultural learning environment norms for both within the classrooms and in various environments throughout the school.

Figure 3.5 is a tool that can help schools in providing equitable learning experiences for students and assist in the process of building common understandings and language around safe and effective learning environments. A kindergarten classroom does not look, feel, or operate the same way as a fifth-grade classroom. Therefore, it is up to each grade-level team to make important decisions about the needed environmental features of their classrooms. You will notice that in our example, the entire school staff first defined and committed to all the checked items on the tool in a staff meeting at the start of the school year, and from those schoolwide collective commitments each team met during one of their planning meetings to talk about what that would specifically look like at their grade level or content area (physical education, music, art, library, and so on). Figure 3.5 highlights a second-grade team using these schoolwide environmental norms to zero in on what that would specifically look like in their classrooms at their grade level. Although teachers have autonomy to show their personalities and respond to the individual learners in their classrooms, the physical and cultural learning environment of each classroom should embody the schoolwide collective commitments the school staff determined. This allows students to access best practices throughout the building and know what to expect in each classroom they enter from year to year. Figure 3.6 (page 122) shows a completed SEL schoolwide action plan tool for the SEL critical elements of safe and effective learning environments. This example shows how schools can create meaningful action plans from those collective commitments focused around the learning environment.

Names of Team Members: Kendra, Joel, Melony Deepak

Grade Level: 2nd Grade

Schoolwide Environments

← SAFETY →

Physical Environment				Cultural Environment		
Learning Spaces	Sensory Features	Storage & Materials	Schoolwide & Classroom Expectations & Organization	Relationship Building	Mindset, Motivation, and Engagement	Learning Experiences
Schoolwide Spaces (including playground, gym, cafeteria, hallways, and classrooms): ☑ Safe & organized ☐ Interactive, well organized, and visually appealing wall space **Classroom Furniture Arrangements & Physical Spaces:** ☐ Designated large-group, small-group, and individual learning spaces ☑ Designated areas where children can go to calm down and use self-regulation strategies ☐ Content-specific spaces (for example, independent reading area with classroom library) ☐ Storage for student belongings ☐ Outdoor learning spaces	**Schoolwide & Classroom Sensory Features:** ☑ Lighting that is not harsh, does not make distracting sounds (effective suggestions include use of natural or LED lighting, and so on) ☐ Good acoustical conditions in all parts of the room as well as positive acoustical strategies ☐ Comfortable temperature ☐ Accessible, clear visuals ☑ Flexible seating to allow students to participate by sitting, standing, or accessing adapted seating options such as stools, exercise balls, wobble chairs, and so on	**Learning Materials and Tools:** ☑ Materials are organized and easy access for teachers and students ☑ Students have choices of provided learning materials ☑ Learning tools promote engagement, exploration, and experimentation ☑ Learning tools showcase diversity and reflect students' cultural backgrounds in read-alouds, bulletin boards, interactive visuals, and other areas	**Procedures & Routines:** ☐ Efficient and clear instructions ☑ Responsive and flexible daily schedule ☑ Transitions maximize instructional time **Behavioral Expectations:** ☑ Community created **Student-Centered Problem Solving:** ☐ Opportunities for both students and staff to brainstorm solutions ☑ Encourage collaborative discussions **Staff Self-Reflection and Self-Regulation:** ☑ Scheduled time for staff reflection ☑ Staff learning opportunities on the importance of monitoring their own emotional responses	**Intentionally Fostering Positive Relationships Between:** ☐ Classroom community ☑ Teachers and students ☑ Students and other students ☐ School staff ☑ Families and school staff	**Positive Atmosphere:** ☑ Positive language and actions of school staff and students **Growth Mindset:** ☐ Teacher classroom practices and behaviors **Respect & Values:** ☑ Involve the ideas and learning of all community members ☑ Reflect diversity and inclusion **Student Voice & Agency:** ☐ Student-centered learning ☐ Students' choice and responsibility in learning ☐ Opportunities for students to give constructive feedback to teachers and peers ☐ Class and individual student goal setting **Engagement & Motivation:** ☐ Effective teacher practices ☑ Measuring and monitoring levels of student engagement	**Learning Activities:** ☑ Differentiated and accessible to all students ☑ Reflect on values and cultures of all learners ☑ Promote diversity ☑ Are rigorous, engaging, and foster critical thinking skills **Rich Classroom Discourse:** ☐ Students engage in productive struggle and practice skills of reasoning and justifying; agreeing and disagreeing; and so on within the classroom community **Teacher-Guided Learning Structures:** ☑ Whole- and small-group guided instruction (for example, workshop model) ☑ Guided play **Student Learning Structures:** ☑ Individual independent learning ☑ Cooperative learning (working with a partner or in a group) ☑ Student-directed activities (student choice, play)

continued →

Figure 3.5: Safe and effective learning environment norms tool.

Schoolwide Environment Norms

- Every classroom will be safe and organized.
- Every classroom will have a designated area where children can go to calm down and use their strategies.
- Every classroom will post visuals from the Zones of Regulation for students to refer to.

- All classrooms will provide flexible seating options for students and for individual students who may need it in places outside classrooms, such as the lunchroom.
- All fluorescent lights will be covered with blue coverings.

- Students will be given choices in the materials they use for their learning (for example, choice of the books they read at their level, mathematics tools, and so on).
- Learning materials will showcase diversity and reflect students' cultural background (read-alouds, bulletin boards, interactive visuals, and so on).

- Transitions will be built into the daily schedule. The daily schedule will be visually posted in all classrooms.
- Together students and teachers will generate classroom community expectations that connect to the schoolwide expectations for behavior.
- Every staff member will commit to using the common language from Zones of Regulation to support students in identifying their emotions.
- Teachers will investigate and implement strategies to support collaborative discussions in the classroom and share what they find works best at team meetings.
- Teams will make time to discuss the importance of self-reflection and self-monitoring at their meetings and will commit to using these strategies during the day.

- Teachers monitor their language with students seeking to connect with each student before the day starts.
- Teachers monitor their own implicit biases and work towards being culturally responsive within relationships.
- Teachers continuously communicate with families regarding what students are learning in SEL and collaborate with parents on student intervention.

- Teachers will use and model positive language and actions with peers, students, and parents.
- Teachers will establish a sense of belonging for all students. Teachers will make respect a constant theme for the school and class community so that all members have explicit understanding around what respect looks like, sounds like, and feels like.
- During instructional planning, teacher teams will find ways to support student engagement.

- Learning activities will be differentiated to meet the needs of all learners.
- Lessons reflect students' cultures, beliefs, and values.
- Learning activities will be rigorous and engaging.
- Staff will implement the mathematics workshop and reading and writing workshops at all grade levels.
- Instruction will include a balance of student independent and cooperative learning as well as teacher-guided practices.
- Evidence of student choice and play will be woven into the weekly schedule.

Grade-Level Team Classroom Environment Norms

- Each grade 2 classroom will designate a calm-down area. Additionally, we will plan SEL instruction around self-regulation strategies that students can utilize in that designated area.

- Each grade 2 classroom will provide flexible seating options for students (standing, clipboards, and carpet squares; wobble stools at the teacher-student small-group table; and so on).

- During mathematics workshop students will have use of mathematics learning toolboxes where students have choice in the tools they want to use to explore new mathematics ideas and solve tasks and problems.

- We will use high- and low-energy transitions in between content areas on the schedule and before and after specials, lunch, and recess.

- Our grade 2 team will greet students each morning as they enter our classrooms and individualize greetings to meet the needs of each student and their level of development with reciprocal engagement skills, and so on.

- Teachers on the grade 2 team will model the use of positive language within our classrooms.

- We will plan for highly engaging learning experiences (inquiry-based learning in social studies and inquiry-based experimentation in science; problem solving with high-cognitive-demand tasks in mathematics; and balanced literacy in language arts).

- During language arts, students will be given individual book baggies for independent and shared reading to use throughout the year. Each week they will get to choose a new set of books they want to read that match their instructional reading level.
- Each classroom will showcase learning materials that promote diversity (classroom libraries; bulletin boards; posters and other pictures used).
- We will highlight holidays and special events on the classroom calendar that appeal to all learners of the classroom.
- When using interactive read-alouds and mentor texts, teachers will use books that reflect various cultures and students' experiences.

- During the first week of school, we will build a list of classroom expectations. All community members will sign it and it will be posted in the classroom.
- Our team will use the common language from Zones of Regulation to support students in identifying their emotions within our classrooms and with students we engage with in the larger school community (lunchroom, hallways, assemblies, and so on).
- In team planning meetings, we will learn about how to facilitate collaborative discussions between students and will share strategies and insights with one another after we implement this strategy.
- Our team will include time for sharing self-reflection moments in team meetings and will encourage one another to reflect and self-monitor throughout the school day.

- Our grade 2 team will incorporate two to three intentional relationship building activities a week into morning meetings.
- As a team we commit to learning about each other and our students and work as a team to consciously recognize and overcome our individual biases and our team biases.
- Our grade 2 team will reach out to families during the first two weeks of school (emails, phone calls, and team newsletter) and continuously throughout the school year.
- Our team will create monthly newsletters to send out to families.

- On a weekly basis during our morning meetings, we will incorporate activities for sharing gratitudes with teachers and peers.
- Our team will find ways (journaling; letter writing; within projects; morning meeting) for our students to share about who they are with teachers and peers.

- On our team instructional planning guide, we will include a new section for student engagement.
- Mathematics problems will be written to reflect student cultures and interests as well as the learning materials we use to model or use with our students.
- We will collaboratively plan lessons designed for mathematics and reading and writing workshops.
- During weekly planning meetings we will plan for:
  + Targeted small-group instruction
  + Independent and cooperative student learning with student choice will occur at student centers and stations during the reading and mathematics workshops.
- We will intentionally plan for and build in daily opportunities for play (at the end of each school day and during the reading and writing workshops).
- We will provide a designated forty-minute block once a week for student-directed play (Friday).

Visit go.SolutionTree.com/instruction for a free blank reproducible version of this figure.

Critical SEL Element: **Safe and Effective Learning Environments**—Learning environments are safe, supportive, culturally responsive, and focused on building relationships and community.

Indicators

Physical Environment			Cultural Environment			
Learning Spaces	Sensory Features	Storage and Materials	Schoolwide and Classroom Expectations and Organization	Relationship Building	Mindset, Motivation, and Engagement	Learning Experiences

See descriptors in figure 2.5 (page 55).

Schoolwide

What it looks like, sounds like, feels like

Physical Environment:

Learning Spaces:

- Well-designed placement of classrooms, small-group learning spaces, and restrooms for both students and staff use throughout the building.
- Displays of student work are distributed throughout the school.
- Designated space for adult relationship building and collaborative learning (staff lounge, conference meeting room).

Sensory Features:

- Thoughtful use of natural light and environmental adaptations for fluorescent light.
- Well-organized, safe, and sensory-sensitive indoor and outdoor learning and non-learning spaces throughout the school (classrooms, gym, cafeteria, playground).
- Available spaces for all students to access sensory breaks or to go on sensory walks to help with regulation.

Storage and Materials:

- Visual displays that promote positive mindsets, kindness, and gratitude (school banners, gratitude boards, and so on).
- Inclusive visuals displayed throughout the school building reflect ideas, values, and cultures of *all* the school's community members (staff, students, and families).
- Systems and structures for sharing learning materials (for example, mathematics, reading, or self-regulation tools) between grade levels.

Classroom

What it looks like, sounds like, feels like

Physical Environment:

Learning Spaces:

- Well-organized learning spaces (safe, clear of clutter, and so on).
- Interactive, organized, visually appealing wall spaces.
- Content-specific spaces (for example, independent reading center, computer station, and so on).
- Space for students' personal belongings.

Sensory Features:

- Sensory-sensitive learning spaces: temperature, lighting, furniture, air quality, and visual wall space are appropriate (for example, light filters; use of natural light; acoustic systems; flexible seating options such as flexible desk or table arrangements, individual desk and chair, standing desk, wobble chair, or whole-class semi-circle).
- Available space for students to take a sensory break or self-regulate within the classroom.

Storage and Materials:

- Materials arranged so students have readable access and choice in learning materials.
- Learning tools promote engagement, exploration, and experimentation; showcase diversity; and reflect students' cultural backgrounds in read-alouds, bulletin boards, interactive visuals, and so on.

Schoolwide	Classroom
What it looks like, sounds like, feels like	What it looks like, sounds like, feels like
Cultural Environment:	**Cultural Environment:**
Expectations:	Expectations:
• Student-centered and brain-based discipline is consistent across the school building.	• Clearly defined, community-built (teacher and student) classroom routines and procedures.
• Schedules, structures, and staffing provide opportunities for school leaders and teachers to enhance family and community engagement.	• Student-centered and brain-based discipline.
• Student expectations are community created and visually posted throughout the school building (lunchroom, playground, hallways, classrooms, and so on).	Relationship Building:
• Students and adults engage in reflective practices (actively listening to one another when there is a problem, identifying possible solutions and working together to implement the agreed-on solution).	• Students have opportunities to collaborate and communicate their ideas with peers and pose questions knowing it is safe to do so.
Relationship Building:	Mindset, Motivation, Engagement:
• Schoolwide common community-building practices are present throughout the school.	• Teachers and students foster positive growth mindsets.
• Administrators form strong relationships with the students, staff members, and families.	• Classrooms are inclusive and culturally and linguistically responsive, including culturally responsive pedagogy.
• The school holds celebrations of the school's diversity and student and adult learning.	Learning Experiences:
Mindset, Motivation, Engagement:	• Learning is teacher-directed and student-empowered (student choice, play, cooperative learning, and so on).
• Positive atmosphere stems from using growth mindset approaches.	• Interactive visual tools, teaching practices, and the curriculum used for learning are inclusive and reflect the students within the classroom.
• Staff use both positive and culturally responsive language.	• Research-based and differentiated rigorous and engaging instructional practices are used during learning.
• All families and community members are engaged in a diverse offering of schoolwide events, assemblies, and opportunities for school-home connections.	• Structures such as the workshop model are used so educators can work with small groups to target student needs.
Learning Experiences:	
• All teachers throughout the building use structures such as the workshop model so they can work with small groups to target student needs.	
• Students have opportunities to collaborate with peers across the grade level and vertically with other grade levels.	

continued →

Figure 3.6: SEL schoolwide action plan tool—safe and effective learning environments example.

Schoolwide examples:

- Students, parents, and staff enter a building with a growth mindset message on a banner hanging over the entrance of the school. Efficient systems are in place throughout the school building, and students and staff members feel psychologically and physically safe in both the indoor and outdoor settings of the school.

- The school staff makes significant efforts to build relationships with families and celebrate diversity and students' cultures are reflected in the school environment (such as flags from countries where students' families have come from hanging in the gym). The school uses a schoolwide common approach to discipline across all settings (cafeteria, playground, gym, and so on).

Classroom examples:

- Teachers use 21st century research-based high-yield instructional practices within their lessons and consistently modify their learning environments to meet the needs of their students. Relationship building is foundational within the classroom, and students are encouraged and feel comfortable sharing their ideas with others. The teacher is a facilitator of learning and students take ownership of their own learning.

- Learning materials and physical displays throughout the classroom incorporate students' cultures (culturally responsive classroom libraries, posters, morning meetings including celebrations and conversations about diversity). There is a positive approach to discipline with natural consequences and a brain-based approach.

Schoolwide nonexamples:

- Rarely are the administrators seen walking the school hallways or appearing within classrooms. When administrators do enter the classrooms, their sole purpose is to observe the teachers rather than getting to know the students. Discipline practices are inconsistent throughout the school building. Teachers are often heard raising their voices with students in various parts of the school building (hallways, lunchroom, playground, and so on). Bullying is a continual topic at faculty meetings.

Classroom nonexamples:

- Teachers use an authoritarian style of teaching and student collaboration is at a minimum. Typical learning formats consist of whole-group nonengaging instruction where the teacher talks and the students listen as well as independent student practices. Ineffective classroom management and punitive discipline approaches are used.

- Students see one another as "smart" or "not smart" or showing "bad behavior" or "good behavior." Students do not use words to describe their feelings or emotions and are not aware of how to use coping strategies to calm themselves. When students are upset teachers send them out of the room or to the office until they are calm and "ready to learn." Misbehavior and difficulties with emotional regulation are treated through punishment or a consequences approach.

Safe and Effective Learning Environment Collective Commitments	Safe and Effective Learning Environment Schoolwide Action Plans?	What Possible Resources are Needed to Carry Out the Plans?	Who is Responsible for Carrying Out the Action Plans?	Who is Responsible for Monitoring and Evaluating the Plans?	What is the Timeline for the Action Plans?	Indicators of Progress and Success	Next Steps
• Determine common important factors of the physical and cultural learning environments (schoolwide settings within the school building and within the classrooms).	• The staff works together to establish a set of physical and cultural learning environment norms for both within the classrooms and in various environments throughout the school.		• The guiding coalition will facilitate schoolwide environmental learning collective commitments with the entire staff during a faculty meeting. • Individual teams will use the schoolwide collective commitments to develop a set of grade-level classroom learning environmental norms during a team meeting. Specialists will meet together to develop a set of norms for music, physical education, library, and art.	• Administration (upon completion, teams will send their environmental norms to admin and save the file in the schoolwide shared drive). • Administration will monitor schoolwide and classroom learning environments throughout the year and during observations.	• Schoolwide collective commitment discussion will occur during the Monday staff meeting prior to students starting school. • Teams will meet during the first week of school to develop a set of classroom environmental team norms.	• August 9 staff meeting (collective commitments). • September 9 check-in: All grade levels have sent copies of their norms, and they are on the shared server (folder name: Grade-Level Classroom Environmental Norms).	• Send email (guiding coalition) to teams to remind them to revisit the classroom environmental norms and identify what they are doing well, what they are having difficulty with, and what is not working.
• Every classroom will provide students with both a quiet space and physical tools to support student engagement.	• The staff will work together to develop a system for sharing social engagement tools across the school setting. • The upstairs closet will house a collection of fidgets and flexible seating options that teachers can check out for individual student use.	• Flexible seating; assorted fidgets; and various attention, focus, and calming tools.	• The SEL team will meet to develop a system and communicate with administration and all staff members regarding the available items for checkout and provide training on their use.	• Administrators and guiding coalition.	• The SEL team will take inventory of the current materials within the school and place a purchase order for additional needed items during the month of September. • During grade-level team meetings, an SEL team member will share the new checkout system and provide professional development to teams during the months of October and November during team meetings.	• SEL team met on September 6 and created an electronic checkout system (Google Drive) for sharing materials. Materials will be housed in the upstairs closet.	• Organize the upstairs closet and place a purchase order for assorted fidgets and focus/calming tools and wobble chairs (two per classroom). • November staff meeting—share with staff how the checkout system will work.

continued →

Safe and Effective Learning Environment Collective Commitments	Safe and Effective Learning Environment Schoolwide Action Plans?	What Possible Resources are Needed to Carry Out the Plans?	Who is Responsible for Carrying Out the Action Plans?	Who is Responsible for Monitoring and Evaluating the Plans?	What is the Timeline for the Action Plans?	Indicators of Progress and Success	Next Steps
• Incorporate culturally responsive books into instruction and visual displays will reflect the diverse backgrounds and cultures of students.	• Every classroom library will feature a diverse selection of books which include characters from various cultures (including the cultures of the students within the classroom). • Physical displays (classroom posters, bulletin boards, and so on) and visual interactive teaching tools (daily calendar, word walls) will reflect diverse backgrounds and cultures, including those of the students within the classroom.	• Books that reflect diversity and various cultures for classroom libraries.	• Teachers will check out books from the school library and rotate them in their classroom libraries throughout the school year. • Each grade-level team (including the specialist team) will take inventory of the books they currently have within their classrooms and develop a system for sharing books across the team. • The school librarian will take inventory of the books in the school library to ensure there is enough literature at the various reading levels and place a school purchase order if necessary. The librarian will also work with the reading specialist to create a list of the books to be checked out and the books' reading levels.	• Administrators and guiding coalition.	• Teams will select books for their classroom library within the first two weeks of school and rotate the books throughout the school year. • Each team will take inventory of the books they have during the month of September and develop a system for sharing across the grade level. • The school librarian and reading specialist will meet during the fall months to create the schoolwide book list with reading levels and send it out to teams during the month of January.	• Guiding coalition sent out an email on October 1 regarding teams' book inventory task. • Librarian (Mr. Traeger) and reading specialist (Mrs. Wilson) met on September 26 (currently working on creating a book list).	• Guiding coalition members will check in with their grade-level teammates about where they are in the process of creating systems for sharing books across the grade level.

Source: Adapted from CASEL, 2019; The National School Climate Council, 2007.

Visit go.SolutionTree.com/instruction for a free blank reproducible version of this figure.

Some schools may start off focusing on the physical environment and then move towards establishing various aspects of the cultural environment. Building safe and effective learning environments is a process, one that takes time and collaboration. As educators we learn some of our best ideas from our peers. Therefore, as we aspire for equity in education, one area of needed focus is in establishing team environmental learning norms. If you can move past the feeling of wanting sole autonomy of both the physical and cultural aspects of your classroom learning environment, you'll begin to notice how it truly is just not your classroom but rather one that you share with your students, other teachers, and students' families. Figure 3.7 contains the SEL rubric regarding the learning environments of the school. Consider where your school, your team, or you are at personally as you complete this rubric, and think about where growth can occur.

Social-Emotional Learning Rubric: Safe and Effective Learning Environments						
Criteria	**Level 1** **Not Yet Observed**	**Level 2** **Beginning**	**Level 3** **Emerging**	**Level 4** **Implementing**	**Level 5** **Developing**	**Level 6** **Proficient**
Team collaboration around the learning environment	• There is no collaboration around planning for the learning environment.	• School administration works in isolation to plan for school physical safety.	• Staff collaboratively agrees on a set of schoolwide commitments around the environments. • Teams do not collaborate on establishing classroom learning environment norms.	• Staff collaboratively agrees on a set of schoolwide collective commitments around the schoolwide environments. • Teams collaborate on establishing classroom learning environment norms. • Individual teachers do not always follow the team norms.	• Staff collaboratively agrees on a set of schoolwide collective commitments around the physical and cultural aspects of the schoolwide environments. • Schoolwide procedures and policies reflect these collective commitments. • Teams collaborate on establishing and using the agreed-on norms to create safe and effective physical and cultural classroom learning environments for students.	• Staff collaboratively agrees on a set of schoolwide collective commitments around physical and cultural aspects of the schoolwide environment. • Schoolwide procedures and policies reflect these collective commitments. • Teams collaborate on establishing and using the agreed-on norms to create safe and effective physical and cultural classroom learning environments for students. • Systems are in place for monitoring learning environments.

Figure 3.7: Social-emotional learning evaluation rubric—safe and effective learning environments.

continued →

Criteria	Level 1 **Not Yet Observed**	Level 2 **Beginning**	Level 3 **Emerging**	Level 4 **Implementing**	Level 5 **Developing**	Level 6 **Proficient**
Physical Environment	• Strategic thought was not put into the physical learning space.	• Furniture arrangement or student seating options are not conducive to collaborative practices. • Flexible seating and sensory-sensitive learning spaces are evident in some classrooms but are not consistent throughout the school. • Teachers purchase their own sensory-friendly materials to support their students. • Material storage and access for students is inconsistent across classrooms.	• Some teachers arrange furniture to promote collaborative practices, but this is not a consistent practice across the school setting. • Individual teams commit to using flexible seating and examining their learning spaces to improve the sensory experience. This work is not yet reflected in the classrooms. • Teams purchase their own sensory-friendly materials and flexible seating and share within the team. • Teams begin to discuss how to best organize and store materials.	• Furniture is arranged for collaborative practices. • Individual teams are committed to using flexible seating and creating sensory-friendly learning spaces. This is evident when visiting the classrooms and walking in the hallways of those teams. • School is willing to purchase sensory-friendly materials and flexible seating for teams who request it. • Individual teams are strategic in their organization of materials specifically so that it allows for student choice in the classroom.	• Furniture is arranged for collaborative practices. • Schoolwide teams are beginning to discuss using flexible seating and creating sensory-friendly learning spaces, but this is not yet evident in the classrooms. • The school is purchasing materials to support the physical environment but does not yet have a process for sharing these materials between grade-level teams. • All teams begin to discuss how to best organize and store materials to maximize student choice and access during learning.	• Schoolwide learning environments are well organized, safe, and clear of clutter and furniture is arranged for collaborative practices. • Schoolwide learning spaces reflect sensory needs: temperature, lighting, furniture, air quality, and visual wall space are appropriate (for example, light filters; use of natural light; acoustic systems; flexible seating options such as a wobble chair, standing desk, and so on). • Schoolwide materials are arranged so students have readable access and choice in learning materials. • Learning and sensory-friendly materials are shared schoolwide through an organized system.

Criteria	Level 1 Not Yet Observed	Level 2 Beginning	Level 3 Emerging	Level 4 Implementing	Level 5 Developing	Level 6 Proficient
Cultural Environment	• Strategic thought was not put into the cultural environment.	• Some teams may work collaboratively, but collaboration is not a part of the school culture or an expectation. • Teachers and students operate from a fixed mindset and schools primarily use an authoritarian approach to behavior and learning. • Classroom routines and expectations vary throughout the school. • Individual teachers work towards being culturally responsive, but it is not a team or schoolwide conversation.	• Collaboration is expected across school teams but is isolated within the teams themselves. • Teachers begin to engage in growth mindset practices. • Teams discuss their rules and student expectations, but these may not be research based. • Some individual teams address becoming more culturally responsive, but it is not consistent throughout the school.	• Teams work collaboratively and are working on developing a shared set of values, beliefs, norms, and behaviors. • Teams are beginning to actively work on including growth mindset practices. • Individual teams commit to using positive research-based rules and expectations. • Teams begin to discuss being culturally responsive but evidence of this is not yet seen in the classrooms.	• Teams work collaboratively and have shared sets of values, beliefs, norms, and behaviors. Teams are committed to having a growth mindset for all students. • Collaboration includes vertical planning, support staff, specialists, and other members of the school staff. • The school begins to discuss whole-school positive, research-based behavior expectations with the goal of maintaining a common language of clearly defined expectations throughout the school. • Teams are committed to being culturally and linguistically responsive and actively work on learning how to improve their practices.	• Collaboration is seen schoolwide and reflected in the staff's collective mindset that all students can learn both academic and SEL skills at high levels and shares a set of values, beliefs, norms, and behaviors. • Clearly defined, community-built (teacher and student) classroom routines and procedures are consistent throughout the school. • Classrooms are inclusive and culturally and linguistically responsive, including culturally responsive pedagogy.

*Visit **go.SolutionTree.com/instruction** for a free reproducible version of this figure.*

Authentic, High-Quality SEL Instruction

The team must also work collaboratively to identify essential social-emotional learning standards and deconstruct their meaning. Through this process, teachers gain collective knowledge about the progression of these social-emotional skills, which can assist them in developing methods and techniques for student goal setting. There is great power in a team creating a blueprint for assimilating social-emotional learning throughout the entire school day and into core academic instruction. No matter the curriculum, it must be equitable—provided to all students and clearly understood by those teaching it. This includes the need for teachers to be culturally competent using culturally responsive practices with all forms of instruction. Table 3.9 contains a sample collective commitment and example action plans relating to collaborative learning around the SEL building blocks.

Table 3.9: Example Collective Commitments—Authentic, High-Quality SEL Instruction (Example 1)

Collective Commitments Focused on SEL	Schoolwide Action Plan Examples
Learn together about all aspects of the SEL building blocks (SEL competencies)	• Schoolwide engagement in professional learning around SEL • Staff-led book studies around social-emotional learning • Collaborative observations of teachers within the building

An essential aspect of becoming a school that truly embeds social-emotional learning is that all members of the staff commit to learning about SEL competencies together. There are a variety of ways schools can engage in this work. As a whole school, they can participate in professional learning that in-house staff members with expertise in the area of SEL, district staff experts, or outside consultants develop. This can manifest in the form of schoolwide courses at the start of the school year, before students enter the building, or during designated staff development days. These learning experiences could even be offered together to both staff and families and provide opportunities for a deeper home-school partnership.

Another option that allows for staff learning and engaging in the topic is to offer a staff-led book study. This practice allows teacher-readers to build a common language, common understanding, and discuss how to apply the book's ideas to the shared school environment.

A highly recommended option comes in the form of observations that occur during the school day, while staff members are working with students. These can occur when school staff members have opportunities to observe one another teach and are provided with time to engage in rich discussions about what was observed. No matter the learning avenue, what is most important is for all staff members to have opportunities to engage in the learning, and not limit access to just a few select teachers.

When teachers take a collaborative approach to student learning, it lays the groundwork for the establishment of a guaranteed and viable curriculum (Eaker & Marzano, 2020). What students learn should not be dependent on the teacher they receive; instead, we need to ensure that we are providing equitable opportunities to all, which includes learning the same rigorous curriculum. Many components of learning, whether academic or social-emotional, tend to be developmental by nature, but that does not mean that we cannot meet a child where they are on their learning path and support them on their journey to meeting grade-level standards. Instructional practices should be grounded in research, and all students should have access to the same content and effective teachers. Table 3.10 contains a sample collective commitment and example action plans relating to a guaranteed and viable SEL curriculum and the identification of essential standards.

Table 3.10: Example Collective Commitments—Authentic, High-Quality SEL Instruction (Example 2)

Collective Commitments Focused on SEL	Schoolwide Action Plan Examples
SEL Instruction: • Use a guaranteed and viable SEL curriculum. • Identify essential SEL standards at each grade level. • Integrate SEL with academic learning throughout the school day and across school settings.	• Each grade-level team works together to identify a set of essential SEL standards. Additionally, vertical teams meet to strengthen the process by providing insight and feedback on the work of the grade-level teams and ensuring that the standards chosen are of the highest priority. This not only allows for vertical alignment of the standards across the grade levels but also offers an opportunity for teachers to learn from one another. • During team meetings, the team plans for how they will integrate academic learning with SEL.

Teams in a professional learning community build shared understanding about what the four critical questions of learning mean and determine the work a team must do to answer them (DuFour et al., 2016). Recall the four critical questions of learning:

1. What do we want all students to know and be able to do?

2. How will we know if they learn it?

3. How will we respond if they do not learn?

4. How will we extend the learning of those who are already proficient?

To authentically teach social-emotional skills, teams must start by answering the first of the four critical questions of learning: *What do we want all students to know and be able to do?* This involves the team committing to using a guaranteed and viable curriculum and identifying essential grade-level SEL standards. A guaranteed and viable curriculum means that *all* students are receiving the same rigorous curriculum focused on the same essential standards. You can learn more about the process of identifying essential standards by visiting **go.SolutionTree.com/PLCbooks** and searching for the book *What About Us? The PLC at Work Process for Grades PreK–2 Teams* by Diane Kerr, Tracey A. Hulen, Jacqueline Heller, and Brian K. Butler (2021). Teams should then commit to collaboratively planning SEL instruction and answering the second critical question of learning: *How will we know if they learn it?* In chapter 5 (page 223), we talk in depth about useful planning tools for incorporating social-emotional skills into the entire school day, integrating them into other academic content areas, and understanding ideas regarding differentiation. Then in chapter 6 (page 293), we share how schools can develop and use developmentally appropriate common formative assessments to monitor students' learning of SEL and improve instructional practices. This allows the team to answer the third and fourth critical questions of learning: *How will we respond if they do not learn?* and *How will we extend the learning of those who are already proficient?*

Figure 3.8 (page 133) shows a schoolwide action plan for how schools can begin to implement highly effective SEL instruction across school settings.

Critical SEL Element: **Authentic, High-Quality SEL Instruction**—Staff and students have opportunities to build social, emotional, and cultural competencies. Educators authentically integrate SEL content with academic instruction through interactive and collaborative pedagogies.

Indicators:

- Building adult SEL competencies
- Implementing a guaranteed and viable curriculum using research-based teaching practices and programs
- Integrating SEL across the school day; aligning SEL and academic learning; generalizing SEL across school settings and into all aspects of daily life

Schoolwide

What it looks like, sounds like, feels like

Building adult SEL competencies:

- School commitment to understanding and integrating SEL is seen in the professional development calendar.
- All adult staff use a common language to model, reinforce, and teach SEL across settings and subjects.
- Teachers engage in self-reflection and self-regulation practices. Teachers model using self-regulation tools during instruction.

Implementing a guaranteed and viable curriculum using research-based teaching practices and programs:

- Teams identify essential SEL standards during team meetings and collaboratively plan for SEL.
- Teachers use research-based SEL practices or programs.
- Developmentally appropriate assessment practices are used with students, and school teams use common formative assessments to support instruction.
- Teacher teams engage in discussions around data and monitor student growth.
- Throughout the year, staff engages in teacher observations (horizontally and vertically) to improve on their practices.

Integration of SEL throughout the school day:

- Teachers collaborate to determine how best to integrate SEL into academic lessons as well as into daily routines and unstructured time with students.

Classroom

What it looks like, sounds like, feels like

Building adult SEL competencies:

- Classroom teachers model self-reflection and self-regulation practices and walk students through using the strategies as well.
- Students recognize that their teacher is committed to SEL.

Implementing a guaranteed and viable curriculum using research-based teaching practices and programs:

- Teachers use the agreed-on SEL lessons and structures and integrate this learning with academics and throughout the school day.
- Classroom teachers use common assessments to observe and record the students' growth in SEL practices.
- Teachers use results from common assessments to inform their practice.

Integration of SEL throughout the school day:

- Students use common SEL language throughout the school day.
- Students discuss SEL skills and use SEL language when learning academic content.
- Students show a growth mindset in learning academic content and honor their mistakes as learning opportunities.
- Students set goals for themselves within the academic context.

Schoolwide examples:	Classroom examples:
• Teams identify essential SEL standards and use a guaranteed and viable curriculum. The school staff collaborates and works together to develop an SEL plan for their school, pulling from multiple sources (research-based SEL practice and programs) while adhering to state, district, or school-based standards. • Teams commit to effective, more equitable approaches as they plan their lessons collaboratively. They ask questions about how best to integrate SEL into their academic instruction and share their successes with one another. Time is also taken to ask questions about students' development in relation to behavior and SEL. • Teacher teams collaborate around developmentally appropriate assessment practices and hold discussions and reflect on recognizing their own unconscious biases in regard to student behavior.	• Growth mindset language is seen throughout the classroom day. Students understand they are practicing and developing their SEL skills in mathematics games, in reading workshops, and on the playground. • The teacher asks SEL reflection questions throughout different lessons. The students know their SEL and academic learning targets and engage in student goal setting. The teacher uses assessment data formatively to support instruction and meet individual student needs. • The teacher communicates with families about students' SEL on an ongoing basis. Students feel respected within their classroom and believe their culture and family backgrounds are honored and included in discussions.
Schoolwide nonexamples:	Classroom nonexamples:
• A few classrooms within the school have a strong SEL focus, and families hope that their student will end up in those classrooms. Some teachers focus on SEL while others just focus on academic learning. • Teachers engaging in SEL practices use different SEL language across the building and different teachers embrace different programs throughout the school. Schoolwide data reflects issues around equity regarding the students sent to the office.	• The school counselor teaches SEL lessons on a weekly basis, and the classroom teacher leaves the classroom during this time to engage in academic lesson planning. Or, a teacher holds "SEL time" as a part of the instructional block, but does not refer back to it for the remainder of the day. • Teachers become frustrated that they taught an SEL skill, and the students do not demonstrate it. Teachers do not recognize that what they perceive as disrespectful behavior is truly a developmental or cultural difference.

Figure 3.8: SEL schoolwide action plan tool—authentic, high-quality SEL instruction example.

continued ↑

Authentic, High-Quality SEL Instruction Collective Commitments	Authentic, High-Quality SEL Instruction Schoolwide Action Plan(s)	What Possible Resources are Needed to Carry Out the Plan(s)?	Who is Responsible for Carrying Out the Action Plan(s)?	Who is Responsible for Monitoring and Evaluating the Plan(s)?	What is the Timeline for the Action Plan(s)?	Indicators of Progress and Success	Next Steps

Learn together and build communitywide common understandings about all aspects of SEL competencies (building blocks or CASEL's core SEL competencies).	• School staff engages in professional learning around SEL.
	
	• School staff engages in staff-led book studies around SEL.
	
	• Teams engage in collaborative observations of one another engaged in SEL instruction.
		• Professional books for all staff members.
		
		• Time and funding for professional development around SEL.
		
		• Possible use of substitutes to provide coverage for SEL training or observations of staff.
			• SEL team will take the lead in identifying topics for professional development.
			
			• SEL team, administration, and guiding coalition will work together to ensure professional development is meaningfully engaging.
				• Administration and guiding coalition will monitor and evaluate the development of teams and professional development of SEL.	• Professional development begins at the beginning of the year during orientation week, ongoing throughout school year.
					   + September—Building blocks
					   + October/ November—Mindset
					   + December—Integrating SEL into academics
					   + January—Reflect on and re-teach routines
					   + February—Critical dive into classroom environment
					   + March—Reflect on culture and climate
					   + April (as we near testing season)—Professional development on co-regulation and self-regulation
					• SEL team will put SEL tips periodically in the administrators' weekly newsletter that goes out to staff (about every two weeks).
						• October 23 first-grade team engaged in lesson study—observing SEL instruction in second grade.
						
						• Exit surveys from September's professional development showed that teachers felt positive about implementing SEL and were growing in their understanding of the building blocks.
							• Plan for all grade levels to engage in SEL lesson study by June.
							
							• Follow up on questions from September's and October's exit surveys in November's staff meeting regarding building blocks and mindset.

Authentic, High-Quality SEL Instruction Collective Commitments	Authentic, High-Quality SEL Instruction Schoolwide Action Plan(s)	What Possible Resources are Needed to Carry Out the Plan(s)?	Who is Responsible for Carrying Out the Action Plan(s)?	Who is Responsible for Monitoring and Evaluating the Plan(s)?	What is the Timeline for the Action Plan(s)?	Indicators of Progress and Success	Next Steps
Use a guaranteed and viable SEL curriculum and identify essential SEL standards at each grade level.	• Each grade-level team works together to identify a set of essential SEL standards. Additionally, vertical teams meet to strengthen the process by providing insight and feedback to the work of the grade-level teams and ensuring that the standards chosen are of the highest priority.	• Substitutes to provide coverage for vertical team meetings if needed. • Funding to pay teachers to come in over the summer.	• Instructional coaches, school counselors, and team members will work together on the vertical and team planning. • SEL team will support teachers in providing the resources and setting the broad agenda of these meetings.	• Administration and SEL team will monitor and evaluate the products of the meetings to ensure aligned standards.	• Teams will meet over the summer to begin planning. • Grade-level teams will meet during a staff meeting to begin the process of identifying and aligning essential SEL standards. Each grade-level team will provide a list of their essential SEL standards to the SEL team by the end of the first quarter.	• September staff meeting had all teachers engaged in the process of identifying SEL essential standards and had the opportunity to have vertical conversations.	• SEL team needs to meet to ensure that all essential standards align vertically.
Teams collaboratively plan for SEL.	• Teams collaboratively plan for SEL on a weekly basis and develop ways to integrate SEL with aspects of academic learning and throughout the school day.	• Common planning time • SEL learning materials (SEL books, SEL research-based programs, and so on)	• Each grade-level team will collaboratively work together to develop plans for teaching SEL instruction.	• Administration will monitor the implementation of SEL instruction across the school, ensuring that what is planned collaboratively in teams is evident across classrooms.	• Teams will develop yearlong outlines (Sep–Jun) for teaching SEL instruction.	• Each team developed a yearlong outline for SEL instruction and placed it in the SEL schoolwide shared folder.	• Additional read-aloud books focused on SEL need to be purchased through library funds.

We have described in great detail how SEL is not just about focusing on teaching a set of SEL skills and concepts. Social-emotional learning additionally involves the process of building a positive culture, maintaining a healthy climate, and establishing safe and effective learning environments. We also know that using a research-based SEL program or learning strategies is a good start, but SEL goes beyond just choosing a highly effective program. To establish a guaranteed and viable curriculum, teacher teams must engage in the work of identifying essential SEL standards and working together to learn together. Equitable practice requires a team, time, and dedication. Therefore, we share with you a rubric (figure 3.9) that schools, teams, or individual teachers can use to ensure students are all receiving the same learning experiences in highly effective learning conditions and with educators who are committed to using best practices and learning themselves.

Social-Emotional Learning Rubric: Authentic, High-Quality SEL Instruction						
Criteria	Level 1 **Not Taught**	Level 2 **Beginning**	Level 3 **Emerging**	Level 4 **Implementing**	Level 5 **Developing**	Level 6 **Proficient**
Learning and collaboration around SEL	• There is not a schoolwide focus on learning about SEL. • There is no collaboration around teaching and planning SEL.	• Individual teachers are dedicated to building their SEL capacities. • Teachers do not collaboratively plan for teaching social-emotional learning.	• Small groups of teachers work together to build their SEL capacity, but it is not shared throughout the school. • Teacher teams collaboratively plan lessons for core content areas (mathematics, language arts, science, social studies) but plan for social-emotional learning on their own. SEL occurs occasionally.	• Individual teams may work together to build their SEL capacity and develop a common language for discussing SEL. • Individual teams may support teacher self-reflection. • Teacher teams collaboratively plan for SEL infrequently.	• Teacher teams work together to build their SEL capacity, including their ability to self-reflect and self-regulate during the day. • The school is beginning to develop a common language around SEL, but it is not yet used by all staff. • Teacher teams collaboratively plan for SEL.	• The school supports a systematic effort for all staff to build their SEL capacity, including a common language. • Systems are in place for teachers to be able to self-regulate and reflect on their work. • Teams collaboratively plan for authentic and highly engaging SEL using essential standards.

Criteria	Level 1 Not Taught	Level 2 Beginning	Level 3 Emerging	Level 4 Implementing	Level 5 Developing	Level 6 Proficient
SEL instruction	• Teachers do not teach social-emotional skills and concepts to students. • An SEL curriculum is not used.	• SEL lessons occur on a limited basis and are solely taught by school counselors. • Lessons are not focused around essential SEL standards. • SEL is not integrated throughout the school day.	• SEL lessons are taught, but instruction is sporadic or depends on the individual teacher or counselors' schedule. • SEL lessons are not focused on essential standards, not highly engaging, and are mostly limited to activity sheets and read-alouds. • SEL is not integrated throughout the school day.	• Lessons occur on a regularly scheduled basis across teams. • Effective research-based SEL programs may be used but not focused around essential SEL standards. • SEL is not integrated into academics or throughout the school day.	• SEL instruction occurs several times a week. Lessons are focused around essential standards of learning and effective research-based SEL programs may be used. • SEL is integrated throughout various school settings (PE, music, art). • SEL is occasionally integrated into academics.	• SEL instruction occurs daily and is integrated into other content areas and throughout the school day. Lessons are focused on essential standards of learning and research-based programs or practices are used with all students.
SEL assessment practices	• There is no SEL assessment in place outside of the special education eligibility evaluations.	• SEL assessment is only considered for students showing difficulties with emotional regulation. It is conducted in the form of observation and anecdotal notes.	• SEL assessment is only done for students showing difficulties with emotional regulation. It is a part of determining if a student requires additional support from a counselor, and not used to inform teaching practices.	• SEL assessments are used for all students but are general and not focused around essential SEL standards. These assessments are not used to inform teaching practices and not co-created by the team.	• SEL assessments are collaboratively created by grade-level teams to ensure they are developmentally appropriate. They consider essential standards and reflect what was taught.	• Developmentally appropriate common formative assessments are used as tools to monitor student learning and inform teaching practices. • These assessments were collaboratively created by the grade-level team (including support from counselor, specialists, and so on). The team determines the next steps for teaching practices collaboratively and with regards to developmental and cultural considerations.

Figure 3.9: Social-emotional learning rubric—authentic, high-quality SEL instruction.

Multilayered Systems Responding to School and Student Needs

Up to this point, we have shared many examples of the work a school does in establishing SEL. Yet before diving into these suggestions, it is essential to acknowledge that much of this work, especially maintaining a positive culture and healthy climate, can be a heavy lift. Although planning celebrations and fun activities for students and staff seems less essential than carefully analyzing academic data and making determinations on how best to support students' academic needs, planning activities that maintain a positive culture and healthy climate and supporting relationship building are just as essential to the school's outcomes. Tackling efforts on equity and planning for providing professional development should not just be the job of the administration or a few school leaders. In fact, developing a support system to meet the various needs of the school community requires the input of all and strategic planning. Table 3.11 contains a sample collective commitment and example action plans relating to establishing multilayered systems responding to school and student needs.

Table 3.11: Example Commitments—Multilayered Systems Responding to School and Student Needs (Example 1)

Collective Commitments Focused on SEL	Schoolwide Action Plan Examples
Implement a social-emotional support system	• Establish teams—guiding coalition and SEL and equity teams—and develop systems for monitoring the school's climate and necessary areas of school growth. • Find ways to communicate that data to the school community; support professional development; and share best practices, policies, and useful tools that the school can use across the school setting.

To ease the burden and to take full advantage of the talent and knowledge within your school building, we recommend forming multiple teams to evenly distribute the workload. Earlier in chapter 3, we share the importance of a school establishing a guiding coalition. In the following section, we will provide information regarding the specific work of additional teams that can support SEL within your school.

The equity team should:

- Monitor the school climate itself and planning activities that allow for positive and healthy interactions, connections, and communication

- Promote an inclusive schoolwide culture

- Monitor inequities in student achievement and access

- Find opportunities to facilitate conversations around equity and social justice

The SEL team should:

- Support professional development around SEL

- Monitor schoolwide student SEL data

- Make recommendations around best practices that may enhance the learning environment of the school and instruction

As these collaborative teams work together, they will have the opportunity to share their unique observations of the school's culture and climate from their individual vantage points and together gain a holistic understanding of the state of the school. Although the work here is done within the two different teams, at times it will be important for these teams to collaborate as well as communicate their thinking and the data to the entire school so that all stakeholders understand and are part of the decision-making process. Table 3.12 contains a sample collective commitment and example action plans relating to the process of monitoring students' social-emotional growth.

Table 3.12: Example Commitment—Multilayered Systems to Support Learner Needs (Example 2)

SEL-Focused Collective Commitment	Schoolwide Action Plan Examples
Monitor students' social-emotional growth.	- Hold progress-monitoring meetings at every grade level throughout the year. - Establish grade-level systems for monitoring SEL growth. - Use goal cards to help students reflect on their own learning and growth.

All students learn and develop at different rates. While we do the best that we can to ensure that our first layer of support—the initial instruction we provide to *all* students—will meet the needs of *all* learners, it is not always the case (see Tier 1 in figure 3.10, page 140). Particularly in social-emotional development, there are some students who will need additional or different supports. School teams can respond to this need the same way they would for academic concerns through the response to intervention (RTI) process (Buffum et al., 2015; Hannigan et al., 2021). Through monitoring their students' progress on the learning targets agreed on by the school team, teachers can begin to recognize when there is a need for further support (see Tier 2 and Tier 3 in figure 3.10, page 140).

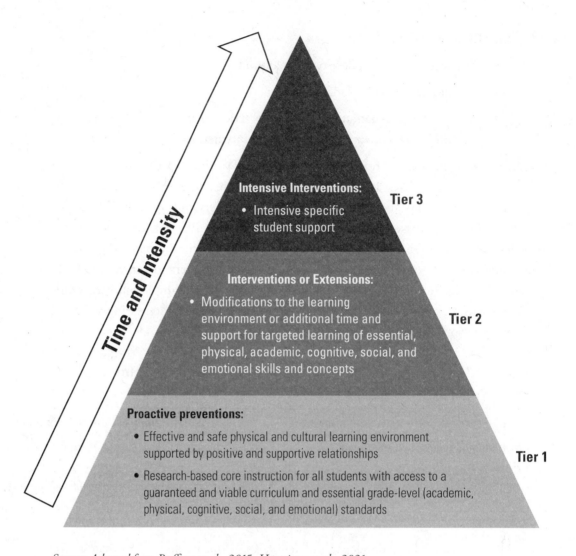

Source: Adapted from Buffum et al., 2015; Hannigan et al., 2021.

Figure 3.10: Response to intervention model for SEL.

In a professional learning community, the school develops a schoolwide approach for monitoring students' overall learning and progress. Grade-level teams work together to answer the four critical questions of learning and create developmentally appropriate common formative assessments and data collection tools, analyze student data, and use those results to make instructional decisions for how to support students. These decisions or overall plans can range from deciding to re-teach a set of lessons to everyone in the class (Tier 1 support), moving to a slightly more intentional plan of changing around guided reading groups to provide specific students with interventions or extensions, adding extra time to practice reading with an additional teacher (Tier 2), or implementing plans which provide students with additional time and more intensive targeted instructional support (Tier 3). So often in schools, this process is limited to academic content areas only. Yet the same practice can, and should, occur with SEL to ensure all students in the school are learning and developing (Hannigan, Hannigan, Mattos, & Buffum, 2021).

Therefore, just as you would for academic learning, grade-level teams should work together to create systems for monitoring students' progress in SEL and development. Once school teams have gone through the process of collaboratively identifying their essential SEL standards and developing plans for how they will monitor students' learning of these standards (see chapter 6, page 293) they will begin to see students who are showing both strengths and difficulties with particular SEL competencies (building blocks of SEL or other core competencies being used). Student SEL goal cards (discussed in chapter 4, page 157), which can be used to help students reflect and monitor their own growth, can also be used as data points. In fact, good assessment practice requires teachers to pull from a variety of sources when making decisions about student needs. As teams collaboratively work to determine a student's area of need, they can turn to the SEL competencies to recognize where they need to additionally strengthen a child's foundation (see figure 3.11).

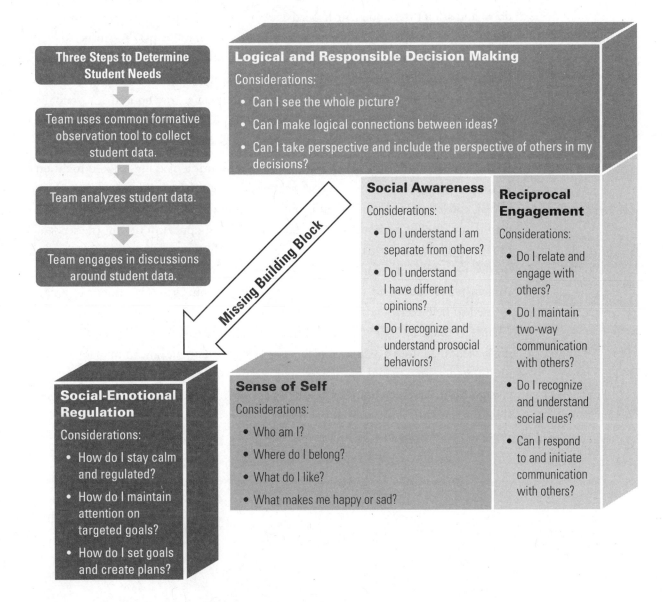

Figure 3.11: Steps to determine focus for intervention.

In collaborative team-based, problem-solving progress-monitoring discussions, staff can create a support plan for students who may be showing difficulty in a particular area (Hannigan et al., 2021). These team progress-monitoring meetings should include multiple members, including a teacher or teachers from the student's specials subjects (art, music, physical education, and so on), particularly if the student excels or struggles in one of these subject areas. This collaborative team should also include the school counselor and other appropriate mental health professionals that work in the school. It is also beneficial for the collaborative team to reach out to the family of the student before the meeting to discuss concerns and hear how the student is doing at home. Has the family noticed changes in behavior? How is the student sleeping and eating? Does the student like school? Has anything changed at home that may be impacting the school behavior?

Before meeting, a staff member with a good relationship with the student may sit down and ask for the student's perspective. As Ross Greene (2008) recommends in his book *Lost at School* and on his website *Lives in the Balance* (https://livesinthebalance .org) students often share their unique perspective with us when we ask in a nonjudgmental, open-ended manner. (Visit **go.SolutionTree.com/instruction** to access live links to the websites mentioned in this book.) Simply state, "I've noticed . . . [state the behavior or concern]. What's up?" and be ready to listen to the child's insights. Visit livesinthebalance.org for more information on this technique.

The discussions occurring in these progress-monitoring meetings should focus on looking at all aspects of the student's school day, identifying which building block or SEL core competency a student is showing difficulty with, and then developing a plan that will offer both support for areas of need and opportunities for the student to receive additional instruction, practice, and feedback in these areas. The collaborative team should record, monitor, and revisit this important information and student plan. Table 3.13 shares a sample progress-monitoring document that can be used to help collaborative teams keep track of students' SEL progress over time. Chapter 5 (page 223) provides an additional planning tool for modifying the learning environment for particular students. To learn more about how to implement this multitiered approach and find additional progress-monitoring tools and examples, visit **go.SolutionTree.com/PLCbooks** and search for the books *Behavior Solutions* (Hannigan et al., 2021) and *What About Us? The PLC at Work Process for Grades PreK–2 Teams* (Kerr et al., 2021).

Table 3.13: Sample SEL Progress-Monitoring Document

Student Name	SEL Core Competency or Building Block of Concern	What This Looks Like in Student Behavior	Interventions	Goals	Timeline & Data Collection Tools	Team Members Responsible	Evidence of Progress
Annika	Social Awareness	• Upset over different opinions • Does not understand when she says something that it hurts someone's feelings • Has difficulty regulating when someone does not agree with her	• Additional focus on ideas around empathy and perspective taking • Opportunities to practice regulating strategies independently or with adult • Secret sign between teachers and Annika to remind her of strategies when she is becoming upset or "stuck"	• When becoming upset, Annika will accept the teacher's cue to use regulating strategies to become calm and return to learning setting. • When Annika disagrees with a peer, she will accept an adult's signal to shift her perspective, or she will remind herself that everyone has different perspectives. • Annika will keep "unfriendly" observations to herself and not state them aloud.	• Collect student data for eight weeks using the RTI observation checklist (see figure 6.8, page 308)	• School counselor and special education teacher work together to provide direct instruction on empathy • School counselor recommends additional books on empathy to classroom teacher • Classroom teacher focuses on perspective taking with Annika • Classroom teacher and Annika develop a silent signaling system to help cue her when she is becoming "stuck"	• RTI checklist (date of observations: Feb 23 and 25)

Visit go.SolutionTree.com/instruction for a free blank reproducible version of this table.

Another critical piece of the schoolwide SEL system is establishing a home-school partnership (Oberle, Domitrovich, Meyers, & Weissberg, 2016). As a part of implementing and maintaining a positive school culture, we, as educators, must also recognize the importance of including students' families as a part of our school community (CASEL, 2017). Students must come into our classrooms knowing that their families trust us as educators and understand what is happening within our school. Families are a key, though often overlooked, aspect of our school communities. Table 3.14 contains sample collective commitments and example action plans relating to establishing a multilayered system responding to school and student needs.

Table 3.14: Example Commitments—Multilayered Systems Responding to School and Student Needs

Collective Commitments Focused on SEL	Schoolwide Action Plan Examples
Establish a home-school partnership	• Maintain clear language (avoiding jargon or eduspeak) when talking with staff and parents. • Focus on using clear, nonjudgmental language when communicating SEL concerns with families. • Commit to positive contact with families early and often throughout the year. • Educate families on SEL through the website, flyers, and information sessions. • Provide opportunities for families and community leaders to collaborate with the school to strengthen SEL so it is culturally responsive.

Social-emotional learning does not just happen within school walls, and it is important to communicate with students and families that the school and the home are a team. Families may not be familiar with the use of SEL language in schools or may not understand why it is being taught along with more traditional academics. In establishing a home-school partnership, staff can monitor their language to ensure they avoid using eduspeak or acronyms when sharing SEL with the families. Share the important vocabulary with families so they can use it at home with their children and commit to helping parents learn about SEL principles alongside the school staff. In turn, listen to families as they share their own SEL language and their cultural practices around this work.

Keep in mind that cultures use different language and have different expectations around SEL. As school teams work with families, they need to maintain an open partnership in the search for finding a common SEL vocabulary. Families should be a part of creating the resources and lessons to ensure that the SEL work the students are exposed to is not from one point of view or created through the lens of an unintentional bias. Listen openly as families share their reactions to SEL and seek to build a common understanding between the school and the family around this work.

Engage in the practice of *cultural humility*, a term originally coined for the medical profession (Tervalon & Murray-Garcia, 1998). This practice asks professionals to be open, lifelong learners of the cultures of the families they work with, committing to self-evaluate and self-critique one's understanding of other cultures. Be willing to engage in open dialogue with families and even community members around cultural expectations of how they expect their children to manage their emotions, behave, follow directions, and engage with adults. Do not approach families with the attitude that any single practices in these areas are superior to those of others. Instead, listen with the intention to understand how these cultural differences can come to support one another toward a common goal.

Schools can share SEL information with families through the school website or flyers sent home. Some schools offer "coffee with the principal" or "family coffee days," where family members can come into the school for an informational session on a relevant topic. These meetings are excellent times to highlight SEL as well as to build a collaborative conversation with families on the work the school is doing on this topic. When scheduling these events, consider the best time to meet the needs of the community. Some families are unable to attend meetings during the day because of their work schedule, while others are unable to attend in the evening. In addition to these in-school events, consider possibilities for using the technological abilities we developed during the COVID-19 crisis. Now that families and teachers are comfortable with virtual meetings, consider how you can use these to connect with families. Often families struggle to get to the school building because of lack of transportation, expensive taxi or ride-share opportunities, or unreliable bus schedules. Virtual conferencing may be what some families need as an option to attend essential meetings, stay in touch, and feel like part of the school community.

As a school seeks to include families to build an SEL-supported culture, it must keep in mind that this family component may look different depending on each school's community, family availability to participate in school activities, and cultural differences within families that attend the school (Lee & Bowen, 2006). In finding the best way to meet families, schools must engage in cultural humility and be genuine in learning the best way to include parents. Remember the isolation we felt as educators during our COVID quarantine? Immigrant families often feel this way—separated from their support systems and unable to physically access the resources needed for support and comfort. In addition to that feeling of isolation most of us are now familiar with, immigrant families can also feel a deep sense of not belonging and not being welcome in our culture and schools. Even providing translated documents may not help with creating clarity and inclusion, as countries' dialects and languages differ even if technically under the umbrella of a prominent language like Spanish. Keep these in mind as you work toward building a true partnership with your families. No matter what type of community the school serves, it is vital that it holds families of students in mind and spends time ensuring that families have the same common understanding of the school's social-emotional expectations and programs, and how these programs are implemented on a day-to-day basis.

Educators can easily become caught up in eduspeak, using acronyms and terms only familiar to those in education (Holland, 2017; Willen, 2015). While educators do not even recognize that they are using terms unfamiliar to the families, this language serves to set a wall between the educators and the families. This is a particular problem in the field of special education. When reaching out to families, whether in person, online, or in back-to-school programs, teachers should monitor their language carefully, making sure that they are using common language and explaining all acronyms or popular education terms. Ask non-educators to review any slides you prepare for families—do they understand everything you are saying? If not, change your language and provide examples and definitions. Just as with our professional learning communities, building a common understanding is the foundation for working together. Schools must determine what is the best method for collaborating with parents based on their community's population and offer multiple ways for families to engage with the information the school presented (Lee & Bowen, 2006).

In addition, it is important to maintain a positive home-school relationship throughout the year. Teachers should start off the year by making positive phone calls to families so that the first individual interaction a family has with the school is a positive one. Teachers should continue to maintain positive interactions throughout the year, welcoming families into their classroom for activities and events, and sharing even small celebrations about a child with the family.

Schools may have communities that want to engage through the Parent Teacher Organizations or Associations (PTOs/PTAs) or through various volunteering opportunities within the school. Schools can respond to each of these unique requests and tailor their home-school communication to meet these needs. While some families may not be comfortable coming into the building or joining Parent Teacher Organizations or Associations, they may be willing to watch videos of back-to-school night or have a video conference. Other families may be from cultures that consider it rude for a parent to question a child's teacher. In cases like this, schools must work to provide open dialogue and be aware that some family members may not be voicing all their concerns (Davis & Yang, 2005). Some families may have a generational mistrust of schools and have had their own negative experience with teachers (Lee & Bowen, 2006). These families may not feel welcome in schools or trust teachers and administrators. It is important to recognize that these families are entering a relationship with the school while not feeling safe. Just as we consider how to create safe environments for all students, we must also create safe environments for our families as well. Do not take it personally if a family does not open up or if they question you. Maintain your professional, welcoming style and be there for the family as they begin to feel more comfortable with your school community. When there is a concern with a child's social-emotional growth or behavior, teachers can monitor their language to reflect a neutral tone so that parents understand the facts of their child's behavior and do not feel the teacher or school staff is placing judgement on the child or the family.

Regardless of the culture or community a school serves, they should follow the same basic tenets for building a home-school partnership (see table 3.15).

Table 3.15: Tenets of Building a Home-School Partnership

Building Common Understandings, Knowledge, and Language With Families	• Build common understanding of the school's social-emotional learning plans, vocabulary, and structure (CASEL, 2017; Oberle et al., 2016). • Take time to ensure families understand what SEL skills are being taught, the language you are teaching around these skills, and most importantly, why the school believes investing time in SEL skills is important. Collaborate with families and community leaders to ensure your SEL is culturally responsive. • Share tips and strategies for families to use at home so that they can model using SEL skills in a natural environment. For more information on sharing SEL learning with families, visit CASEL's website and their guide for caregivers (available at https://casel.org/wp-content/uploads/2017/11/CASELCaregiverGuide_English.pdf).
Communication and Connections Between School and Home	• Positively communicate with each family in the beginning of the year so that the family's first interaction with the teacher is a positive one. • Establish additional routines to provide positive connections with families throughout the year (Davis & Yang, 2005). These routines could involve sending each family a quarterly postcard, email, or letters home.
Sharing Student Concerns With Families	• When there is a behavior or social-emotional concern, share the concerns with the family in a truthful and objective manner. These communications can include both positive information about the child as well as the clear facts of what the child is struggling with. Though a student's behavior may frustrate a teacher, that frustration should not be communicated to the family. Instead, the teacher should share specific information without adding in judgmental comments.
Partnering to Establish Student Supports	• Collaborate with the parent to find solutions or to establish interventions (Davis & Yang, 2005). Do not forget that the family is a significant part of the student's educational team and may have insights into the student's behavior the school does not have. • Ask the family what works or does not work at home. What sort of behavior does the child show at home? Have they noticed a pattern for the behavior? These questions serve to not just dive deeper into discovering the reason behind the child's behavior but also maintain a collaborative relationship with the family.

Overall, to achieve the desired outcomes in social-emotional learning, schools must commit to multilayered support systems. These systems will ensure the work is completed and that staff, families, and students feel supported and do not fall through the cracks. This work includes monitoring students' progress in the areas taught, making space for team-based problem solving for students who need more support, and creating opportunities for true family collaboration. Figure 3.12 (page 148) contains an example SEL schoolwide action plan tool that you can use to support your school's efforts in taking action in doing this important work.

Critical SEL Element: **Multilayered Systems Responding to School and Student Needs**—Teams work together in developing systems to monitor all students' SEL growth and to determine how to address learners who need additional time and support as well as finding ways to support a home-school partnership.

Indicators:

- Schoolwide social-emotional support system to monitor SEL growth; the climate of the school; and the usage of best practices, policies, and professional development.
- Systems to monitor individual students' SEL growth and development.
- Collaborative communication with families about student progress and learning needs.

Schoolwide
What it looks like, sounds like, feels like

Schoolwide SEL Support System:

- The school develops a common system to monitor the overall SEL growth and climate of the school and support the usage of best practices, policies, and professional development.

Systems to Monitor Student Growth:

- School teams use a problem-solving-based approach and common language to discuss student behavior, learning, and development.
- School teams meet every six to eight weeks to monitor student progress in academics and SEL.
- In progress-monitoring meetings, school teams use additional knowledgeable staff within the building to identify positive interventions to support a student's ability to feel safe, regulated, and connected.
- School teams identify which building block a child may be having difficulty with and work together to develop plans to support that child.

Communication with Families:

- Families understand that every teacher their child works with understands their child's development and SEL.
- School staff continuously communicates with families throughout the year (in person or virtually).

Classroom
What it looks like, sounds like, feels like

Schoolwide SEL Support System:

- Individual classroom reflects the schoolwide commitments to best practices, policies, and professional development.
- Teams use schoolwide common systems and tools for monitoring students' growth of SEL.

Systems to Monitor Student Growth:

- Classroom teachers model and support their students in identifying and monitoring SEL goals.
- Students engage in goal-setting practices to monitor their own growth in both academic and social-emotional learning.
- Teachers monitor students' behavior and collect data as agreed on by their team.
- Teachers collect data, analyze the data within their team, and use them to inform teaching practices and target student learning.

Communication with Families:

- Teachers connect and collaborate with parents and communicate what students are learning, their overall progress, and their individual needs throughout the year.

Schoolwide examples:

- Administration ensures grade-level teams have opportunities to engage in embedded professional development (weekly common planning meetings to plan instruction and meetings throughout the year to monitor student progress). Additional professional development around monitoring students' SEL occurs during designated teacher professional development days throughout the year, or in other job-embedded professional development (for example, teacher or team observations).
- Teams (guiding coalition, SEL team, or equity team) support the development of common schoolwide tools that can be used across the school for monitoring students' progress.
- Teachers discuss student behavior with an inquisitive, problem-solving lens. The school has a common schoolwide approach to monitoring SEL, and teams develop systems to support intervention.
- When discussing students' learning, development, and behaviors, teachers use common language and knowledge, are mindful of their language, and speak respectfully to peers and about students.
- Families feel welcomed and part of the school community, and every team develops systems for communicating with families about students' SEL. The school has multiple layers of supports (guiding coalition, SEL and equity teams, and so on). All teams are diverse and find time to collaborate and support the school's mission and vision.

Classroom examples:

- Teachers use a balance of informal formative assessments and team-developed common formative assessments to monitor students' learning of SEL and inform their daily instruction. The classroom teacher collaborates and plans with the grade-level team, administrators, counselors, specialists, and various other staff members to support all student needs.
- Students use SEL vocabulary and can identify their feelings and ways to support their own social-emotional regulation, including when to ask for help in regulating themselves.
- Teachers assist students in individual goal setting and find unique ways of celebrating student growth. Teachers continually collaborate with families about what students are learning and their progress.

Schoolwide nonexamples:

- Teachers use different vocabulary and terminology when discussing student behavior and SEL learning across the school setting and with parents. Student behavior and emotional development is not discussed at progress-monitoring meetings, and behavior is simply seen as interfering with academics.
- Common tools for monitoring students' SEL growth are not used; rather individual teachers or teams create their own systems.
- A select group of staff members receives training on SEL, and these individuals are not always given the opportunity to share information schoolwide. Teachers vary in their SEL competencies, and student SEL outcomes are based on teacher effectiveness and level of SEL knowledge.
- The school has designated various teams to support learning but the teams all operate in silos and have very little opportunity to collaborate with one another. When teams do collaborate, it is around academic learning and not SEL.

Classroom nonexamples:

- SEL is taught to students, but not monitored. Or, SEL is taught to students and assessed, but the teacher does not engage in meaningful data discussions with colleagues to support student needs or use it to direct their instruction.
- Students' learning of social-emotional skills and knowledge is not monitored, nor is any aspect communicated with parents.

Figure 3.12: SEL schoolwide action plan tool—multilayered systems.

continued →

Multilayered Systems Collective Commitment(s):	Multilayered Systems Schoolwide Action Plan(s):	What Possible Resources are Needed to Carry Out the Plan(s)?	Who is Responsible for Carrying Out the Action Plan(s)?	Who is Responsible for Monitoring and Evaluating the Plan(s)?	What is the Timeline for the Action Plan(s)?	Indicators of Progress and Success:	Next Steps:
Implement a social-emotional support system.	• Establish teams—SEL team, guiding coalition, and equity team—to develop systems for monitoring the school's climate and determine needed areas of school growth; find ways to communicate that data to the school community; support professional development; and share best practices, policies, and useful tools which can be used across the school.	• Professional development materials, books, and training on learning best practices.	• Members of the SEL, equity, and guiding coalition teams. • School staff is responsible for participating in professional development and implementing agreed-on best practices and policies.	• Administration is responsible for monitoring and supporting the work of the guiding coalition and the SEL and equity teams.	• Guiding coalition, SEL, and school equity teams are formed prior to students entering school. • In September, the teams will determine when they will meet and how often. During this time, the administration will meet with both teams to help in mapping out a yearlong plan for the work of both the teams.	• SEL team and guiding coalition teams began meeting in August and each determined they will hold biweekly meetings. • The equity team first met in September and determined they will meet every month. • The equity team is actively working on the SEL needs assessment.	• Equity team will conduct needs assessment in October. • Both the guiding coalition and SEL teams will present a new schoolwide individual student monitoring system focusing on the whole child at the October staff meeting.

Monitor students' social-emotional growth.					
• Hold progress-monitoring meetings every 4–8 weeks.	• Organized and sharable computer-based system for recording and monitoring SEL progress of students	• Administration, guiding coalition, and SEL team will determine what common schoolwide tools will be used to monitor the growth of the whole child.	• Administration will ensure that all aspects of learning are being monitored using a multitiered approach.	• August: Progress-monitoring plan developed.	• In early September all grade-level teams determined which SEL and academic essential standards will be assessed and how to assess them.	• After October staff meeting teams will incorporate new schoolwide system into their progress-monitoring work.
• Establish grade-level systems for monitoring SEL growth.	• Materials to make goal cards (index cards, hole punches for each classroom)	• Individual grade-level teams will determine how they will monitor and assess SEL learning.		+ September: Teams determine which essential social-emotional and academic standards will be assessed and how.	• Kindergarten, second, and fifth grade have begun using goal cards.	• Kindergarten, second-, and fifth-grade teams will visit team meetings for first, third, fourth, and sixth grades and the specialist teachers to share how goal cards are working.
• Have teams use collaborative, formative assessments to measure SEL growth.		• Grade-level teams are responsible for monitoring, recording, and discussing progress in meetings.		+ October: First progress-monitoring meeting. Identify students who need additional support with SEL and academic learning.		
• Use goal cards to help students reflect on their own growth.		• School counselors, special education teachers, English as a second language teachers, and additional support staff will participate in discussions around specific students and how their social-emotional development may be impacted.		+ December: Second progress-monitoring meeting.		
		• Administrators will participate in progress-monitoring discussions.		+ February, May: Progress monitoring.		
		• Grade-level teams and students are responsible for implementing and managing goal cards.				

continued

Multilayered Systems Collective Commitment(s):	Multilayered Systems Schoolwide Action Plan(s):	What Possible Resources are Needed to Carry Out the Plan(s)?	Who is Responsible for Carrying Out the Action Plan(s)?	Who is Responsible for Monitoring and Evaluating the Plan(s)?	What is the Timeline for the Action Plan(s)?	Indicators of Progress and Success:	Next Steps:
Establish a home-school partnership.	• Maintain clear language and avoid eduspeak when talking with staff and parents. • Educate families on SEL through the website, flyers, and information sessions. • Build in opportunities throughout the year for family engagement. • Commit to positive contact with families early and often throughout the year. • Focus on using clear, non-judgmental language when communicating SEL concerns with families. • Communicate with families regarding students' SEL progress and find ways to collaborate with families regarding student interventions.	• Examples of non-eduspeak language and non-judgmental language for staff. • Access to translation services if needed. • Paper, technology needed for development of flyers.	• Staff members and the school's equity team with understanding of cultural biases will work with the guiding coalition and SEL team to provide professional development to the staff on cultural awareness. • Special education team will create non-eduspeak documents to help families understand the special education eligibility and IEP process. • School counselors and the SEL team will create non-judgmental language example cards. • SEL team and ESL team will create flyers to communicate SEL program to families.	• Administration and guiding coalition will monitor and evaluate the home-school partnership.	• Orientation week—share positive language with staff + September: School staff makes positive contact with families. + October: Classrooms invite parents in for visits. + November: Flyers sent home explaining SEL curriculum. + December: Classrooms invite parents in for learning celebrations.	• By September 20th every student had a positive phone call home as recorded in the schoolwide phone call recording list. • At back-to-school night, the special education team presented on the special education eligibility process using non-eduspeak. This received high praise from parents as reported in emails to administration. • School counselors, special education team, and ESL team began working on SEL flyers for families.	• Classroom teachers plan on holding classroom visits for parents. • SEL flyers are set to be distributed in November.

Source: Adapted from CASEL, 2019; The National School Climate Council, 2007.
*Visit **go.SolutionTree.com/instruction** for a free reproducible version of this figure.*

Take a moment to look at the social-emotional learning rubric in figure 3.13 (page 154). Think about where you or your school is at in the overall process. Are there schoolwide systems in place for monitoring the growth of the whole child? Do you already engage in monitoring students' SEL growth and progress? If not, what might that look like for you and your team? No matter where you are in this process, remember it is most important to think about the great practices you are doing and to take small steady steps to improve what is already in place.

Conclusion

Building a foundation for SEL in elementary school requires schools to establish a collaborative positive culture and maintain a healthy climate where both the adults and students feel safe and respected. To provide equitable learning experiences for all our students, schools need discussions around effective schoolwide learning environments and a guaranteed and viable SEL curriculum. Yet, as we have previously explained, SEL is not just a standalone curriculum. If your school uses a research-based SEL program, it is likely that it may not cover all four critical SEL elements (see figure 3.2, page 99). Therefore, the school must determine what is not included and what it needs to supplement. For example, if the school chooses a program that primarily focuses on building a positive schoolwide culture, healthy climate, and effective learning environments, then teams must still determine what daily SEL instruction and assessment will look like for students. Or, if the SEL program only focuses on SEL standards, lessons, and ways to monitor students' learning of SEL skills and concepts, the teams will still need to determine how teachers will integrate SEL into academic learning and throughout the entire school and decide how to build the necessary conditions (a positive culture, healthy climate, and an effective classroom learning environment) for learning.

In chapter 4 (page 157), we will take time to dig into various instructional practices for integrating SEL into academic learning and throughout the school day. Then in chapters 5 (page 223) and 6 (page 293), we will share various planning tools teachers can use to support the planning and assessing of SEL skills and concepts.

Social-Emotional Learning Rubric: Multilayered Systems Responding to School and Student Needs

Criteria	Level 1 Not Yet Observed	Level 2 Beginning	Level 3 Emerging	Level 4 Implementing	Level 5 Developing	Level 6 Proficient
System for schoolwide SEL support	• The school does not have common systems in place monitoring the school's culture and climate and schoolwide equity efforts.	• The school has minimal schoolwide common practices and policies for monitoring the school's culture and climate and schoolwide equity efforts.	• The bulk of the work around maintaining and monitoring the school's climate and promoting equity efforts resides on the principles of a small leadership team.	• The school has designated teams to monitor the climate of the school and promote schoolwide equity, but the teams operate as silos; do not work together; and do not make efforts to reach out to the community for support and guidance. • There is not a system for sharing out the work from the designated teams with the whole school.	• The school has systems in place and designated teams to monitor the climate of the school and promote schoolwide equity efforts, and supporting efforts toward SEL. The teams meet infrequently and only occasionally reach out to the community for support and guidance. • Occasionally the designated teams share their work schoolwide to staff and families, but it is not consistent.	• The school has common systems in place for monitoring the school's culture and climate and schoolwide equity efforts. • Designated teams frequently meet and reach out to the community for support and guidance when establishing schoolwide practices and policies as well as the overall growth of the school throughout the year. • Systems are in place to regularly communicate efforts with staff and families.
System for monitoring SEL instructional practices and student growth	• Monitoring student SEL progress is not a part of the schoolwide focus.	• Teachers are individually responsible for monitoring all areas of student progress.	• Teachers engage in collaborative practices of monitoring students' academic progress but are individually responsible for monitoring students' progress in the area of SEL.	• Grade-level teams develop their own systems for monitoring student growth and evaluating the effectiveness of SEL instructional practices (administrators and teachers who specialize in specific fields are not typically part of the process). • There is not a schoolwide common and collective approach to monitoring student learning.	• Teams (consisting of administrators, general education teachers, specialists, and others where appropriate) collaboratively work together using team-generated tools and practices for evaluating the effectiveness of SEL instruction and monitoring individual student SEL growth. • There is not a schoolwide common and collective approach to monitoring student learning.	• There are schoolwide common and collective approaches and tools used across grade levels to monitor individual SEL growth. • Teams (consisting of administrators, general education teachers, specialists, and others where appropriate) collaboratively work together using common schoolwide and team-generated tools and practices for evaluating the effectiveness of SEL instruction and monitoring individual student SEL growth.

Home-school partnership				
• Building a home-school partnership is not a schoolwide focus.	• Schools communicate with parents and families, but only around academic student learning and student behavior concerns.	• Schools communicate with parents and families about all aspects of learning, but it is one-sided and focused on telling the parent about the child versus gaining parental input.	• Some teams and individual teachers work closely with families and provide regular feedback on student learning. However, this is not consistent throughout the school building.	• Families are involved in the process of supporting student needs, and teams collaborate on effective ways to communicate and work with parents and families. • Families understand the work the school is doing around academic and SEL instruction but there is not a structured way for families to provide feedback or collaborate with teachers around this work.	• The school develops a strong home-school partnership where families are invited and involved in supporting student learning. • Teams carefully monitor their language with families and avoid eduspeak. • Families understand the work the school is doing around academic and SEL instruction and feel they are able to share their ideas and concerns with the school. • Teams develop systems for effectively communicating with families regarding what students are learning, progress, and specific individual needs throughout the year.

Figure 3.13: Social-emotional learning rubric—multilayered systems.

Visit go.SolutionTree.com/instruction for a free reproducible version of this figure.

Tips for Administrators, Teachers, and Support Staff

Figure 3.14 contains tips and reflection questions relating to the contents of this chapter. As you consider these questions and next steps, reflect on your current practices in your own classroom and school.

Administrators	Teachers	Support Staff
• As your teams work, ensure all members understand their roles and have ownership over the process. • Provide common planning time for teams to plan and implement SEL. Carefully consider the school's schedule—does it provide teachers with time to meet to address SEL as well as to follow through on the plans themselves? • Share your collective commitments with the staff for supporting the work of establishing SEL in your school. • Build time into the calendar and possibly provide funding for teams to collaborate and develop systems for monitoring students' social-emotional and academic learning. • Disperse leadership across the school and give staff members the opportunities to use their talents and strengths to support the needs of the school and share in the workload.	• As you come together with collaborative teams to plan for SEL, be open to new ideas and procedures. Although conversations about making these changes can be uncomfortable, they can go a long way to supporting the students as well as the overall culture and climate of the school. • Be supportive of your students as well as your co-workers as you dive into SEL. • Continuously communicate with families about SEL and take steps to involve families in students' learning.	• Understand the valuable contribution you make to the collaborative teams and students. Be familiar with the norms of each team you are a part of. Become familiar with the language and routines the collaborative teams are using and implementing throughout the building. • Find opportunities to support the school's effort in developing common understandings and using a common language as a vertical lens while working with teams. • Be mindful of how your work supports the consistency of the school's mission. • When interacting with your colleagues, be models of prosocial behaviors and skills for students. • Find opportunities for engaging with families and the community.

Figure 3.14: Tips for administrators, teachers, and support staff from chapter 3.

CHAPTER 4

Effective SEL Teaching Practices and Strategies in Elementary Schools

Vignette: Teaching and Supporting Daniel

Maria found herself thinking about Daniel and students like him often. He had so much potential, and yet so often had difficulty participating in her lessons. She knew he should be doing better in school than he was, but he barely produced work due to his emotional outbursts. She didn't feel like the solution was to create an individualized program for Daniel, and she knew she couldn't just send him to the office every time he was upset. In fact, there were too many students like Daniel who needed her to shift her own teaching practices. After an episode, Daniel could label exactly what he should do next time. He could identify emotions and talk about using calm-down strategies, but he couldn't seem to bring himself to use them in the moment. There had to be a better way to support Daniel's social-emotional learning, along with *all* students in her classroom, throughout the regular school day.

As educators, we are skilled at teaching students new skills and building their knowledge. We can look at students' work on what we just taught and easily assess whether the student has a firm sense of the academic content or needs reteaching. When it comes to social-emotional learning, we must use a different approach, as much of students' true understanding develops through movement paired with cognition (Lillas & Turnbull, 2009). With this learning domain, some students can easily learn the vocabulary and concrete information we teach them but still not fully comprehend what these isolated skills mean or apply the learning when upset unless they have practiced these skills and acted them out in an interactive, action-oriented method. Asking a child to identify the meaning of happy, sad, and angry and match a series of emotional pictures with the vocabulary word associated with them does not mean that the child is able to actually apply that concrete knowledge in day-to-day life. Instead, to fully support students in learning SEL skills, these lessons must be both directly taught to the students and then, more importantly, modeled, supported, and integrated consistently into the daily tasks that already exist in the classroom (Jones et al., 2021; Jones & Kahn, 2017; Lillas & Turnbull, 2009). As students develop in their learning of various skills and concepts throughout elementary school, the goal is for them to gradually take ownership of their own learning and apply these skills to their daily actions.

When teachers act as facilitators of students' learning and find ways for students to learn by doing, students are more engaged in their own learning and have opportunities to make deeper connections. In this chapter we specifically focus on SEL instruction and what it can look like to support SEL skills and concepts (see figure 4.1). This chapter provides you with ten instructional practices that will allow you to embed SEL into instruction, practice, and guidance in your already busy schedule to make a true, meaningful impact on your students (and save you time!).

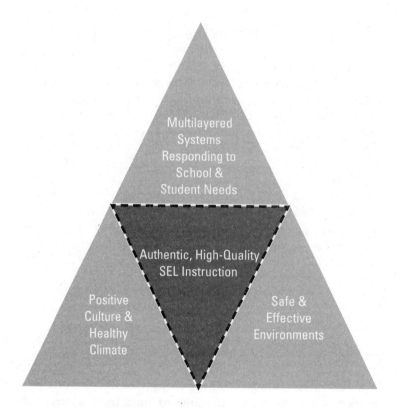

Figure 4.1: SEL schoolwide pyramid.

Ten Practices to Teach and Integrate Social-Emotional Skills

The following sections will introduce ten instructional practices you can use to teach and integrate social-emotional skills into academic and social settings throughout the school day.

1. Transitions

2. Student goal setting

3. SEL daily routines

4. Picture book read-alouds and reading comprehension strategies

5. Social-emotional learning during play

6. SEL-focused partner or group games

7. SEL journal writing

8. SEL projects

9. Teachable moments

10. SEL classroom learning centers and menus

1. Transitions

It was time for reading workshop to end, and Maria dreaded stopping the class from their work to ask them to clean up. *Transitions—* or moving from one activity to another as a class—were difficult for all the students in her class, but particularly Daniel. Ending one activity and moving to a new one always seemed to create power struggles and cause the class to lose instructional time. What's more, she felt like these moments were wasted opportunities. She was interacting with the students during this time, but more like a traffic cop—correcting their behavior, monitoring their safety, and directing them where to go—and less like a teacher. When she thought about how to adapt her school day to support Daniel and her other students with "big feelings," she wondered about transitions. Could these be opportunities to change her interactions from simply being a behavior monitor to meaningful teaching? Would that make transitions smoother for the whole class?

What are transitions and why are they important? Teachers often use transitions when students finish learning from one content area to another (for example, from a science lesson to a mathematics lesson). Sometimes teachers refer to transitions when students are moving from whole-group instruction to small-group learning within a content-focused lesson (for example, when a teacher is at the carpet with all her students teaching a mathematics focus lesson, then students transition or move from the carpet to tables and engage in small-group work). We also refer to transitions when students are moving from classroom to classroom or to other parts of the school building (for example, students transition from the classroom to lunch or recess and then back to the classroom). Typically, when discussing good classroom management techniques, classroom transitions are considered time when students are moving from place to place between learning opportunities (Finley, 2017). A teacher would be considered highly effective in their classroom management if their transitions were short and students followed the teacher's directions.

Transitions can become difficult for students who need support in the lower SEL building blocks. A student who is still developing SEL building block components 1 (*self-awareness*), 2 (*reciprocal engagement*), or 3 (*social awareness*) may have difficulty managing to control their body in relation to those around them. This student may see transitions as a stressful time when they may bump into peers as they move about the classroom. These times can also be difficult for students who are still developing emotional regulation and the cognitive skills that involve executive planning abilities, as they struggle to end one activity and move to the next. Also, students with processing difficulties (visual or sensory) may struggle with this task. Therefore, additional anxiety added to transition periods can result in prolonged transitions and reduced instructional time.

We have started to see teachers maximize this noninstructional time to now include short spurts of instruction. For example, a kindergarten teacher may have students count back from ten each time they move from one learning station to another during their mathematics workshop versus just having them walk from station to station after the teacher rings a chime. Or a teacher may have their kindergarten students transition from the science instructional block to the language arts block by asking students to move from their seats to the carpet. In this scenario, students sometimes have an additional minute or two where they are expected to wait at the carpet quietly. A teacher might capitalize on this time to include instruction, such as having students find objects in the classroom that start with a "p" sound (for example, pencils or pattern blocks) as they quietly wait for the science lesson to begin. Purposeful transitions allow for the learning and practicing of skills and concepts and serve as a useful management strategy, engaging students in a task and limiting the opportunity for classroom behavioral issues to arise.

Now take a moment to think about if teachers began to incorporate purposeful transitions around social-emotional learning. Using transitional periods of time to have students learn and practice SEL skills can be a great way to find time to teach social-emotional learning and integrate academics and SEL learning. It allows teachers to interact with students in a more meaningful way during these short moments rather than simply monitoring behavior. Most importantly, it directly teaches students what tools they can use to make these moments of transition less stressful.

There are multiple possibilities for integrating SEL learning into transitions. On a basic level, teachers can use this opportunity to label how their students feel about changing subjects, supporting the social-emotional building block the class is focused on. The teacher might say the following: "It is time to clean up. Take a moment and think about how you are feeling right now. Are you frustrated that you are not finished? Are you excited to move on? Think about what strategy you can use to help you with those feelings."

Labeling these feelings during transitions is perfect modeling for helping children recognize that adults have emotions around transitions as well. Therefore, a teacher could use a *think-aloud* strategy, stating, "It's time to clean up. I'm so frustrated right now because I want to keep reading with you all. I don't want us to have to clean up, but it is time for lunch. I am going to take two deep breaths and think about what I need to do to get ready for lunch. Breathe with me . . . one, two . . . "

Moving beyond modeling and labeling emotions around transitions, teachers can also use these opportunities for guided practice. Take the scenario where students in kindergarten are counting backwards as they transition from learning station to learning station in their mathematics workshop. What if the teacher has them use deep breathing along with counting back from five?

Picture the students coming back from recess and sitting at the carpet. The teachers recognize they need to gather the students' attention as well as help them have calm bodies and be ready and focused for academic learning. What strategy or transition can the teachers put into place to achieve this goal? Figure 4.2 (page 162) shows another counting-backward strategy where students pretend their five fingers are five candles and they use deep, slow, long breaths to blow out a candle and count back with each breath from five to zero. Deep breathing slows down our body responses, lowers our cortisol levels, and moves us away from our fight, flight, or freeze response so that we can once again access our decision-making abilities in our prefrontal cortex (Ma et al., 2017). These breathing strategies support the development of SEL building block component 4 (*emotional regulation*) and cognitive executive functioning skills and give students a tool toward being in control of their own emotional responses. After practicing this a few times, it will become part of a classroom routine as well as a management strategy the teacher uses. In addition, students will hopefully begin to make connections and this self-regulation skill will transfer, becoming a strategy that some may choose to access and use when they experience a moment of fight, flight, or freeze.

Figure 4.2: Blowing out candles self-regulation strategy.

Figure 4.3 provides examples of additional, powerful transition activities that can be used with students to help teachers with classroom management and teach students social-emotional skills. These are short transitions that can either be used to help decrease energy (calm students down) or increase energy (energize students), depending on the needs of the group. We also include mixed-energy transitions that specifically teach SEL concepts and skills that focus on the five SEL building blocks components. You can find descriptions of these general SEL transition activities for younger and upper elementary students in the appendix (figures A.2–A.7, pages 318–326). It is important to keep in mind that the transitions you use with your students should be developmentally appropriate and connect to your grade-level SEL standards.

Virtual Learning Tip

These transitions can also be adapted to the virtual setting. As you provide a short break for your students, you can use these transition activities as students are returning to their computers to gather the group back together and create joint attention for the next lesson.

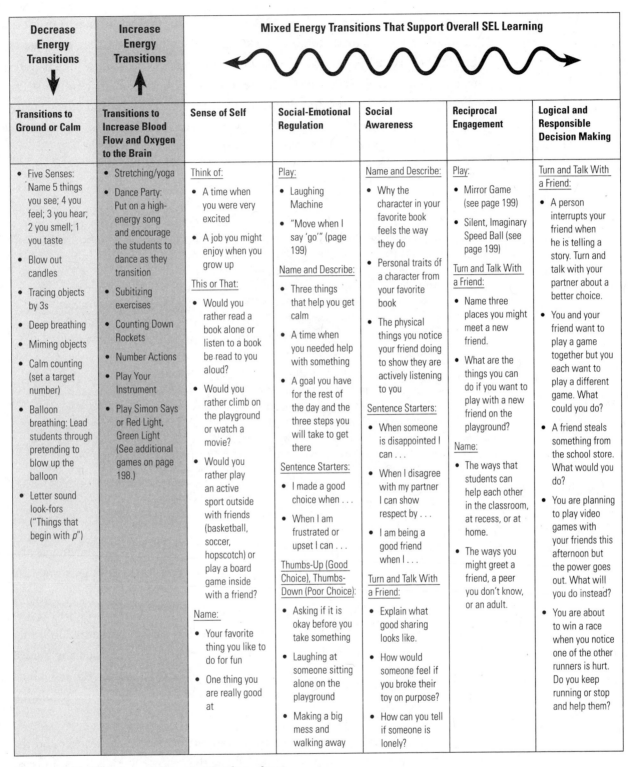

Decrease Energy Transitions ↓	Increase Energy Transitions ↑	Mixed Energy Transitions That Support Overall SEL Learning				
Transitions to Ground or Calm	Transitions to Increase Blood Flow and Oxygen to the Brain	Sense of Self	Social-Emotional Regulation	Social Awareness	Reciprocal Engagement	Logical and Responsible Decision Making
• Five Senses: Name 5 things you see; 4 you feel; 3 you hear; 2 you smell; 1 you taste • Blow out candles • Tracing objects by 3s • Deep breathing • Miming objects • Calm counting (set a target number) • Balloon breathing: Lead students through pretending to blow up the balloon • Letter sound look-fors ("Things that begin with *p*")	• Stretching/yoga • Dance Party: Put on a high-energy song and encourage the students to dance as they transition • Subitizing exercises • Counting Down Rockets • Number Actions • Play Your Instrument • Play Simon Says or Red Light, Green Light (See additional games on page 198.)	Think of: • A time when you were very excited • A job you might enjoy when you grow up This or That: • Would you rather read a book alone or listen to a book be read to you aloud? • Would you rather climb on the playground or watch a movie? • Would you rather play an active sport outside with friends (basketball, soccer, hopscotch) or play a board game inside with a friend? Name: • Your favorite thing you like to do for fun • One thing you are really good at	Play: • Laughing Machine • "Move when I say 'go'" (page 199) Name and Describe: • Three things that help you get calm • A time when you needed help with something • A goal you have for the rest of the day and the three steps you will take to get there Sentence Starters: • I made a good choice when . . . • When I am frustrated or upset I can . . . Thumbs-Up (Good Choice), Thumbs-Down (Poor Choice): • Asking if it is okay before you take something • Laughing at someone sitting alone on the playground • Making a big mess and walking away	Name and Describe: • Why the character in your favorite book feels the way they do • Personal traits of a character from your favorite book • The physical things you notice your friend doing to show they are actively listening to you Sentence Starters: • When someone is disappointed I can . . . • When I disagree with my partner I can show respect by . . . • I am being a good friend when I . . . Turn and Talk With a Friend: • Explain what good sharing looks like. • How would someone feel if you broke their toy on purpose? • How can you tell if someone is lonely?	Play: • Mirror Game (see page 199) • Silent, Imaginary Speed Ball (see page 199) Turn and Talk With a Friend: • Name three places you might meet a new friend. • What are the things you can do if you want to play with a new friend on the playground? Name: • The ways that students can help each other in the classroom, at recess, or at home. • The ways you might greet a friend, a peer you don't know, or an adult.	Turn and Talk With a Friend: • A person interrupts your friend when he is telling a story. Turn and talk with your partner about a better choice. • You and your friend want to play a game together but you each want to play a different game. What could you do? • A friend steals something from the school store. What would you do? • You are planning to play video games with your friends this afternoon but the power goes out. What will you do instead? • You are about to win a race when you notice one of the other runners is hurt. Do you keep running or stop and help them?

Figure 4.3: SEL transition strategies chart.

*Visit **go.SolutionTree.com/instruction** for a free reproducible version of this figure.*

Think of the value of a team of teachers working together to generate transitions that focus on the five SEL building block components that specifically correlate to SEL grade-level essential standards. This type of focused, intentional teaching requires proactive purposeful planning. Therefore, in chapter 5 (page 223) we discuss the importance of planning SEL transitions throughout the school day and provide planning tools and specific ideas for making this manageable for teachers.

2. Student Goal Setting

> Maria watched as Daniel and Maggie cleaned up from their reading center using the breathing exercises she was leading the class through during the transition. She smiled as the two of them laughed together at blowing out their finger-candles. Later in the day, while Daniel was working on his writing, he threw his paper across the room. "It's *not perfect!*" he cried. Maria went to him and suggested he try breathing, but he just put his head down and sobbed. "I can't! I try to be perfect and not get upset and everyone else is perfect, and I just can't!"
>
> Reflecting on this made Maria realize that Daniel is putting a lot of pressure on himself to "be perfect" but he does not necessarily know what this means. It seems like an unattainable goal. To even learn to use these self-regulation strategies, Daniel must begin to understand how to set a goal and achieve it through small steps so that he can celebrate his successes along the way. *Come to think of it, all students benefit from goal setting*, Maria thought. *What if we incorporate goal setting into our classroom?*

Essential SEL standards can be made into student-friendly "I can" statements and used for student goal setting. When students know their learning targets, they are not only more likely to learn the skill but are also using and practicing a cognitive executive functioning skill (namely, goal setting) needed for academic learning and something that is a lifelong skill. Edwin A. Locke and Gary P. Latham (2002) find that setting higher goals yields greater effort and performance. Experiencing guided goal setting with a teacher helps to develop the child's executive functioning which supports the academic cognitive skill area as well as the area of emotional regulation (SEL building block component 4).

Goal setting should require shared ownership on the part of the teacher and the student. It is important for the teacher to facilitate the process, but it is just as important for the student to take personal ownership in the act of goal setting. Student goal setting becomes meaningless if the student is not part of the process. Matthews (2015) shows that people are 33 percent more likely to accomplish a goal when the goals are recorded, shared with others, and frequently updated.

The question becomes, How can teachers help facilitate social-emotional goal setting so it is meaningful and manageable for the teacher and the students? Look at the goal card in figure 4.4. These are four essential learning targets that progress and build on one another. They could be four core essential learning targets at kindergarten that students focus on for the entire school year, or they could be goals to focus on for one to two months such that all lessons connect and build on these four essential learning targets. To learn more about how to create goal cards using learning progressions, visit **go.SolutionTree.com/PLCbooks** and refer to the book *What About Us? The PLC at Work Process for Grades PreK–2 Teams* (Kerr et al., 2021).

Self-Awareness and Self-Management Skills

Source: Kerr et al., 2021, p. 81.

Figure 4.4: Self-awareness and self-management skills goal card.

Let's take the first learning target and think about how we would monitor if students have achieved their social-emotional goals. At a planning meeting, a team of kindergarten teachers determined they would use goal setting with the students and would monitor the children's ability to identify feelings and emotions (SEL building block 1: *self-awareness*). The team introduced the concept to the students by reading books connected to feelings and emotions, and students engaged in learning activities that required them to identify and label a variety of feelings. The team then decided to create a chart that included visual examples of various feelings and emotions for the students to use when they entered the classroom each morning. The students would each take a clothespin with their name and picture on it and place it on the feelings chart. If the student wishes to keep their feelings private from the class but wants to share with the teacher, they may place their clothespin backwards so their name is hidden from public display. This activity would not only take attendance and allow the students to practice identifying and sharing their feelings but would also communicate to the teacher which children may need a check-in before the day starts.

During the two or three weeks of this unit, the teacher can make general student observations and plan for specific days to engage with students by asking them questions like, "Can you point to the excited face on the chart?" or "Can you make an excited face?" This quick check-in then serves as an informal assessment to help the teacher determine which students can or cannot identify and label feelings and emotions. For students who can accurately identify feelings and emotions, the teacher can quickly conference with them sometime during the week and have them place a sticker on or punch a hole in the applicable star on their goal card. For students still learning, the teacher might decide to use small-group targeted instruction to support them with extra time and guidance to learn the skill.

It is important to know that although these skills have a natural progression, they are developmental and may take some students longer than others. Also, students may show inconsistency with demonstrating certain skills based on their current emotional and physiological states. Many of these skills are built over time through life experiences. Keep in mind, the components are building blocks and some students may not have a strong base to support secure SEL growth in the higher blocks. The object is not to expect mastery, but rather for a student to demonstrate knowledge of the concepts and skills and show growth. The age and independence of the students will determine the level of support they need in monitoring their own goals. Teachers with younger students might strategically house and organize students' goal cards, whereas older students may take more responsibility in maintaining and monitoring them. Or, the teacher may just use this as an interactive teaching tool used during instruction. We share additional information about monitoring students' growth of SEL in chapter 6 (page 293).

Student goal setting can be more individualized for students as well. For instance, teacher teams can use universal screeners, common formative assessments, or informal observations to help students with individualized SEL needed areas of growth. Look at the individual SEL student goal card in figure 4.5). This teacher used an assessment tool to determine that a student was struggling with keeping her hands and feet to herself at the carpet, in line, and at recess. The teacher created a personal goal card for the student and conferenced with her regarding its use and purpose. The teacher then decided that the student's goal card would be taped onto her desk, so it was a consistent visual reminder. When the student was able to keep her hands and feet to herself at the carpet, in line, and at recess, the teacher would check in with the student and give positive verbal praise. The student would then be given a star sticker to be put on the goal card. When the student modeled the behavior five times, the goal card would be completed and sent home for the student to share with her parents. The goal card also became the teacher's informal data collection tool, serving as a record that demonstration of the skill was observed.

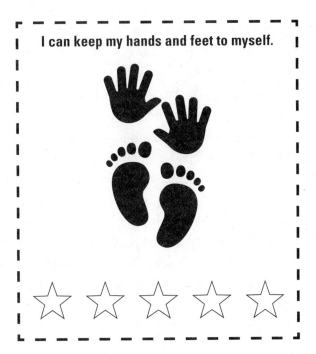

I can keep my hands and feet to myself.

Figure 4.5: Individual SEL student goal card.

·Although most of the students may be working on one goal card over the course of one to two weeks, children who require more individual and targeted goals may need to have their goal tracking broken down into more concrete periods of time. They will require a higher level of positive and specific reinforcement for their behaviors to change (Fosco, Hawk Jr., Rosch, & Bubnik, 2015). In these situations, teachers can give the students a new goal card each day, with the intention of the child demonstrating the targeted behavior at least five times in one day. In these cases, the child will not master the goal by achieving the five stars but instead will see themselves as continuing to be on their way toward the goal. These daily cards can be tangible evidence for the child and their family of the progress the child is making and should be a source of daily celebration and reflection. Be sure to date each goal card and note how many stars the child achieved before sending the card home. This information can serve as data to reflect the child's overall progress toward this goal.

Some students may need a more complex goal-tracking system. We recommend talking with the school counselor, behavior specialists, or special education teacher to develop a meaningful individual behavior plan. In these cases, it is often helpful for the team to take pre-data, or data before an intervention begins, to determine patterns in the student's behavior, identify common antecedents or triggers, and note the typical consequences of the behavior. These data are often called *ABC data*, which stands for antecedent, behavior, and consequence.

It's important to consider how goal cards will be managed and maintained by the teachers and students. Some teachers might not have assigned seats for students within their classroom, so goal cards can be placed in the students' cubbies where they keep their personal belongings, put in the students' personal classroom mailboxes, stored in a special folder to serve as student goal portfolios, or hung on rings in a designated area of the classroom set aside for student goal cards. Again, in this situation, the expectation is student growth and learning.

At this point, you might be saying, "Wait, you want me to create personalized individual social-emotional learning goals for each of my students? How is that manageable?" Imagine that at a meeting your whole team identifies a list of expected essential social-emotional skills and generates corresponding *I can* statements. Next, one or two team members volunteer to make a template and add pictures to the various student goal cards you created. You'll notice that in figure 4.6 the SEL skill is about asking for help when needed. The team used student-friendly language and changed the wording to *I can ask for help from a friend or a trusted adult when needed.* Some students may consistently already ask for help when needed, while others may really struggle in this area. These students may get a different student goal card that better fits their needs, such as the example in figure 4.7. These two goal cards help students reflect on their goals and give personal examples of when they use that SEL skill in real life.

SEL Skill:

Asking for help when needed

I can statement in student-friendly words:

- I can ask a friend or trusted adult for help when I need it.

> I can ask a friend or trusted adult for help when needed.
>
> X X ★ ★ ★
>
> At recess when I fell I asked Akash if he would take me to the nurse to get a Band-Aid.
>
> I didn't understand the directions on the 3-D shapes math task and asked Mrs. Gupta if she could help me.

Figure 4.6: Reflective student goal card—asking for help.

Practicing self-talk in different situations (to calm or to praise self for accomplishments)

I can statement in student-friendly words:

- I can practice self-talk in different situations (to help calm me or to praise myself for accomplishments).

I can practice self-talk in different situations (to help calm myself, to praise myself for my accomplishments or maybe when I need to do hard things).

I can do hard things.

Writing is really hard for me and I didn't want to get started but I kept saying in my brain, "Liam you can do hard things."

I was playing a game at recess and my partner won and I was really upset, but I said in my brain, "Liam it's ok, maybe you'll win next time."

Figure 4.7: Reflective student goal card—practicing self-talk.

Teachers can decide what works best for scheduling time for students to reflect and share their progress. Some may make time with a daily routine during the last five minutes of the day, where students are given time to reflect on their student goal cards. During this time, students can make real-life connections, put meaning to context, and monitor their own goals. Alternatively, other teachers may offer a weekly routine on Fridays during morning meeting when students have opportunities to reflect on their week, share with a friend the various times they used that skill, and also have time to hear and celebrate their friend's accomplishments or struggles. After a few weeks, students are given time to reflect on their goal in a journal-writing activity at the start of the day or during writing time and describe how and when they used these skills over the course of a few weeks or during the month.

It is not realistic to think that a teacher will generate every personalized goal card needed for their students, but it is a start, and something the team can share electronically, store in a shared file, and add to over time. Instead of just randomly assigning goal cards to students, teachers can use data gathered from team-generated common formative SEL assessment tools (see chapter 6, page 293) to help determine students' areas of need. When doing this, we make the learning more focused and targeted for our students.

We suggest when trying something new to start off small. Therefore, you just may want to try this out with a few students and over time build up to include SEL goal setting with all students. For this to be sustainable, the process must be well thought out by the teacher, clearly understood by the students, and consistently monitored by both teacher and students. Overall, student SEL goal setting should be a positive experience and something that is accessible to all students.

Virtual Learning Tip

During virtual learning experiences, teachers may want to show the goal card visual at the start of the lesson or learning so students know their learning expectations. They can show the visual again at the end and ask students to reflect on their learning and any goals they accomplished throughout the lesson, during that day, or within the week. Students who can write may create their own goal cards under the direction of the teacher.

---

3. SEL Daily Routines

Teachers can create SEL daily routines or incorporate SEL into any existing routines that are part of the regular school day. The following sections will focus on incorporating SEL into the following typical teacher routines.

- Morning meetings

- Social-emotional calendar routines

- SEL interactive whiteboard activities

Morning Meetings

Daniel and Maggie dragged themselves into their classroom looking rather glum. Maria greeted them happily and reminded them to go through their daily morning routine. She was glad they seemed to be becoming such good friends. She was worried about how today would go for them based on their emotions this morning. She had been noticing that she could predict how the day would go for both of them based on how their mornings went. On days when one of them appeared to be disorganized and dysregulated and had difficulty remembering the classroom routines, she knew the rest of the day would be like this as well. Maria had come to realize that on days when they came in so glumly, Daniel could end up with negative thinking that would lead to an outburst if she did not step in. *Luckily*, Maria thought, *we have morning meeting to help us mentally transition into our school day and organize ourselves for the day.* Maria had begun increasing social-emotional learning into her morning meeting. It was saving her time, changing the tone of her school day, and teaching vocabulary she could refer back to when students had big emotions.

Many elementary school classrooms start each day with a variation of a morning meeting, opening circle, or family meeting. No matter the terminology, this familiar, daily structure allows the students within each classroom to develop a community, connect with the teacher as well as their peers, share their thoughts and perspectives, and review the daily routine. This one routine promotes the development of SEL building block components 1 (*self-awareness*), 2 (*reciprocal engagement*), 3 (*social awareness*), and 4 (*emotional regulation*) and executive functioning. Morning meetings provide a safe, comfortable start for each school day (Dabbs, 2017; Williams, 2011). This already-established daily routine gives teachers an excellent opportunity to teach, model, and practice social-emotional learning skills.

Virtual Learning Tip

Teachers are easily able to follow the same pattern of activities for morning meeting and can occasionally utilize breakout groups to allow for students to feel more connected to others during the greeting and share patterns. In the virtual setting, this routine will be invaluable for building community (Kelly, 2020).

Table 4.1 describes each SEL building blocks component in a traditional morning meeting routine following the Responsive Classroom's evidence-based approach and provides examples of how to directly embed SEL skills.

Table 4.1: Embedding SEL Skills Into Morning Meeting Example

Morning Meeting Component	What It Looks Like	Where to Embed SEL Skills
Greeting	Students greet one another by passing a handshake or high five around the circle.	• Directly teach behaviors of eye contact, speaking voice level, and smiling to greet someone. • Ask the class to think about how they feel when a peer smiles at them. Build awareness of emotional responses to being greeted. • Add in silly greetings to connect with taught SEL skills.
Message	Teacher writes a message to greet students and discuss what will happen that school day. Often involves engaging questions to encourage student participation.	• Embed SEL questions directly related to what is being taught and discussed into the morning message. • Include model statements of how the teacher is feeling and why, based on the targeted SEL skill. • Ask students to think ahead in their day and predict what SEL skills they may need and how they will react in different situations.
Activity	Teacher uses a fun activity, song, or game to allow students to get up and move. The goal is to build community while having fun.	• Play games directly related to SEL skills. • Ask students to reflect on how they feel during games.
Share	Students have opportunities to share something about themselves.	• Specifically teach presentation behaviors of voice level, body placement, and eye contact when sharing. • Ask students to share events from their past that correspond with the SEL skills being taught.

Source: Adapted from Bechtel, Clayton, & Denton, 2003.

These morning meeting routines begin with students greeting one another (SEL building block 2: *reciprocal engagement*) followed by a shared reading of an opening written message from the classroom teacher. There is then an opportunity for students to review the schedule, set goals for the day (SEL building block 4: *emotional regulation* and executive functioning), share something about themselves, and participate in a game or an activity (SEL building block 3: *social awareness*).

The following is a vignette that shows what this might look like in the classroom and how it could possibly play out.

> Maria gathered her class on the rug they use for a meeting area each day. The students sat around the edge of the rug, facing inward. "Good morning!" Maria announced. "It's wonderful to see you today! Let's begin our greeting. Today we'll say hello in Spanish—*Hola!* When it is your turn to greet your friend, turn your body all the way around so you are knee to knee. Look your friend in the eyes and smile so they feel that you are happy to see them. In a big voice, greet your friend by using their name." Maria's directions reminded the students of the specific social behaviors she expected them to use during this time. "Who can show me what that looks like?"
>
> Johnny raised his hand, and Maria asked him to greet his neighbor. As the greeting spread around the circle, Maria smiled at the students and provided gentle reminders to make eye contact, turn, and use their friendly voices. When the greeting reached everyone, she addressed the class. "Wonderful. This week we have been talking about identifying our emotions. Give me a quick thumbs-up if you noticed that you felt happy when your friend looked at you and smiled." This whole-group response encouraged everyone to participate, without taking time to listen to individual answers. Maria kept the pace of her morning meeting going. "Turn your bodies to see today's message," she told the class, and because this is a practiced skill, the class quickly moved to their spots on the rug where they could see the message.
>
> "Dear Fantastic First Graders! Today is Tuesday, October 28th, 2019. Today we have PE and music. I noticed I have two feelings about book character day on Friday. I am excited to share my costume with you, but I am also a little nervous that I'll be wearing a costume to school. Who else feels that way?
>
> Have a great day!
>
> Love, Mrs. Smith."
>
> The class read the message two times. As they read, Maria changed her voice to reflect how she was feeling with each emotion word. "I wonder if anyone else is feeling this way about Friday. Without talking, put up two fingers in front of your chest if you are feeling two feelings about Friday. Put up one finger if you are feeling one feeling, and three if you have three feelings!" She waited while the students thought and then shared their fingers.

"Johnny, put your fingers in front of your chest, don't wave them in the air! Wow—I see some people just have one feeling, while others have two or three! We have a lot of feelings in this room! It is normal to feel two or more feelings about one event. It feels mixed up inside, but events can make us feel many different things. Time for our game. Who wants to lead *Simon Says*?"

After the game, Maria again asked for a show of fingers of how many emotions they felt during the game. "*Simon Says* always makes me nervous! I'm worried that I'll miss something," she shared. "Did anyone else have a different feeling?" She chose one student to share, and then moved on to the sharing portion of morning meeting.

Maria has her class sign up for when they have something they would like to share with the class and allows three students to share a day. Each child shares quickly, and then the class moves on to its next subject. On this day, Maria decided not to add any additional social-emotional skills to the share period. Tomorrow, she'll give a reminder on the specific social skills needed for this share time and may ask a student to elaborate on how they felt during the story they shared. She worked to keep her morning meetings to no more than twenty minutes, which means making professional decisions about when to emphasize social-emotional learning and when to move on. Teachers or teacher teams can use the template in figure 4.8 to specifically plan where to embed the SEL building block components, standards, and learning targets into morning meetings.

Morning Meeting SEL Activities Template			
Social-Emotional Learning Target	Morning Meeting: Message (suggested phrases to embed in the message)	Morning Meeting: Group Questions	Morning Meeting: Activities, Games, or Share
I can identify and label feelings and emotions.	"Today I feel happy." "Yesterday we read *Knuffle Bunny*. I think Trixie must have been worried when she lost her bunny."	"Look at the picture. How does this animal feel?"	Match that emotion freeze dance: The teacher plays music while the class dances. When the music stops, the teacher puts up a picture of an emotion and the class makes that expression (usually with exaggerated, fun but silent actions).

Figure 4.8: Morning meeting planning template—example.

continued →

Social-Emotional Learning Target	Morning Meeting: Message (suggested phrases to embed in the message)	Morning Meeting: Group Questions	Morning Meeting: Activities, Games, or Share
I can identify my feelings and emotions.	"I am feeling excited to be here this morning!" "I am happy because we are going to have fun in math today!" "I am feeling frustrated because we can't go outside for recess today." "I am feeling nervous about trying something new in science today, but I think it will be great!"	"How are you feeling this morning?" "How are you feeling about going to PE today?" "How did you feel when your mom told you to get out of bed this morning?" (Attaching emotions to past events) "How do you think I felt when the fire alarm went off during our math lesson yesterday?" (Attaching emotions to someone else)	Feelings charades: One person chooses a feeling to act out silently. The class gets to guess what the student is acting out. Provide a feelings chart to give concrete feeling words. "I'm feeling _____ because _____."
I can identify how my body feels with different emotions.	"I feel like dancing today because I am so excited for math!" "My stomach is tight today. I am nervous about what will happen in our read-aloud." "My arms feel tight and stiff. I am frustrated we cannot go out to recess again because of the rain."	"When you feel happy, where do you feel it in your body? Head, stomach, arms, or feet?" "When you feel frustrated, where do you feel it in your body?"	Mindfulness moment: Students can do a mindful moment where the teacher walks them through paying attention to each part of their body—from the feet to their head—to notice any particular feelings that might be linked to different emotions (Waterford, 2019). This calm activity does not need to involve sharing out observations unless students chose to. The teacher may opt to make her observations aloud, so the students understand the process.
I can express my feelings and emotions with appropriate words or actions.	"I am feeling happy about our dance party this afternoon, so I am smiling." "I am so frustrated about the rain today! I will take some deep breaths and think about good choices for indoor recess."	"When you are happy, how do you show it? Smiling, dancing, friendly voice, or laughing?" "When you are feeling angry, what strategies do you like to use? Take a deep breath, get a drink of water, go for a walk, or talk to someone?" "When you are feeling sad, what helps you feel better? Talking to someone, being alone, getting a hug, or moving around?"	Act, pause, rewind, and act again: Student groups can create skits to share during morning meeting around a character not recognizing and expressing their emotions and then "rewinding" and changing the scenario with the character expressing their emotion to others (Copeland, 2015).

*Visit **go.SolutionTree.com/instruction** for a free blank reproducible version of this figure.*

Social-Emotional Calendar Routines

Embedding the SEL skills into morning meeting is working well, but I need more of a routine to make it more powerful, Maria thinks. *It cannot just be me using the vocabulary. Images are so much more meaningful. How can I bring visuals into teaching SEL skills in morning meeting and keep it brief?*

Many teachers have students interact with the monthly calendar as part of their daily routine. Interactions may include questions about the date or a special holiday, or connect to the mathematics curriculum (for example, "Today is November 4th; Sanjay's birthday is two weeks later. When is Sanjay's birthday?"). A great way to incorporate social-emotional learning is using a daily calendar routine with the use of visuals. Using visuals to ignite rich classroom discussions can be very powerful. Ghulam Shabiralyani, Khuram Shahzad Hasan, Naqvi Hamad, and Nadeem Iqbal (2015) share results from research where using visual aids ignites thinking and strengthens the learning environment within the classroom. John Hattie's book, *Visible Learning* (2009; see also Hattie & Donoghue, 2016), supports the use of meta-cognitive strategies as a teaching practice, which has been proven to positively impact student learning. Therefore, an SEL calendar routine which involves the use of higher-order thinking skills to analyze one's own thoughts, ideas, emotions, and feelings can be a powerful and useful practice. This routine should move quickly to not take up core instructional time. Pictures centered around social-emotional learning can be printed and displayed on a classroom calendar. As you can see, the sample calendar in figure 4.9 (page 176) has a theme. Each week of the calendar focuses on a different essential SEL standard and correlates to the student-friendly goal card seen in figure 4.4 (page 165). Teachers can make this a daily or weekly routine depending on their students' needs.

The goal of the SEL calendar is to use the embedded pictures as tools to help engage students in rich discussions about social-emotional learning concepts and provide a time when students can build and practice SEL skills. Figure 4.10 (page 177) is a sample graphic organizer which contains various teacher questions and prompts that correlate to each picture on week one and two of the monthly calendar. To make this an interactive and engaging activity, teachers can have students turn and talk to a partner and then share out their ideas with the whole group.

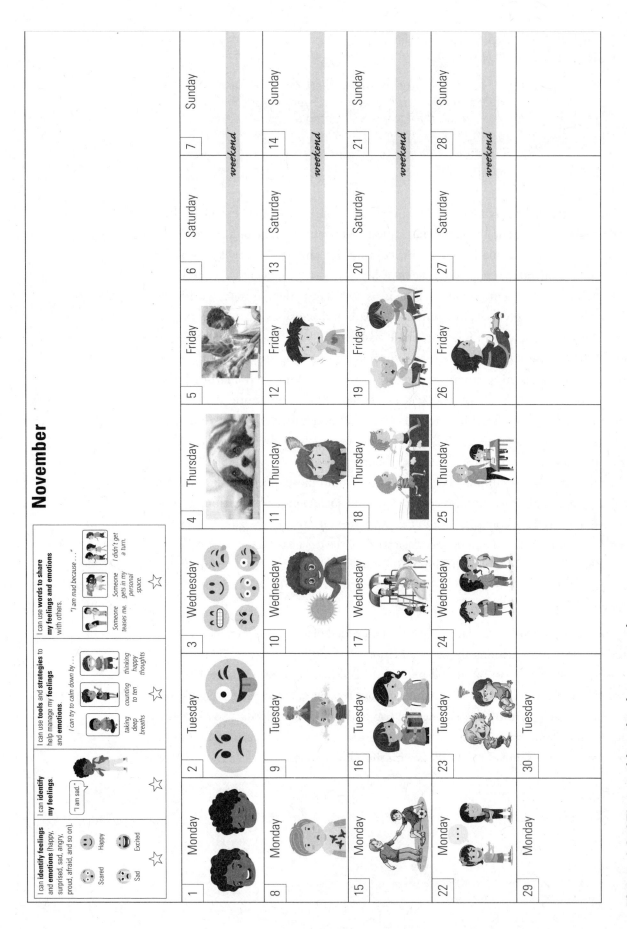

Figure 4.9: SEL monthly calendar—example.

Teacher Questions and Prompts

November Calendar

Week 1:	Day 1:	Day 2:	Day 3:	Day 4:	Day 5:
SEL Focal Area: Self-Awareness **SEL Standards:** I can identify and label feelings and emotions (happy, surprised, sad, angry, proud, afraid, silly). Scared · Happy Sad · Excited	 What do you notice about the expressions on each of the faces? How are they similar? How are they different? What do you think the child is thinking about? What is something that could have made this student happy?	 What do you notice about each of the faces? How are they similar? How are they different? Can you make a silly face? How do you know that this is a mad face?	 Can you identify each of the six emotions? How are you able to tell the differences between each emoji? What helped you determine which is happy and which surprised? Turn to your partner, and model different emotions and see if your partner can guess.	 How do you think the dog feels? What clues did you use to help your best guess? What are other words that can be used to also mean sad?	 Look at the picture. Describe what you see. Thumbs up or down if you think the boy is scared or nervous. What clues did you use to help you determine he was happy? Turn to your partner and show them your scared face versus your happy face.

continued ↑

Figure 4.10: Weekly calendar teacher questions and prompts—example.

Teacher Questions and Prompts
November Calendar

Week 2:	Day 8:	Day 9:	Day 10:	Day 11:	Day 12:
SEL Focal Area: Self-Awareness **SEL Standards:**	How are you able to recognize when you are worried or nervous? What differences do you feel in your body when you are happy versus when you are worried or nervous? What can you do to help calm your body when you are worried or nervous?	What types of things can make someone angry or mad? What reaction happens in your body when you start getting angry? Thumbs up or down that it is OK to feel angry. (Share that it's OK to have any feeling you have, but not OK to hurt yourself or others when you are mad or angry.) What does angry look like, and what can you do when you are angry?	Turn to your partner and share one thing that makes you happy while you are at school and one thing that makes you happy outside of school. How can you tell when you are happy? How do you feel inside and how can other people identify when you are happy?	What are some words that can be used to describe this person's emotions? What body feelings match this emotion? When you experience this emotion what body feelings do you have? What things can you do to help calm your body? If your friend is feeling this emotion, what actions can you take to be a good friend?	How do you think this person is feeling? How do you know? Who are the people in your life who you can ask for help when you feel afraid or scared? What are the things that can help a person when they are scared or fearful?

*Visit **go.SolutionTree.com/instruction** for a free blank reproducible version of this figure.*

Teachers can use the planning tool in figure 4.10 (page 177) to jot down prompts and questions that correlate to the weekly calendar. This routine is flexible and can be adapted to meet the classroom's needs. Teachers may choose to ask one quick question each day when viewing the calendar but then spend more time (maybe five to eight minutes) on one SEL picture during one particular day during the week. Or, teachers may begin the school year only showing one picture each week on the calendar, with the goal of increasing the frequency of this routine throughout the school year. The routine nature of this discussion will support the students' understanding of SEL across time. Again, at this point you might be thinking to yourself that this seems like a lot of work! Now view this through the lens of having your whole team engage in this practice. Each teacher can be assigned one or two months (depending on the size of your team), find the pictures, generate the prompts, and share them with the entire team. This way, instead of each teacher having to find pictures and create prompts for each month, they will only have to do it one or two times during the entire school year.

Virtual Learning Tip

In a virtual learning environment, you can make virtual calendars or include these pictures on a shared slide deck. Students can share their responses in the chat box. Depending on your time, you may choose to put students in breakout rooms to engage in rich discussions and even use a collaborative and interactive shared electronic document (Wills, 2021) as a way to engage students and help them process the content.

SEL Interactive Whiteboard Activities

Teachers can use technology to engage students in daily routines. Instead of just talking about social-emotional skills and concepts, interactive whiteboards allow for students to explore the learning through a variety of sensory experiences—visual, auditory, and kinesthetic—that can often occur simultaneously. We enhance the learning experience and provide opportunities for students to practice certain skills when we add in opportunities for students to collaborate and communicate with each other.

Imagine students who come in and greet their teacher as part of their morning routine and then, after putting away their belongings and setting themselves up for the day, look to the interactive whiteboard for their daily morning task. What if each morning students have an opportunity to come up to the interactive whiteboard and answer a daily question focused on social-emotional learning? For instance, during planning, teacher teams could create an interactive presentation with multiple slides. Each slide could contain a different message to allow the students to come up to the interactive whiteboard, write their response, and read the responses of their peers. The teacher can then share student responses to the posed questions during the morning meeting as a positive task that helps set the tone and mood for the day.

Figure 4.11 shows an example of a daily routine in the form of an interactive whiteboard slide with questions and prompts. This example asks students to first jot down on a sticky note a kindness they did sometime during their week either at home or in school (SEL building block 3: *social awareness*) and share it with another student nearby. Next, they are asked to think about how engaging in that activity made them feel and to then go up to the interactive whiteboard and add their data on the class graph (SEL building block 1: *self-awareness*). After the teacher has finished greeting the students and all students have finished their morning routine, the teacher takes time to pose questions about the graph: How many more students feel excited than proud (SEL building block 3: *social awareness*; mathematics concepts: measurement & data)? How were you able to decide if you felt more excited versus proud (SEL building block 1: *self-awareness*)? Did any of you feel nervous or worried before you engaged in the act of kindness, but then feel happy or excited afterward? How does your body feel when it is excited versus proud, or does it feel the same? You will notice how the teachers also included mathematics concepts with the social-emotional concepts in the daily routine. In this example, during planning, the team looked at their mathematics standards related to measurement and data and considered all of the graphic representations related to their grade-level standards—in this case, object, picture, and pico-graphs—as well as standards which require students to read, interpret, and answer questions relating to the graphs. The team decided to create a different whiteboard daily routine for each month (namely, September: object graph; October: picture graph; November: pico-graph, and so on) focusing on both mathematics and social-emotional standards.

1. Use a sticky note to jot down one kindness you did for someone else during this week. How did this action or event make you feel?

2. After you jot down the kindness, raise your hand. Find another person with their hand raised and partner up. Use your listening skills to hear your partner's act of kindness, and then share your act of kindness with your partner.

3. Next, go up to the interactive whiteboard and use your data to fill in the picture graph.

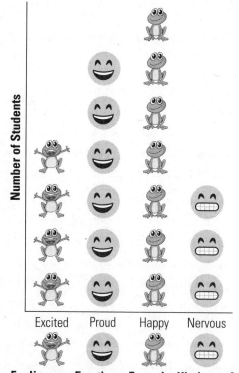

Figure 4.11: Interactive whiteboard daily routine.

We provide additional examples of daily SEL routines in the appendix (figure A.8, page 328). Each of these examples includes visuals, questions and prompts, and connections to additional academic content areas. With limited classroom wall space, the interactive whiteboard allows a space for routines with minimal materials and preparation. If you are without this technology, the routine can still occur, but you may think about keeping one structure for a longer period with the same graphic representation but where just the SEL concepts, questions, and prompts change. Think about how students get the opportunity to practice and learn both social-emotional skills and academic skills in these short daily routines. Students are communicating their ideas in writing and orally. They are also interacting with mathematics skills by using graphs and answering questions about the data within the graph. Consider planning a few routines together as a team in a meeting and then asking each team member to create one outside of the meeting to share with their teammates in a shared team electronic folder.

Teachers can also create these interactive whiteboard routines by embedding digital SEL videos into interactive whiteboard slides and using them in a daily or weekly routine. When using SEL videos in daily routines, how can we make them engaging and interactive for our students? For starters, students are not just watching a video; rather, they are watching a video and answering higher-order questions about the video. Embedded in the interactive whiteboard presentation might be a slide which requires students to reflect on the video and prompts the teachers to use thoughtful questioning techniques, serving as a great way to engage students in social-emotional learning. Requiring students to "turn and talk" allows for cooperative learning, metacognitive thinking, and oral language skills. In this scenario, the interactive whiteboard routine might ask students to first partner, discuss, and generate ideas together before sharing out their ideas and having a whole-class discussion.

Virtual Learning Tip

In a virtual learning setting, teachers can share their screens as the students are entering the virtual room. The shared slide can include the morning message with the question of the day—perhaps asking students to respond about how they are feeling that morning. Students can share their thoughts in the chat box or through a collaborative, interactive digital document. These responses can be turned into a graph for discussion. While the virtual classroom makes it difficult for students to "turn and talk," it does offer a variety of possibilities for students to respond to a question. Teachers can assign groups of students to breakout groups to encourage more interaction and engagement between students (Wills, 2021).

4. Picture Book Read-Alouds and Reading Comprehension Strategies

> With an extra five minutes to spare before lunch, Maria grabbed the class's favorite book—*The Pigeon Has to Go to School!* by Mo Willems (2019). *It's such a silly book*, Maria thought, *but the students really seem to connect with it. Especially when I act like the pigeon—and ask the class to do the same. It's funny*, she thought, *Daniel and Maggie are often the most engaged during read-alouds, especially when the characters have big emotions. I wonder how I can use these to further teach and practice our SEL skills?*

Another natural place to embed SEL learning into already-set classroom routines is during picture book read-alouds. Storybook read-alouds provide multiple benefits to classroom communities. They create a shared experience and language as a class listens and responds to a story together. Stories can provide a narrative for academic content, illustrate a concept, or simply provide a quiet time for students to become immersed in language. Yet during a busy classroom day, read-alouds can often be overlooked or under-planned for, especially in the upper elementary grades. As teachers, we tend to grab a read-aloud when there is a surprise free ten minutes in the day, or when we are building interest and background in a new concept. Well-planned, interactive read-alouds increase students' abilities to interact with the text, engage with their teacher and the concepts the book presents, and heighten deeper-level thinking (van Druten-Frietman, Strating, Denessen, & Verhoeven, 2016; see figure 4.12).

Read-Aloud Planning Template			
Book: *Squanto*			
Page Number	**Question**	**Focus**	**Notes**
2	When did this story take place? In the present or the past? How do you know?	Identifying genre: language arts Identifying past and present: social studies	Refer to the student's timelines that were created at the beginning of the year as a reference for the vocabulary terms past, present, and future.
3	Squanto is meeting the pilgrims. Who are the pilgrims?	Social studies: recalling facts	
4	Look at the faces in these pictures. How do you think Squanto is feeling? How do you think the pilgrims are feeling?	SEL Learning: identifying emotions	

Page Number	Question	Focus	Notes
5	Have you ever met someone who dressed differently or looked differently than you? How did you feel?	SEL: perspective taking	
6	What did Squanto teach the pilgrims to do?	Social studies: recalling fact Language arts: comprehension	
7	How do you think the pilgrims felt after Squanto helped them? How many different emotions can you think they may have felt?	SEL: We feel many emotions at the same time. Emotions change over time.	

Figure 4.12: Interactive read-aloud SEL planning tool.

*Visit **go.SolutionTree.com/instruction** for a free blank reproducible version of this figure.*

Read-alouds deepen students' understanding of social and emotional learning. Stories allow students to experience another point of view, consider new information, or develop empathy for characters (SEL building block 3: *social awareness*). As teachers intentionally plan their read-alouds, they can embed social-emotional lessons and examples into their planned concepts as well as their academic questions (see figure 4.12).

Read-alouds support social-emotional learning in two specific ways. First, books can be intentionally chosen to specifically teach or enhance a social-emotional concept. When the class is working on identifying emotions and using calming strategies (SEL building block 4: *emotional regulation*), teachers can read books like *When Sophie Gets Angry—Really, Really Angry* by Molly Bang (1999) to help illustrate the concept. Elephant and Piggie books, by Mo Willems, are excellent for encouraging students to identify emotions within a text. In these books, the characters become overcome with emotions that are easy to identify through the illustrations and dramatic words. By the end of the book, the characters are once again calm, providing classrooms with the opportunity to discuss how the characters used calm-down strategies before resolving their problem.

Alternatively, teachers can include social-emotional questioning into the read-alouds they are using for their academic areas. If the class is learning about fractions and fair-shares, they may read *The Cookie Fiasco* by Dan Santat (2016). In addition to planning interactive questions to encourage the students' problem solving and deeper-level mathematics thinking, teachers can embed social-emotional questioning here as well. In this story, four friends are panicking because they have three cookies and cannot figure out how to fairly share the cookies. While discussing the mathematics components of the story, the students can also track the characters' emotions as the story progresses. As the class notices how the characters' emotions change with each event, they will be able to connect the events of the story that cause emotional responses (SEL building block component 4: *emotional regulation* and executive functioning). This will build heightened interest for how the characters solve the problem (in this case, using mathematics). In almost all fiction stories, the characters' decisions and actions are driven by their emotions. Having students track these emotions and the events around them also supports students' reading comprehension.

A critical factor of learning to read is the ability to understand the meaning behind what we read. In addition to focusing on decoding words and understanding word principles, students must be able to decode while keeping the story's events and plot in their mind. Many reading comprehension assessments ask students to be able to independently tell what happened in a story from beginning to end. In supporting reading comprehension in fiction texts, teachers can encourage students to identify and track the characters' emotions and how they change throughout the book. Although students can often retell a story without identifying how the characters feel, the reasons behind the characters' actions and decisions are usually emotionally driven. Students can retell specific events if they are able to remember the characters' emotional response that led to or resulted from the event. This also allows the students to begin to infer the reason behind the characters' actions. If the girl missed her mother and then left the house to look for her, a student can be supported in understanding that the girl left the house *because* she missed her mother. This basic understanding of how emotions drive our decisions and actions is the foundation of the reading comprehension skills of inferring and identifying cause and effect, as well as understanding the emotions of the world around us.

As students read, they may jot down each time a character's emotions change. These jots can be on a sticky note and placed anywhere in the text this occurred. After the child has finished reading, ask them to review the character's emotional journey. Often, the character begins happy, but a conflict arises where the character's emotions change. This change pushes the events of the story onward, until at least the character's emotions change again for the story's resolution. Figure 4.13 provides a graphic organizer to help students track a character's emotional journey.

Virtual Learning Tip

When teaching in a virtual classroom, read-alouds and picture books can be used in the same manner they are used in the in-person classroom. Often, teachers can find digital copies of the picture book, making it possible for the teacher to share their screen and project the book. If a teacher is not able to access a digital copy, a hard copy will work if the teacher ensures the students can see the pictures in the book they are holding and reading aloud. The reading responses can be assigned through an interactive platform; in fact, even in an in-person classroom students will enjoy responding to books using technology such as collaborative, interactive digital platforms.

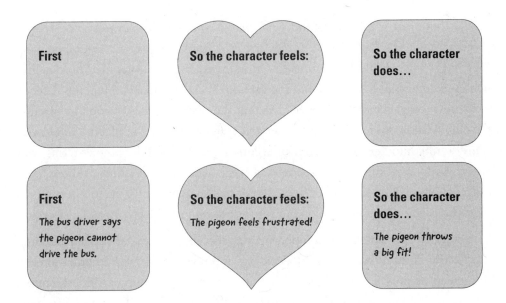

Figure 4.13: Event, feelings, action graphic organizer (template and student example).

*Visit **go.SolutionTree.com/instruction** for a free blank reproducible version of this figure.*

5. Social-Emotional Learning During Play

> "Play is often talked about as if it were a relief from serious learning. But for children play is serious learning. Play is really the work of childhood."
>
> —Fred Rogers
>
> Although there was no specific time to play in Maria's first-grade classroom, she recognized that her students had a hard time sitting still for her lessons. *If only they were as engaged with me as they are when they play house or soccer at recess*, she often found herself thinking. *Of course, that would probably lead to more frustration from Daniel. But what if I used these moments of play as a way to help him practice calming down, use strategies, and interact with his peers? Is play—when he is the most engaged—an opportunity to guide him in this practice?*

Although we often focus on the academic aspects of the school day, from reading, writing, and mathematics to science and social studies, play is a key period during a child's day where they are actively learning. Whether this is a free play period in a kindergarten classroom, indoor recess in a fourth-grade room, outside recess for fifth graders, or silly moments during second-grade lunch, students are often more actively engaged in their environment during play (Brown, 2009). The very nature of play allows students to engage in SEL component 2: *reciprocal engagement* (Porges, 2017). This makes these play periods the perfect time to capitalize on teaching and guiding social and emotional learning.

The first piece is to understand what play is and why it is important. Stephen Porges writes in the *Pocket Guide to the Polyvagal Theory* that play is a "neural exercise" (2017). Play, he explains, allows us to naturally experience co-regulation, synchronous and reciprocal behaviors, and increase our social awareness. He states, "Access to the social engagement system ensures that the sympathetic activation involved in the mobilization does not hijack the nervous system, resulting in playful movements transitioning into aggressive behavior" (Porges, 2017, p. 22). In simpler terms, play allows our internal systems to experience a range of different emotions without being triggered into the fight, flight, or freeze response. Play is where we practice having our big feelings and where we develop our safe responses to those emotions.

In addition to its emotional component, play also allows us to develop our executive functioning skills of setting a goal, deciding, and revising the plan in order to meet the agreed-on goal. I (Ann-Bailey) remember watching a group of kindergarteners play in the housekeeping center during their free choice time. The group was playing that they were making dinner for a funeral, but they kept running out of food. They kept sending someone to the store to get more food. As an outsider, the play seemed monotonous, but the funeral theme of the play allowed the students to make sense of something that recently happened to them while also exercising their reciprocal engagement and executive functioning skills. By the end of their play they had covered half the classroom in items that represented food for the funeral. Together they decided on their goal (dinner for a funeral) and then worked together to gather anything they could that would make the meal just right, despite obstacles real (not enough toy food) or imaginary (not enough food for all the imaginary funeral guests).

Teachers can incorporate SEL during play in two ways: (1) supporting SEL during unstructured play, or (2) directly guiding play.

Supporting SEL During Unstructured Play

When teachers take time to observe children at play, without interrupting or guiding the play, they will have an opportunity to see a variety of skills in multiple learning domains (language, motor, social-emotional, cognitive-academic and executive function, and so on) in action. In addition to making observations during this time, teachers can strategically join in with children's existing play schemes to add additional social and emotional learning themes that the child may otherwise experience in real life. If a group of students is playing in the classroom's kitchen, the teacher can enter the play and add a new event for the students to react to. If a group of students are pretending to have a picnic, the teacher may add in that a thunderstorm is coming. Through the safety of play, the children will be able to experience reacting to the unplanned change and comforting each other from the storm. Perhaps the teacher pretends to be a family member coming home from school after a bad day, or acts out running out of milk and not being able to go to the store to get more.

When the teacher joins in the play, the teacher provides a natural opportunity for the children to playfully respond after processing the newly introduced imaginary emotional situation (SEL building blocks 2: *reciprocal engagement*, and 4: *emotional regulation* and executive functioning). In these examples, the teacher has joined the students as a play partner rather than as an adult integrating academics into play. The teacher's role in these examples has not caused the students to shift from their pretend world to respond to the teacher as a teacher; rather, the students are able to respond from the safety of the pretend play. This allows for authentic problem solving and practice of SEL skills within the play.

Just as we challenge children with slightly more difficult reading books, we can challenge children to push beyond their current play schemes (Levine & Chedd, 2007). At times, the teacher can pause the play and suggest an event within the children's existing, chosen play scheme. For example, the teacher might say, "Let's pretend we are late for school and we can't find our book bags. What will we do? How will we act? Show me the face you are going to use!" The students can then go forward with the play scheme, already having been given support and forward planning in the situation (SEL building block 4: *emotional regulation* and executive functioning).

When something upsetting happens in a child's life, they will often process it through play. It is not uncommon to see a kindergarten student recreating a funeral during free-play periods after a grandparent has died, playing doctor to give a stuffed animal a shot after a traumatic flu shot experience, or even having dolls fight in a way that echoes an argument they overheard between their parents. It is important to not judge the play or tell a child they are being too mean in their play. Instead, adult observers or play partners can comment that, "Wow, you must be feeling really angry to want to hit that doll like that," or "Your stuffed animal has some big feelings about not getting that flu shot! I can't believe he wants to destroy the doctor's office." These comments do not pass judgement but rather draw the child's attention to their larger emotion to help them process their feelings.

Older elementary students are not as likely to pull out a doctor's kit to help themselves process a parent's cancer diagnosis. Instead, provide students opportunities to role play different scenarios (which we discuss in more detail in the section "Directly Guiding Play," page 188). Role playing games or different theater improvisation games can give older children the same sense of emotional release while allowing them to save face. With older students, teachers can also be aware of how their emotions will come out on the playground. After recess, allow time for the students to process their different emotions. Comment, without judgement, on what you observed: "You looked really angry after missing that goal. That looked pretty important to you. Do you need a moment to get a drink of water before we regroup in the classroom?" Your nonjudgmental observations allow students to recognize their emotions (SEL building block 1: *self-awareness*) and apply what you have taught them in the classroom.

Virtual Learning Tip

While the virtual environment can make unstructured play difficult, it is not impossible. In this case it will be important to communicate to parents the value of play. Encourage parents to support their child through optional assignments that involve playing together. They can recreate a story together by acting it out and filming it to share with the teacher. Older students can be assigned breakout rooms to create skits in the virtual environment. Interactive play over the computer screen can become as exciting as participating in an improv activity—students enjoy "taking" objects through the computer and pretending to use them before passing them back.

Directly Guiding Play

What is guided play? According to Tamara Spiewak Toub, Vinaya Rajan, Roberta Michnick Golinkoff, and Kathy Hirsh-Pasek (2016), "Guided play maintains most traditional elements of play, especially the enjoyable and engaging nature and the child's own agency but adds a focus on the extrinsic goal of developing children's skills and knowledge" (p. 121). The authors describe guided play as being a balance between complete free play and direct instruction. Teachers can specifically set up play schemes for students to play out the social-emotional focus of the week. After a classroom reads a book, the teacher can provide toys or regalia that correspond with the story and make these available during play time or allow them to be accessed during reading workshop as a retelling station. The children can act out the story with the toy characters, emphasizing the characters' emotional responses. This is a great opportunity for children to explore what it may feel like to have an out-of-control tantrum like the pigeon in Mo Willems's *Pigeon* series without actually having a risky emotional tantrum themselves. Often, when given access to toys to retell a story, children will begin with the original story and then change the ending. This exploration of alternative endings allows them to ask "what if" questions and explore alternative emotional responses of the characters. Teachers can support this exploration by asking children how the new ending changes the characters' thoughts, feelings, and decisions (SEL building block component 4: *emotional regulation* and executive functioning), allowing students to openly explore in these areas to fully enhance their emotional learning. Guided play allows the teachers to informally assess and teach concepts and skills simultaneously in more than one learning domain (language, social-emotional, academic, physical, and so on).

I (Tracey) had the opportunity to work with preschool students in an elementary school. Each morning when the student came into the classroom, they would routinely put away their belongings and engage in *networking time*. This was a time they could take out play materials and engage in play, and they were encouraged to communicate with their peers (building block 2: *reciprocal engagement*). Sometimes I took the opportunity to just sit and watch them at play to get to know them better (likes or dislikes) or take notice of their social-emotional strengths or areas of need. At other times, I would engage in their play schemes and use probing or guiding questions to either informally assess, teach specific mathematics concepts focused on essential mathematics standards, or build their mathematics background knowledge and vocabulary. When I made that shift from observer to play partner, the child moved from engaging in unstructured self or peer partner play to guided play with a teacher.

In one of my guiding play experiences, two students were in the play kitchen, and I joined in their play scheme. At first I observed to see what they were doing, and then I gradually began to engage in their play scheme. I posed carefully crafted questions directed at their essential mathematics standards (sorting and counting) and modeled prosocial skills (using manners, sharing, and so on). In this scenario, students began to bring me all kinds of foods to pretend eat. After I had about twenty items, I said, "Wow, there are so many things here, and I'm noticing they are all different colors. I wonder if we could sort all the food." Immediately the students began to sort the objects by color, and I just sat back and observed. Next, I said, "Wow, I want to eat all the red foods! They look so yummy. Which ones do you want to eat?" The little girl took the yellow foods and the little boy took the green foods. Finally, I posed the question, "I wonder who has the most food?" In that moment, the students started counting their food items and communicating about how many they had and who had more. During this play experience, I was mindful to continuously model prosocial skills and behaviors. This didn't take very long, and when I left the play kitchen area, I heard one of the students say, "How many more do you have than me?" In that moment I was able to observe that this higher-level question being posed was very difficult for both students and they were not able to accurately determine "how many more" one student had over another. In this little time, I was able to see them use their social, emotional, and cognitive skills and skills relating to sorting and counting, as well as determine their needed next steps in mathematics concepts relating to comparison.

Often when we hear the word *play,* we think of our youngest learners, but what about the older elementary grades? Where does play come in there? While older students may be unsure of letting go and free playing in a way that lets out their emotional responses, there are many opportunities to allow them to play as well. Offering them opportunities to write and perform skits is an excellent way to let them act out those bigger feelings. I (Ann-Bailey) once worked with a fourth-grade teacher whose students would not sit quietly or engage in work with her unless they were participating in skits. Putting them in groups and allowing them to write and perform skits suddenly opened them up to sharing about themselves in a way they otherwise avoided. Their skits around SEL or when they reenacted stories for their literature reflected their daily lives.

You can embed play through role playing into lessons by acting out different events from history, putting on skits to retell a story read aloud (or adding a new ending to a familiar story the class read), or even acting out word problems. Small, short skits can allow children to engage with the material or act silly or even angry within a controlled environment. We discuss additional detail about the use of skits in the section on "SEL Projects" (page 204). Role playing is also an excellent way to allow students to problem solve and practice different social-emotional scenarios. Include these role plays into your weekly social-emotional lessons and ask students to identify multiple ways to solve a problem, identify an emotion, or be a friend. Often, allowing a child with pent-up anxiety to act as the "wrong" example gives that child permission to let their feelings out in a controlled and appropriate way. While it is not OK to yell at a teacher, it is OK to pretend to yell at the play teacher in one of these skits.

A weekly or monthly "Creative Thinking and Building" time is one play approach for upper elementary students that has the potential to also incorporate academic learning. This is a time during the week or month where students are given time and materials (old boxes, empty plastic containers, empty paper towel rolls, tape, scissors, markers, string, and so on) to engage in engineering and creatively design and build something. This is where students get to be creative and practice using social skills while working with a partner or group of peers. It is also a time where students might get a chance to practice previously learned science and mathematics skills (for example, estimating, measuring, or using knowledge about force or simple machines). In these situations, students are provided with an open-ended challenge such as "make a bridge that can hold a human's weight"—a direct instruction lesson on physics and engineering—and then given open-ended time to experiment with as many materials as they can. These labs lend themselves perfectly to developing the executive functioning skills of setting a goal, creating a plan to meet that goal, and pivoting from the plan as one becomes frustrated and recognizes that the original plan, materials, or goal was not going to work. While students are designing, building, and creating, the teacher is acting as a facilitator of social-emotional learning. The teacher can ask students to identify their goal and reflect on their plans to achieve that goal, comment on how the group is working together, recognize the emotional journey the students are on as they try and fail at their projects, and offer support for emotional-regulation strategies (SEL building block 4: *emotional regulation*) as students become frustrated. When students complete their creations, they can use literacy skills to write about what they created. They could simply engage in journaling about what was created or be guided to complete a more formal writing task during the language arts block. For example, if third graders are learning about persuasive letter writing, the students could write a persuasive letter to a company telling them why they should buy and sell what they made during their "Creative Thinking and Building" time.

Virtual Learning Tip

In the virtual setting, teachers can provide students with an open-ended challenge and a list of suggested materials students are likely to have around the house (such as cardboard cereal boxes, paper towel tubes, and newspaper). Students can create their projects in front of the camera while they work together, and the teacher is able to label and coach them through the executive functioning and self-regulation skills they are using. Alternatively, students can work on these projects during their asynchronous time and share their final projects when they return to the synchronous digital classroom.

Table 4.2 is a chart that shares examples of guided and unstructured play in various situations. Please note that we are not limiting play to these few areas; rather, this is just a sample so you can begin to see what guided or unstructured play might look like for your students.

Table 4.2: Opportunities and Examples of Play Throughout the School Day

Topic	Guided Play	Unstructured Play
Retelling or Reenactment Play	Teacher provides figures to act out a story with a group and participates in the retelling. The teacher may act out one of the characters or be the narrator to start the story.	The teacher provides figures that correspond with a book the class has read but does not stay in the area to guide the play. The students may use the characters to act out the book exactly, or may alter the story of the book, change a character's response to a problem in the book, or have the characters experience a new challenge.
Mathematics Games	The teacher assigns partners to play a specific game or offers the choice of specific games to play during a set amount of time. The teacher may monitor the game to ensure the students are on task and playing the game the correct way. The teacher may play with the students and model good sportsmanship, turn taking, and fair play.	During an open-ended block of time, students are allowed to access the mathematics games they are already familiar with. They choose their partners and may play the game as assigned or may create their own rules or variations. Students can also be given opportunities to create their own mathematics games using the skills they have learned. Teachers can provide a bin of materials that students may want to choose from when creating their game (blank gameboards, blank spinners they can write on, dice, and so on).
Dramatic Play	A teacher assigns students into groups and provides a general topic for the students to write and perform a skit around. The teacher may sit with a group to help them plan out the skit.	A group of students forms independently and creates a skit, play, or dramatic performance around a topic of their choice. The students may choose to record themselves outside of the classroom and share it with the class.
Makerspace or TinkerLab	The teacher provides instruction on an engineering or physics topic and then gives the students a challenge with set parameters. The students are given a set amount of time to use the materials in the makerspace or lab to fulfill the challenge.	A teacher provides students open-ended time in the makerspace or TinkerLab where they can explore the materials and create whatever they want.

Whether you are supporting unstructured play or guided play, many teachers struggle to find the time to incorporate play in their rigorous academic schedules. See chapter 5 (page 223) to learn about how to plan for the various types of play within your daily, weekly, or monthly schedule.

6. SEL-Focused Partner or Group Games

Maria inwardly groaned as she watched Maggie and Daniel team up to play the mathematics partner game she'd assigned. She normally assigned partners to prevent this from happening, but she'd forgotten this time. *I suppose,* she thought, *that this will be a good opportunity for them to practice their SEL skills. I hope there is not a big outburst.* Playing games throughout the day tended to be a cause of problems with many of her students who want to win. For Daniel, games often caused frustration with waiting his turn, deciding who will go first, and playing fairly. Losing seemed to be so upsetting to him. *Yet,* Maria thought, *games are a part of life, and being able to lose is a fairly critical life skill. I can't just send Daniel to the office every time we are going to play a game, and I know that using games in mathematics can be a very powerful and effective teaching strategy. Something has to change here.*

Another interactive teaching strategy already embedded into classroom routines is group and partner games. As with play, these games allow students to naturally engage in SEL building block 2: *reciprocal engagement.* These games are also an avenue for directly teaching social-emotional learning skills to students. There are several ways to use partner or group games to either teach SEL skills or provide opportunities for students to practice these skills with their peers. In figure 4.14, we list five different ways to use partner or group games to teach SEL to elementary students. We will discuss each of these five ways in the following sections.

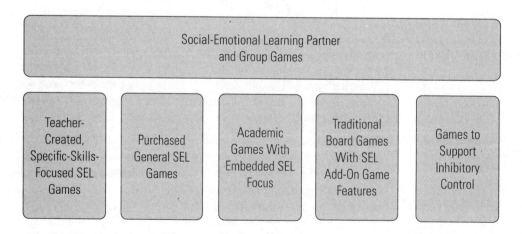

Figure 4.14: Types of SEL partner or group games.

The following sections will go into further detail on these five types of SEL partner or group games: (1) teacher-created, specific-skills-focused SEL games; (2) purchased general SEL games; (3) academic games with embedded SEL focus; (4) traditional board games with SEL add-on game features; and (5) games to support inhibitory control.

Teacher-Created, Specific-Skills-Focused SEL Games

A teacher team can use social-emotional games to teach students specific SEL skills within the targeted SEL building blocks. For example, figure 4.15 depicts an SEL standard, written in student-friendly language, that we shared in the student SEL goal card in figure 4.4 (page 165).

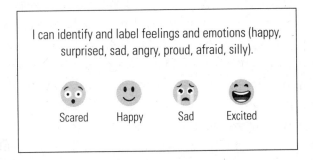

Figure 4.15: Essential SEL standard in student-friendly language.

Imagine a team of teachers creating a set of cards that have a scenario that matches a picture of an emotion (see figure 4.16). Students can use this one set of cards for multiple games. They can work together to simply match the scenario with the emotion. Give each student a card and ask them to find someone in the classroom that has the corresponding card, or use the set of cards to play the games Go Fish and Memory. Once you create your cards, you can place the set of cards in a plastic baggie and label it with the student-friendly SEL *I can* statement so it is visible to students.

Figure 4.16: SEL matching emotions card game example.

You can use games like this, which the team creates and specifically focuses around grade-level SEL skills and concepts, during designated playtime, student choice time, or indoor recess, or use them for small-group instruction. You can also send cards home for students to use and play with their families.

Purchased General SEL Games

In addition to creating specific targeted social-emotional learning games, there are social-emotional board games or various SEL learning activities students can use with a computer or a tablet that schools can purchase for student use. Keep in mind that using digital platforms to teach SEL skills does not include SEL building block 2 (*reciprocal engagement*). While there is value in these games and activities, they cannot serve in place of meaningful interactions with the teacher and peers.

With so much academic content to teach, it can be difficult to find time for students to play SEL games. We suggest having students play these games during embedded playtime (indoor recess, scheduled choice time built into the daily schedule, or at the end of the day during dismissal). Another time could be when students are finished with their independent work. Often teachers suggest that students read a book if they have completed their assigned task. As an alternative, a student could play a digital SEL game independently or find a partner (someone else who is also finished with their assigned task) to play the SEL board game. Additionally, teachers might want to find time to build specific SEL learning time into their daily or weekly schedule. In this scenario, using a workshop model, students could engage in independent learning with the use of a computer or tablet, or students could play an SEL board game with a partner or small group. This structure would then free up the teacher to work with smaller groups of students who may need more targeted SEL-focused instruction.

We remind teachers that it is important to seek out quality social-emotional learning games that specifically connect to your grade-level SEL standards and match students' skill levels. Therefore, we suggest consulting the school counselor, the special education teacher, or the school's SEL team for advice on which games to use with students; or seeking out research-based SEL programs with embedded digital gaming components. Having students play SEL computer or tablet games, even daily, is not enough to support a student's learning of social-emotional concepts and skills. Rather, it is just one piece that has the potential to strengthen students' social-emotional learning when implemented effectively and used in addition to other effective teaching methods.

Academic Games With Embedded SEL Focus

Social-emotional learning can also happen when students engage in academic partner games. As anyone who has spent time around children can attest, games that involve winning and losing often cause big emotions. And at times, those big emotions can become distractions in the classroom. Teachers can be proactive in supporting these moments by embedding social-emotional learning supports within their academic game routines. For example, a teacher might use sentence frames or sentence starters to help students engage in fair play (SEL building blocks 3: *social awareness*;

and 5: *logical and responsible decision making*) and practice social communication skills (SEL building block 2: *reciprocal engagement*) with one another during specific content-focused game playing with a group or partner (see figure 4.17).

While playing a game with a friend, I can:

1. Greet my partner

2. Take turns

3. Ask questions using a kind tone

4. Use kind and encouraging words during the game, such as "Can you please give me the dice?" or "Your turn."

5. Use self-talk and my strategies to stay calm and focused

6. Win or lose—use encouraging, kind words after the game or shake hands (or fist bump, elbow tap, or air high-five) with my partner: "Nice game!" or "You can go first this time since I went first last time."

Figure 4.17: SEL partner game guide.

If students are to learn these skills, teachers must directly teach and model these skills before allowing students to practice with teacher guidance. On an anchor chart, the students and the teacher can create a set of prosocial skills or regulation strategies (see figure 4.17) to use while playing games. Next, the teacher can play and model the skills listed on the anchor chart with a student partner. In this scenario, the game-playing partners sit in the center as the rest of the class sits around them in a circle, observing them play the game (fishbowl modeling activity). The teacher can stop along the way asking the students in the class questions: *What did I do to greet my partner before we started the game? Why do you think greeting your partner is important? What did you notice about my tone of voice throughout the game?* The teacher will also want to model examples of fair appropriate play and unfair inappropriate play, as well as examples of *self-talk*. To do this, the teacher might pause during the game and turn to the student audience and say, "This is what I'm thinking in my brain: *Right now at this part of the game, I'm noticing that I'm getting really anxious, I can feel my palms beginning to get a little sweaty, and I'm holding my breath a little bit more than usual on each of my turns. I feel like I might lose this game, and I'm feeling really frustrated. Last time I didn't win I got really upset and flipped the game board; maybe this time I shouldn't do that. It's OK if I don't win this one time; maybe I can ask my partner if we can play another round and maybe I'll win in the next round.*"

For routine practice, the teacher can print out the prosocial skills and regulation strategies the students generated onto small cards and store them with the academic games that students play. Or, teachers can create one larger card that students can use with any game they play within the classroom. It is important to teach students this classroom routine and have them practice getting the SEL Partner Game Guide during any type of partner or group play. This guide serves as a visual reminder to the students. These *I can* cards should include more visuals and fewer words for younger students. Students can reflect on their own game play if this list is given to them on small paper copies with check boxes. After a few rounds, students can use this as a self-reflection tool to help them recognize their own actions during the game (see figure 4.18). Paper copies can be created and collected as data and evidence of students using SEL skills or these templates can be laminated or put into dry-erase sleeves for repeated use.

While playing a game with a friend, I can:

☐ Greet my partner

☐ Take turns

☐ Ask questions using a kind tone

☐ Use kind and encouraging words during the game such as "Can you please give me the dice?" or "Your turn."

☐ Use self-talk and my strategies to stay calm and focused

☐ Win or lose—use encouraging, kind words after the game or shake hands with my partner: "Nice game!" or "You can go first this time since I went first last time."

☐ Other skills I used

Figure 4.18: SEL partner game self-assessment card.

*Visit **go.SolutionTree.com/instruction** for a free reproducible version of this figure.*

Traditional Board Games With SEL Add-On Game Features

Social-emotional skills can be taught through the use of traditional strategic board games like Monopoly, Chutes and Ladders, and others. Traditional board games innately require students to use wait time and take turns, use communication and listening skills, and follow a set of directions. The use of these board games supports the building of social-emotional skills as well as important mathematics and literacy skills (such as oral communication). To create better student awareness of these social-emotional skills, teachers can add on additional social-emotional components to traditional board games. For instance, teachers can introduce a set of SEL game cards to go along with traditional board games (see figure 4.19 and figure 4.20). In this example, each student starts a board game with six social-emotional skills cards (figure 4.19) and a social-emotional game board mat (figure 4.20). The goal is to receive and give away social-emotional cards throughout the game. By both receiving and giving away cards during the game, students can earn an extra turn or move spaces ahead or back to strategically help them win the game.

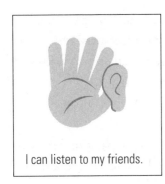

I can listen to my friends.

I can show good sportsmanship.

I can be patient and wait my turn.

I can follow directions.

I can show honesty.

I can use a respectful tone/voice and words.

Figure 4.19: Social-emotional "I can" game cards.

*Visit **go.SolutionTree.com/instruction** for a free reproducible version of this figure.*

Place the 1st card that you receive here.	Place the 2nd card that you receive here.	Place the 3rd card that you receive here.	Place the 4th card that you receive here.
Check off a star or place a marker on a star every time you give out a card during the game.			
⭐	⭐	⭐	⭐
You get an extra turn if you gave 1 card and got 1 card. . . . Extra turn!	You get an extra turn or get to move ahead 1 space if you gave 2 cards and got 2 cards. . . . Extra turn or move up 1 space	You get an extra turn or get to move ahead 2 spaces if you gave 3 cards and got 3 cards. . . . Extra turn or move up 2 spaces	You get to choose if you get an extra turn or move up or back 1, 2, or 3 spaces if you gave 4 cards and got 4 cards. YOU CHOOSE . . . Extra turn or move up or back 1, 2, or 3 spaces

Figure 4.20: Social-emotional game board mat.

*Visit **go.SolutionTree.com/instruction** for a free reproducible version of this figure.*

This is just one idea of adding on SEL features to traditional board games. We encourage and challenge you and your teammates to use your creativity and talents to come up with other ideas where students can practice social-emotional skills and prosocial behaviors across the school setting.

Games to Support Inhibitory Control

Not all games require the use of tangible items or extensive preparation. You can use playful whole-group games or organized activities like obstacle courses (Lillas & Turnbull, 2009) to support students' ability to control their impulses, stop on demand, and attend to social cues. You can embed these games into morning meeting or shorten and use them during transitions. Games like Red Light, Green Light are prevalent in early childhood classrooms but are not seen as often in middle and upper elementary classrooms. Yet these games are often exactly what students need to support their social-emotional regulation in a safe setting. The disappointment or frustration a child feels during a game when they lose their impulse control and act without thinking is a smaller version of their emotional response when faced with a larger problem. Aside from asking the child to practice using impulse control, these games allow children to experience those moments of frustration, practice using self-calming strategies, and develop competence in coping with those emotions.

You can also incorporate these games into the transition periods discussed previously (page 159). The following are some games that you can include throughout your day that are appropriate for all ages.

- **Stop, Watch, Follow Along:** One student leaves the room and the class begins to mime a pattern by clapping, foot stomping, and so on (two claps, two foot stomps, tap shoulders, repeat). Once the class has learned the pattern, the student outside the room is invited back in to join. The goal for this student is to first stop and watch the group to learn the pattern and then to follow along. Students who try to jump in before watching will often get the pattern wrong. This game supports the inhibitory response as well as social awareness of following the cues of others (Bellini, 2016, pp. 167–168).

- **Find the Leader:** This game is similar to Stop, Watch, and Follow Along as one student leaves the room. This time, the teacher chooses a leader to create a pattern and change it sporadically. The rest of the class must copy the leader and change when the leader changes. (For instance, the leader might start with a clap, stomp, clap pattern but change to clapping twice and stomping once.) The student returns to the room and must watch the group to identify who the leader is. This game encourages the student to use the social cues of others to find the leader, while the other students must also use social cues to copy the movement patterns (social awareness building block).

- **Silent Imaginary Speed Ball:** The students stand in a circle large enough so that everyone can see each other. The teacher throws an imaginary ball to someone in the circle, and that person is expected to throw it to someone else. Because there is not a real ball, this game requires students to track social cues and eye contact, as well as use impulse control to not just jump at the pretend ball. The game becomes more fun once the teacher models funny catches or throwing the ball in dramatic ways, such as catching the ball as though it hurt.

- **Mirror Game:** In this game students can either be in pairs or follow one group leader. The idea is for one person to act as the mirror of the partner or leader and to copy their movements and behaviors exactly. This works skills within the reciprocal engagement, social awareness, and social-emotional regulation blocks, particularly in the area of inhibitory control.

- **Laughing Tissue:** The teacher stands on a chair and releases a tissue into the air. The class is allowed to laugh as hard as they can as long as the tissue is falling, but as soon as it touches the ground everyone must be silent. This works on inhibitory control in the social-emotional regulation building block.

- **Freeze Dance:** The teacher plays music as the class dances, and when the music stops, the class freezes. Anyone moving after the music stops must sit down. This targets the students' ability to control their movements and stop on demand (social-emotional regulation). These dance parties can also include going from dancing quickly to suddenly moving slowly. Asking students to shift movements from fast to slow or from fast to freezing allows them to practice this modulation of movements (Lillas & Turnbull, 2009).

- **"Do _____ when I say _____":** Teachers can use this version of Simon Says for preparing students to listen and attend to the teacher for transitions. The teacher gives students a set of directions (for example, hop up and down, do jumping jacks, find a partner) and tells them not to move until they say "go" (or the targeted word). The teacher then says anything besides go (goldfish, gold, gopher) and the students must listen carefully to hear the correct word. This game works best if it is used during a transition when the teacher begins using an animated voice and high affect and then slowly down-regulates their body language and voice until they finally whisper "go."

- **Obstacle Courses:** Obstacle course games and activities ask students to practice their ability to follow a sequence of movement activities while regulating themselves and modulating their movements to follow the course (Lillas & Turnbull, 2009).

> **Virtual Learning Tip**
>
> There are many interactive partner games available to use in the virtual classroom. Though the setting is different, the concept is the same. We recommend exploring Theresa Will's website (www.theresawills.com/games) for virtual interactive game recommendations.

7. SEL Journal Writing

> "Today is the *worst day ever!*" Maggie yelled as she stormed to her seat after Maria asked her to take a break from playing a partner game. Maria sighed. For Maggie, every day was the worst day ever. Maria mentioned this to the school counselor, who suggested having Maggie start journaling about her day to reflect on both the good and the challenging times of the day. *That's a great idea,* Maria thought, *for my students that like to write. In fact, I'm going to try that with all my students. But Maggie and Daniel hate writing! How can I help them to journal their feelings as well?*

As you introduce the new SEL building blocks or SEL competencies in your SEL curriculum, students can reflect on these ideas in journals. Journaling is an excellent way for students to individually show what these new concepts mean to them. This can become a daily or weekly routine done at the start of a student's day or after a student finishes an assigned learning task (for example, instead of reading a book when a student completes an assigned task, they can journal). We have provided a list of general SEL-focused journal prompts in the appendix as guidance (figure A.9, page 331), but we feel strongly that the prompts should be team generated and specifically designed to target essential SEL grade-level standards or to support students' individual SEL needs.

Also, consider allowing students to pair drawing with their writing, or encourage them to create a graphic novel that portrays their feelings and thoughts on the given topic (see figure 4.21). Graphic novels break down thoughts into small boxes, encouraging students to think in a linear, cause-and-effect manner, which is essential for comprehending SEL. In using the graphic novel approach, you can place the main problem-solving situation in the center of a pre-created comic strip. Then, ask the students to draw and write what happened before and after that social situation (see figure 4.22). This supports the students' SEL building blocks 4 (*social-emotional regulation*) and 5 (*logical and responsible decision making*).

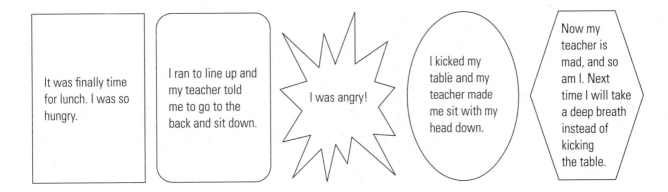

Figure 4.21: SEL comic strip journaling activity (student example).

*Visit **go.SolutionTree.com/instruction** for a free blank reproducible version of this figure.*

Figure 4.22: SEL comic strip journaling activity—template.

Outside of specific journaling, include SEL skills in your traditional writing workshop. Encourage your students to reflect on how their character feels, what made their character feel that way, and how the character is going to solve their problems. If the student is writing a personal narrative, use graphic organizers to have the student draw out their emotions from a specific event and record them on the paper (see figure 4.23, page 202, and figure 4.24, page 202). Remind them that including what a character is thinking and feeling creates a more powerful experience for the reader.

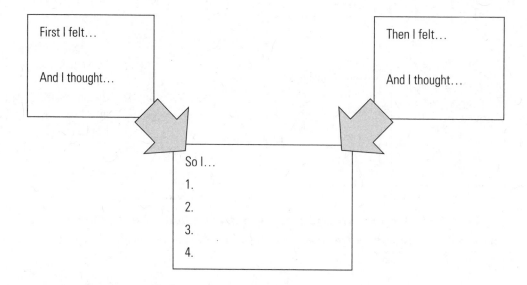

Figure 4.23: First/then feelings organizer.

*Visit **go.SolutionTree.com/instruction** for a free reproducible version of this figure.*

Figure 4.24: Emotion and action chain graphic organizer.

*Visit **go.SolutionTree.com/instruction** for a free reproducible version of this figure.*

Students also benefit from maintaining daily journals that allow them to track their day-to-day emotions (SEL building block 1: *self-awareness*). This is especially useful for students with all-or-nothing thinking, who may end their day thinking, "This was the worst day, ever!" even though they had a great day until someone stepped on their foot at the end of the day.

Emotional tracking journals will also support your goal-setting work. Ask students to reflect on how they feel after they get back a test, and have them make a goal and plan for the upcoming unit (see figures 4.25 and 4.26).

Figure 4.25: Daily emotional tracking journal.

*Visit **go.SolutionTree.com/instruction** for a free reproducible version of this figure.*

Date: 1/12

A.M.:

I felt:
Happy

Big event:
Fun in math!

P.M.:

I felt:
Lonely

Big event:
No one to talk to at lunch

Figure 4.26: Daily emotional tracking journal—student example.

Virtual Learning Tip

In the virtual classroom, teacher teams can provide their students with journaling templates through collaborative digital platforms such as interactive boards, slides, or documents. Students may enjoy these digital journals' font, color, and template options as a way to better express themselves. Or, using paper or a blank notebook, students can create a physical journal, which can include personal drawings and personal artwork.

8. SEL Projects

> *Man,* Maria found herself thinking, *it has been one long year! But I'm so proud of how I've been able to notice what my students need and can embed it into the day. The end of the year is going much smoother than the beginning did, and I see real change in Daniel and overall SEL growth in all my students. Now that our team has done this work together, it should be easier to put into place next year.*
>
> *One team goal for next year is to increase our use of projects. I shared with my team how Daniel took so much ownership of the project I gave the class at the end of the year, and my teammates also noticed the same for many of the students in their classrooms as well. In fact, it was the most engaged we saw some of our students. As I reflected with my teammates, I wondered aloud if I could have used project-based learning earlier in the year to not just engage Daniel but help him develop his emotional regulation. We all agreed that this would have truly been good for all our students and not just Daniel, so we decided that we would plan for putting project-based learning earlier in the year and find ways to continuously incorporate it into our current curriculum.*

The use of projects and presentations is a great way to engage learners and integrate multiple curriculum areas, including SEL. These presentations could be done independently or within a small group or with a partner. John Hattie (2009), in his book *Visible Learning*, states that reciprocal teaching is an effective practice used for student learning. In addition to supporting student learning, this work also creates opportunities for students to practice SEL building blocks 2 (*reciprocal engagement*) and 5 (*logical and responsible decision making*). Using this learning structure, students learn through the process of creating and teaching concepts and ideas to their peers, and in turn by being taught the concepts and skills through presentations and projects their peers create. Instead of the traditional model of the teacher instructing the students, in this scenario the students are teaching each other, and the teacher is acting as a facilitator. Students can teach their peers and present the social-emotional learning in various formats. Students can create SEL presentations (see figure 4.27) using various digital presentation software and videos. Also, students could present SEL skills and concepts by using visual poster presentations, acting out social situations in skits or plays, or creating their own SEL-focused songs.

Students can also engage themselves in learning through various SEL projects that specifically support literacy and writing skills (see figure 4.28). Ideas may include creating comic strips, bookmarks, magazines or newspaper articles, and stories that teach specific SEL concepts or skills.

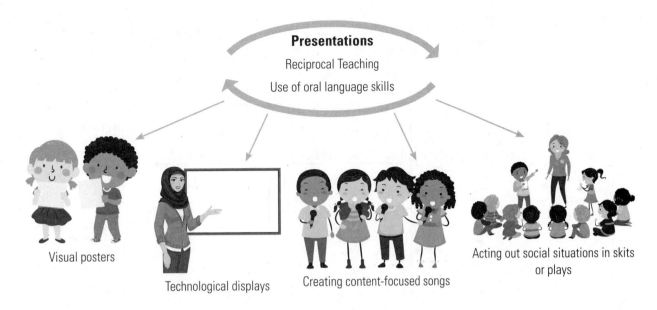

Figure 4.27: Using reciprocal teaching methods with SEL presentations.

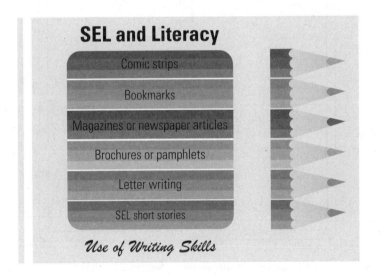

Figure 4.28: Connecting SEL and literacy with SEL projects.

Some upper elementary teachers have their classes pair up with younger primary classes and have their students read to younger students (or the younger students read to the older students). Another option is having upper-grade-level students gear their SEL projects toward younger students instead of creating and presenting them to their grade-level peers. It might also be important to use scaffolds to help students create their SEL projects. Figure 4.29 (page 206) is a graphic organizer that students can use when creating social stories. Dexter and Hughes (2011) find that using graphic organizers can support students (particularly students with learning disabilities) with making abstract concepts more concrete and help in transferring knowledge and ideas in new or unusual situations. Christopher Kaufman (2010) breaks down the executive functioning skills necessary during the writing process and states that teachers should require all students to use prewriting processes and organizers, not just those with learning disabilities.

SEL Short Stories

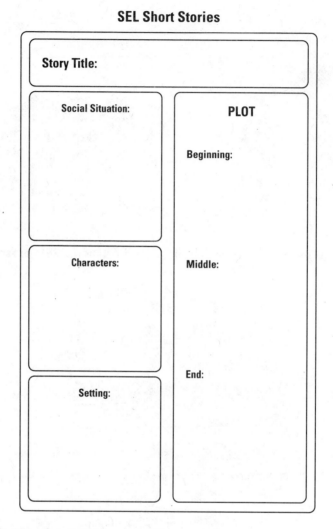

Figure 4.29: SEL short stories graphic organizer.
*Visit **go.SolutionTree.com/instruction** for a free reproducible version of this figure.*

Social stories help to describe social situations in life and can be used to teach students about social behaviors and social expectations in everyday life (SEL building block 3: *social awareness*). They can also be used to help students learn about self-concepts and emotions and how our actions (both positive and negative) can affect ourselves and those around us. Historically, social stories have been used to teach students who have difficulty understanding social situations and communicating. However, we argue that social stories are effective for all students.

In addition to writing social stories, students can create their own SEL skits. Figure 4.30 is a sample graphic organizer that students could use to create short SEL skits with several scenes. In addition to these graphic organizers, students may need additional scaffolds to be put into place. Martha Larkin (2002) states:

The ultimate academic goal is for students to become independent lifetime learners, so that they can continue to learn on their own or with limited support. Scaffolding instruction optimizes student learning by providing a supportive environment while facilitating student independence.

Therefore, we feel that at first students may need examples of social scenarios (see figure 4.31, page 208) that they can choose from as they begin to generate their own social stories or social scenes in skits. These social scenarios should align to the grade-level SEL essential standards. In fact, it is best practice to have all SEL projects align to the grade-level essential standards. The samples we provide for you are just that—examples—so that your team can begin to see what this work can look like. The real work and learning come from what you generate together as a team.

SEL Skit or Play

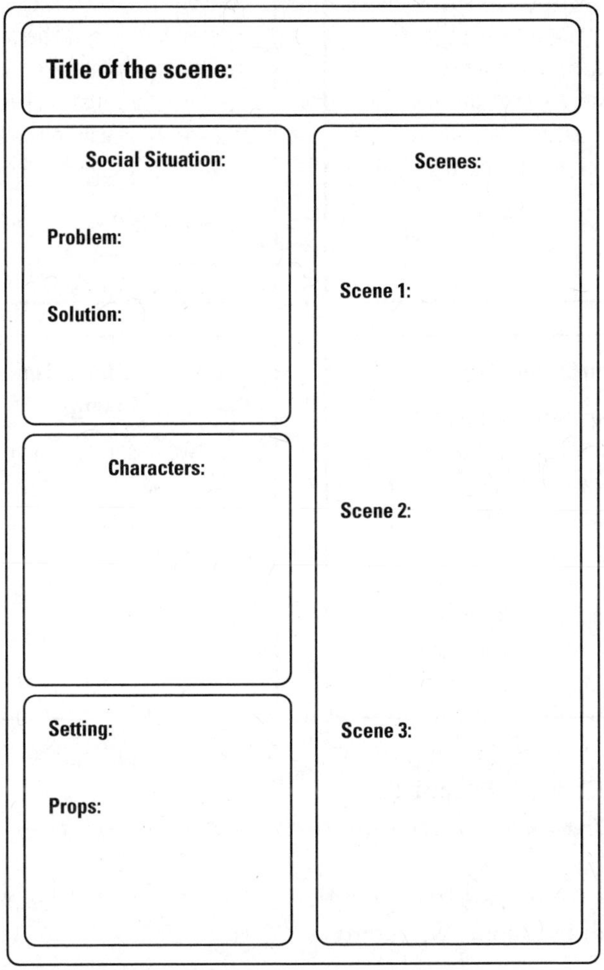

Title of the scene:

Social Situation:	Scenes:
Problem:	
Solution:	Scene 1:
Characters:	Scene 2:
Setting:	Scene 3:
Props:	

Figure 4.30: SEL skit or play organizer.

*Visit **go.SolutionTree.com/instruction** for a free reproducible version of this figure.*

SEL Social Scenarios

Social Situation 1: Joining in Play

A student is out at recess and wants to join in playing with a group of students playing basketball. What can the student do to join in? What shouldn't the student do?

Social Situation 2: Changing Plans

You and your friends have a plan to play soccer at recess, but no one brought out the soccer balls today. What are you thinking and feeling? What can you and your friends do instead?

Social Situation 3: Active Listening

A student in class wants to share what happened to her this weekend. She is talking, but there is a substitute teacher and some students are not listening to her. What is active listening? What does active listening look like? What does it not look like?

Social Situation 4: Taking Perspective

Everyone is excited to eat pizza and watch a movie for the class party but your best friend. She has allergies and cannot eat the pizza with the class. How is she feeling? What can you do to help her feel included and still have fun?

Social Situation 5: Fair Play

What does *being fair* during play look like? Think about examples of fair play in school and outside of school. What are nonexamples of fair play? What emotions do people feel during fair play, and what emotions do people feel when play is not fair? What strategies can a person use if they are in a situation where play is not fair?

Social Situation 6: Logical Decision Making

Your two best friends both want to play different games during recess. How can you talk to both of them to find a solution all three of you are happy with?

Figure 4.31: SEL social scenarios.

*Visit **go.SolutionTree.com/instruction** for a free reproducible version of this figure.*

Project-based learning (PBL) is another great way to integrate social-emotional learning. According to John W. Thomas (2000):

> Project-based learning (PBL) is a model that organizes learning around projects. According to the definitions found in PBL handbooks for teachers, projects are complex tasks, based on challenging questions or problems, that involve students in design, problem-solving, decision making, or investigative activities; give

students the opportunity to work relatively autonomously over extended periods of time; and culminate in realistic products or presentations (Jones, Rasmussen, & Moffitt, 1997; Thomas, Mergendoller, & Michaelson, 1999). (p. 1)

Often project-based learning incorporates multiple academic content areas. Social-emotional learning typically occurs naturally through the process of project-based learning, but it can also be directly planned for and embedded into PBL. Projects can also be an avenue for building relationships with families as families can be encouraged to contribute to the process. Additionally, students can use technology to enhance their projects.

In fact, in the 21st century, technology has become a huge part of our everyday lives. In fact, if not for technology, our students' ability to learn and stay connected during the COVID-19 quarantine period would have been very limited. Despite the necessity of technology to connect us, there continues to be much debate about the use of technology by our youngest learners: How does it affect their health? How long should children be allowed on devices? And how does technology impact children's learning itself? As we learned during the pandemic, the use of technology should not be an either-or situation; rather, it should be a discussion of how we teach with and without technology in today's education system and how we can use technology to enhance student communication and teach the skills students need in our ever-changing world full of advancing technology.

Technology should not replace good instruction facilitated by a classroom teacher, but teachers can use it to engage students and enhance the learning of skills and concepts. In fact, Linda Darling-Hammond, Molly B. Zielezinski, and Shelley Goldman (2014) found that for the use of technology to have an impact on student learning, it must be effectively implemented, interactive, and used by students to explore and create.

Previously we discussed the possibility of using technology with daily or weekly routines (videos and interactive whiteboard presentations). Interactive whiteboard programs, various computer-presentation-based software, or online programs that offer digital presentation platforms or slideshows can all be used to support students in creating SEL presentations and projects with or for their peers. We also previously discussed the instructional practice of journaling (page 200). Teachers may consider having students use digital journals and store them on a shared server where the teacher can engage in the *reciprocal engagement* building block with students by responding to or commenting on their journal entries. Teachers can also show SEL videos in either large or small groups and then facilitate rich and meaningful discussions around what the students viewed, or students can embed these SEL videos in their projects.

Virtual Learning Tip

Ongoing SEL projects can be assigned in the virtual environment as well, encouraging students to become creative when they are away from the screen. This can be an opportunity to encourage them to build their relationships with their families.

---

9. Teachable Moments

Maria's class came to gather for morning meeting, but as they sat down, the circle they made was not big enough for Daniel to fit. Maria inwardly groaned, knowing that this small problem could set Daniel's day on the wrong foot. Suddenly, she had an idea.

"Hmmm . . ." she said, modeling thinking aloud. "I notice that there is not enough room for everyone on the carpet. I notice that Daniel is still coming to join us but there is not enough room for him." As the class glanced around at each other, Maria turned to Daniel. "Daniel, when you walk over here, I wonder what you can do? First, I bet you can look at the circle and see where there might be room for someone to move. It looks like there is room between Imron and Sally. Do you think you could tap Imron on the shoulder and ask if he can scoot over?" Daniel looked confused by this, as he normally pushes his way into the circle, causing yelling and complaining from the other students. Imron turned to look at him and nodded, preferring this idea to being pushed. Maria continued, "Daniel, let's try. Carefully walk up to Imron and put out one finger. Yes, just like that. OK, now tap him lightly on the shoulder. You can say quietly, 'Can you move over?'" Maria coached Daniel through asking for space on the carpet and waited patiently while the class all shifted their positions so that Daniel had room. Once everyone was situated, Maria turned to her class and said, "Wow, you all were problem solvers today. We had a problem—there was not enough room for everyone—and you worked together to solve it. Daniel, you did a great job recognizing there was a problem and calmly finding a solution." Daniel, clearly proud of this, beamed. "Now," Maria continued, "we are ready to begin morning meeting. Make sure your eyes are on me!"

To herself, Maria laughed. *That could have been a disaster!* she thought. *In the moment, it felt like it took an hour to get everyone situated, but it was only about ninety seconds. If I'd let them work it out themselves, or if I had just told Imron to move over, there still would have been pushing, and in the end I would have given up a lot more time than ninety seconds—only to repeat the same chaos tomorrow. Hopefully, now that they feel ownership of this problem-solving routine, they will try it out again tomorrow!*

Leading experts and researchers in the field of SEL (Greenberg et al., 2017) share that educators should not only teach social-emotional skills, but they also model them and provide students with opportunities to practice and apply these skills throughout the school day in various settings and situations. Although we often carefully plan our specific SEL lessons, true learning moments happen throughout the day, whether we plan for them or not. These are moments we can use to support our students' SEL development. At times, taking advantage of these moments may require spontaneous responses to a situation that arises in our classroom, or pausing from a lesson to address a social-emotional need, but often allowing for this spontaneity means that the real learning can occur.

We have placed these teachable-moment strategies into three categories: (1) teacher modeling, (2) student modeling, and (3) student problem solving. In figure 4.32 you will note some of the specific strategies you can implement during your day to respond to students' needs.

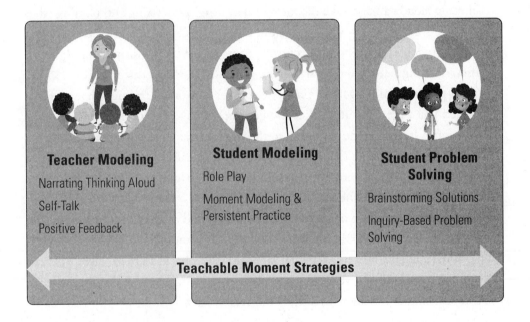

Figure 4.32: Teachable moment strategies.

Teacher Modeling: Narrating Thinking Aloud, Self-Talk, and Positive Feedback

As teachers, we know that we almost always have students' eyes on us throughout the day, even when we are trying to take a moment to ourselves. One way to reinforce social-emotional learning is to outwardly model applying those SEL strategies yourself. Students are far more likely to learn from watching you than they are from being told what to do.

This can happen in little moments. Imagine trying to start a lesson, but you cannot find a dry-erase marker that is not dried out. Say that aloud to the class—a strategy called *narrating aloud.* "Man, this is frustrating. All of these markers are dried out!

Every time I think 'OK, here is one that will work,' I find another one that does not work. I'm getting so frustrated. I'd better take a deep breath. I'm going to take a sip from my water bottle and think about a backup plan. Oh! Now I remember! I have other markers in the cabinet." While this sounds like a lot of talking in front of the class, it fills the time when you are looking for the marker (when students are likely to become off-task anyway) and models how you identify your emotion, use a calm-down strategy, and problem solve. This strategy also builds your relationship with the students because you are sharing your real-life secret: that you are human, just like them.

Narrating your thoughts aloud models two strategies we want the students to apply. It shows how adults identify their own emotions and then use *self-talk* to walk themselves through a problem. This can happen in both academic and social situations. In academics, this may look like showing a mathematics problem on the board and saying, "Wow, I wonder how I should start this. What if I . . ." In academic settings, this type of modeling during lessons can be planned ahead of time.

Thinking aloud can also take the form of narrating, or noticing and naming what you observe students doing well (Johnston, 2004). This is particularly helpful when you notice students making positive choices, using their SEL skills, applying a growth mindset, or using self-regulating strategies. For some students this may come in the form of a private comment like, "Carlos, I notice you worked through that problem even when you were frustrated. Nice job getting a drink of water and then coming back to work." It can also be addressed to the whole class: "I notice there are students who are carefully checking their work before handing it in. I know I like to get work finished quickly and it is hard to pause and take time to look at my work. That takes self-control." Be careful when you are providing positive feedback to students that you are not publicly calling on the same student over and over again (Denton, 2007). Attempt to keep your observations broad and address what you notice the whole class doing. Some students may not want verbal positive feedback. In these cases, you can develop a secret signal to give them when they are showing these skills, or even write the compliment on a sticky note so they can read it later.

Utilizing this thinking aloud strategy may particularly help the areas of *social awareness* and *reciprocal engagement*. Some students who have difficulty with social awareness or maintaining a back-and-forth engagement with another person may benefit the most from being able to hear someone else's thoughts. To support reading social cues, the teacher models playing a new partner game. She may narrate, "I'm excited to play this partner game! First, I'm going to look at my partner's face. He looks really excited. I hope he doesn't want to go first because I want to go first. He is already holding the dice. I'd better ask him. Diego, do you want to go first because I want to go first. What should we do?" A teacher supporting extending reciprocal engagement may model having a fake conversation with someone and mid-conversation say "I'm thinking I need to go to the bathroom, and I am bored. Should I say that? Hmm . . . no, I'll answer his question first, and then say, 'excuse me' before I tell him I need to go to the bathroom."

Student Modeling: Role Play, Modeling in the Moment, and Persistent Practice

Having students model and practice using their SEL skills is necessary so that students are able to learn and apply the strategies. As we talked about in previous sections of this book, fully developing executive functioning and self-regulation strategies involves a motor (movement) component along with the cognitive component (Lillas & Turnbull, 2009). This can take on a variety of forms in the classroom.

In the beginning of the year or after longer breaks, it is beneficial to have students model and practice the rules and routines you expect them to follow. Ask them to go through the routine themselves and provide positive feedback of what they are doing. I (Ann-Bailey) often feel as though I am an announcer for a little-known Olympic sport: "Look how they carefully push in their chairs and come to the rug. I notice no one is going to the water fountain or trying to sharpen a pencil. They are walking directly to the carpet. I don't even hear their footsteps. I see that they want to talk to each other, but they don't! Look at that self-control!" After labeling what you observe, ask the students to label what they noticed the peer models doing.

A *role play* strategy, sometimes referred to as a *fishbowl activity*, can also be used when students are learning a new partner game, learning to use new classroom materials appropriately, or learning prosocial skills such as how to get someone's attention, how to ask for help, what to do if you accidentally spill something, or what to do after a classmate pushes you. Ask the students role playing to sit in the center or front of the group with the rest of the class sitting around them observing (as though in a glass fishbowl). Give the observing students the job of labeling what they notice is occurring inside the fishbowl. During this time, the teacher can act as the facilitator of the learning, by asking the students who are modeling to pause, and pose reflective questions to the group, or highlight important things that are happening with the student models.

Student modeling or role play can also be used to problem solve as a group. Assign students to small groups and give them a problem the class may be familiar with (for example, there are not enough glue sticks for each person to have one, it is too loud during indoor recess, or the basketball game at recess is becoming too competitive). Give the groups opportunities to generate possible solutions, and then ask them to create a skit using their solution. Bring the group back together and have them model the solutions for one another. This will reinforce the idea that there are multiple ways to solve a problem and will let more students have an opportunity to practice the solution through movement.

The strategy of student modeling and practicing can also be effective when done *in the moment*. After a student or the class makes a mistake, the teacher may want to ask them to model using a strategy the right way. This can be as simple as saying "Show me how you walk in the halls," or, "That was a lot of noise! Let's pause, take a breath, and try that again. This time look at your friend's face. What do you notice? He looks pretty upset that you took the marker from his hand. Show us how you can ask for the marker without making him upset." During these in-the-moment modeling and practice sessions, it is essential to keep your teacher emotions in check. Use a calm, neutral voice to show that we are all learning and that this is a part of the learning process.

This strategy can be especially helpful to bring a noisy or chaotic group of students back together, regulate them, and send them back to work. Bring the students to the gathering area and in a calm, low voice, let them know that they need to *practice* that transition. "We are a loud and active group today! Let's do some of our breathing exercises before we get back to work. We have a lot of high energy right now, and we need to lower that energy if we are going to do our independent reading." After walking through the regulating exercise, one by one, ask the students to model moving quietly to their workspace. Keep your voice calm and encouraging, and provide positive feedback as needed. Be sure to later reinforce what you did as a group to regain calm: "You all did a great job this afternoon during independent reading. We all started off as a bit crazy but once we recognized that we had too much energy to work we were able to use our strategies to calm down and accomplish our goal of a quiet independent reading block. Nicely done. That is not always easy."

Guided Student Problem Solving

As educators, we can support students' social-emotional development, particularly in the blocks of social-emotional regulation and logical and responsible decision making, by giving them the opportunity to solve problems themselves in a supported environment. This may look like holding a whole-group discussion to look at all sides of a question in an academic context like, "Should we, the American colonists, tell the British king we want to be our own country, or should we try to work it out and stay a part of Britain?" Teachers can also pose *inquiry-based* questions and facilitate discussions around historical injustices as well as real-world current events and inequities that impact students and their communities.

It can also be used as a way to solve real problems occurring in the classroom. One year I (Ann-Bailey) had a very active first-grade class. At one point in the year, I brought up to the class that the room arrangement was not working and asked them what they saw as some of the problems. We held this discussion in both whole and small groups to identify exactly what was not working about our room setup and how we could fix it. Being first graders, they had very elaborate ideas to fix some of the simpler problems, but in the end, we did end up with a room that flowed better for our specific needs (and had engaged in a powerful SEL opportunity).

When engaging students in these *brainstorming problem-solving discussions*, be sure to use the strategy listed previously of narrating your thoughts and observations about the process (see page 211). These are the moments where students may feel genuine frustration with the problem or each other. This is an excellent time to provide meaningful, in-the-moment positive feedback as students grapple with the problem at hand. Honor their frustration—it is a real feeling!—and gently coach them on using calm-down strategies to refocus. As a part of your narration, be sure to include labeling when you see students try an idea that does not work. This is a wonderful time to honor the idea and the attempt made, and to walk the students through identifying why the idea did not work and how they can build on the mistake to improve their idea.

Virtual Learning Tip

For virtual learning, you can use teacher modeling throughout lessons. It may be beneficial to use a visual cue, like touching your finger to your face, to differentiate between thinking aloud and the lesson itself. You can also easily adapt guided student problem solving to the virtual format, utilizing discussions in either the large group or small breakout rooms. Student modeling is a bit more difficult but can take the form of students recording themselves (with the help of their families) acting out solving problems such as solving connection difficulties, navigating the digital classroom interface, or finding needed school supplies. This is an opportunity to engage families in creating social-emotional learning skits so that students can practice these SEL skills with the support of their families. Involving the family has the added benefit of providing the student's outside-of-school support system with language to support the student in these skills. Be mindful of families' limitations in time and technology accessibility and make recording video skits a choice activity.

---

10. SEL Classroom Learning Centers and Menus

Daniel groaned loudly when he saw the assigned work. Although Maria knew he was capable of completing it, something about the assignment itself seemed daunting. *Why didn't Daniel have this reaction to the independent work this morning?* Maria wondered. Oh! The team had decided to try using a menu for students to choose how they wanted to practice their skills. Daniel, and really all the students, had responded so much better to having choice.

Setting up an SEL center within your classroom and teaching students about what they can do when they are finished with their work is a great way to embed SEL. Often teachers have set routines and procedures for students after they finish their assigned learning tasks within a particular subject area. In these situations, students don't need to ask the teacher what to do next as they already know what is expected. While some teachers allow students to read a book or complete additional work, another option is to have students use the SEL center or learning menus.

The SEL center can contain a menu of learning options that connect with SEL essential standards. These can include SEL-focused books to read, SEL partner games,

SEL games from a computer or tablet, and SEL projects. These projects can also connect with the academic curriculum so that students are connecting the topics together and synthesizing their learning (see chapter 5, page 223). Offering a menu is essential in this process because teachers have a better chance of students being engaged in SEL when the students are given the choice of the type of activity. Figure 4.33 shows a sample SEL learning center menu that students can choose from. The key to setting up a structure like this is to critically think through the organization of materials, provide students with clear expectations, and teach them specific procedures and routines. Teachers can set up a weekly routine of allowing students to share their projects. This could occur one day each week during morning meeting or at the end of the day on Fridays.

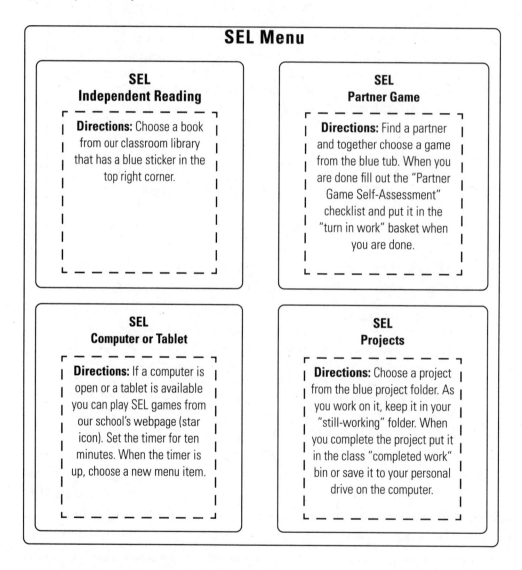

Figure 4.33: Learning center SEL menu.

> **Virtual Learning Tip**
>
> In the virtual environment, students may feel an additional need for agency and autonomy. Learning menus provide students with an opportunity to engage in the virtual classroom while making choices. Teachers can share these menus with both families and the students so there is a shared understanding of the students' choices.

By embedding your SEL instructional practices into your day-to-day academics through these ten strategies, you will maximize your students' access to SEL and increase their ability to generalize what they are learning throughout the school day. These strategies can either allow you to continue to teach your academic subjects without necessarily rearranging your day to add a separate SEL time frame, or enhance or support the existing current SEL curriculum you are using.

Connecting Multiple Practices to Deepen SEL

In this chapter, we offered ten instructional practices that teachers can use to teach and integrate social-emotional skills into academics and throughout the school day. Instructional approaches to teaching SEL should be based on the current needs of the students and align to the instructional strengths of a teacher and with the classroom environment. So, let's take a moment to think about what it would look like to pull multiple instructional practices together and plan for SEL instruction. Table 4.3 (page 218) provides a few examples of how a teacher might use and implement multiple SEL teaching practices and strategies within their classroom. Teachers may just start off focusing on one or two SEL practices and build in more practices and strategies over time. These practices may shift and change throughout the school year based on the needs of the students within the classroom. We suggest that teachers start off small, gradually build on what is working, and modify practices and strategies if needed.

Table 4.3: SEL Sample Classroom Scenarios

Sample Classroom Scenarios	SEL Teaching Practices and Strategies		
Classroom Teacher A	SEL transitions used throughout the entire school day	Daily SEL routine (displayed on interactive whiteboard)	Integrating SEL into morning meetings
Classroom Teacher B	SEL transitions used when students are moving to various parts of the school only (PE, music, art, lunch, recess, dismissal)	Daily calendar routine	Monthly planned PBL with academic and SEL focus
Classroom Teacher C	SEL student goal setting	Students reflect on a weekly SEL journal prompt on Friday mornings as their morning work	Integrate SEL reading comprehension strategies into all read-alouds

In figure 4.34, we display a teacher's planning approach to teaching SEL with the use of a learning progression and with student goal setting as a central theme for the learning. In this approach, each learning target is taught over the course of one week. All teaching resources connect to that one particular learning target. In this scenario, the teacher reads a book relating to the learning target, and while reading, focuses on reading comprehension strategies that we discussed earlier in the chapter (page 182). The teacher also focuses on a quick calendar routine and integrates SEL into the morning meetings each day. In addition to these instructional approaches, the teacher uses daily transitions as a way to integrate SEL throughout the day. Notice how targeted and connected to SEL this teacher's approach is in this scenario. When teachers and teacher teams meaningfully plan for SEL, they have a better chance of students making authentic connections to the learning, and save overall instructional time. In chapter 5 (page 223), we will discuss various planning tools that teachers can utilize to support SEL planning.

As teachers, we have limited time available to us during the school day. If we teach social-emotional learning skills through ineffective practices that do not deepen our students' understanding or connect with their daily lives, we can end up wasting time and not seeing meaningful change in our students. We must both directly teach these skills and then consistently integrate the skills into our daily routines and academic work to fully support students' SEL growth (Lillas & Turnbull, 2009).

November

Social-Emotional Learning Standards:

Monday	Tuesday	Wednesday	Thursday	Friday
I can identify and label feelings and emotions.	I can identify and label feelings and emotions.	I can identify and label feelings and emotions.	I can identify and label feelings and emotions.	I can identify and label feelings and emotions.

Book: *Glad Monster Sad Monster* by Ed Emberley and Anne Miranda Morning Meeting Activity or Calendar Activity	Book: *The Feelings Book* by Todd Parr Morning Meeting Activity or Calendar Activity	Book: *Lots of Feelings* by Shelley Rotner Morning Meeting Activity or Calendar Activity	Book: *The Color Monsters: A Story About Emotions* Morning Meeting Activity or Calendar Activity	Book: *Feelings and Dealings: The ABC's of Emotions: An SEL Storybook to Build Intelligence, Social Skills, and Empathy* Morning Meeting Activity or Calendar Activity
Monday	**Tuesday**	**Wednesday**	**Thursday**	**Friday**
I can identify what body feelings happen with different emotions.	I can identify what body feelings happen with different emotions.	I can identify what body feelings happen with different emotions.	I can identify what body feelings happen with different emotions.	I can identify what body feelings happen with different emotions.

Book: *Listening to My Feelings* by Michael Gordon Morning Meeting Activity or Calendar Activity	Book: *Listening to My Body* by Gabi Garcia Morning Meeting Activity or Calendar Activity	Book: *1–2–3, My Feelings and Me* by Goldie Millar and Lisa Berger Morning Meeting Activity or Calendar Activity	Book: *Exploring Emotions* by Paul Christelis Morning Meeting Activity or Calendar Activity	Book: *Wilma Jean, Worry Machine* by Julia Cook Morning Meeting Activity or Calendar Activity

Figure 4.34: SEL monthly theme.

continued →

Monday	**Tuesday**	**Wednesday**	**Thursday**	**Friday**
I can identify my feelings and emotions.	I can identify my feelings and emotions.	I can identify my feelings and emotions.	I can identify my feelings and emotions.	I can identify my feelings and emotions.

Book: *My Feelings and Me* by Holde Kreul	Book: *Today I Feel Silly and Other Moods That Make My Day* by Jamie Lee Curtis	Book: *I Feel: A Book About Recognizing and Understanding Emotions* by Cheri Meiners	Book: *The Way I Feel* by Janan Cain	Book: *The Boy With Big, Big Feelings* by Britney Winn Lee
Morning Meeting Activity or Calendar Activity	Morning Meeting Activity or Calendar Activity	Morning Meeting Activity or Calendar Activity	Morning Meeting Activity or Calendar Activity	Morning Meeting Activity or Calendar Activity
Monday	**Tuesday**	**Wednesday**	**Thursday**	**Friday**
I can express my feelings and emotions with appropriate words or actions.	I can express my feelings and emotions with appropriate words or actions.	I can express my feelings and emotions with appropriate words or actions.	I can express my feelings and emotions with appropriate words or actions.	I can express my feelings and emotions with appropriate words or actions.

Book: *The Angry Dragon* by Michael Gordon	Book: *Little Monkey Calms Down* by Michael Dahl	Book: *The Very Frustrated Monster* by Andi Green	Book: *Don't Feed the Worry Bug* by Andi Green	Books: *Hands Are Not for Hitting, Feet Are Not for Kicking,* or *Voices Are Not for Yelling* all by Elizabeth Verdick
Morning Meeting Activity or Calendar Activity	Morning Meeting Activity or Calendar Activity	Morning Meeting Activity and Calendar Activity	Morning Meeting Activity or Calendar Activity	Morning Meeting Activity or Calendar Activity

Conclusion

Chapter 4 provided ten practices to embed SEL into your classrooms: (1) transitions, (2) SEL student goal setting, (3) SEL daily routines, (4) picture book read-alouds and reading comprehension strategies, (5) social-emotional learning during play, (6) SEL-focused partner or group games, (7) SEL journal writing, (8) SEL projects, (9) teachable moments, and (10) SEL classroom learning centers and menus. The challenge for us as educators, of course, is planning for SEL so that our lessons and activities are purposeful and connected to students' lives. Chapter 5 (page 223) provides planning templates so that teams can create both yearlong and weekly plans, as well as templates to support intentionally planning how to integrate SEL into academics.

Tips for Administrators, Teachers, and Support Staff

Figure 4.35 contains tips and reflection questions relating to the contents of this chapter. As you consider these questions and next steps, reflect on your current practices in your own classroom and school.

Administrators	Teachers	Support Staff	Virtual Teaching Tips
• Check in with your teachers and teams to ensure they understand the purpose behind the activities and practices they choose to implement. If they are unsure of the reason behind a practice, how can your leadership team support them in building a stronger understanding? • In building your growth-mindset culture, do your teachers and teams feel comfortable in trying out these new practices? How can you model the expectation of trying, failing, reflecting, and trying again so that teams feel safe exploring new practices?	• Think about your current SEL practices within your classroom and determine what is working and effective. Think about one of the ten new SEL practices you may want to try. Consider which practice is the most manageable to integrate into your current routines. • Think about how you can use a team approach to implement these practices to share the workload and make the practices more manageable.	• How can you support teachers and students in trying out the new practices? What can you offer to the daily routine that will make the practices go smoothly? • Think about how the relationships you build with students support the activities in these routines. How can you maintain your positive interactions while encouraging students in goal setting, participating in transitions, morning meeting expectations, and other new challenges?	• Utilize your digital platform to encourage interactive participation throughout SEL activities. Encourage participation through chat boxes, interactive shared documents within a digital platform. • Digital activities are expanding daily for students! Explore ways to facilitate interactive game play. Keep in mind our students are often more comfortable with technology than we are! • Remember that your affect and connection with your students is even more important in this virtual world. As you read to students, share the morning message, or respond to their emotions, be sure you are using your facial expressions and voice to convey love and warmth.

Figure 4.35: Tips for administrators, teachers, and support staff from chapter 4.

CHAPTER 5

Effective SEL Lesson Planning

Vignette: Team Planning for SEL

Ana, a first-grade teacher on Maria's team, sits down at her team planning meeting on Wednesday afternoon. She feels exhausted after a busy day of keeping up with her class. After fifteen years of teaching, somehow it feels like the job is getting harder. She always told herself she wouldn't be one of those teachers who complained about "kids today" but now she's started to catch herself thinking it. She spends more time breaking up arguments and teaching children how to calm down and recover from disappointment than she did when she first started teaching. What's going on? And now she must somehow facilitate her team meeting. Luckily, they are going to be addressing exactly what she's worried about—how to teach social-emotional skills.

Padmaja (School counselor): *I'm looking forward to diving into how we can teach and embed the social-emotional learning standards into your day and within your daily lessons. I think that it is more valuable if we incorporate this learning into students' daily learning versus me just coming in each week to teach one lesson. I still plan on coming into each of your classrooms one time per week, but I'd like us to plan these lessons together, and I'd like to team-teach with each of you. We most likely are going to find that devoting time to these skills in your up-front lessons will save you time in the long run.*

Maria (First-grade teacher): *It had better. I can't add anything else into my day. Our students need every second of instruction to close the gap in reading and mathematics.*

Ana (First-grade teacher): *True. This overwhelms me, but I also know that most of my instruction is interrupted by the missing skills we are discussing here. Something must change. Our reading and mathematics lessons can be great, but if our students are missing social-emotional skills they will not be able to have full access to the learning within our lessons.*

Tom (English language learner teacher): *Think of it as an equity issue. We can't control what happens outside our school walls when our students go home. We'll waste our time thinking about what we can't control, so we may as well look at how we can help our students with these skills within our classrooms.*

Padmaja: *So, let's start with the first essential standard we identi-fied—we want the students to recognize different emotions. Let's use the planning tool and figure out what we'll directly teach and what we can support within our other academic subjects.*

Dave (First-grade teacher): *Based on our initial observations, most of the students in my class can identify emotions, but they can't always recognize when they feel that way. They are quick to tell me when someone else is mad but never recognize when they are angry with someone. It is always someone else's problem.*

Maria: *My class is the same way. I don't see how we teach that.*

Padmaja: *Sounds like most first graders. Being able to label some-one else's emotions is the first step! So, let's start with building a common vocabulary of these emotions. While we're laying that framework, we'll also model identifying our own emotions through-out the day. Your students will start to apply that to themselves, and they'll be ready for our next essential standard of identifying their own emotions. So, how do we want to introduce this?*

Ana: *I love starting with the book,* How Am I Peeling? *Students always seem to identify with the pictures.*

Dave: *OK, I'll record these in our shared planning document. Our focus will be to recognize different emotions. So, for Monday, our lesson will be reading that book and making a list of all the differ-ent emotion words we can think of on an anchor chart. I'll write that here for Monday.*

Maria: *This planning tool confuses me. What goes into the "when" box?*

Ana: *That's for when you want to teach it. Leave it blank for the team, and we can each decide "when" we will read the book during our day to our students. I'm going to read mine during the morning meeting, but I know Dave likes to read aloud after recess.*

Tom: *Maria, let's do it when I'm in your room between our reading and writing lessons. Then I'll be able to recognize when the stu-dents who are learning English are having difficulty with the English words. If we need sentence starters or additional visuals, I'll help differentiate on the spot. Then we'll come back and share those with the team at our next meeting.*

Ana: *That would be great—thank you. OK, so our connect for Monday . . . when can we integrate these emotional words into the rest of the day?*

Padmaja: *For this lesson, there are so many opportunities. Let's brainstorm ways to connect these ideas into other subject areas throughout each day of our week. Then, we can go back into the planning tool and add our ideas into each day.*

Integration:

Maria: *Well, for reading this week we're already planning on using* Knuffle Bunny *as a mentor text. Trixie has so many big emotions in that one—that's easy to connect to language arts. We can have the students recognize Trixie's emotions. At first, she is happy to be with her daddy at the laundromat, then she is sad to lose her Knuffle Bunny, next she becomes angry because her daddy cannot understand her, but at the end of the story she is excited to have her bunny back.*

Dave: *I'll write that down. And for writing we are working on our revising unit. That seems harder . . .*

Tom: *Wait, I think that fits in. We want them to "show, not tell," so they need to think about what emotions their characters have. We can use one day to identify the emotions they show in their writing and talk about whether they are labeling the emotion or describing it.*

Maria: *Yes, that's a great idea! I'm so tired of the typical writing of "And I was so happy." I think they are ready to describe and write about more emotions in their work.*

Ana: *What about mathematics? I don't really see how it connects . . . I mean, numbers aren't happy or sad.*

Dave: *No but losing in a partner game sure makes my students angry. Who knew mathematics could be such an emotional experience?*

Tom: *Ha! OK, perfect. When we're introducing the partner game for this week, let's do a quick statement about how we feel when we win and lose. It is a good reminder of being a good partner. We'll give them model sentences, "Oh man, I lost the game! Better luck next time!"*

Clara: *I'll make model sentences with visuals for each of you. Send me an email with some ideas, and I'll drop them off in your rooms before we introduce the partner games. Since we have some non-readers, I'll use my computer program to add pictures.*

Ana: *Thank you. That will also connect with games in PE, but the other specials are tough.*

Maria: *Maybe not. We can let the specialist teachers know what we are doing. In art, they can discuss the colors they are using and how those colors make them feel. In music, they are singing some upbeat songs. They can do the same thing there. I'll send the email to the specialist teachers to let them know our key vocabulary words this week and share the model sentence and visuals we will be using. They can either use the words themselves, or they can send us an email about their lessons and additional ideas they might have that we can incorporate into our lessons. We can easily chat with our class about the happy songs, colors, or books as we transition back from the specials classes.*

Dave: *And that brings us to the transitions. How do we connect identifying emotions into our transitions throughout our day?*

Maria: *I don't know about you, but by the time reading is over, I'm so late for lunch that I don't have time to think about having a* *planned, structured transition. It's "everyone for themselves—just get in line, students!"*

Ana: *I know. I feel like that too, but I've learned that if I line my class up quietly and calmly, lunch itself goes smoothly. They really pick up on our energy level here.*

Clara: *So, what if when we dismiss them to line up, we say, "If you are wearing red, make a sad face and line up," "If you are wearing blue, make an angry face and line up . . ." We can go through all the emotions, and then have them all make their happy faces before going into the hallway.*

Maria: *I will never remember that.*

Dave: *Ha! Me neither. Not if I don't write it down. I'll write these down on popsicle sticks for each classroom teacher. We can pull a popsicle stick out for each transition. The students will be excited by the anticipation of which stick I will pull out, and we won't have to remember it—it will just be routine. As we come up with more transitions that connect with social-emotional learning, we can add them to a new popsicle stick. Each week at planning we can generate more, and then if we develop new ones during our teaching then we can share what we are doing in our classrooms each week at planning.*

Ana: *Excellent idea about transitions, Dave! Moving on to recess, we can tell them what we noticed about their emotions on the playground. Like, "Kelly, I noticed you had a big smile when you were on the swings. You looked so happy. And Johnny, you looked frustrated when you missed that goal, but you took a deep breath and didn't get upset."*

Maria: *"And Daniel . . . I noticed you were mad when you punched your friend during the soccer game."*

Dave: *Truth. Well, while that's an unfortunate example, it is what happens, and Daniel needs to know he was angry. Hopefully, if this works, eventually Daniel will know he's angry and then he'll be able to identify that and calm down before using his fists.*

Maria: *Eventually . . .*

Padmaja: *Exactly. That's the hope. Spending time in the office today does not mean he will not punch anyone tomorrow. Instead, we must teach him the skills he's missing. It won't happen overnight, but it will happen over time as he builds needed social-emotional skills.*

Ana: *OK, time check—back on topic. For content, we are talking about the pilgrims. We can talk a lot about what the pilgrims felt like in the new world and how the Wampanoag Indian tribe felt about the pilgrim's arrival. That's easy. And for the end of the day . . .*

Dave: *Let's do a quick "Which emotions did you feel today?" check.*

Maria: *I'll make an interactive whiteboard slide that will let them put their name under the emotion they felt the most during the day. Then tomorrow, it will be ready for the morning meeting question. I'll put it in our shared folder. I will also include this into the email to the specialist teachers. They might want to use this idea as well.*

Padmaja: *Awesome—thank you! I am going to share this with other teams in our school as well.*

Maria: *So, we have our connections done, but we don't have specific social-emotional lessons planned for the rest of the week.*

Direct Instruction:

Padmaja: *Well, if we read the book on Monday, Tuesday we can write down different emotions we read about in the book. Wednesday, we can read another book, and on Thursday we can sort and compare the emotions we noticed in those books.*

Dave: *Wait! Before just reading them, let's think carefully about which questions we can ask. Here is the read-aloud planning sheet. Each of us can take a book and fill it out and share it with the team. And on Friday we can read a book that doesn't specifically list emotions and see if the students can identify what the characters are feeling.*

Ana: *Let's choose our favorite Elephant and Piggie book. Those characters always have big feelings.*

Padmaja: *This is great. I know you have so much overall content to cover so these should not be long, additional lessons. The strength of this is that you are introducing the vocabulary as a group, and then using it throughout the day to generalize it and give it meaning. You could have a great, in-depth lesson about each emotional word, but if you didn't give it meaning to students' lives, your lesson would be meaningless. Remember it's about building the common language and then giving it meaning.*

Maria: *I was skeptical about all of this at first, but I'm feeling like this is actually manageable.*

Ana: *I'll be excited to see how this goes. Something must happen. I know it's not an overnight change, but it's too much to keep going with academics and not support our students with their missing social-emotional skills. I can't afford to give any more academic time to breaking up student arguments.*

Padmaja: *Let's give this a try, and when we meet next week for planning, we can make any necessary modifications to our new planning tool. How about we start our next team meeting with a reflection on the week and talk about what went well and what needed adjustments? This is going to be a new learning experience for all of us, but let's have a growth mindset.*

As teams like the one in the vignette move to collaboratively establish social-emotional learning norms, create lessons, and answer the first critical question of learning—*What do we want all students to know and be able to do?*—they will be looking for specific ways to directly teach, model, and guide their SEL expectations. If your district or school is using a program to support the instruction of SEL, collaborative planning by the grade-level team is still required to provide quality integrated instruction.

When social skills are taught in isolation, out of context, or in a small, controlled environment, children are less likely to use these skills independently or generalize them to other contexts throughout their lives (McIntosh & MacKay, 2008). The goal in teaching SEL is for students to independently apply these skills throughout a variety of settings and contexts. Therefore, teachers must be strategic in how and when they address these skills during the school day. It is important to seize these teaching opportunities when they happen in the moment with our students, but we also must plan for directly teaching these skills and concepts in an authentic way (see "Teachable Moments," page 210).

In this chapter, our primary focus is on the SEL instruction element of the pyramid and providing teams with teacher tools to support the instructional planning of social-emotional concepts and skills (figure 5.1). First we discuss how to plan for differentiation when teaching SEL. Next, we present an abundance of SEL planning tools for elementary teachers. We provide a yearlong planning template to aid school teams in determining when they will be teaching SEL standards throughout the school year and highlight a tool for helping teachers plan out a well-balanced daily schedule to support engagement and behavior, through the use of transitions or modifications to the learning environment, and with the use of specific well-structured activities. Additionally, we share a planning template that can support the direct teaching of SEL skills and concepts in the form of focus lessons, as well as embedding social-emotional supporting moments into academic learning and already established routines, to further enhance students' understanding and internalization of these skills. Finally, we provide ideas for planning and organizing play in your classroom.

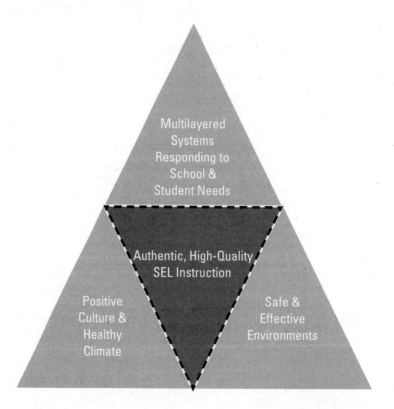

Figure 5.1: SEL schoolwide pyramid.

Supporting the Differentiation of SEL in Elementary School

Historically, educators have spent a great deal of their time immersing themselves into all aspects of academic learning (teaching the academic learning standards, assessing these standards, and using data to determine what concepts need to be retaught and reassessed as well as interventions to support or extend learners). Nevertheless, it is important to remember that teaching social-emotional learning is different from our traditional academic learning cycle. Although in this chapter we will advocate for you to follow similar processes as you do for planning academic instruction, we also note that SEL is different. Students enter our classrooms with a variety of different SEL skills for a variety of reasons. Some may be slow to develop, others may be experiencing ongoing trauma. Others may be from families or cultures that place different values on social norms than the school does. Others may simply have a late birthday and be the youngest in the grade, putting them developmentally behind their grade-level peers, but on track for their developmental age. As educators, we must remember that when it comes to SEL it is our job to teach, support, and guide, but *not to judge* the students or their families. While we want to help our students gain the SEL skills needed to be successful throughout their life, we must also keep in mind that there are a variety of reasons a child may not be successful in demonstrating SEL skills throughout the school day. Unlike learning basic mathematics facts, identifying or analyzing geometric shapes, or being able to match letters and sounds, students may fluctuate in their ability to demonstrate the SEL skills you have taught.

When we consider how to teach these SEL skills, keep in mind that SEL is a continuum of skills that build on one another. Often, what we are able to identify as a weak skill is actually weak because the foundational SEL building block supporting that skill is weak. The best, most effective work you can do for your students is to create a safe learning environment, build positive relationships with them and between them, and monitor them throughout the days for subtle or overt cues of feeling unsafe or dysregulated.

In chapter 2 (page 45), we discussed how a differentiated classroom in all domains of learning is part of creating a safe physical and cultural environment for all students. Planning lessons to intentionally engage the harder-to-reach students, providing alternative or flexible seating, and offering academic choice, tiered questioning, and visual supports when possible are examples we discussed. These supports should happen throughout the day, not just when addressing social-emotional learning.

When considering how to differentiate for SEL, teachers must take into account the students in their classroom. While last year's lesson may have worked well for last year's students, teachers must carefully consider the students in their classroom this year. What do these individual students need, and what are their individual stories? Each classroom community is a unique makeup of individuals, and teachers may need to be sensitive to the nuances of their group. They can take this into account when planning, as they determine what standards they need to spend the most time on and which foundational skills they may need to address first.

Differentiation is also something that shouldn't just happen on occasion; rather, it should become a teaching mindset and practice that enters into all aspects of instruction. According to Carol Ann Tomlinson and Tonya R. Moon (2013), teachers can differentiate instruction in four ways: (1) content, (2) process, (3) product, and (4) the learning environment. In figure 5.2, we share a few ideas for what that might look like for SEL, and it is important to note that whatever the strategy you use, it is imperative that you know your students well in order to determine the differentiation strategies needed for your learners.

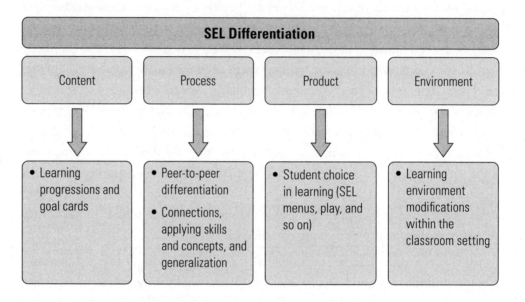

Figure 5.2: SEL differentiation.

Content

Differentiating instruction includes meeting the needs of all learners, not just considering how to create repetition and more accessible information for students who may have difficulty with the initial concept. Teachers must consider how to reach a variety of learners, such as their language learners, their learners who are ready to learn more advanced concepts, and their students with academic and social-emotional delays. Luckily, what benefits these diverse learners also benefits all students, making differentiation a key part of a teacher's ability to engage an entire class. When planning, we encourage teacher teams to use the four critical questions of a PLC to help focus their work on student learning and results. This involves teams thinking through how they will reach each set of learners, asking themselves, "How can I make this more accessible to students learning English?" "How can I make this more accessible to students with learning differences?" and "How can I extend the learning for students who may already understand the concepts?"

In the introduction (see page 6), we discuss the four critical questions of the PLC process (DuFour et al., 2016). In this chapter, we will share how teacher teams can engage in the process of answering critical question one (What do we want our students to learn?) by identifying essential SEL standards and unpacking those standards into student-friendly learning targets. To build on this, the team will need to answer the second critical question of learning (How will we know if each student has learned it?) by creating developmentally appropriate common formative assessments to determine students' needs (see chapter 6, page 293). Next, we follow with the remaining two critical questions of learning (How will we respond when some students do not learn it? and How will we extend learning for students who already have learned it?). Therefore, we suggest that, when planning, teams determine those correlating *foundational SEL learning targets* that connect with the essential grade-level SEL standards. From these essential grade-level SEL standards, teachers should then incorporate both *foundational SEL learning targets* as well as the grade-level *developing SEL learning targets* into their lessons to ensure that each student's needs are met. The amount of time on each SEL learning target may vary depending on the individual needs of the students. It is important for us to know those skills that come before (*foundational SEL learning targets*), but it is just as important to know the correlating concepts and skills that connect to the essential standards that come after or next (*expanding learning targets*; see figure 5.3, page 232). When we know this progression of learning, we can meet the students where they are and either scaffold and support using foundational skills and concepts, or look ahead and teach additional concepts and skills when ready. When students know their learning targets and their learning paths, they can begin to make deep connections and set goals for themselves.

In chapter 4 (page 157), we discussed how students can use goal setting as a strategy for learning social-emotional skills and use it as a tool for monitoring their own growth. These goal cards lend themselves to natural differentiation as each student can have a unique goal related to their individual needs. While one student may have a goal related to a broader skill of "using calm-down strategies when upset," another may have the goal of "recognize when I am feeling angry and tell an adult." In this case, the first student is already able to identify when she is upset while the second student is still working on recognizing that he feels anger in his body.

Second-Grade Social Awareness Learning Targets

Standard: Demonstrate an awareness of different cultures and a respect for human dignity

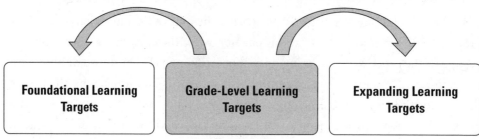

Foundational Learning Targets	Grade-Level Learning Targets	Expanding Learning Targets
Grades PreK–K:	**Grades K–2:**	**Grades 3–5:**
• Recognize respectfully the similarities and differences in people	• Use listening and attention skills to identify the feelings and perspectives of others (face, body, voice)	• Predict how their own behavior affects the emotions of others
• Show an increasing capacity to take into account another's perspective	• Recognize that words and actions can hurt others	• Define and understand perspective or point of view
• Show increasing respect for the rights of others		• Use listening skills to identify the feelings or perspectives of others
• Recognize and respect similarities and differences in people (gender expression, family, race, culture, language)		• Recognize how words and actions can hurt others in different ways

Source for standards: Michigan SEL State Standards, 2017.

Figure 5.3: Second-grade learning targets progression.

Process

In thinking about how to differentiate for students, we cannot forget how students are able to support and learn from one another in the classroom (peer-to-peer differentiation). Our students learn not just from us as teachers but from their interactions with each other as well. I (Ann-Bailey) had the opportunity to observe this firsthand while teaching in an inclusive pod during the COVID-19 shutdown. After doing work in the *sense of self* and *social awareness* building blocks in the areas of identifying emotions, I attempted to transition into mathematics games. Unfortunately, I transitioned too quickly, and one first-grade girl had difficulty shifting topics and regulating her frustration over ending the first task. Her assigned partner for the mathematics game was a first-grade boy with cerebral palsy who used an AAC eye-gaze device to communicate. He watched her with great concern as she struggled to regulate herself. Once she came over to him, he locked his eyes with hers and matched his breathing to hers. Though unable to speak oral words, he was able to regulate the upset student in a way the adults in the room had not been able to. Although the two students had different communication abilities and needed teacher support to play a mathematics game together, they were able to strengthen their SEL skills when they were together because each had different strengths and needs within the SEL building block components. It was an excellent reminder to me that all students in the room are both teachers and learners.

To best support peer-to-peer differentiation, we must be intentional about how we group students. Consider pairing students together for partner games who have different sets of emotional regulation skills. Two students who both have difficulty with skills in the same SEL building block or SEL competency are going to have a difficult time completing a task together because one of them will not be able to support the other in the weaker area. Perhaps they both struggle with the building block of *reciprocal engagement*—in this case, that partnership may not talk with each other, not consult or listen to one another, and not have an opportunity to practice those important skills. Pairing students who have difficulty with emotional regulation together may result in the two dysregulating one another and neither student completing the task. Alternatively, pairing two students together who are highly adept at reciprocal engagement may result in extended off-task talking, with neither student taking a leadership role nor initiating the work. Two students who have strong self-regulation skills may perform well but will not challenge one another in a way that results in any social-emotional skill growth. Keep in mind, as social beings we respond to those around us. Although we do not highlight every possible scenario, figure 5.4 highlights a few partnering models previously described.

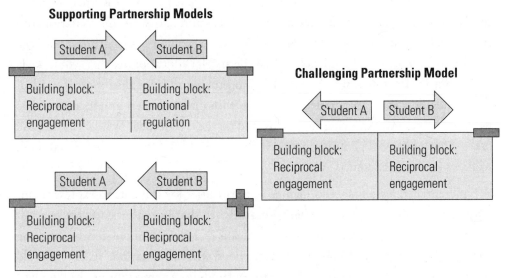

Key: ▬ symbol represents difficulty in the SEL building block; ✚ symbol represents strength in the SEL building block

Figure 5.4: Examples of student partnership models.

Perhaps what is most important in differentiating SEL is to remember that *all* students benefit from differentiation. It may be tempting to only approach a small group of students with differentiated lessons or to leave a group of students out because of their disabilities or advanced skills. Keep in mind that students will strengthen their

SEL skills through interacting with one another. It is vital to plan inclusive lessons and encourage students to interact with others whose SEL strengths and weaknesses may be different than theirs.

In our own experiences, we have seen co-teachers structure small groups of learners or partners in a way that may support the adult needs over the student needs. When forming partners or small groups, teachers may put all the learners with language needs or those who have specific learning goals together in one group, to work with the guidance of a teacher who specializes in either language learning or special education. In these cases, it is important to consider what type of community the teacher is creating through this grouping. These practices of consistently grouping language learners or special education students together send a message to the whole class that there are subgroups within the larger class community.

I (Tracey) witnessed this when supporting mathematics in a classroom where the teacher used the mathematics workshop model. The teacher and her special education co-teacher used this practice as a way to support smaller groups of students. Although this is an excellent opportunity to strategically pair students together; create smaller, more focused groups; and utilize the knowledge of both teachers throughout the classroom, this team consistently partnered the four students with Individual Education Plans (IEPs) together. This allowed the special education teacher to work with the four students on her caseload, but it also limited these students' ability to be a part of the larger classroom community. A more supportive, alternative approach would have been to carefully pair partners together based on their mathematical and social-emotional strengths and needs. In this scenario, both the general education and special education teacher would circulate throughout the classroom supporting all students. While the special education teacher would keep an eye out for the four students with IEPs to provide additional support if needed, she would allow them to experience working with different peers and to attempt the work independently, knowing support would be there if needed. While this method takes some additional planning between the co-teachers, it is more beneficial to all students in the classroom.

Differentiated lessons should include opportunities for students to express themselves in a variety of methods—whether orally when sharing with the teacher or a seat partner; in writing, on a whiteboard or by means of a project; or possibly by selecting an image from an array of choices that correspond with the question. Teachers should be selective about the books they choose to read and discuss, monitoring the language level and attention span of their students as well as whether or not the books reflect the cultural identity and lived experiences of the students. If a recommended book is too long, is not engaging for the given group of students, or reflects a cultural bias, a teacher should consider how they might teach the same lesson, address the same standard, or achieve the same message in a different way.

Students can maintain and generalize information best when it is presented in a variety of formats, across different settings, and with frequent reviews (Council for Exceptional Children, 2017). Teachers can consider which multiple methods work best for their students. If the topic is originally presented in a class discussion and read aloud, the teacher can follow up with an art project, asking groups of students to put on a skit around the concept or describe how they used the concept at recess or at lunch. Later in this chapter (page 278), we address how teachers can create weekly plans to embed SEL skills throughout the school day. The power of embedding this material is not just that it makes our teacher lives easier, or that it generalizes the material for students. Embedding and spiraling the material allows students to review what they learned or consider it in a new light. Students who may not need the original lesson because it was a concept they were already familiar with may be struck by a question during science about how scientists must monitor their own self-regulation skills when conducting experiments in the lab. Students who struggled with understanding concepts the first time around in a lesson may need the concepts repeated or used in a different context. These students benefit from hearing their peers' answers as well as responding on their own. Having the opportunity to hear the material in a variety of ways provides differentiation for students (see figure 5.5).

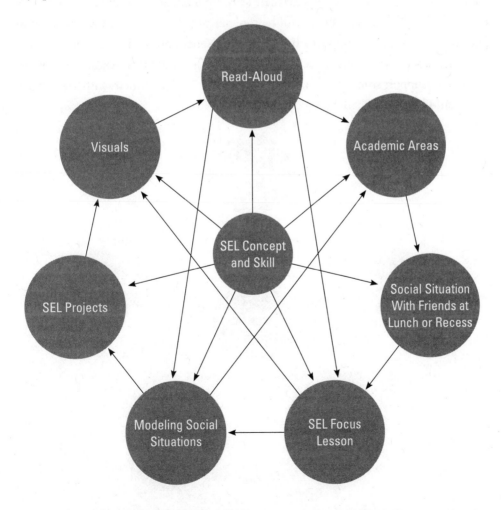

Source: Adapted from Lesh, Post, & Behr, 1987.

Figure: 5.5: Building deeper understanding through multiple experiences.

Product

In the previous section, we described how students can generalize information best when it is presented in a variety of formats. In chapter 2 (page 45) and chapter 4 (page 157) we discussed the importance of student choice in learning. We shared one strategy in the form of a learning menu (see figure 4.33, page 216), where students have choice in how they demonstrate their learning. In addition to providing tangible projects to demonstrate their understanding, students may engage in learning experiences that are intangible, such as a play or a skit. Intangible products allow students who may have difficulty with fine motor skills an opportunity to demonstrate their knowledge without being limited by the writing or drawing requirement. No matter the product, when the element of choice is offered, differentiation occurs (see figure 5.6), although how it occurs and to what degree can vary. Students might all be focusing on the same grade-level essential standard but have choice in how they demonstrate their learning (choice of product). Or, the differentiation may occur when all students are working on a project at the same time but are focusing on different skills based on their own individual needs (determined by teachers through the use of common formative assessments), and the learning is further differentiated when providing choice in how students demonstrate their learning (choice of product). If we provide choice first, students most likely will be more engaged and invested in the learning and therefore may have opportunities to form deeper connections to the concepts. If we start there, we can then use supports and scaffolds to bridge these ideas to new learning or support students in making connections or helping them with generalizing information in more challenging contexts.

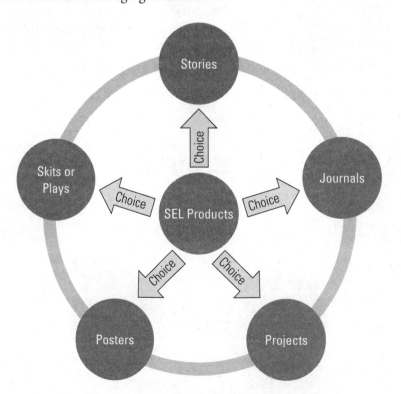

Figure 5.6: Differentiating through the use of products.

Environment

We shared both physical and cultural features of the classroom learning environment in chapters 2 (page 45) and 3 (page 93). Figure 5.7 shows how these learning environments can be modified to support students' individual needs. In fact, environmental features of the learning environment can affect student behavior and their attention levels on learning tasks (Guardino, 2010). Sometimes this differentiation strategy is the simplest, yet often the most overlooked. Modifications such as changing a daily routine, a student's seating, or classroom lighting; providing visual symbols or labels within the classroom; or changing how we store and make materials accessible to students can make a big impact on classroom learners. Adjusting the learning environment for the whole class or individual students can be just as important as providing the differentiation of an academic learning task. As we continuously adapt the learning environment to meet students' needs, we need to sit back and reflect on what is working and what is not working and make the modifications needed. Relying on co-teachers to help with this reflective process is not only important but necessary. Later in the chapter (page 238), we will share ideas for how to proactively plan for modifying the learning environment.

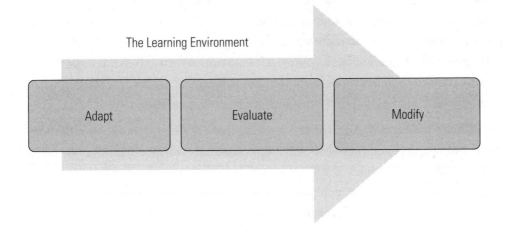

Figure 5.7: Differentiating the learning environment.

When a teacher or teacher team is struggling to reach a particular student or group of students, the answer tends to be in looking deeper into the differentiation. Often, the teacher can make seemingly easy changes to help the student learn the standards, skills, or concepts, through either the content, process, product, or environment. In moments of frustration, it can be difficult to identify the exact differentiation strategies needed, yet talking through the problem and needs with a teacher team often helps identify the right differentiation approach needed.

SEL Planning Tools for Elementary Teachers

How do we bridge knowing to actually doing? The link that binds the two is often *planning*. Planning can help us reach our goals and be more efficient with our allotted instructional time. As teachers, we know that time is something we value immensely. If you carefully and strategically plan for SEL, not only can you achieve your goals but you will also find that you are not taking excessive amounts of instructional time away from academic-focused areas. In this section, we will share a variety of planning tools to support elementary teachers in providing authentic forms of SEL. First, we will discuss purposeful and proactive planning to lift engagement, provide differentiation, and support behavior. Next, we will introduce several tools and templates to guide you in planning for SEL direct instruction and integrating SEL with academic learning.

Purposeful and Proactive Planning to Lift Engagement, Provide Differentiation, and Support Behavior

In chapters 2 (page 45) and 3 (page 93), we discussed ideas around engagement and the learning environment, which are both areas closely tied to instruction and planning, and in chapter 4 (page 157), we described how transitions can be used as valuable teaching opportunities for SEL skills, or as opportunities to support students in co-regulation. Here, we share some simple suggestions for how these transitions can be easily put into daily practice. We must take time to proactively plan for the daily use of transitions, make modifications to the learning environment when needed, and use specific activities that support student engagement and behavior.

When planning our daily instruction, it is important that we think about the flow of the daily schedule and possibly build in opportunities for increasing or decreasing students' energy levels. Look at the sample schedule for day one in figure 5.8 and notice how students are engaged in many high-energy activities throughout their day. Next, look at the sample schedule for day two and see how the students' day mainly consists of several low-energy activities. In either scenario, students might find it challenging or actually become dysregulated—either if they are sitting and occupied with a series of low-energy activities throughout most of their day, or if they are exposed to consistent high-energy activities without built-in breaks. Take time to look at your daily schedule and determine if it contains an overabundance of overlapping high- or low-energy routines or academic blocks that may prove to be a challenge for your class or individual students. If so, decide what adjustments or modification you can make to support regulation and engagement. We know that sometimes we don't always have control over all aspects of the daily schedule, and it might not be possible to make certain shifts. Nevertheless, what we can do is plan and build in opportunities for getting students up and moving and their blood flowing to their brains, or provide periods of needed rest or calm, as well as finding moments, possibly during transitions, to teach and practice needed social-emotional or academic skills. All these things are not only critical to students' learning, but they also require careful thought and planning.

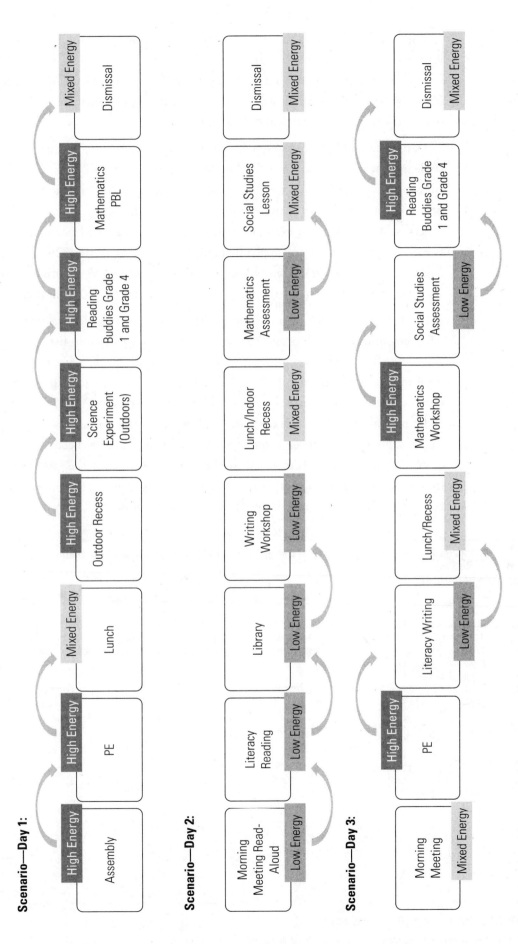

Scenario—Day 1:

Assembly — High Energy

PE — High Energy

Lunch — Mixed Energy

Outdoor Recess — High Energy

Science Experiment (Outdoors) — High Energy

Reading Buddies Grade 1 and Grade 4 — High Energy

Mathematics PBL — High Energy

Dismissal — Mixed Energy

Scenario—Day 2:

Morning Meeting Read-Aloud — Low Energy

Literacy Reading — Low Energy

Library — Low Energy

Writing Workshop — Low Energy

Lunch/Indoor Recess — Mixed Energy

Mathematics Assessment — Low Energy

Social Studies Lesson — Mixed Energy

Dismissal — Mixed Energy

Scenario—Day 3:

Morning Meeting — Mixed Energy

PE — High Energy

Literacy Writing — Low Energy

Lunch/Recess — Mixed Energy

Mathematics Workshop — High Energy

Social Studies Assessment — Low Energy

Reading Buddies Grade 1 and Grade 4 — High Energy

Dismissal — Mixed Energy

Figure 5.8: Example daily schedules showing energy levels.

When we take time to carefully plan for transitions, make modifications to the learning environment, and incorporate well-thought-out activities, we actually have the opportunity to support students' engagement levels and behavior. When planning, it's important to think about ways to purposefully plan for a balance of low-, high-, or mixed-energy activities within our lessons.

Transitions can be useful when shifting from one subject area to the next or when students move throughout the school building to specials, lunch, or recess, and so on. In chapter 4 (page 157), we described how transitions have the ability to help calm students, increase blood flow to the brain, or be used to teach and practice SEL skills and concepts. We shared many examples of activities that can be used as useful transitions (see figure 4.3, page 163, and appendix figures A.2–A.7, pages 318–326) to target specific areas. These transition examples are just that—examples. We recommend that you try some of our suggested transitions as well as take time to create your own.

Figure 5.9 is a blank SEL transition tool that you or your grade-level teams can use when engaging in this process. You may want to use this tool to list out just a few transitions from each area you want to try for a week or during a month, or you may want to generate some of your own ideas that specifically align to the SEL or academic content you are currently teaching. You and your team will also want to think about management strategies for making these transitions an easy part of your daily routines. For example, if you want a few particular transitions to become part of your daily routine, use them consistently and possibly even during the same time of the day or with the same subject area. We suggest trying them a few times, or possibly tweaking them before determining if they are useful or not.

Decrease Energy Transitions ↓	Increase Energy Transitions ↑	Mixed Energy Transitions That Support Overall SEL Learning				
Transitions to Ground or Calm	Transitions to Increase Blood Flow and Oxygen to the Brain	Sense of Self	Social-Emotional Regulation	Social Awareness	Reciprocal Engagement	Logical and Responsible Decision Making
Management strategies and ideas:						

Figure 5.9: SEL transition planning tool.

*Visit **go.SolutionTree.com/instruction** for a free reproducible version of this figure.*

It is also beneficial to think about management strategies that you can use to incorporate several transitions throughout your day, strategies that require little to no pre-planning. For example, you could record transitions that your students really respond to on popsicle sticks, and label them with colors (calm energy—green, high energy—red, and mixed energy—yellow). Then you can put them all in a cup, and as you read the energy level cues of your class, you can easily pull out the labeled popsicle stick needed. This would especially be helpful if you are trying to use transitions that relate to SEL content that you want to teach. For example, imagine your students are finishing up with mathematics workshop and you want them to transition to the carpet and get ready to start a social studies lesson. In the mathematics workshop, students were working collaboratively on a group project, and you notice that the class's overall energy level is currently high. You decide you need a calming transition to support with co-regulation. Therefore, you pull out a green (calm energy) popsicle stick and read it to yourself—*Skip count breathing activity*. After reading the popsicle stick, you give students directions: "It's time to clean up from your mathematics project and transition to the carpet. When you get to the carpet and find your space, I want you to close your eyes and begin skip counting by 3s in your brain. As you are skip counting, inhale on the odd numbers and slowly exhale on the even numbers."

As teachers we build our teacher toolkits over time and continue to fill these toolkits year to year as we try new ideas, modify our practices, and hone our best and most useful skills. Yet, in order for these to become practices that just become what we do, we first must take time to engage in inquiry-based learning, which often consists of many failures. Though discouraging, these failures are what will eventually bring us to successful teaching if we persist using a growth mindset. It is not realistic to consistently plan out every daily transition with great detail, but if we engage in doing it several times and build in structures to support these teaching practices, it will eventually just be something we do consistently and naturally, and without the need for much prep or planning.

Beyond the use of transitions, we also know that playing quiet music or dimming the lights can be simple strategies that can support our students. When we plan our daily schedule, we know the value of overall consistency with our routines and the need to also be responsive to students' individual needs. Table 5.1 (page 242) describes characteristics of various energy levels and figure 5.10 (page 243) is a planning tool that teachers can use as they begin to think about their class needs and the individual needs of their students. We have provided a list of sample ideas in the planning tool (figure 5.10), but recommend you fill it out using your own daily schedule and with your class and students in mind. As we shared previously, what might be calming for some might actually be dysregulating for others, so getting to know your students and their needs is vital. We suggest you start small, reflect on the routines implemented within your schedule, and observe your students over time to look for trends. Then make plans for testing and trying various new strategies, or modify existing ones. For example, if you notice that when students come back from recess the class struggles to engage themselves in the lesson that follows, it would be important to think about strategies, transitions, or modifications to the learning environment that might support students in gaining focus and attention.

Table 5.1: Characteristics of Student Energy Levels and Optimal Settings for Each Level

Energy Level	Description	Optimal Setting
High	Student is moving and thinking quickly. Student may feel joyful, angry, or frustrated, but their feeling is seen through movement within the body. The student appears present and alert, though may be easily distracted.	Settings: • Recess • Physical education • Classroom games
Balanced	Student is alert and engaged with stimuli in the room. Student's head is up, eyes are alert, and posture is erect. Student responds quickly either to a question or interaction, either verbally or through a gesture or facial expression.	• Focus lessons • Independent or group work • Lunch time
Low	Student appears tired and moving slowly. Student may appear to daydream or look out the window or around the classroom. Student takes longer than expected to respond to others, even with facial expressions or gestures.	• Quiet times in the classroom • Classroom opportunities for breathing • Independent reading or drawing time (not related to school assignments)
Mixed	We are using this term to refer to the energy levels of the class itself—when some students have high energy levels and others are low. This may happen when the class is just entering the room in the morning or when groups of students are returning from different classes.	• Morning or afternoon transitions when students are unpacking or packing their bags • Recess, when each student is taking a break and meeting their own individual needs to come back to the room refreshed

Daily Schedule	Students' Energy Level	Target for Balance	All Student Supports	Individual Supports
Arrival	High	Ground students in school day	Supports: • Play quiet music • Give a warm, low-energy greeting • Provide quiet, independent task	Supports: • Check in • Review visual schedule for day • Set self-regulation goals

Daily Schedule	Students' Energy Level	Target for Balance	All Student Supports	Individual Supports
Morning Meeting	Mixed	Balanced energy with shared attention	Supports: • Engage in a whole-group choral reading; recite poems or song • Conduct a fun, community-building activity • Provide opportunities for students to share and listen to one another • Establish predictable questions and routines	Supports: • Provide opportunities to transition to the group late • Display visual schedule of morning meeting • Be prepared with planned responses to routine questions • Allow for participation by choice in fun activities
Focus Lesson (No more than fifteen minutes)	Low	Increase energy for optimal engagement	Supports: • Have a brain break after ten to fifteen minutes of sitting • Give a class cheer • Hold a quick one- or two-song dance party or play freeze-dance by playing a song and randomly pausing it at different points where the students have to freeze • Sing silly songs • Incorporate meaningful transitions	Supports: • Offer heavy work* • Take a note to another classroom • Have a sensory break • Offer flexible seating
Group, Partner, or Independent Work	Mixed	Balanced energy for optimal engagement	Supports: • Hold frequent whole-class check-ins to refocus • Incorporate meaningful transitions • Monitor learning activity times • Offer flexible seating • Give students choice of assigned activities	Supports: • Give chunked tasks with increased reinforcement • Provide opportunities for sensory break and self-regulation • Monitor use of technology and set time limits • Offer flexible seating opportunities

Figure 5.10: Evaluating and strengthening the daily schedule—planning tool.   continued →

Daily Schedule	Students' Energy Level	Target for Balance	All Student Supports	Individual Supports
Lesson Reflection	High	Balanced for refocus and support joint attention	Supports: • Hold whole-class calm breathing • Conduct visualizing activities* • Have a choral reading or recite a poem or song*	Supports: • Provide visuals • Reflect on previous and upcoming tasks
Before Lunch	High	Calm energy	Supports: • Conduct whole-class calm breathing • Talk through transition before lining up • Conduct a quiet, controlled transition—individually call students to line up	Supports: • Provide heavy work* during walking in the hall • Give a reminder about earphones • Plan on what to buy for lunch • Provide clear boundaries for individual lunch belongings
After Lunch/Recess	High	Low energy	Supports: • Provide silent work time to transition back to classroom • Play calm, quiet music • Reduce lights • Conduct an independent, low-stress activity (looking at books, coloring, drawing) • Incorporate meaningful transitions such as whole-class calm breathing*	Supports: • Provide individual direction on making quiet choice • Give opportunities to access sensory items • Review schedule for afternoon • Reflect on self-regulation strategies
Before Specials	High	Calm, focused energy	Supports: • Conduct whole-class calm breathing • Talk through transition before lining up • Conduct a quiet, controlled transition—individually call students to line up • Provide positive reinforcement in hallway • Conduct purposeful transitions while walking in the hallways*	Supports: • Provide heavy work* during walking in the hall • Give a reminder about earphones if needed • Talk through upcoming specials and what child may expect • Communicate with specials teachers on student needs

Daily Schedule	Students' Energy Level	Target for Balance	All Student Supports	Individual Supports
After Specials	High	Balanced for refocus and support joint attention	Supports: • Whole-class calm breathing • Conduct visualizing activities* • Hold a choral reading or recite a poem or song* • Provide additional quiet time if class is coming from a high-energy special	Supports: • Provide visuals • Reflect on previous and upcoming tasks
Academic Block	See Above			
Pack-Up and Dismissal	High	Calm, focused energy	Supports: • Engage in whole-class reflection • Make goals for tomorrow • Play quiet, calm music • Conduct independent activities while waiting for dismissal	Supports: • Check in on self-regulation during the day • Provide quiet reflection time • Provide access to sensory supports • Review upcoming day's schedule

*Visit **go.SolutionTree.com/instruction** for a free blank reproducible version of this figure.*

Consider the power of sitting with your team and filling out this planning tool together. Most likely you would end up with more ideas than if you worked on it in isolation. This planning tool can also serve as a record-keeping tool for the individual supports you provide and use with your students. It is important to note that each school and classroom of students is unique. Therefore, in our example, *arrival* may not create high energy within your classroom, or maybe it does for one of your teammates but not for your class of students. Although your daily schedules, procedures, and routines may vary at times, we still believe there is great value in sitting down with your team as you evaluate your daily schedule and generate ideas for how to enhance the learning environment and instruction.

Planning for SEL Direct Instruction and Integrating SEL With Academic Learning

Planning for social-emotional learning in many ways may look like planning academic content (language arts, mathematics, science, and social studies), yet it might also look and feel very different. We need to avoid unauthentic forms of teaching social-emotional learning. Just having a school counselor come in weekly, biweekly, or monthly to teach a set of SEL lessons isn't enough. It is not enough to guarantee strong SEL by just planning to teach a set of SEL lessons on a given schedule without responding to the needs of your students. Likewise, randomly choosing a few read-alouds that you think might be good for your students, and having your students complete a few worksheets focused around SEL skills, are not best practices. First and foremost, it is best to teach social-emotional learning by means of our students' daily social interactions with their teachers and peers, as well as helping students to become cognizant of their own self-awareness and emotions. Furthermore, it is beneficial to directly plan for and teach SEL skills and concepts during the school week and weave the learning into each school day. In the previous section, we demonstrated how teams can begin to engage in this process with the use of intentionally focused targeted transitions.

CASEL (n.d.d) recommends adopting an evidence-based program for SEL. According to CASEL:

> Evidence-based SEL programs are grounded in research and principles of child and adolescent development, and scientifically evaluated and shown to produce positive student outcomes. The goals of schoolwide SEL are more likely to be achieved when evidence-based approaches are used to reach students in all settings where they spend their time.
>
> Effective SEL approaches often incorporate four elements represented by the acronym SAFE:
>
> • *SEQUENCED*: Connected and coordinated activities to foster skills development.
> • *ACTIVE*: Employing active forms of learning to help students master new skills and attitudes.
> • *FOCUSED*: Dedicated time and attention to developing personal and social skills.
> • *EXPLICIT*: Targeting specific social and emotional skills.

The challenge becomes when those district or state standards do not directly align with the selected SEL program. Therefore, teachers must first know the expected student outcomes (state or province or district standards) and then determine if they need to supplement the chosen SEL program. For instance, if the program only addresses skills-based instruction and does not focus on school climate, culture, learning environments, and systems for monitoring SEL, then the school must also determine what that needs to look like at the school and classroom levels (as discussed in chapter 3, page 93). Additionally, if the program provides teachers with specific targeted learning outcomes but not all state or district learning outcomes are covered in the program, then, again, the team must supplement and ensure all standards are taught at the grade level.

SEL might be new for you or your school and you may be at the start of your journey, yet working in a team not only allows for equitable practices but also gives teachers the support and guidance they need for providing quality SEL instruction. CASEL (https://casel.org), along with Harvard's EASEL Lab (n.d.), provides schools with extensive resources, and teachers and teams can also use the social-emotional learning rubrics in chapter 3 (page 93) as tools for evaluating current practices and guiding teachers and teams in planning for high-quality SEL.

The following sections will provide strategies and tools in the following areas:

- Developing an SEL yearlong planning outline

- Integrating SEL and academic learning using weekly lesson-planning tools

- Planning for play

SEL Yearlong Planning Outline

At the start of the year, the team needs to develop a plan for teaching social-emotional instruction. Part of that plan should involve the development of a yearlong outline. We note that if your school is using an SEL program it may already have a suggested timeline, but we still think it is best practice for teams to work collaboratively and develop plans and tools that specifically meet the needs of the students within the school and at the grade level. If you are using a structured program with a pacing guide or outline, you may decide as a team that you want to add or supplement additional ideas and correlate SEL activities and lessons with various academic areas you are specifically teaching. For example, before teaching students specific skills and concepts outlined in a selected program chosen by the school, the team may first consider taking time to build community and relationships during the first month of school. The team itself may develop these ideas based on its previous teaching experiences or additional research-based practices and structures. If we truly want to integrate SEL with our academic instruction, we need to evaluate both our academic curricula as well as our selected SEL curriculum or programs and determine where we can make them authentically align.

To do this, you first need to determine what standards your state, district, or school expects you to teach. The next step is to create a timeline for when you will teach these standards, how long you will teach them, and how you can integrate them with other academic areas. To support teachers in this effort, we created a protocol for teams to use as guidance (see figure 5.11, page 248). In this section, we will share examples and describe the process teachers and teams can take in creating this yearlong planning tool. It is important to note that when planning, your state or district might focus instruction around CASEL's five competencies, or possibly similar but different SEL frameworks. In the following examples, we use the five building blocks of SEL discussed in the introduction (page 1) and chapter 1 (page 23), and a set of correlating learning standards with specific learning targets that have been adapted from CASEL and social-emotional learning standards the state of Illinois created.

SEL Yearlong Instructional Planning Protocol	
1	Determine the amount of time you will spend on each overarching SEL focal area over the course of the year.
2	Identify essential and non-essential SEL standards at your grade level.
3	Identify *developing* learning targets and correlating *foundational* learning targets for each standard.
4	Cluster SEL standards *within* and *across* each of the overarching SEL focal areas (for example, the five SEL building block components; CASEL's five SEL core competencies).
5	Determine which SEL standards and learning targets correlate with academic units or structures.
6	Form SEL units of study.
7	Create a timeline by ordering the units of study and determine the duration of each unit of study.

Figure 5.11: SEL yearlong instructional planning protocol.

*Visit **go.SolutionTree.com/instruction** for a free reproducible version of this figure.*

Step 1: Determine the Amount of Time You Will Spend on Each Overarching SEL Focal Area Over the Course of a Year

First, the team needs to consider the amount of time it will spend on each SEL focal area (five building blocks, CASEL's five core competencies, other SEL frameworks, and so on) over the course of the year. During this stage of planning, it is essential for teams to take student development into account. In kindergarten and first grade, teachers must account for the fact that their students are undergoing critical brain development in their prefrontal cortex—the area that supports executive functioning and cognitive skills (Jones, Barnes, Bailey, & Doolittle, 2017; Wood, 2015). To fully develop the age-appropriate self-regulation skills they need to be successful in school, students at this stage require supportive relationships where they can learn about themselves through their relationships with others. Kindergarten and first-grade teachers, therefore, should focus their time on those foundational SEL building blocks, such as sense of self, reciprocal engagement, and social-emotional regulation, while keeping in mind that they must support these through strong relationships. Teachers in middle grades can begin a focus on the later developing building blocks such as social awareness (with the lens of perspective taking) and logical and responsible decision making. Although you can address each component in a developmentally appropriate way at each grade level, it is important to recognize the developmental progression across the grades. Spending a significant amount of time on social awareness in first grade may teach students isolated skills like making eye contact and saying, "good game," but these rote skills are not indicative of a strong social-emotional foundation.

Step 2: Identify Essential and Non-Essential SEL Standards at Your Grade Level

Next, teams can begin identifying essential SEL standards at their grade level. As is often the case in education, standards are packed in various learning domains. Teachers who attempt to cover each and every standard to the full depth of knowledge may find that their students only have basic knowledge and not a true understanding of the standards by the end of the year. Instead, teams should determine which standards require the most amount of focus and attention. So, we suggest school teams sit down together and look at each standard with a critical eye. They must identify which standards are essential (which require teachers to provide students with direct instruction and which may require teachers to spend additional time teaching) and which standards may be approached through guided support during groups, read-alouds, or interactive play experiences. Teams should consistently revisit these decisions throughout the year. For instance, notice how in the example in figure 5.12, a team of teachers, using their state's mandated learning standards, determined a set of essential and non-essential standards at their grade level around self-awareness. The standards the team deemed *essential* were those that require students to identify interests and strengths as well as label positive values. They could teach these essential standards in one or two lessons, whereas they could address the other, non-essential standards in the chart during a read-aloud, when reviewing a dispute on the playground, or when working with students in a writing conference.

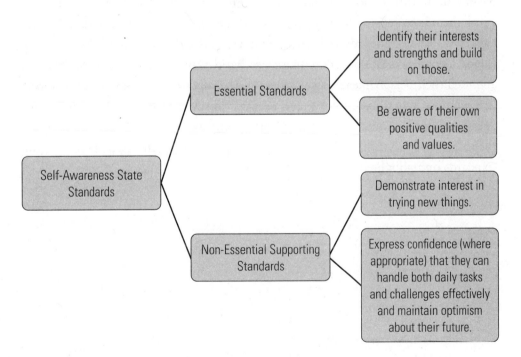

Source for standards: Adapted from CASEL, 2017; Illinois Board of Education, 2020.

Figure 5.12: Example of selecting essential standards.

To complete this task, school teams must look at what their school, district, county, or state requires. Some states already have specific SEL standards identified, but if school teams do not already have state or province or district standards, we recommend exploring CASEL's resources and looking at states that do provide comprehensive SEL standards as guidance. See Butler and colleagues' (Kerr et al., 2021) *What About Us?*, or visit www.solutiontree.com/free-resources/plcbooks/wau, to learn more about the process of identifying essential standards.

Step 3: Identify Developing Learning Targets and Correlating Foundational Learning Targets

Once teachers and teams clarify which standards are essential, it is also important to dig into each of their associated learning targets and come to common understandings about what they are asking of students. Additionally, teachers and teams need to determine the foundational concepts and skills that precede the essential grade-level standards and their correlated learning targets. When teaching, we may first need to start with the foundational concepts and skills and then support students in bridging many of these ideas to the grade-level skills and concepts. Figure 5.13 is an example of the work a third-grade team conducted in first identifying a set of essential standards from a larger set of SEL standards Michigan's Department of Education adopted. You'll notice that the Michigan Department of Education framed their SEL standards around CASEL's five core competencies We have also included an example of a set of third-grade standards that align with our five SEL building blocks, which include correlating foundational and developing learning targets (see table 5.2, page 259). These standards and learning targets were adapted from CASEL and the Illinois Department of Education. In each scenario, teams engaged in rich discussions and used their personal teaching experiences, the expertise of certain team members (for example, school counselors), and research to select those standards the teams deemed essential. You can see that in both examples, the team simply highlighted those standards that they identified as essential and left non-essential supporting standards unhighlighted.

CASEL Core Competencies: *Self-Awareness*	
Michigan State Standards	
SEL Essential Standard	Learning Targets
1A. Demonstrate an awareness of their emotions	PreK–K: • Show an emerging sense of self • Continue to develop personal preferences • Identify a variety of feelings and moods in themselves Grades K–2: • Recognize and label their emotions and feelings • Describe their emotions and the situations that cause them (triggers) Grades 3–5: • Recognize intensity levels of their emotions • Recognize how emotion can change • Recognize how thoughts are linked with emotions and emotions are linked to behavior • Describe ways emotions impact their behavior or behaviors • Draw an "anger thermometer" and discuss why they might move along the thermometer
1B. Demonstrate an awareness of their personal traits, including their strengths and interests*	PreK–K: • Identify their own strengths • Demonstrate positive feelings about their own gender, race, ethnicity, disability, national origin, and language, as well as community and family cultural practices • Demonstrate growing confidence in expressing their feelings, needs, and opinions Grades K–2: • Identify their likes and dislikes • Describe things they do well or the knowledge that they have • Describe an activity or task in which they may need help to improve Grades 3–5: • Describe their personal identities (for example, gender identity, race, ethnicity, national origin, disabilities, and so on) • Describe the personal traits they possess that make them successful members of their classroom and school community • Describe their growth areas; prioritize the personal traits and interests they want to develop and explore opportunities to develop them

Figure 5.13: Essential third-grade SEL standards.

continued →

Highlighting indicates an essential standard.

SEL Essential Standard	Learning Targets
1C. Demonstrate awareness of their external supports	PreK–K: • Learn from and through relationships and interactions • Demonstrate an increasing sense of belonging and awareness of their roles as members of families, classrooms, and communities Grades K–2: • Identify at least one adult they trust • Identify situations they need to seek help from an adult (big problem or small problem) • Recognize how and where to get help in an emergency Grades 3–5: • Recognize qualities of positive role models in their lives • Identify positive adults in various facets of their lives • Identify peer, home, and school supports and resources they can access to help solve problems
1D. Demonstrate a sense of personal responsibility	PreK–K: • Begin to organize projects or play; make and carry out plans • Exhibit a growing capacity to self-regulate, demonstrate self-efficacy, and know acceptable boundaries • Show an increasing ability to follow simple, clear, and consistent directions and rules • Begin to take action to fix their mistakes, solve problems with materials, and resolve conflicts with others Grades K–2: • Understand their responsibility to meet schoolwide safety expectations knowing it promotes a safe and productive environment • Recognize that there are positive and negative consequences for their choices and actions Grades 3–5: • Define what it means to be responsible and can identify things for which they are responsible • Explain the benefits of being responsible • Demonstrate ability to say "no" to negative peer pressure

CASEL Core Competencies: *Self-Management*	
Michigan State Standards	
SEL Essential Standard	Learning Targets
2A. Identify and manage their emotions and behavior constructively	PreK–K: • Grow in their capacity to avoid harming themselves, others, or things around them when expressing feelings, needs, and opinions • Manage reasonable frustration • Address stress in a reasonable and age-appropriate way Grades K–2: • Utilize techniques that allow them to calm themselves • Practice using words to share their feelings about an interaction or situation rather than physically aggressively expressing feelings • Practice moving to a "calm down" space in the room after a triggering event Grades 3–5: • Use self-monitoring strategies such as self-talk to regulate emotions • Respond effectively to pressure situations (for example, walk away, seek help, or use mediation) • Communicate their perspective on triggering behaviors or situations using "I" messages • Express emotions in a respectful manner
2B. Demonstrate honesty and integrity	Grades PreK–K: • Show increasing respect for the rights of others • Understand the prosocial value of honesty and truthfulness to the extent their perception of reality permits it Grades K–2: • Describe a situation when they could have lied but they told the truth • Share reasons why they follow classroom or school rules (their own safety, the safety of others, reducing chance of damaging property, and so on) • Describe the differences between and consequences or benefits of lying and truth telling Grades 3–5: • Tell the truth in a difficult situation, while honoring personal boundaries • Follow through on their commitments

continued →

SEL Essential Standard	Learning Targets
2C. Set, monitor, adapt, and evaluate goals to achieve success in school and life	**Grades PreK–K:** • Approach tasks and activities with increased flexibility, imagination inventiveness, and confidence • Demonstrate increasing ability to set goals and to develop and follow through on plans • Demonstrate a reasonable self-perception of confidence; can make choices and explain discoveries • Grow in their ability to follow simple, clear, and consistent directions and rules **Grades K–2:** • Identify a short-term goal (wish, dream) • Determine whether the goal is under their control or someone else's control; identify and take steps needed to accomplish a short-term goal • Identify people who can support them in reaching their short-term goal **Grades 3–5:** • Distinguish between long-term and short-term goals • Describe why learning is important in achieving personal goals • Evaluate the action steps taken to accomplish a goal and identify what, if anything, they could have done differently to facilitate that • Identify resources that help them achieve their goals (home, school, and community support)

CASEL Core Competencies: *Social Awareness*

Michigan State Standards

SEL Essential Standard	Learning Targets
3A. Demonstrate awareness of other people's emotions and perspectives	**Grades PreK–K:** • Show increasing respect for the rights of others • Demonstrate the ability to care; can respond with sensitivity or sincerity (later empathy) • Identify a variety of feelings and moods in others • Increase their capacity to take another's perspective **Grades K–2:** • Use listening and attention skills to identify the feelings and perspectives of others (face, body, voice) • Recognize that words and actions can hurt others **Grades 3–5:** • Predict how their own behavior affects the emotions of others • Define and understand perspective or point of view • Use listening skills to identify the feelings or perspectives of others • Recognize how words and actions can hurt others in different ways

SEL Essential Standard	Learning Targets
3B. Demonstrate consideration for others and a desire to positively contribute to the school and community	Grades PreK–K: • Participate successfully as a group member • Demonstrate an increasing sense of belonging and awareness of their role as a member of a family, classroom, and community • Increase understanding of the relationship between people and their environment and begin to recognize the importance of taking care of the resources in the environment • Show increasing respect for the rights of others • Grow in their ability to follow simple, clear, and consistent directions and rules Grades K–2: • Recognize and name how they can help others within their school, home, and community • Identify how they help others and how they feel about helping (for example, feed the dog, share, clean up when asked) Grades 3–5: • Share reasons for helping others • Identify roles they have that contribute to their school, home, and neighboring community • Work together with peers to address a need
3C. Demonstrate an awareness of different cultures and a respect for human dignity	Grades PreK–K: • Recognize respectfully the similarities and differences in people • Show an increasing capacity to consider another's perspective • Show increasing respect for the rights of others • Recognize and respect similarities and differences in people (gender expression, family, race, culture, language) Grades K–2: • Describe ways that people are similar and different • Name positive qualities in people that cross all cultures and groups Grades 3–5: • Identify contributions of various social and cultural groups • Recognize that people from different cultural and social groups share many things in common and identify similarities and differences • Define stereotyping, discrimination, and prejudice

continued →

SEL Essential Standard	Learning Targets
3D. Demonstrate the ability to read social cues and respond constructively	**Grades PreK–K:** • Make connections with situations or events, people, or stories • Contribute individual strengths, imagination, or interests to a group • Extend offers of help to peers or adults, to help them feel that they belong to the group • Can adapt to different environments **Grades K–2:** • Understand the importance of and demonstrate respect for personal space • Appropriately engage in play with others (for example, introduce self, ask permission, join in, and invite others to join in) • Wait their turn, observe the situation, and know when it's appropriate to respond **Grades 3–5:** • Describe tone and how it is used to communicate to others • Describe the impact of body language and facial expressions in communication; develop awareness that social cues may be different among various groups

CASEL Core Competencies: *Relationship Skills*

Michigan State Standards

SEL Essential Standard	Learning Targets
4A. Use positive communication and social skills to interact effectively with others	**Grades PreK–K:** • Successfully develop and keep friendships • Use positive communication and behaviors • Show progress in developing and keeping friendships • Resolve conflicts respectfully with the help of supportive adults **Grades K–2:** • Pay attention to others when they are speaking • Demonstrate the use of verbal etiquette (use please, thank you, excuse me, and so on; take turns and share with others) • Effectively and appropriately communicate needs, wants, and ideas in a respectful manner **Grades 3–5:** • Give and receive compliments in a genuine manner • Use attentive listening skills to foster better communication • Demonstrate good sportsmanship • Demonstrate cooperative behaviors in a group (for example, listen, encourage, acknowledge opinions, compromise, reach consensus)

SEL Essential Standard	Learning Targets
4B. Develop and maintain positive relationships	Grades PreK–K: • Show an increasing ability to initiate and sustain age-appropriate play and interactions with peers and adults; successfully develop and keep friendships • Use positive communication and behaviors Grades K–2: • Identify the multiple types of relationships they have with others • List traits that characterize a good friend • Demonstrate ability to make new friends • Identify and practice behaviors such as active listening and sharing to maintain positive relationships Grades 3–5: • Recognize the difference between helpful and harmful behaviors in relationships; identify a problem in a relationship and seek appropriate assistance • Understand the positive and negative impact of peer pressure on self and others
4C. Demonstrate an ability to prevent, manage, and resolve interpersonal conflicts in helpful ways	Grades PreK–K: • Show an increasing capacity to take another's perspective • Begin to develop and practice the use of problem solving and conflict resolution skills Grades K–2: • Identify interpersonal problems they need adult help to resolve and appropriately ask for help • Recognize there are many ways to solve conflicts and practice solving problems using a menu of choices, including the use of "I" messages • Identify and state feelings and problem in conflict Grades 3–5: • Show an understanding of conflict as a natural part of life • Describe causes and effects of conflicts, including how their behavior impacts others' emotions • Distinguish between destructive and constructive ways of dealing with conflict; activate the steps of a peaceful conflict resolution process (listen, express feelings, discuss solutions, make amends, and so on)

continued →

CASEL Core Competencies: *Responsible Decision Making*	
Michigan State Standards	
SEL Essential Standard	**Learning Targets**
5A. Consider personal, ethical, safety, and cultural factors in making decisions	PreK–K: • Positive and accepting attitudes toward people of a variety of backgrounds or characteristics (for example, race, ethnicity, national origin, physical characteristics, disability, economic status, language spoken, or signed background) • An increasing ability to take another's point of view and to empathize with others K–2: • Recognize that one has choices in how to respond • Identify ways to promote safety for oneself and others • Identify ways to respond to unfamiliar adults in different settings • Stand up for a friend or peer and let others know when a person is being treated unfairly 3–5: • Identify social norms that affect decision making • Define cyber-bullying and response strategies • Identify when someone is targeted and how to respond to a situation to support the individual • Recognize and describe how the media can influence one's behavior • Stand up for self or a peer who is being disrespected
5B. Develop, implement, and model effective decision-making skills to deal responsibly with daily academic and social situations	Grades PreK–K: • Begin to hypothesize or make inferences • Attempt a variety of ways and demonstrate enjoyment of solving problems • Use materials purposefully, safely, and respectfully more and more of the time • Manage transitions and follow routines most of the time Grades K–2: • Recognize that they have choices in how to respond to situations • Implement *stop, think, and act* strategies in solving problems • Demonstrate social and classroom behavior (ask permission, listen to speaker, ask for help, offer to help, participate) • Demonstrate constructive academic behaviors and self-regulation (listen, pay attention, follow directions, ignore distractions) Grades 3–5: • Describe the steps of a decision-making model • Generate alternative solutions to problems and predict possible outcomes; effectively participate in group decision-making processes • Demonstrate academic behaviors and self-regulation skills such as organization, completing assignments, and planning

SEL Essential Standard	Learning Targets
5C. Contribute a developmentally appropriate role in classroom management and positive school climate	**Grades PreK–K:** • Contribute individual strengths, imagination, or interests to a group • Demonstrate an increasing sense of belonging and awareness of their role as a member of a family, classroom, and community **Grades K–2:** • Recognize the various roles of the personnel that govern the school (all staff); participate in individual roles and responsibilities in the classroom and in school **Grades 3–5:** • Identify and organize materials needed to be prepared for class • Understand personal relationships with personnel that govern the school • Discuss and model appropriate classroom behavior individually and collectively

Source: Michigan Department of Education, 2017.

Table 5.2: Building Block—Third-Grade Essential Standards Chart

Building Block: *Sense of Self*		
SEL Essential Standard	**Foundational SEL Learning Targets**	**Developing SEL Learning Targets**
SS1. Recognizing individual traits and qualities of oneself*	SS1.F.a. Identify likes and dislikes SS1.F.b. Identify wants and needs SS1.F.c. Feel proud of oneself for specific tasks and achievements	SS1.D.a. Identify personal strengths and challenges SS1.D.b. Identify personal qualities one wants to develop or improve SS1.D.c. Identify own needs and values
SS2. Identifying Emotions	SS2.F.a. Recognize names of emotions SS2.F.b. Label one's own emotions SS2.F.c. Understand how one can feel emotions in different physical areas in their body	SS2.D.a. Understand how one can feel one or more emotion at the same time SS2.D.b. Identify the physical effects of emotions
SS3. Identify cause-and-effect nature of events and emotions	SS3.F.a. Recognize which events make one feel specific emotions	SS3.D.a. Recognize cause and effect of events that lead to emotions, and emotions that lead to events

Highlighting indicates an essential standard.

continued →

Building Block: *Reciprocal Engagement*		
SEL Essential Standard	**Foundational SEL Learning Targets**	**Developing SEL Learning Targets**
RE1. Participate in an extended reciprocal interaction, either nonverbal or verbal	RE.1.F.a. Respond to others' initiations. RE.1.F.b. Initiate conversation. RE.1.F.c. Maintain back and forth communication for an extended time without walking away.	RE.1.D.a. Evaluate own skills to communicate with others. RE.1.D.b. Recognize ways to initiate conversation with an unfamiliar peer or adult. RE.1.D.c. Monitor ebb and flow of conversation in response to conversation partner.
RE2. Interact with peers in structured and unstructured settings for extended periods of time	RE.2.F.a. Take turns in game play and in conversation RE.2.F.b. Include others' ideas in play schemes and activities	RE.2.D.a. Group work—Participate in cooperative learning (partner play or group work) RE.2.D.b. Communicate thoughts and ideas with others and work toward a common goal
RE3. Appropriately share one's own emotions and respond to the emotions of others	RE.3.F.a. Share emotions with others in a socially appropriate way. RE.3.F.b. Recognize the emotions of others and respond appropriately. RE.3.F.c. Respond to verbal and nonverbal cues of others.	RE.3.D.a. Describe and demonstrate one's own emotions. RE.3.D.b. Recognize the emotions of others and what events led the person to feel this way. RE.3.D.c. Recognize nonverbal cues that indicate someone's emotions. RE.3.D.d. Respond to the emotional needs of others appropriately.
RE4. Identify needs and advocate for self (ask for help)	RE.4.F.a. Identify personal needs. RE.4.b. Appropriately ask for help or let others know about these needs (for example, ask to go to the bathroom, ask to get water at the appropriate time). RE.4.c. Make choices about when to ask for help or self-advocate and when to wait.	RE.4.D.a. Identify personal needs and self-advocate when appropriate. RE.4.D.b. Recognize needs of others in both verbal and nonverbal cues and respond appropriately, in either offering help or allowing someone to have appropriate processing time.
RE5. Recognize and respect boundaries between self and others	RE.5.Fa. Label own emotions and the reason behind those emotions. RE.5.Fb. Understand that individuals may be experiencing different emotions from one another.	RE.5.D.a. Recognize that people can respond to the same event with different emotions. RE.5.D.b. Listen to another person's perspective and respond without judgement.

Building Block: *Social Awareness*		
SEL Essential Standard	**Foundational SEL Learning Targets**	**Developing SEL Learning Targets**
SA1. Identify similarities and differences in self and others	SA.1.F.a. Understand that individuals have different likes, dislikes, and emotional reactions to events. SA.1.F.b. Observes others and recognizes feelings from others' facial expression, body language, and tone of voice.	SA.1.D.a. Describe positive qualities in others. SA.1.D.b. Recognize similarities and differences in viewpoints and opinions. SA.1.D.c. Seek to find common understanding even within a disagreement.
SA2. Recognize and appreciate differences in cultures	SA.2.F.a. Identify similarities and differences in cultures. SA.2.F.b. Recognize how different cultures contribute to a community.	SA.2.D.a. Identify similarities and differences in cultures. SA.2.D.b. Recognize how different cultures can work together to help one another within the same community. SA.2.D.c. Understand that differences and similarities exist within different groups, even when those groups do not agree.
SA3. Take perspective and "put self in someone else's shoes"	SA.3.F.a. Explain how a character in a book may feel and why. SA.3.F.b. Listen to a peer's view of a situation and understand how the peer may have responded to that situation. SA.3.F.c. Understand another person's thoughts, feelings, and why that person may feel that way.	SA.3.D.a. Explain the cause-and-effect relationship of events and emotions and how these differ for individuals. SA.3.D.b. Understand that each person brings a different viewpoint to the group; listen to different perspectives and be open to new ideas when working with peers in collaborative projects. SA.3.D.c. Ask questions to find a common ground or to understand where the peer is coming from, when one does not agree with a peer.
SA4. Recognize how one's actions may harm or interfere with another's well-being.	SA.4.F.a. Understand that one's words and actions can help or hurt others. SA.4.F.b. Describe words, phrases, and actions that can help others, as well as those that may hurt others. SA.4.F.c. Use active listening skills.	SA.4.D.a. Recognize how one's strengths and characteristics can benefit the larger community. SA.4.D.b. Identify ways to work effectively with others that may be different from oneself or disagree with one's ideas.

continued →

Building Block: *Social-Emotional Regulation*		
SEL Essential Standard	**Foundational SEL Learning Targets**	**Developing SEL Learning Targets**
SR.1. Monitor personal emotions and use strategies to regulate emotions	SR.1.F.a. Explore different calm-down strategies and identify which works best for the individual. SR.1.F.b. Recognize situations when upset and when one may need to use the calm-down strategies. SR.1.F.c. Use calm-down strategies with an adult when upset or dysregulated.	SR.1.D.a. Explore different calm-down strategies and identify which works best for the individual. SR.1.D.b. Recognize situations when upset and when one may need to use the calm-down strategies. SR.1.D.c. Use calm-down strategies with an adult or independently when upset or dysregulated.
SR.2. Exercise self-control	SR.2.F.a. Recognize that sometimes we all want to do something that we cannot do. SR.2.F.b. Practice using self-talk and self-regulation strategies to pause before acting and think about one's actions. SR.2.F.c. Accept coaching from an adult on refraining from impulses.	SR.2.D.a. Identify times when it is difficult but necessary to use self-control. SR.2.D.b. Use self-talk and self-regulation strategies to pause before acting to calm self and make predictions of possible consequences of actions.
SR.3. Demonstrate ability to recover from challenges	SR.3.F.a. Recognize when something is difficult, did not work, or did not go their way. SR.3.F.b. Identify strategies to use when faced with challenges. SR.3.F.c. Accept coaching and co-regulation from peers or adults when recovering from a challenge.	SR.3.D.a. Reflect on events that did not turn out as intended. Identify setbacks and ways to improve in the future. SR.3.D.b. Use calming strategies when recovering from a challenge in order to move forward.
SR.4. Self-motivate	SR.4.F.a. Identify a goal or task needed to be achieved and use self-talk to get started. SR.4.F.b. Accept coaching and co-regulation to return to the task at hand in order to complete the task.	SR.4.D.a. Identify, begin, and complete the required task while using self-regulation strategies such as self-talk when needed.
Building Block: *Logical and Responsible Decision Making*		
SEL Essential Standard	**Foundational SEL Learning Targets**	**Developing SEL Learning Targets**
DM.1. Follow a systematic process to make decisions and choices	DM.1.F.a. Identify a goal in making a decision and list a plan to achieve that goal. DM.1.F.b. Take multiple pieces of information, make an informed decision, and act on it.	DM.1.D.a. Consider ethical standards, safety concerns, and social norms as they impact decision making.
DM.2. Revise opinions and plans based on new information	DM.2.F.a. Identify an original opinion or plan as "Plan A" and understand that sometimes we have to change to a "plan B" or "plan C" once there is new information.	DM.2.D.a. Recognize the need to change plans or opinions based on new information.

SEL Essential Standard	Foundational SEL Learning Targets	Developing SEL Learning Targets
DM.3. Consider the perspectives and needs of others when decision making	DM.3.F.a. Identify people who the outcome may impact before making a final decision. DM.3.F.b. "Fast forward" to consider how they might feel about the plan or action.	DM.3.D.a. Describe how each stakeholder may be impacted by a decision, and how those impacts may cause both long-term and short-term effects.
DM.4. Apply a shared norm for treating others how you would like to be treated	DM.4.F.a. Think about treating others like they want to be treated when making decisions that may impact others.	DM.4.D.a. Reflect on the repercussions of one's decisions and determine if they reflect how one would want to be treated for all stakeholders when thinking about making decisions that will impact a large community.

Source: Standards and learning targets adapted from CASEL, 2017; Illinois Department of Education, n.d.; Michigan Department of Education, 2017.

In figure 5.13 (page 251), the Michigan Department of Education directly aligns learning targets to grade-level bands. In table 5.2 (page 259), the *developing* learning targets are the grade-level learning targets (in this example, that would be for third grade). Yet the team recognized that some of its students may be missing skills or may not have the foundational understandings needed to learn some of these grade-level learning targets. So, using SEL standards from grade levels below third grade, the team identified a set of correlating learning targets, which it labeled as *foundational*. Therefore, if a student or group of students shows difficulty with the developing learning targets, the teacher knows to build work around the foundational learning targets within lessons. Because students develop SEL skills at different rates it is important to consider where each student is working within each of these standards and recognize which learning target to focus on first.

Step 4: Cluster SEL Standards Within and Across Each of the Overarching SEL Focal Areas

Next, the team can look at the learning targets within each SEL focal area (five SEL building blocks, CASEL core competencies, and so on) and see which standards it can teach simultaneously. Then, it is equally important to look across the SEL focal areas to determine which standards could be taught together to strengthen students' understanding and build deeper connections. As seen in the third-grade yearlong-planning tool example (figure 5.13, page 251), the team decided to create a unit around self-regulation strategies to teach in October. The team recognized that to teach self-regulation, the students must first be able to share emotions with others in an appropriate way (*reciprocal engagement*) and recognize the impact of one's emotions (*sense of self*), and only then will students be ready to begin learning self-regulation strategies. Therefore, this unit will begin with using an essential standard the team placed within the *reciprocal engagement* building block component and then move into focusing on an essential standard from the *sense of self* building block. This will be followed by teaching some of the essential standards within the emotional regulation strategies.

Step 5: Determine Which SEL Learning Targets Correlate with Academic Units or Structures

In doing this work, the team should consider other curriculum areas and how it can embed or align SEL lessons with the academic learning. For instance, if a third-grade team will be teaching about ancient civilizations in February and March, they can align their SEL curriculum so that they also teach social awareness between different cultures during this time. The content students are learning in world history provides an excellent framework to begin to discuss cultural differences among civilizations and how those cultures influence us today. Conversely, if a team focuses on character traits in fiction literature in November and December, it can pair the SEL standards with social awareness of the emotions of others, cause-and-effect of events and emotions, and perspective taking. Teachers may want to teach group work skills and reciprocal engagement before or in conjunction with group projects or introduce partner games in mathematics. Pairing SEL standards with academic standards will make the SEL skills more meaningful to the students.

Steps 6 and 7: Form and Order Units of Study and Determine the Duration of Each Unit of Study

The third-grade team's yearlong planning tool (figure 5.13, page 251) shows that after sequencing its essential standards into a yearlong plan the team then created separate units to organize students' thinking. At this stage, the team can look at how the standards build on one another and possibly use pacing guide tools in the school's selected SEL program or SEL research as guides in doing this work. Each unit of study should contain a balance of essential and non-essential standards, and the essential standards should spiral throughout the year and may appear in more than one unit of study. While each unit dives into a core concept and related skills, standards from different SEL competencies or building blocks are taught together. These units may also be paired with the academic units the team is discussing. During this time, teams should keep in mind that some standards may need additional time or repetition. Providing direct instruction on self-regulation skills in October will most likely not be enough to sustain the students throughout the school year. These are essential standards that should be focused on throughout the year and reviewed or examined in more depth later in the year.

Next, it is time to order the units of study (figure 5.14). If the units correlate with specific academic areas, it is important to align them at the same time of the school year (when possible). Finally, the team needs to determine the duration of each unit of study. Some skills and concepts might be new or students may need more or less time based on students' background knowledge or the rigor of the content being taught. Decide how many instructional days are needed for each unit of study.

Unit 1: Introduction to Routines, Community, and Reciprocal Engagement September/October *Six weeks*				
Topic and Standards	Duration	Foundational Learning Targets	Developing Learning Targets	Curriculum Connection
Building SEL routines	August/September: one to two weeks		Building SEL routines, community, and the positive learning environment	Social studies: 3.1. The student will demonstrate skills for historical thinking, geographical analysis, economic decision making, and responsible citizenship by practicing good citizenship skills and respect for rules and laws while collaborating, compromising, and participating in classroom activities
RE1. Participate in an extended reciprocal interaction, either nonverbal or verbal	One day	RE.1.F.a. Respond to others' initiations. RE.1.F.b. Initiate conversation. RE.1.F.c. Maintain back and forth communication for an extended time without walking away.	RE.D.a. Evaluate own skills to communicate with others. RE.1.D.b. Recognize ways to initiate conversation with an unfamiliar peer or adult. RE.1.D.c. Monitor ebb and flow of conversation in response to conversation partner.	Mathematics: Partner game Recess: Collaborative play 3.1. The student will demonstrate skills for historical thinking, geographical analysis, economic decision making, and responsible citizenship by practicing good citizenship skills and respect for rules and laws while collaborating, compromising, and participating in classroom activities

Figure 5.14: Third-grade yearlong SEL planning tool—example (based on table 5.2).

continued →

Highlighting indicates an essential standard.

Topic and Standards	Duration	Foundational Learning Targets	Developing Learning Targets	Curriculum Connection
RE2. Interact with peers in structured and unstructured settings for extended periods of time*	One week	RE.2.F.a. Take turns in game play and in conversation RE.2.F.b. Include others' ideas in play schemes and activities	RE.2.D.a. Participate in cooperative learning (partner play or group work) RE.2.D.b. Communicate thoughts, ideas with others and work towards a common goal	Mathematics: Partner game Social studies: 3.1. The student will demonstrate skills for historical thinking, geographical analysis, economic decision making, and responsible citizenship by practicing good citizenship skills and respect for rules and laws while collaborating, compromising, and participating in classroom activities
SS1. Recognizing individual traits and qualities of oneself SA4. Recognize how one's actions may harm or interfere with another's well-being	One week	SS1.F.a. Identify likes and dislikes SS1.F.b. Identify wants and needs SS1.F.c. Feel proud of oneself for specific tasks and achievements	SS1.D.a. Identify personal strengths and challenges. SS1.D.b. Identify personal qualities one wants to develop or improve. SS1.D.c. Identify own needs and values. SA.4.D.a. Recognize how one's strengths and characteristics can benefit the larger community.	Language arts: 3.6. The student will continue to read and demonstrate comprehension of nonfiction texts. That is, compare and contrast the characteristics of biographies and autobiographies. Social studies: 3.13. Student will recognize that Americans are a people of diverse ethnic origins, customs, and traditions and are united by the basic principles of a republican form of government and respect for individual rights and freedoms.

Topic and Standards	Duration	Foundational Learning Targets	Developing Learning Targets	Curriculum Connection
SS2. Identifying Emotions	One week	SS2.F.a. Recognize names of emotions SS2.F.b. Label one's own emotions SS2.F.c. Understand how one can feel emotions in different physical areas in their body	SS2.D.a. Understand how one can feel one or more emotion at the same time SS2.D.b. Identify the physical effects of emotions	Pair with novel study on E. B. White's *Charlotte's Web* Language arts: 3.5. The student will read and demonstrate comprehension of fictional text and poetry. • Compare and contrast settings, characters, and events. • Draw conclusions about text.
RE3. Appropriately share one's own emotions and respond to the emotions of others	One week	RE.3.F.a. Share emotions with others in a socially appropriate way. RE.3.F.b. Recognize the emotions of others and respond appropriately. RE.3.F.c. Respond to verbal and nonverbal cues of others.	RE.3.D.a. Describe and demonstrate one's own emotions. RE.3.D.b. Recognize the emotions of others and what events led the person to feel this way. RE.3.D.c. Recognize nonverbal cues that indicate someone's emotions. RE.3.D.d. Respond to the emotional needs of others appropriately.	Social studies: 3.2. Recognize direct cause-and-effect relationships.
SS3. Identify cause-and-effect nature of events and emotion	One week	SS3.F.a. Recognize which events make one feel specific emotions	SS3.D.a. Recognize cause and effect of events that lead to emotions, and emotions that lead to events	Language arts: 3.5. The student will read and demonstrate comprehension of fictional text and poetry. That is, the student will identify the problem and solution. Social studies: 3.2. Recognize direct cause-and-effect relationships.

continued →

Unit 2: Identifying and Using Self-Regulation Strategies October/November *Five weeks*				
Topic and Standards	Duration	Foundational Learning Targets	Developing Learning Targets	Curriculum Connection
RE3. Appropriately share one's own emotions and respond to the emotions of others	One week	RE.3.F.a. Share emotions with others in a socially appropriate way. RE.3.F.b. Recognize the emotions of others and respond appropriately. RE.3.F.c. Respond to verbal and nonverbal cues of others.	RE.3.D.a. Describe and demonstrate one's own emotions. RE.3.D.b. Recognize the emotions of others and what events led the person to feel this way. RE.3.D.c. Recognize nonverbal cues that indicate someone's emotions. RE.3.D.d. Respond to the emotional needs of others appropriately.	Language arts: 3.5. The student will read and demonstrate comprehension of fictional text and poetry. (d) compare and contrast settings, characters, and events.
SS3. Identify cause-and-effect nature of events and emotion	One week	SS3.F.a. Recognize which events make one feel specific emotions	SS3.D.a. Recognize cause and effect of events that lead to emotions, and emotions that lead to events. SS3.D.a. Recognize cause and effect of events that lead to emotions, and emotions that lead to events.	Fiction unit on cause and effect: Language arts: 3.5. The student will read and demonstrate comprehension of fictional text and poetry. (h) identify the problem and solution. Social studies: 3.2. Recognize direct cause-and-effect relationships.

Topic and Standards	Duration	Foundational Learning Targets	Developing Learning Targets	Curriculum Connection
SR 1. Monitor personal emotions and use strategies to regulate emotions SR 3. Demonstrate ability to recover from challenges	Two weeks	SR.1.F.a. Explore different calm-down strategies and identify which works best for the individual. SR.1.F.b. Recognize situations when upset and when one may need to use the calm-down strategies. SR.1.F.c. Use calm-down strategies with an adult when upset or dysregulated. SR.3.F.a. Recognize when something is difficult, did not work, or did not go one's way. SR.3.F.b. Identify strategies to use when faced with challenges. SR.3.F.c. Accept coaching and co-regulation from peers or adults when recovering from a challenge.	SR.1.D.c. Use calm-down strategies with an adult or independently when upset or dysregulated. SR.3.D.a. Reflect on events that did not turn out as intended. Identify setbacks and ways to improve in the future. SR.3.D.b. Use calming strategies when recovering from a challenge in order to move forward.	Pair with science—when the simple machines projects do not go as planned. What if your plan does not work? Science and engineering: 3.1. The student will demonstrate an understanding of scientific and engineering practices by (a) asking questions and defining problems, (b) asking questions that they can investigate and predicting reasonable outcomes, (c) asking questions about what happens if a variable is changed, and (d) defining a simple design problem that they can solve through the development of an object, tool, process, or system. Mathematics: Partner games—use self-talk and teacher and student modeling.

continued →

Topic and Standards	Duration	Foundational Learning Targets	Developing Learning Targets	Curriculum Connection
SR 2. Exercise self-control	One week	SR.2.F.a. Recognize that sometimes we all want to do something that we cannot do. SR.2.F.b. Practice using self-talk and self-regulation strategies to pause before acting and think about one's actions. SR.2.F.c. Accept coaching from an adult on refraining from impulses.	SR.2.D.a. Identify times when it is difficult but necessary to use self-control. SR.2.D.b. Use self-talk and self-regulation strategies to pause before acting to calm self and make predictions of possible consequences of actions.	Social studies: 3.10. The student will identify examples of making an economic choice and will explain the idea of opportunity cost (what is given up when making a choice). Civics: 3.11. The student will explain the responsibilities of a good citizen, with emphasis on (d) demonstrating self-discipline and self-reliance. Mathematics: Partner games—use self-talk and teacher and student modeling.
Unit 3: Developing Social Awareness November/December *Six weeks*				
Topic and Standards	Duration	Foundational Learning Targets	Developing Learning Targets	Curriculum Connection
SA1. Identify similarities and differences in self and others	One week	SA.1.F.a. Understand that individuals have different likes, dislikes, and emotional reactions to events. SA.1.F.b. Observes others and recognizes feelings from others' facial expression, body language, and tone of voice.	SA.1.D.a. Describe positive qualities in others. SA.1.D.b. Recognize similarities and differences in viewpoints and opinions.	Fiction unit: Character traits Language arts: 3.5. The student will read and demonstrate comprehension of fictional text and poetry. That is, the student can compare and contrast settings, characters, and events.

Topic and Standards	Duration	Foundational Learning Targets	Developing Learning Targets	Curriculum Connection
RE5. Recognize and respect boundaries between self and others	One week	RE.5.F.a. Label own emotions and the reason behind those emotions. RE.5.F.b. Understand that individuals may be experiencing different emotions from one another.	RE.5.D.a. Recognize that people can respond to the same event with different emotions. RE.5.D.b. Listen to another person's perspective and respond without judgement.	Civics: 3.11. The student will explain the responsibilities of a good citizen, with emphasis on (d) demonstrating self-discipline and self-reliance.
RE1. Participate in an extended reciprocal interaction, either nonverbal or verbal RE2. Interact with peers in structured and unstructured settings for extended periods of time	Two weeks	RE.1.F.a. Respond to others' initiations. RE.1.F.b. Initiate conversation. RE.1.F.c. Maintain back-and-forth communication for an extended time without walking away. RE.2.F.a. Take turns in game play and in conversation. RE.2.F.b. Include others' ideas in play schemes and activities.	RE.1.D.a. Evaluate own skills to communicate with others. RE.1.D.b. Recognize ways to initiate conversation with an unfamiliar peer or adult. RE.1.D.c. Monitor ebb and flow of conversation in response to conversation partner. RE.2.D.a. Participate in cooperative learning (partner play or group work). RE.2.D.b. Communicate thoughts and ideas with others and work towards a common goal.	Language arts: 3.1. The student will use effective communication skills in group activities. a) Listen attentively by making eye contact, facing the speaker, asking questions, and summarizing what is said. b) Ask and respond to questions from teachers and other group members. c) Explain what has been learned. d) Use language appropriate for context. e) Increase listening and speaking vocabularies. Apply these skills during collaborative work in economics: Project-Based Learning on SOL Social Studies 3.9 regarding bartering and trade.

continued →

Topic and Standards	Duration	Foundational Learning Targets	Developing Learning Targets	Curriculum Connection
SA3. Take perspective and put self in someone else's shoes.	One week	SA.3.F.a. Explain how a character in a book may feel and why. SA.3.F.b. Listen to a peer's view of a situation and understand how the peer may have responded to that situation. SA.3.F.c. Understand another person's thoughts and feelings, and why that person may feel that way.	SA.3.D.a. Explain the cause-and-effect relationship of events and emotions and how these differ for individuals. SA.3.D.b. Understand that each person brings a different viewpoint to the group; listen to different perspectives and be open to new ideas when working with peers in collaborative projects. SA.3.D.c. Ask questions to find a common ground or to understand where the peer is coming from, when one does not agree with the peer.	Perspective taking in character development: Language arts: 3.5. The student will read and demonstrate comprehension of fictional text and poetry. b) Make connections between previous experiences and reading selections. d) Compare and contrast settings, characters, and events.
SA4. Recognize how one's actions may harm or interfere with another's well-being.	One week	SA.4.F.a. Understand that one's words and actions can help or hurt others. SA.4.F.b. Describe words, phrases, and actions that can help others as well as those that may hurt others.	SA.4.D.a. Recognize how one's strengths and characteristics can benefit the larger community.	Social studies: 3.1. The student will demonstrate skills for historical thinking, geographical analysis, economic decision making, and responsible citizenship by (f) determining relationships with multiple causes or effects; (h) using a decision-making model to make informed decisions.

Unit 4: Review Routines and Exercising Self-Control January *Four weeks*				
Topic and Standards	Duration	Foundational Learning Targets	Developing Learning Targets	Curriculum Connection
SR.3. Demonstrate ability to recover from challenges	Three weeks	SR.3.F.a. Recognize when something is difficult, did not work, or did not go one's way. SR.3.F.b. Identify strategies to use when faced with challenges. SR.3.F.c. Accept coaching and co-regulation from peers or adults when recovering from a challenge.	SR.3.D.a. Reflect on events that did not turn out as intended. Identify setbacks and ways to improve in the future. SR.3.D.b. Use calming strategies when recovering from a challenge in order to move forward.	3.1. The student will demonstrate skills for historical thinking, geographical analysis, economic decision making, and responsible citizenship by (h) using a decision-making model to make informed decisions.
SR.4. Self-Motivate	One week	SR.4.F.a. Identify a goal or task you need to achieve and use self-talk to get started.	SR.4.D.a. Identify, begin, and complete the required task while using self-regulation strategies such as self-talk when needed. (Use self-talk to get started)	Connect with teaching reading strategies and self-monitoring: Language arts: 3.5. The student will read and demonstrate comprehension of fictional text and poetry. k) Use reading strategies to monitor comprehension throughout the reading process. Mathematics: 3.3.b. Create and solve single-step and multistep practical problems involving sums or differences of two whole numbers, each 9,999 or less (model self-talk during focus lesson and implement use of student goal cards).

continued →

Unit 5: Understanding Social Awareness Within Different Cultures				
February				
Three weeks				
Topic and Standards	Duration	Foundational Learning Targets	Developing Learning Targets	Curriculum Connection
SA2. Recognize and appreciate differences in cultures	Three weeks	SA.2.F.a. Identify similarities and differences in cultures. SA.2.F.b. Recognize how different cultures contribute to a community.	SA.2.D.a. Identify similarities and differences in cultures. SA.2.D.b. Recognize how different cultures can work together to help one another within the same community. SA.2.D.c. Understand that differences and similarities exist within different groups, even when those groups do not agree.	Social studies: 3.1. The student will demonstrate skills for historical thinking, geographical analysis, economic decision making, and responsible citizenship by comparing and contrasting ideas and perspectives to better understand people or events in world cultures. Social studies: 3.13. The student will recognize that Americans are a people of diverse ethnic origins, customs, and traditions and are united by the basic principles of a republican form of government and respect for individual rights and freedoms.

Unit 6: Revisit Self-Regulation Strategies				
March				
Three weeks				
Topic and Standards	Duration	Foundational Learning Targets	Developing Learning Targets	Curriculum Connection
SR 1. Monitor personal emotions and use strategies to regulate emotions SR 3. Demonstrate ability to recover from challenges	Two weeks	SR.1.F.a. Explore different calm-down strategies and identify which works best for the individual. SER.1.F.b. Recognize situations when upset and when one may need to use the calm-down strategies. SR.1.F.c. Use calm-down strategies with an adult when upset or dysregulated. SR.3.F.a. Recognize when something is difficult, did not work, or did not go one's way. SR.3.F.b. Identify strategies to use when faced with challenges. SR.3.F.c. Accept coaching and co-regulation from peers or adults when recovering from a challenge.	SR.1.D.c. Use calm-down strategies with an adult or independently when upset or dysregulated. SR.3.D.a. Reflect on events that did not turn out as intended. Identify setbacks and ways to improve in the future. SR.3.D.b. Use calming strategies when recovering from a challenge in order to move forward.	Connect emotional regulation cycle to adaptations Science: 3.4. The student will investigate and understand that adaptations allow organisms to satisfy life needs and respond to the environment. Key ideas include (a) populations may adapt over time; (b) adaptations may be behavioral or physical. Geography: 3.5. The student will develop map skills and an understanding of change over time by locating major ancient world cultures on world maps (a) at the beginning of their culture, (b) during their period of greatest influence, and (c) today.

continued →

Topic and Standards	Duration	Foundational Learning Targets	Developing Learning Targets	Curriculum Connection
SR 2. Exercise self-control	One week	SR.2.F.a. Recognize that sometimes we all want to do something that we cannot do. SR.2.F.b. Practice using self-talk and self-regulation strategies to pause before acting and think about one's actions. SR.2.F.c. Accept coaching from an adult on refraining from impulses.	SR.2.D.a. Identify times when it is difficult but necessary to use self-control. SR.2.D.b. Use self-talk and self-regulation strategies to pause before acting to calm self and make predictions of possible consequences of actions.	Connect to economic lessons of scarcity, supply, and demand. Economics: 3.9. The student will recognize that because people and regions cannot produce everything they want, they specialize in what they do best and trade for the rest. 3.10. The student will identify examples of making an economic choice and will explain the idea of opportunity cost (what does one give up when making a choice).
Unit 7: Goal Setting and Planning April *Four weeks*				
Topic and Standards	Duration	Foundational Learning Targets	Developing Learning Targets	Curriculum Connection
DM.1. Follow a systematic process to make decisions and choices DM.2. Revise opinions and plans based on new information	One and a half weeks	DM.1.F.a. Identify a goal in making a decision and list a plan to achieve that goal. DM.1.F.b. Take multiple pieces of information, make an informed decision, and act on it. DM.2.F.a. Identify an original opinion or plan as "Plan A" and understand that sometimes we have to change to a "plan B" or "plan C" once there is new information.	DM.1.D.a. Consider ethical standards, safety concerns, and social norms as they impact decision making. DM.2.D.a. Recognize the need to change plans or opinions based on new information.	Project-based learning science projects—use goal setting and plans to guide process. Social studies: 3.1. The student will demonstrate skills for historical thinking, geographical analysis, economic decision making, and responsible citizenship by (h) using a decision-making model to make informed decisions. Multiplication unit: Setting goal for learning multiplication facts; 3.4.c. Demonstrate fluency with multiplication facts of 0, 1, 2, 5, and 10.

Topic and Standards	Duration	Foundational Learning Targets	Developing Learning Targets	Curriculum Connection
SR.4. Self-Motivate	Half week (review)	SR.4.F.a. Identify a goal or task needed to be achieved and use self-talk to get started.	SR.4.D.a. Identify, begin, and complete the required task while using self-regulation strategies such as self-talk when needed. (Use self-talk to get started)	Social studies: 3.1. The student will demonstrate skills for historical thinking, geographical analysis, economic decision making, and responsible citizenship by (h) using a decision-making model to make informed decisions.
RE4. Identify needs and advocate for self (ask for help)	Two weeks	RE.4.F.a. Identify personal needs. RE.4.b. Appropriately ask for help or let others know about these needs (ask to go to the bathroom, ask to get water at the appropriate time). RE.4.c. Make choices about when to ask for help or self-advocate and when to wait.	RE.4.D.a. Identify personal needs and self-advocate when appropriate. RE.4.D.b. Recognize needs of others in both verbal and nonverbal cues and respond appropriately, in either offering help or allowing someone to have appropriate processing time.	Social studies: 3.9. The student will recognize that because people and regions cannot produce everything they want, they specialize in what they do best and trade for the rest.

continued →

Unit 8: Making Logical and Responsible Decisions				
May/June				
Three weeks				
Topic and Standards	Duration	Foundational Learning Targets	Developing Learning Targets	Curriculum Connection
DM.3. Consider the perspectives and needs of others when decision making DM.4. Apply a shared norm for treating others how you would like to be treated	Three weeks	DM.3.F.a. Identify people who the outcome may impact before making a final decision. DM.3.F.b. Fast forward to consider how they might feel about the plan or action. DM.4.F.a. Think about treating others like they want to be treated when making decisions that may impact others.	DM.3.D.a. Describe how each stakeholder may be impacted by a decision, and how. DM.4.D.a. Reflect on the repercussions of one's decisions and determine if they reflect how one would want to be treated for all stakeholders, when thinking about making decisions that will impact a large community.	Cumulative project on three ancient cultures. Social studies: 3.2. The student will explain how the contributions of ancient China and Egypt have influenced the present world in terms of architecture, inventions, the calendar, and written language. 3.3. The student will explain how the contributions of ancient Greece and Rome have influenced the present world in terms of architecture, government (direct and representative democracy), and sports. 3.4. The student will describe the oral tradition (storytelling), government (kings), and economic development (trade) of the early West African empire of Mali.

Source: Standards and learning targets adapted from CASEL, 2017; Illinois Department of Education, n.d.; Michigan Department of Education, 2017; Virginia Department of Education, 2015.

Weekly Lesson Planning

No matter what standards you are using, the most important work is collaborating with a team—digging in and learning about what students need to know and understand. We can't expect students to learn and understand if we don't first have clarity ourselves. Others refer to this process as unwrapping, unpacking, or deconstructing the standards. Figure 5.15 is an SEL standards unpacking tool teachers can use as an initial first step to lesson planning, which ultimately is knowing the ins and outs of the standards you'll be teaching. This tool can help teachers identify what students need to understand and demonstrate and then determine how the learning might progress and build. It will also help teams generate ideas for teaching skills and concepts and measuring student growth through developmentally appropriate formative assessments (see chapter 6, page 293). Teachers might find that it is most useful to use a tool like this prior to teaching a new unit of study. They can take time to gain a deeper understanding about the essential SEL standards they will be teaching during the unit of study, and when they do this with their team, common understandings of what they need to teach and assess become a driving force for providing a guaranteed and viable curriculum.

SEL Focal Area: *Reciprocal Engagement*

Essential Standard: RC2. Interact with peers in structured and unstructured settings for extended periods of time

What do students need to know:	What do students need to be able to do:
• Friends, classmates, and teachers like when we take turns listening and talking • When we listen to our friends, they feel that we care about them and their ideas • When we share our ideas with friends, they know we are a part of the conversation	• Take turns in conversations and when playing games in the classroom or on the playground • Maintain a topic of conversation in the classroom during "Turn and Talk" or on the playground with friends • Share thoughts and ideas during group work within the classroom or during guided or unstructured play

Learning Progression:

Foundational Skills:	Developing Skills:	Expanding Skills:
• RE.2.F.a. Take turns in game play and in conversation • RE.2.F.b. Include others' ideas in play schemes and activities	• RE.2.D.a. Participate in cooperative learning (partner play or group work) • RE.2.D.b. Communicate thoughts and ideas with others and work towards a common goal	Listen to the ideas of others, share one's own ideas, and then combine the ideas of others and own idea to form a compromise.

Teaching strategies and tools:

- Utilize group gathering times such as morning meeting or an end-of-day reflection time to provide conversational instruction, modeling, and practice.

- Model a back-and-forth conversation. Ask students what they notice.

- Have students practice conversations in skits.

- Provide feedback during group work and during unstructured times.

- Offer reflection questions such as, "How did you feel at lunch during your conversation with your friend? What made you feel good? What made you sad?"

Monitoring student growth:

- Observation checklist

- Student self-reflection

- Student goal-setting cards

Figure 5.15: SEL standard unpacking tool.

*Visit **go.SolutionTree.com/instruction** for a free blank reproducible version of this figure.*

SEL Weekly Planning Tool

Once teams have mapped out their yearlong SEL plans and have a clear understanding of the essential standards they are teaching within a given unit, they are ready to create their weekly plans (see figure 5.16). The SEL standards in the weekly planning tool (figure 5.16) align with the SEL building blocks framework. At first glance, some teachers may assume that certain planning elements in the SEL weekly planning tool are "obvious" and not worth writing down, but these pieces are key to ensuring that each member of the team understands the concepts being addressed and that each individual teacher recognizes where the essential standard falls in importance in connection to the greater picture.

Team:				
SEL Focus Areas:				
SEL Essential Standards:				
SEL Foundational Learning Targets:		**SEL Developing Learning Targets:**		**SEL Expanding Learning Targets:**
SEL Supporting Standards (non-essential):				
SEL Foundational Learning Targets:		**SEL Developing Learning Targets:**		**SEL Expanding Learning Targets:**
	Monday	Tuesday	Wednesday	Thursday	Friday
Instruction (Consider using instructional SEL practices—daily routines, read-alouds, games, goal setting, play, journal writing, projects, teachable moments, or learning menus)					

	Monday	Tuesday	Wednesday	Thursday	Friday
When Instruction Occurs					
Connection					

Connections Throughout the Day:					

Time Period	Connecting Activities
Mathematics	
Language Arts	
Other Content Areas	
Lunch/Recess	
Transitions	
Specials (Music, PE, Art, and so on)	
End-of-Day Reflection	
Look-Fors	

Figure 5.16: SEL weekly planning tool.

Visit go.SolutionTree.com/instruction for a free reproducible version of this figure.

To plan for the week using the SEL weekly planning tool, teachers note what they will directly teach each day regarding SEL, when they will teach it, and how they will connect that specific SEL skill to the broader school day. Because SEL skills are often not given a set block of academic time in the daily schedule like reading, writing, or mathematics is, each teacher may choose to structure their SEL time with what works best for their classroom. After identifying when each teacher will teach the direct lessons, the planning tool provides space where the team can note how it will connect SEL learning to the rest of their day. This section of the planning document allows teams to identify which SEL connection (in mathematics, reading, recess, transitions, and so on) they will teach each day. The connection does not need to happen in every academic lesson during the week. Instead, teachers can be intentional in determining which day they will connect SEL to mathematics, recess, end-of-day routines, and so on.

The next step after identifying the direct instruction of the SEL essential standards and how to address these each day is for teachers and teams to complete the *Connections Throughout the Day* section found in the week-at-a-glance (figure 5.16, page 281). This part of the SEL weekly planning tool allows teams to fluidly and easily map out how they will create an interconnected SEL curriculum with what they are already teaching. Planning should include looking at each learning domain and individual subject area and finding possible connections. Mathematics may be an ideal time to review social awareness and reciprocal engagement building block components when working on games, or to review goal setting when looking at a more challenging topic. Already-planned read-alouds in language arts may easily lend themselves to a question or two that connect with the SEL curriculum, or it may be natural to connect a reflective writing assignment to standards within the *sense of self* building block. Science may lend itself to observations of the world around us, or to social awareness, goal setting, sense of self, and our five senses. Social studies can be connected to the study of different cultures, stories of famous figures fulfilling their goals, or historical problems that could have been solved with better reciprocal engagement. In the area of mathematics, teachers can take time to support ideas around self-motivation, persistence, and goal setting as students are engaging in rigorous problem solving. Teachers can use their creativity and consider different ways they may be able to interweave one or two SEL questions or concepts into each academic area throughout the week.

Note that the SEL weekly planning tool also includes connection opportunities at recess, lunch, and specials. SEL cannot be completed in a vacuum (Burt & Whitney, 2018), and many lessons will not resonate unless teachers are able to connect the SEL skill with the soccer game at recess that ended in tears, or to take a moment before and after lunch to challenge students to consider how they responded to their peers' conversations as they ate. Teams can even directly plan for how to teach SEL skills during daily school transitions, such as walking in the hallway or lining up for dismissal at the end of the day, as we previously mentioned. As teams talk through how they will deliberately turn these teachable moments into SEL lessons, they will find the connections come easily and do not take much time (see "Teachable Moments," page 210).

In addition, each team should plan for an end-of-day reflection that will allow students to review and reflect on how their social-emotional capacity was that day. Are they proud of what they achieved? Do they see areas where they can make improvements tomorrow? This is an excellent time to utilize the reflective student goal-setting cards discussed in chapter 4. This natural and nonjudgmental reflection time will allow students to feel safe and connected, reminding them that with a growth mindset each of us can identify ways we can continue to grow.

Finally, at the end of the planning for the week, teams note the teachable moments they should look for that week. These may include friendly language during partner game play, or a disagreement over a game that a teacher can use to turn into a lesson on the exact SEL topic for that week. Thinking through these look-fors ahead of time helps teachers to be on the lookout for the valuable real-world moments when they can naturally coach students on the very work the students need help with in a meaningful, tangible way, outside of the direct instruction within the lesson. This support in real time allows students to generalize SEL skills to all environments, not just within the classroom setting (Burt & Whitney, 2018). If your school is using an SEL curriculum that includes a series of scripted lessons, you can use those for direct instruction, but we still recommend that you think about the standards you are teaching within the lesson. Determine if the lessons fully encapsulate the entire standard or if you may need to supplement the lesson with additional resources. As a team, determine how these ideas can connect to your students' learning in other content areas and real-life experiences throughout the day.

Figure 5.17 contains an example of a completed weekly lesson planning tool for second grade. The SEL standards in the weekly planning tool (see figure 5.15, page 279) align with the SEL building blocks framework (figure I.2, page 10). We have also included two additional weekly planning tools in the online materials for this book (visit **go.SolutionTree.com/instruction** to access these examples).

Team: Second Grade
SEL Focus Areas: Building Blocks *Sense of Self* and *Social Awareness*
SEL Essential Standards: SS2. Identifying Emotions SA3. Take perspective and put self in someone else's shoes.

Figure 5.17: Second-grade SEL weekly lesson planning tool—example.

continued →

SEL Foundational Learning Targets:	SEL Developing Learning Targets:	SEL Expanding Learning Targets:
SS1.F.a. Identify likes and dislikes. SS1.F.b. Identify wants and needs. SS1.F.c. Feel proud of oneself for specific tasks and achievements. SA.3.F.a. Explain how a character in a book may feel and why. SA.3.F.c. Understand another person's thoughts and feelings, and why that person may feel that way.	SS1.D.a. Identify personal strengths and challenges. SS1.D.b. Identify personal qualities one wants to develop or improve. SS1.D.c. Identify own needs and values. SA.3.D.a. Explain the cause-and-effect relationship of events and emotions and how these differ for individuals.	Not applicable at this grade level; Strengthen Developing Skills

SEL Supporting Standards (non-essential):

SA1. Identify similarities and differences in self and others

SEL Foundational Learning Targets:	SEL Developing Learning Targets:	SEL Expanding Learning Targets:
SA.1.F.b. Observe and recognize feelings from others' facial expression, body language, and tone of voice.	SA.1.D.b. Recognize similarities and differences in viewpoints and opinions.	Not applicable at this grade level; Strengthen Developing Skills

Day:	Monday	Tuesday	Wednesday	Thursday	Friday
Instruction (Consider using instructional SEL practices—daily routines, read-alouds, games, goal setting, play, journal writing, projects, teachable moments, or learning menus)	Read book: *Today I Feel Silly*	Record different emotions in book	Read *The Way I Feel*	Venn diagram on the different emotions in each book	Read *Waiting Is Not Easy* by Mo Willems and identify the emotions
When Instruction Occurs	Teacher A—After lunch Teacher B—After recess Teacher C—After lunch Teacher D—End of the day	Teacher A—After lunch Teacher B—After recess Teacher C—After lunch Teacher D—End of the day	Teacher A—After lunch Teacher B—After recess Teacher C—After lunch Teacher D—End of the day	Teacher A—After lunch Teacher B—After recess Teacher C—After lunch Teacher D—End of the day	Teacher A—After lunch Teacher B—After recess Teacher C—After lunch Teacher D—End of the day
Connection	Language Arts Specials	Recess and Transitions Specials	Mathematics Transitions Specials	Language Arts Transitions Specials End of day	Social Studies Transitions Specials

Connections Throughout the Day:	
Time Period	**Connecting Activities**

Mathematics	• Focus on partner games:
	  + Describe how we feel when we win and lose.
	  + Provide model sentences—"Oh man, I lost the game! Better luck next time!"

Language Arts	• Reading:
	  + Read *Knuffle Bunny*
	  + Identify Trixie's emotions throughout the book
	• Writing:
	  + "Show, don't tell"—identify what emotions characters are feeling
	  + Write the character's actions that show that emotion

Other Content Areas	Social Studies: Pilgrims—How did the pilgrims feel in the new world? Why would they feel that way?
Recess	Label the physical features that showed emotions observed on the playground ("I noticed a big smile on Kelly's face. She must have been feeling very happy playing soccer.")
Transitions	Line up by color and make an emotional face: "If you are wearing red, make a sad face and line up," "If you are wearing blue, make an angry face and line up."
Specials	• Art—Students identify how each color makes them feel • Music—Students notice how different music tempos can reflect different emotions • PE—Identify how they feel before and after physical exercise. Does physical exercise change their emotions?
End-of-the-Day Reflection	• Ask "Which emotions did you feel today?" at check in.
Look-Fors	
• Students using emotion words to label their experiences • Students using emotion words to retell stories • Students able to explain why they feel a certain emotion • Students recognizing and accepting similarities and differences in one another's opinions and perspectives	

Incorporating Play Into Academic Schedules

In chapter 4 (page 157), we described what play is, its value, and its overall purpose. While much has been written about the importance of play in children, and while many teachers want to add play into their daily routines, it is difficult to do in an academically rigorous environment. A co-teacher I (Ann-Bailey) deeply admire once lamented, "Maybe we'd be able to do more play if we were teaching in a middle- or upper-class neighborhood. But our students come to us so behind their middle-class peers, it feels wrong to give them time to play when it is my job to make sure they catch up." Even as she said it, we both recognized that while that was true, what the students we were teaching needed more than anything was to have opportunities for free play. There was much we could teach them in our highly rigorous kindergarten class, but the one element we could not do was to give them hours of unstructured play where they could naturally learn and practice all these SEL skills. Deeply struck by what my co-teacher had said, I became determined to embed play into my daily schedule. If play was something beneficial for some students, then it should be offered to *all* students—and it was my job to find that time.

Play can have a powerful place within our academic rigor, but how do we make time for it? Scheduling time for play can be difficult for teachers at first. Once teachers recognize that play is an aspect of learning they want to incorporate in their classrooms, they can often find time to embed both guided and unstructured play. In chapter 4 (page 157), we defined types of play in two ways—guided play, where a teacher directs or guides the play; and unstructured play, where students may be given materials and time but with no constraints on what to do.

For teachers who would like to include unstructured play in their classrooms, we recommend making it a part of the daily or weekly routine (see figure 5.18). If it is routine, students will know what is expected during this set time. Fred Jones recommended having students earn *preferential activity time*, or PAT (Jones, 2000). While this strategy may feel very 1990s, it can provide an excellent way of incorporating play. As a first-grade teacher, I (Ann-Bailey) recognized that the last twenty minutes of the day were the worst. Somehow pack-up could last forever. I turned it around and told the students that those twenty minutes were "their time." As soon as they were packed up, they could access their free time, which was, for lack of a better term, unstructured playtime. While I did not let them get out all the games and toys used in indoor recess, I did let them use art supplies, mathematics games and materials, books, and any of our work from our language arts centers. They packed up quickly and happily engaged in the open-ended, unstructured play. They also cleaned up their play quickly, knowing that if they did not, their free time for the next day would be reduced. Those daily twenty minutes gave me a window into the lives of my students and allowed me to see creativity I otherwise would not have observed.

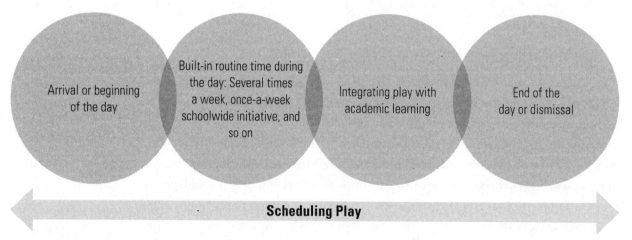

Figure 5.18: Scheduling play into the day.

While play can easily be implemented at the end of the school day, we have seen some teachers use the beginning of their day during students' arrival as a "networking time" for students to engage in reciprocal engagement while at play. The teachers were strategic in the play materials they offered to students and chose items that paired with their current read-alouds or the academic content currently being taught (three-dimensional shapes, sound and light materials, and so on). The teachers would also use this time to engage with students in guided play scenarios, making observations and collecting informative student data.

We also know of schools who have Friday afternoon *wonder time*, when students in the entire school are given an open-ended block of time on Fridays to tinker or explore. While this does not need to be a whole-school commitment, a weekly unstructured free time to allow students to play is one way to schedule in this play opportunity. Also, teams can look at their schedule, be creative, and think outside of the box, and find time (possibly even several times a week) to schedule blocks of play.

Scheduling guided play may come easier to some teachers, as it is able to be tied to lessons already being taught in the classroom. A *retelling station* can be incorporated into the literacy block. This station would allow students to act out or retell what they are reading using symbolic objects that represent characters from the book. In older grades, this may look like creating videos using figures that represent historical time periods they are studying or using small figures to act as scientists to explain the concepts behind a science project in a silly video. These videos (if appropriate) could be shown to younger grades.

Planning for Play

After you have built in time to your schedule to provide students with the opportunity to engage in play, next you must plan for play. Figure 5.19 (page 288) is a play protocol that provides teachers with the steps they can take to implement play. Teachers must first determine the academic or SEL standards and correlating learning targets students need to learn. Then they will determine when the play will occur in the schedule. Following that, they will decide on the type of play they will incorporate into their schedule—either unstructured play or guided play, or possibly even a combination of both. Next, teachers will need to decide what parameters they will provide for the experience, such as: Will they assign groups? Will they limit the number of students in an area? What routine procedures and structures will they establish ahead of time (for example, explaining ahead of time where students can access play materials and where in the classroom they can engage in unstructured play)? Finally, teachers can determine look-fors (observable behaviors that demonstrate if the student is using the SEL objectives within the play) or behaviors that indicate it is a good time for a teacher to provide coaching and feedback.

Play Protocol
1. Identify Learning Standards
What standards will students be learning?
2. Type of Play
Decide what type of play you are trying to incorporate: unstructured play or guided play.
3. Scheduling Play

Unstructured play: Determine when your daily or weekly routine will provide unstructured play.	Guided play: Determine when you will schedule guided play and what topics in your weekly schedule lend themselves to guided play.

4. Parameters of Play
Next, decide what parameters you will provide for the experience. Will you assign groups? Will you limit the number of students in an area? Will you require students to tell you what area they go to before they begin? What play materials will you provide?
5. Look-Fors
Now identify what academic or social-emotional "look-fors" or observable behaviors you will be monitoring for, either to positively reinforce or to use as a teachable moment.
6. Share
How will students share their work?

For both structured and unstructured work, there may be opportunities for students to share their creations with others. Will you provide time to share this work, or will you offer a place in the room where students can put their work on display in a class "museum"? |

Figure 5.19: Play protocol.

*Visit **go.SolutionTree.com/instruction** for a free reproducible version of this figure.*

Figure 5.20 is a sample template for planning unstructured and guided play (a blank template is available online at **go.SolutionTree.com/instruction**). To ensure equity, all teachers at the grade level should be providing play, not just some, but how they structure this time may differ from teacher to teacher. We always recommend starting from a team approach and then encouraging teachers to think about their own students and making modifications to support students' needs.

Planning Play Template

1. Identify Standards

SEL learning targets: Social Awareness

- SA.3.D.b. Understand that each person brings a different viewpoint to the group. Listen to different perspectives and be open to new ideas when working with peers in collaborative projects.
- SA.3.D.c. Ask questions to find a common ground or to understand where the peer is coming from when one does not agree with the peer.

Academic learning targets:

VA SOL Science 3.2—Investigation of Force, Matter, and Simple Machines

3.2 The student will investigate and understand that the direction and size of force affects the motion of an object.

3.2(a) multiple forces may act on an object

3.2(b) the net force on an object determines how an object moves

3.2(c) simple machines increase or change the direction of a force

2. Type of Play

What type of play you are trying to incorporate:

☐ Unstructured play

☑ Guided play

3. Scheduling Play

Unstructured play: Determine when your daily or weekly routine will provide unstructured play:	**Guided play: Determine when you will schedule guided play and what topics in your weekly schedule lend themselves to guided play:**
When:	*When:* Fourth-Grade Science Topics: Science—Simple Machines

Figure 5.20: Sample planning play template—example.

continued →

4. Parameters of Play

What parameters will you provide for the experience? Will you assign groups? Will you limit the number of students in an area? Will you require students to tell you what area they go to before they begin? What play materials will you provide?

Parameters: Assign groups.

Provide students with a variety of common objects such as paper towel rolls, cardboard boxes, rubber bands, rulers, tape, plastic straws, and a marble.

Give students twenty minutes to explore how they can move the marble without touching it.

5. Look-Fors

Identify what specific skills and observable behaviors you will be monitoring for, either to positively reinforce or to use as a teachable moment:

Observable Skills:

- Reinforceable look-fors: Listening to one another's ideas and building onto different ideas.
- Teachable moment look-fors: A student shutting down when others do not take their idea.

Academic look-fors:

- Students discover marbles roll faster with a steeper incline.
- Students apply taught-knowledge of simple machine vocabulary while building.
- Students identify multiple ways to create force to move the marble.

6. Share

In both structured and unstructured work, there may be opportunities for students to share their creations with others. Will you provide time to share this work or will you offer a place in the room where students can put their work on display in a class "museum"?

Will students share their work? _Y_ *If so, how:*

Yes—each group will showcase what they learned at the end of the twenty-minute block and answer the questions about what simple machine they used as well as what aspect of the project was the most challenging and how they overcame that challenge.

Source for standard: Virginia Standards of Learning, Third Grade Science 2018.
*Visit **go.SolutionTree.com/instruction** for a free blank reproducible version of this figure.*

Conclusion

While it can be tempting to only use a stand-alone SEL curriculum that is pre-planned and gives you a clear roadmap for the entire year, doing so will not necessarily meet the needs of your students, your classroom, or your school's unique community. The time collaborative teams are able to commit to careful SEL planning will ensure that the work teachers do with their students around this topic is not wasted. Meaningful learning and development will come from collaborative, thoughtful plans and purposeful differentiation.

After a team has made the commitment to dive into SEL planning and learning, it is time to take the next step of monitoring students' development of these skills. Yet social-emotional learning presents a unique challenge in creating assessments as it differs from typical academic skills. Chapter 6 (page 293) provides insight into collaboratively creating these meaningful monitoring tools and purposefully selecting data and measurement tools that will ensure the teams' ability to answer the second through fourth critical questions of the PLC process: How will we know if they learn it, and how will we respond when some students do not learn and how will we extend learning for students who already have learned it? (DuFour et al., 2016).

Tips for Administrators, Teachers, and Support Staff

Figure 5.21 (page 292) contains tips and reflection questions relating to the contents of this chapter. As you consider these questions and next steps, reflect on your current practices in your own classroom and school.

Administrators	Teachers	Support Staff
• Support teacher teams in making time for SEL throughout their day. • Be understanding of the importance of play embedded into academics. • Provide common planning time for collaborative teams to address SEL work together. Find creative ways for specialist teachers to attend these meetings as well so that they are a part of the conversation. • Model using SEL language throughout different topics during the day, both for students and staff, to bring awareness to how simply embedding SEL awareness questions into the day will connect academics and SEL.	• Look for ways to work better, not harder. How can you embed SEL into your already busy schedules? Rely on your collaborative team for discussing creative ways to make connections with SEL so that it enhances and does not add onto your already busy plate. • Look for ways to embed the 10 teaching strategies—daily routines, transitions, read-alouds, games, goal setting, play, journal writing, projects, teachable moments, and learning menus— into your weekly plans to embed SEL throughout your day. • While planning, consider the unique profiles of the students you are teaching. How can you provide differentiation in either the content, process, product, or environment? • Share your long-range SEL plans with the specialist teachers and support staff who work with your students. Invite them to your meetings to discuss how they can include the SEL topics and vocabulary into their work. • With your collaborative team, create a list of open-ended SEL questions that can be used throughout the school day. Consider how your language and carefully worded questions can be used to bring student focus from academic to SEL.	• Ask to have access to your teams' SEL plans. Be familiar with the connections the team plans so that you can use the language and transitions along with the teachers. • If you are unsure of why a teacher or collaborative team is using certain vocabulary or phrasing, ask for clarification. Once everyone is on the same page the program is stronger and more successful for the students. • Be mindful of the language you use with students throughout the school day. Regardless of the subject, you can embed SEL questions and reflections into your interactions with students to encourage their awareness of their own skills.

Figure 5.21: Tips for administrators, teachers, and support staff from chapter 5.

CHAPTER 6

Monitoring Student Learning of SEL

Vignette: Determining If Teaching SEL Is Actually Making a Difference

Maria sat uncomfortably during her team meeting that focused on how to assess the social-emotional skills they were teaching. She was fully on board for constantly assessing academic skills and using that information to inform their instruction, planning, and grouping, but how would that work with SEL? These skills were different than simply introducing a concept and having the student demonstrate they know it. Some of what they would assess were skills that adults struggle with. Some of the skills were developmental and would take time along with adult support to perform, while some had cultural components. This whole process felt subjective and like the team could end up punishing students for elements they could not control. Maria wasn't sure she liked where this conversation could go.

"Before we start," the school counselor participating in their meeting said, "I want to make sure we first talk about what we want to do with this data. We are so accustomed to constantly assessing academics, but we know exactly how we will use those data. Let's make sure we are on the same page with how we will use what we learn. Are we taking data to report to parents or so we can change what we are doing to help our students be more successful?"

Maria breathed a sigh of relief. This sounded like the right start. "I think," she began, "that we want to take data to know if what we are doing is effective—are our students making improvements on their SEL skills? We also want to know if there is a group of students we can better support by creating groups or shifting our differentiation within our whole-group lessons."

"What we don't want," the English language teacher added, "is to create an assessment that will negatively reflect on students from different cultures and make our students look as though they have social deficits."

> "OK," the special education teacher said. "We also need to ensure that we are not just measuring an SEL skill in one moment during the day. Many of us can demonstrate these skills, but we do not always do it when we are under stress. That's normal human behavior. How do we account for that?"
>
> As Maria listened to her team carefully identify what they wanted from these assessments and what they did not want from assessing SEL skills, she began to feel hopeful. If they did these assessments well, they would have excellent data to inform them of how their teaching was going, along with information on how to best help individual students. Best of all, analyzing these assessments may give the team more insight into which skills they need to spend more time on. Hopefully this would help team members know which of these social-emotional skills are influenced by culture and which are developmental across all students. That knowledge alone would help improve the team's work in future years.

In chapter 3 (page 93), we discussed how schools can use the PLC process to support SEL throughout the school. Part of this involves creating multilayered systems to continuously improve schoolwide efforts relating to SEL. In this chapter, we focus on the multilayered systems that need to be in place to respond and support the needs of individual students (see figure 6.1) and the work of teams in answer to the remaining three critical questions of the PLC process: How will we know if they learn it? How will we respond if they do not learn? And, How will we extend learning for students who already have learned it ? (DuFour et al., 2016).

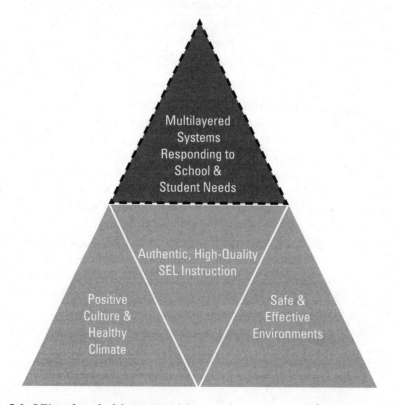

Figure 6.1: SEL schoolwide pyramid.

While the field of social-emotional learning is expanding, the creation and productive use of SEL assessment is still catching up. There are universal screeners and SEL assessments available to purchase, but school teams must be mindful about using SEL assessment. As Herman and McKown (n.d.) note in their article about SEL assessments, before embarking on measuring SEL for the sake of creating data, teachers must first answer the question of what they wish to accomplish with the data and what the purpose of the assessment should be. Are we using this data to determine the next steps in teaching SEL skills? Will we use these data to determine grades on progress reports or what we communicate to parents? Will we use these data to allow school teams to reflect on their work in the area of SEL and determine what practices are and are not benefiting their students?

We would be remiss as educators if we dedicated ourselves to creating a strong, viable curriculum but failed to recognize how all students learn the curriculum. Just as with academics, when some students do not learn the content the first time around, it is our obligation to intervene and make sure students learn it. At this point, it is necessary to provide additional time and support to learn social-emotional learning standards. Some students might even need more intensive interventions in addition to the essential grade-level standards. We can't just intervene on academically focused concepts and skills. In fact, we argue that social-emotional learning is just as important if not more. If social-emotional learning is of great importance, then what does that extra support look like, and will a purchased program be effective in targeting and supporting students' specific needs?

In traditional academic areas, collaborative teams develop common formative assessments to allow teachers to determine which instructional practices are working. While there are universal behavior screeners currently available to schools that provide teachers with useful information, we believe there is significant value found in the school's reflective process of creating and reflecting on SEL assessments. In this chapter, we share specific ideas for teacher teams to look beyond behavior and develop team common formative assessments that focus on the social-emotional skills they are teaching to students at the grade level. These common formative assessments, which the team creates, are intended to measure the skills the team determined to be essential in its SEL work. Based on their yearlong planning, the team can use the essential standards and create common formative assessments to inform how all students grow in the area of SEL. As teacher teams engage in rich discussions around these data from common formative assessments, they have opportunities not only to learn and gain new ideas from each other but also to make important instructional decisions based on results versus opinion.

Understanding the Value of Collaboratively Created Common Formative SEL Assessments

Commercially available universal screeners that specifically focus on social-emotional skills serve an overall purpose and provide teachers with information. Yet, as CASEL notes on the blog *Measuring SEL*, just having information on students is not enough—teacher teams need a clear purpose for collecting this data (Herman & McKown, n.d.). What will teachers do with this information, and why is it important to their work? We believe that common formative assessments should embed the essential social-emotional learning standards the grade-level team identified and be used to support the social-emotional learning of all students, not just some.

Creating common formative assessments also allows teams to address the systematic behavior gap John Hannigan, Jessica Djabrayan Hannigan, Mike Mattos, and Austin Buffum (2021) describe when the decisions of the leadership and intervention teams are somehow not connected to the collaborative teacher teams in practice. As this team describes, schools often take on programs or make collective commitments but are not able to give their staff the full training or translate the importance of the commitments to the school team. This may be from lack of communication, collaboration, coordination, capacity building, or collective ownership. Yet if teams come together to create both their yearlong lesson plans and common formative assessments, they will be addressing this systematic gap through their collaborative discussions and decision making. The work of these common formative assessments allows teams to operate within the Plan—Do—Study—Act framework (Hannigan et al., 2021; Herman & McKown, n.d.), which is what leads schools to making better decisions about SEL.

What is important to keep in mind as we discuss creating common formative SEL assessments is that these assessments are for *all* students. Because the mission of a PLC is for all students to perform at grade level or higher (Hannigan et al., 2021), it is essential we include *all* students in our Tier 1 work. As we learn more about our students and begin to better understand which students need additional time and support, teams can begin to target instruction for students at the Tiers 2 and 3 levels (keep in mind this is additional to what is being taught in Tier 1).

Creating SEL Common Formative Assessments

As teams sit down to determine how to measure the essential SEL standards, they must keep in mind the following questions.

- What SEL skill do we want to measure?

- Why do we want to measure this SEL skill?

- What will we do with the information?

- What will be the best way to get a true measurement?

Unlike academic skills, measuring SEL skills can be a bit less black and white. In figure 6.2, we provide an SEL common formative assessment team planning template for teams to use to guide their decision-making process. As teams become more comfortable with discussing how to measure SEL skills they will move faster through this process.

SEL Common Formative Assessment—Team Planning Template
Target Essential SEL Standards to Measure
Essential Standard: SA3. Take perspective and put self in someone else's shoes. **Learning targets:** SA.3.F.a. Explain how a character in a book may feel and why. SA.3.F.b. Listen to a peer's view of a situation and understand how the peer may have responded to that situation. SA.3.F.c. Understand another person's thoughts, feelings, and why that person may feel that way.
What opportunities do we have to observe our students using those skills?
Options: • Discussing character traits in literature • Talking with peers at lunch and recess • Sharing reactions to situations during morning meetings • Participating in project-based learning
Who will conduct SEL student observations?
Team members: ☑ Classroom teacher: For this assessment we will each make our own observations of our students ☐ Grade-level team member: _____ ☐ Support teacher (English language teacher, special education teacher, and so on): _____ ☐ Specialist teacher (physical education, art, music, librarian): _____
Brainstorm ways to measure the learning of SEL standards and learning targets
Options: • Ask students to respond orally, in writing, or in drawing about how a character from a story is feeling and to identify what they would do in that character's place. • Embed SEL skills into social studies project-based learning. • Create an SEL comic strip scenario and ask students to consider the main character's view of a situation and understand how another character may have responded to that situation. • Create a checklist for yes or no when the student observes the skill: *Understand another person's thoughts, and feelings, and why that person may feel that way.* (Use three data points over the course of two weeks.)

Figure 6.2: Common formative assessment team planning template—example. continued →

Which method is most reliable and free from unbiased judgement?

- Read three literature books; literacy or SEL exit ticket (characters' emotions)—Allow students to show thinking in writing or orally if needed.

- Comic strip journaling activity— Allow students to show thinking in writing or orally if needed.

- Three data points in observation with yes-or-no criteria

What factors may negatively influence a student's social-emotional responses?

- If students come to school dysregulated, they may not be as open to sharing (we may not know what happened at home).

- Students feel hungry before lunch.

- Distractions

Which method will provide us with the *most useful and unbiased* information?

Methods:

Literacy or SEL exit tickets—We will read each of the three books over the unit, and after each book students will answer questions. We will create three literacy or SEL exit tickets focused on essential literacy target: *Tell stories beginning-middle-end,* and essential SEL learning target: *Explain how a character in a book may feel and why.*

Comic strip journal writing activity—We will create a comic strip journal with pictures, and students will reflect on the situation and answer questions relating to SEL learning target: *Listen to a peer's view of a situation and understand how the peer may have responded to that situation.*

Observation and checklist—We will observe how many times students demonstrated this learning target: *Understand another person's thoughts and feelings, and why that person may feel that way,* over the course of two weeks and take notes on the observation sheet.

Team discussion—We will compare the data across classrooms and determine if we need to spend additional time on empathy and perspective taking with all students. We will plan for re-teaching (Tier 1). We will also determine which students are developing the skills and which student may need extra support with these skills (Tier 2 and Tier 3).

What specific materials and tools are needed?

Are there specific tools and materials students will need?	**What materials and tools will the observer use to make the student assessment?**

• Read-aloud books:
  + *A Tale of Two Beasts*
  + *Enemy Pie*
  + *Each Kindness*
• 3 exit tickets
• Comic strip activity:
• Lined and unlined paper for reader responses
• Graphic organizer of perspective taking
	Student observation sheet—Common formative assessment tool

Timeline and Dates	
Dates of assessments: Begin on 10/5 and end on 10/20.	**Date of data discussion:** • Bring raw data to team meeting on 10/22. • Prepare to share one statement of what you observed from your data. Were there surprises? Did this data collection method work for you? Do you feel it was fair and reliable?

*Visit **go.SolutionTree.com/instruction** for a free blank reproducible version of this figure.*

To begin, teams must first determine which essential standards and learning targets they want to measure as well as how they will use the information they gather. How they plan to use it will determine what type of data to collect. Teams may decide the purpose of gathering information is to demonstrate the SEL skills the students are focusing on and provide evidence of learning for families. In this case, they may want to discuss opportunities for students to produce a work sample through writing, drawing, or creating a product displaying the target skill. Alternatively, if a team would like to assess how often the students within the class are using the designated skills, an observation sheet or checklist may be helpful.

When making these decisions, keep in mind that while creating tangible evidence of an SEL skill can be useful, it does not provide a full picture of the child's ability. It gives a snapshot of what the student was able to produce at one point in time. Another facet of SEL skills is that some students can correctly answer questions around these skills, write about them, and demonstrate them in skits and during lessons. However, this cognitive ability to discuss the skill does not always translate to the student's ability to apply it to themselves in a real-life experience or use the skill when under stress.

If a team decides to measure what targeted SEL skills students are using, the team may develop a checklist or observation scale. This will allow team members to observe which skills students use when playing a game, working in a group, or discussing a particular topic. Figure 6.3 (page 300) shows a sample of a team-generated data collection tool that correlates with the assessment ideas in figure 6.2 (page 297). In this scenario, a third-grade team decided they would create exit tickets connected to three read-alouds they were using in their literacy unit. The team decided that each exit ticket would focus on essential literacy and SEL learning targets. After each read-aloud, the students would complete an exit ticket asking students to describe what happened in the *beginning, middle, and end of the story* (literacy essential learning target) and to *identify the emotion of a character in the story and then explain how they would feel in a similar situation* (SEL learning target SA.3.F.a). The team also gave the students a comic strip journal activity where students would be required to *consider another person's view point of a situation and understand how that person may have responded to that situation* (SEL learning target SA.3.F.b). The team created a rubric for this activity (3: shows full understanding of the concept; 2: shows partial understanding of the concept; 1: shows no understanding of the concept). The team

SEL Common Formative Assessment Data Collection Tool

Essential Standard:

SA3. Take perspective and "put self in someone else's shoes."

Look-fors:

SA.3.F.a. Student identifies the emotions of a character in a story

SA.3.F.b. Listen to a peer's view of a situation and understand how the peer may have responded to that situation

SA.3.F.c. Student empathizes with a peer's emotions

Student Name	A Tale of Two Beasts (Literacy or SEL exit ticket 1)		Enemy Pie (Literacy or SEL exit ticket 2)		Each Kindness (Questions 1 and 2 on literacy exit ticket 3)		Comic Strip Journal Activity	Teacher Observation	Notes	Baseline
	SA.3.F.A Q1	SA.3.F.A Q2	SA.3.F.A Q2	SA.3.F.A Q3	SA.3.F.A Q3	SA.3.F.A Q4	SA.3.F.B	SA.3.F.C		-Developing -Need support
	Y/N	Y/N	Y/N	Y/N	Y/N	Y/N	3 2 1	Date: Y/N		
	Y/N	Y/N	Y/N	Y/N	Y/N	Y/N	3 2 1	Date: Y/N		
	Y/N	Y/N	Y/N	Y/N	Y/N	Y/N	3 2 1	Date: Y/N		
	Y/N	Y/N	Y/N	Y/N	Y/N	Y/N	3 2 1	Date: Y/N		

Figure 6.3: SEL common formative assessment tool—example.

Visit go.SolutionTree.com/instruction for a free blank reproducible version of this figure.

then determined they would ask follow-up, clarifying questions to any student who fell within the two or one range, knowing that some students may show more understanding of the SEL concept in a verbal response than in writing.

Additionally, the team realized it needed to observe a third learning target (SA.3.F.c: *Understand another person's thoughts and feelings, and why that person may feel that way*) over time. Therefore, the team planned for observing students and using the tool as a means of collecting data over the course of the entire unit. The benefit of taking data over a prolonged period is that it gives the team a greater window into what the students can do. As we know, when it comes to SEL, there are many factors that influence a student's ability to demonstrate and show the skill. A student may be calm and regulated one day and able to use a skill fluidly, but be unable to even co-regulate with an adult coaching them when a task frustrates them. Taking data over time gives teams a broader sense of whether the students are using and applying the skills.

After creating the data collection tool, the team had to think about what opportunities it had to observe learning target SA.3.F.c: *Understand another person's thoughts and feelings, and why that person may feel that way.* Is this a skill that is easily measured during morning meeting activities and whole-group questioning? Can this skill be observed during a recess or lunch block? Is this a skill that is already shown in students' daily journal writing? As teams review when they can observe the skill, the discussion of when students most often use this skill and when it is most valuable to take data will emerge.

Another element of this conversation is what the team is comfortable with in terms of taking reliable data. Some teachers with more challenging students may have a hard time taking data without judgement. While everyone wants to be nonjudgmental toward students, it can be difficult to view a student impartially when the student has been creating additional stress on the teacher and class. In these cases, teams may decide to observe one another's students. Switching classes one day during mathematics partner game time or by observing one another's classes at recess are solutions. Additionally, the special education, English language, or support teachers may be able to come in and observe during a lesson. Also, specialist teachers (music, art, PE, librarian) can collect student data. Once teams can openly talk about how to truly collect nonjudgmental data on students' SEL skills, they will be able to see natural opportunities to work together in this area.

Another element of the discussion should include what aspects of the school day may impact a student's ability to demonstrate a specific skill. This discussion may become a part of whether to take data once or over multiple opportunities that will show students using the skills in a variety of settings. Although this conversation may not change how the team decides to take the data, it is important to be conscious of how different times of day may influence a student's emotional responses. For instance, when students arrive at school the teams do not know what happened to them that morning. Therefore, a student may be agitated and appear to be frustrated over something small when in fact they are reacting to something that occurred at home. Simply being aware of this and the nature of how we learn and apply SEL skills throughout our lives will remind the team of the unique nature of measuring these skills.

Once teams have made the decision of what skills to assess and why, and how to assess these skills, they must determine when they will collect the data and when they will reconvene to discuss the data. This timeframe discussion also lends itself to the next task of what to look for in the data. When individual teachers bring their data back to the team, there are some critical questions they should already be thinking about. These questions, which may be as simple as "What surprised you?" or "What was expected?" should be tied to the team's original goal of how these data can inform next steps.

Ways to Measure SEL Skills Throughout the School Day

Figures 6.4 and 6.5 (page 304) describe possible opportunities teachers have to observe SEL skills throughout the school day. Teams can consider this list when determining when to observe students using SEL skills and when they are able to measure these skills. Quick observation checklists or carefully crafted data collection tools will allow teachers to collect evidence of student learning throughout the day without taking time away from academic work. This will also allow teachers to observe whether students are using these skills in real-world situations.

Ideas for Assessing SEL Skills Embedded Within the School Day	
Time of Day	Description
Arrival Routines	Ask students to answer a daily question regarding how they are feeling that morning. As students enter the room, they can place a picture of themselves under a picture of a particular emotion. This not only signals to the teacher how the student feels that day and if the teacher needs to check in with that student before getting started but can also be used as a data point of whether the student can accurately identify their emotions and understand feelings vocabulary.
Morning Meeting	Ask daily routine questions encouraging SEL vocabulary. Observe how students interact with one another and greet each other. Pay attention to how the students respond to the morning meeting activity. Can they follow the directions or do they need to follow peer models? Do they demonstrate self-control?
Transitions	Daily transition routines that involve SEL questions can become a part of an observation checklist (see chapter 4, page 157).
Partner Games	Observe how students interact with one another. How do they react when they lose a game? How do they react when they win? Can they take turns? Do they empathize with a peer when a peer loses?
Challenging Academic Work	Observe how a student handles an academic challenge. Does a student ask for help or communicate their emotions with others? How do the students persevere? Try another strategy? Give up?
Lunch and Recess	Observe how students interact with one another. Do they take turns in conversation? Do they change the topic or stay on topic? Do students identify a game to play and play it without adult intervention?
Participation in Specials	Observe students in PE, music, art, and library. Do the students demonstrate the same SEL skills in these settings that they demonstrate in the classroom?
Play	Observe how students engage in play. Do they build on one another's ideas or have a difficult time accepting a new play scheme? Do they include emotions during pretend play?
End-of-Day Reflection	Observe how students reflect on their day. If the day was difficult, were they able to reflect at the end of the day, or did they not recognize that there was a problem? Can they make goals or identify areas to work on for the next day? Assign students to complete the self-reflection tools in chapter 4, figures 4.5 (page 167) and 4.6 (page 168).

Figure 6.4: Ideas for measuring SEL skills embedded within daily routines.

*Visit **go.SolutionTree.com/instruction** for a free reproducible version of this figure.*

Ideas for Assessing SEL Skills Within Academic Work	
Academic Assignment or Task	**Look-Fors**
Reading Reflection Assignments	Are students able to identify a character's feelings?
	Can the students identify the cause-and-effect actions that led to the character's feelings?
	Can the student identify an emotional connection they have with the character? What is a time in their life they felt the same way?
Writing Assignments	Read through student journals to look for the use of a variety of feelings vocabulary.
	Do students identify their feelings and the reasons behind those feelings?
	Can students accept revisions to their work? Can they take the perspective of the reader?
Project-Based Learning Assignments	Can students identify a goal and create steps to work towards that goal?
	Do students show flexible thinking when their original plans for the project do not work?
	Do students use collaborative language when talking with peers?
	Do students build on one another's ideas if working in a group?
	Are students persistent in achieving their goal even when it is not going as planned?
Collaborative Partner or Group Work and Games	Can students take turns during a structured partner game?
	If a student is upset at losing the game, can they use strategies to calm down and play again? Will they accept calm-down strategies from a peer or adult?
	Can students take the perspective of their partner?
	Do students recognize when a peer is upset about losing a game and respond in a socially appropriate way?

Figure 6.5: Ideas for measuring SEL skills within academic work.
Visit go.SolutionTree.com/instruction for a free reproducible version of this figure.

Analyzing Data From Common Formative Assessments

Once all the data have been collected, the team must come back together and analyze the data to determine what the data say and how to use them to inform their next practice. Figure 6.6 shows a sample of one classroom's data. To ensure interrater reliability, the team decided that together it would talk through these data of a few students to determine if students were developing in their understandings of these skills and concepts or if they felt like the data were showing that a student needed extra support. You'll notice that Juanita was able to demonstrate the learning of each of the three learning targets. The teacher described that she observed Juanita spontaneously comparing the different characters' perspectives during the read-aloud, before any questions were asked. In fact, the teacher realized, Juanita often makes observations about how others are thinking and feeling and is usually the first to help a classmate who is upset.

SEL Common Formative Assessment Data Collection Tool—Example

Essential Standard:

SA3. Take perspective and "put self in someone else's shoes."

Look-fors:

SA.3.F.a. Student identifies the emotions of a character in a story

SA.3.F.b. Listen to a peer's view of a situation and understand how the peer may have responded to that situation

SA.3.F.c. Student empathizes with a peer's emotions

Student Name	A Tale of Two Beasts (Literacy or SEL exit ticket 1)		Enemy Pie (Literacy or SEL exit ticket 2)		Each Kindness (Questions 1 and 2 on literacy exit ticket 3)		Comic Strip Journal Activity	Teacher Observation			Notes	Baseline
	SA.3.F.A Q1	SA.3.F.A Q2	SA.3.F.A Q2	SA.3.F.A Q3	SA.3.F.A Q3	SA.3.F.A Q4	SA.3.F.B	SA.3.F.C				Developing / Need support
Juanita	**Ⓨ**/N	**Ⓨ**/N	**Ⓨ**/N	**Ⓨ**/N	**Ⓨ**/N	**Ⓨ**/N	**③** 2 1	Date: 10/13 **Ⓨ**/N	Date: 10/25 **Ⓨ**/N	Date: 11/02 **Ⓨ**/N		Developing
Bilal	**Ⓨ**/N	**Ⓨ**/N	**Ⓨ**/N	**Ⓨ**/N	**Ⓨ**/N	**Ⓨ**/N	3 **②** 1	Date: 10/11 **Ⓨ**/N	Date: 10/21 **Ⓨ**/N	Date: 1/03 **Ⓨ**/N		Developing
Monica	**Ⓨ**/N	**Ⓨ**/N	**Ⓨ**/N	**Ⓨ**/N	Y/**Ⓝ**	Y/**Ⓝ**	3 **②** 1	Date: 10/13 Y/**Ⓝ**	Date: 10/24 **Ⓨ**/N	Date: 11/04 **Ⓨ**/N	Changes in home life on date of last exit ticket	Developing
Aaron	**Ⓨ**/N	Y/**Ⓝ**	**Ⓨ**/N	Y/**Ⓝ**	**Ⓨ**/N	**Ⓨ**/N	3 2 **①**	Date: 10/17 **Ⓨ**/N	Date: 10/28 **Ⓨ**/N	Date: 11/03 **Ⓨ**/N		Developing

Figure 6.6: Common formative assessment data collection tool—example.

Bilal showed understanding of the skills and concepts in the written tasks, but the teacher noted that while Bilal is readily able to take the perspectives of characters in books, he has a more difficult time taking the perspective of a classmate when he and the classmate disagree. Although Bilal understands the concept of taking another's perspective, he is not consistently able to apply it in his own life, particularly when he is upset. Bilal will continue to work on this skill. The team agrees he is developing the skill and will continue to develop it with Tier 1 instruction.

Monica showed evidence of understanding perspective taking and empathy in the first two exit tickets but had more difficulty with the task on the third. She was also inconsistent during the teacher observations. Her teacher shared that Monica's father was recently deported. Monica's family was undergoing significant stress in their home at the time of the last exit ticket and observation. While Monica currently needs more support from teachers and school staff to support her feelings of belonging and her sense of safety in school, when it comes to perspective taking, she is showing that she is developing the skill appropriately.

Aaron was able to identify the emotions of the characters in each of the books, but he was not able to describe how the character in a book may have felt or why the character acted the way they did. During the observations the teacher observed that Aaron often acted impulsively with his peers and did not attend to their faces when he played with them. He often missed social cues when his friends were mad or frustrated, and needed an adult to support him in his frequent peer conflicts. After looking at Aaron's birthdate to determine that he is the same age as most of his peers, the team determined that Aaron would benefit from additional support. Aaron's difficulty in taking others' perspectives is impacting him both socially and academically.

While a class total and a class average are not an ideal way to compare classrooms because of the unique individuals within each classroom, this tool will allow teachers to gain a quick sense of whether certain teachers' instructional strategies and practices may have differed from one another. In this example scenario, the teachers calculated the percentage of the students who were developing the skills (see figure 6.7). This data analysis and rich discussion between team members can help teachers improve on their practices and gain ideas from their peers, which in turn has the potential to benefit all students. We also recommend looking at the data as a whole grade level and setting a team goal to increase student achievement. In this scenario, the team decided that after eight weeks they would reassess the students who needed support, and their goal was to have 80 percent of their students working on grade-level developing skills. Teachers need to remember that all students belong to all teachers and that the individual classroom scores should not be taken personally. It should be the mindset of the entire team to support all students' learning of SEL skills and concepts.

Teacher	SEL Data Essential Standard: SA.3. Take perspective and put self in someone else's shoes.
Elmo	70% of the students are working at grade level.
Kristin	52% of the students are working at grade level.
Tyrell	88% of the students work at grade level.
Analisa	72% of students are working at grade level.
Overall Grade Level	71% of students are working at grade level.

Figure 6.7: Third-grade SEL data for essential standard SA.3.

Data analysis is important work for the team, and when they structure and thoughtfully plan this process out with targeted questions, the team can start to really understand what students know and are able to do (see figure 6.8, page 308). Teams should reflect on those students who they consider are developing the SEL skills and ask, "What do the students have in common?" as well as asking themselves, "What do the students who need support have in common?" This provides an opportunity for teams to be culturally reflective. If they notice that those students who need support have the same cultural background or racial similarity, they may need to examine either their own implicit bias when observing student behavior, or whether the skill they are measuring is culturally sensitive (Collado et al., 2021). Is this a skill expected and taught in some cultures but not in others? Is this a skill that only certain communities see as valuable? This reflective work may lead the team to consider whether they need to re-examine which essential standards they are teaching and where they are spending the most instructional time. Aside from examining the cultural aspect of the skill, teams should also look at the birthdates of the students who need extra support. If this was a skill that the younger students in the grade had difficulty with but the older students easily demonstrated, teams may need to reconsider the age-appropriateness of assessing this skill. If most students in this grade are not developmentally ready for a skill, this is an opportune time for the grade-level team to reach out to the grades above and below them. These vital discussions should include sharing this observation and creating shared knowledge in vertical planning of the developmental nature of this skill. This is also a time to reach out to other professionals in the building, such as the English language teachers, special education teachers, counselors, and school social worker or psychologist, to gain more insight into the cultural and developmental factors to determine more appropriate expectations.

Team Data Discussion-Guiding Questions
What do we notice about the data of the students who scored in the lowest percentile range? What do these students have in common?
What are the birthdates of each set of these students?
What are the students' cultural backgrounds?
What was successful in teaching and supporting this skill development?
What was not successful?
Do we need to continue embedding the standard into our weekly plans?   If so, what is our plan?
Do we need to address the students who showed difficulty with this target skill? If so, what is the plan for supporting these students?   How can we best do that, respectfully, and allow for developmental and cultural differences?
Are there students who are ready to learn the expanding learning targets (those skills and concepts that come next in students' learning)? If so, what is the plan for supporting these students?

Source: Adapted from Kerr et al., 2021.

Figure 6.8: Data review team discussion—guiding questions.

Visit go.SolutionTree.com/instruction for a free reproducible version of this figure.

In looking at the overall data, teams must reflect on whether the work they did in teaching their initial lessons was effective. If so, what made it effective? What does that tell the team about their planning moving forward? What worked best for this group of students? But what if it was not effective for all students? If most students only showed the essential SEL target skill once in a three-part observation, what did not work? Were the students able to demonstrate the skill on academic exit tickets but unable to use the skill at recess or lunch? Did students understand the skill and know how to use it? Was there enough time for students to practice the skill between the initial introduction and the observation? In looking at the data, teams must reflect on what they can improve in their practice for the next unit, but also in whether they need to extend their current unit, re-teach or re-emphasize the target skill (see figure 6.8). If a team chooses to move on with the next unit, how can they continue to support and coach this essential SEL skill throughout the day? Is this an SEL skill that can be practiced and monitored daily during mathematics games, or should it be used to coach the students on this SEL skill during recess?

In addition, discussion around this data will also lend itself to addressing which students may require additional time and support in these areas (Hannigan et al., 2021). These discussions will lead teams to determining which students need access to Tier 2 and Tier 3 interventions. For more information in working with teams to form Tiers 2 and 3 support, refer to *Behavior Solutions: Teaching Academic and Social Skills Through RTI at Work* (Hannigan et al., 2021). Figure 6.9 and figure 6.10 (page 311) provide templates for teams to use when planning and taking additional student data on Tier 1 and Tier 2 supports when considering the needs of individual students. Figure 6.9 will guide a team's planning and decision making for monitoring the progress of students' SEL skills, while figure 6.10 provides an example of a student observational tool used to collect the data. As the team comes together to determine a student's needs, they can record their plan in figure 6.9. Figure 6.10 allows teachers to quickly take observational data of whether a student is demonstrating the targeted SEL skill, with or without help.

SEL Student Progress-Monitoring Tool			
Student name:	Yair J.	Grade:	3
Teacher:	Ms. Kem	Birth date:	January 5
Team members:	Ms. Kem, Mr. Jennings, and Ms. Colton	Assessment dates:	Initial date: 2/19 — Follow-up date: 3/21

Figure 6.9: Common formative assessment team planning template—example. continued →

Concerns
Yair shows difficulty maintaining self-control throughout the school day. Although he often shows remorse for his actions, when he is upset with another student or situation he displays behaviors of walking away, shouting at peers, and throwing objects around the room.

Essential SEL Standards (Foundational Goals)

Initial goals:

- SS.2. Identify emotions.
- SS.3. Identify cause-and-effect nature of events and emotions.
- SR.2. Exercise self-control.

Foundational learning targets within initial goals:

- SR.2.F.b. Practice using self-talk and self-regulation strategies to pause before acting and think about one's actions.
- SR.2.F.c. Accept coaching from an adult on refraining from impulses.
- SS.2.F.b. Label their own emotions.
- SS.3.F.a. Recognize which events make them feel specific emotions.

Secondary SEL Standards
(Developing goals—to focus on after the foundational goals have been accomplished)

Secondary goals:

- SR.1. Monitor personal emotions and use strategies to regulate emotions.
- SR.3. Demonstrate ability to recover from challenges.
- SR.3.D.b. Use calming strategies when recovering from a challenge in order to move forward.

Foundational skills within secondary goals:

- SR.1.F.a. Explore different calm-down strategies and identify which works best for the individual.
- SR.1.F.b. Recognize situations when upset and when one may need to use the calm-down strategies.
- SR.1.F.c. Use calm-down strategies with an adult when upset or dysregulated.

Intervention Plan

Who is responsible for the plan:

Classroom teacher, reading teacher, and school counselor

When will the intervention occur:

- Lunch two days a week with school counselor
- Morning check-ins with reading teacher
- Frequent check-ins with classroom teacher for in-the-moment coaching

What are the intervention strategies being used:

- Lunch—social group with three other students
- Morning check-ins to preview the day and predict possible emotional responses
- In-the-moment coaching with classroom teacher to apply skills throughout the day

What assessments will be used with the students:

- Observation checklist (completed by classroom teacher, classroom assistant, and reading teacher).

What is the duration of the intervention, and when will the students be reassessed:

- Intervention will last four weeks, and teachers will use the student observation tool over a two-week period to collect data.

Visit **go.SolutionTree.com/instruction** *for a free blank reproducible version of this figure.*

SEL Student Observational Tool				
Student: Yair J.				
Grade: 3				
Teacher: Ms. Kem				
Date: January 20				
Foundational Learning Target: SR.2.F.b. Practice using self-talk and self-regulation strategies to pause before acting and think about one's actions.				

Date	Setting and Event	Standard Demonstrated	With Help?	Notes
2/18	Classroom—Morning work	Y	Y	Yair was upset with peer; he identified he was angry.
2/19	Recess: lost at soccer	N	Y	He was upset over losing game. Yair did not accept help to calm down.
2/19	Mathematics	N	Y	Frustrated with difficult mathematics problem, so he ripped up work and did not accept help.
2/20	Morning meeting	Y	Y	Yair identified feelings when peer accidently tripped him.
2/20	Recess	Y	Y	With coaching, he identified frustration over losing a game.
2/23	Morning meeting	N	N	Yair was upset with sub and spent time with counselor until calm.
2/24	Mathematics	Y	N	Yair identified feelings and self-calmed.
2/25	Mathematics	Y	Y	Yair accepted help to calm when frustrated.
Total:	Demonstrates 5 of 8 opportunities	5 Y 3 N	6 Y 2 N	Yair met standard 4 of 5 times; student had help meeting the goal.

Figure 6.10: SEL student observational tool.

*Visit **go.SolutionTree.com/instruction** for a free blank reproducible version of this figure.*

Individual Student Data Considerations

To monitor the growth of students' learning of SEL concepts and skills, using a learning progression might help keep track of where students are in their learning. As you collect data over time, you can determine a student's current skill level and use that information to determine their instructional level. In the scenario in figure 6.3 (page 300), the teachers are using the learning progression as a tool to keep track of each student's instructional learning, and this will help them target students' individual needs. Again, the goal is not to push students to the next level or even consider mastery; rather, it is to help teachers determine what skills a student learned and still needs to learn and then use this information to inform the teachers' instruction. Figure 6.11 shows data from October and November. Notice how some students were learning foundational skills in October and many were still working on these foundational skills in November, while some were now ready to learn developing skills in November, and one student was even ready to explore skills and concepts beyond grade-level expectations. In chapter 4 (page 157), we shared ideas around using goal cards as a way for students to keep track of their own learning of skills and concepts. This goal card is a visual learning progression for teachers to use as a support during instruction and for students to use to monitor their own learning and overall growth. When students know their learning goals, they are more apt to hit their learning targets.

Date: 10/12	Self-Awareness Instructional Levels	
Foundational Learning Targets	**Developing Learning Targets**	**Expanding Learning Targets**
Identify a variety of feelings and moods in themselves	Recognize and label their emotions or feelings	Recognize intensity levels of their emotions
10/12 (Clara, Tarik, Anna, Saaid, Elisa, Janice, John, Bonnie, Sarah, Aaron, Carter, Deon, Hannah)	10/12 (Omar, Alex, Jenna, Tonisha, Lavar, Janice, Miguel, Romeo, Bella, Juan, Lakesha, Keyton, Ronnie, Mackenzie)	

Date: 11/28	Self-Awareness Instructional Levels	
Foundational Learning Targets	**Developing Learning Targets**	**Expanding Learning Targets**
Identify a variety of feelings and moods in themselves	Recognize and label their emotions or feelings	Recognize intensity levels of their emotions
11/28 (Clara, Tarik, ~~Anna~~, Saaid, Elisa, Janice, John, ~~Bonnie~~, Sarah, Aaron, Carter, ~~Deon~~, Hannah)	11/28 (~~Omar~~, Alex, Jenna, Tonisha, Lavar, Janice, Miguel, Romeo, Bella, Juan, Lakesha, Keyton, Ronnie, Mackenzie) Anna, Deon, Bonnie	11/28 Omar

Source for standards: The Michigan Department of Education, 2017.

Figure 6.11: Using learning progressions to monitor student growth.

When teams begin to examine the data of individual students, they must also consider the student's individual differences before determining whether intervention is needed, and if so, what next steps may occur. If the student in question is younger than the rest of the grade level, this skill may not be developmentally appropriate for them. In this case, teachers can discuss ways to support this student until they gain the skill. How can they help the student still be successful socially in this grade level until the skill develops? Is it possible to focus on those foundational skills that typically develop first and support the student in bridging to the grade-level expected concepts and skills? Another aspect to consider is the student's cultural background and family dynamics. If a student's culture influences the development of this skill, teachers should seek to understand and familiarize themselves with this culture. Is this a cultural expectation that is acceptable in the classroom?

I (Ann-Bailey) once watched a very kind boy who had just entered the United States spit on the floor of the cafeteria. The cafeteria manager was outraged, and her behavior made the boy feel threatened. He reacted poorly, having been accustomed to teacher beatings in his previous country. In talking with the boy, we learned that he had no idea that it was not acceptable to spit on the floor, as that had been common practice back home. He was mortified when he realized he had broken an unspoken social norm. That is an obvious example of an easily fixable time in addressing cultural differences outright. Most of the time, however, cultural differences are more nuanced. Students may not make eye contact with adults or may only refer to adults by *Ma'am* or *Sir* because that is how they have been brought up. They may interrupt the speaker as a sign of respect because it shows they were listening and engaged, as their family does at home. In these situations, it is important to honor the family's culture and not judge or attempt to remediate the student's behaviors. Conversations about clear school expectations (without making a statement that these expectations are better or superior to a student's home expectations) will support this area.

School expectations are also important to keep in mind. I once had a student tell me that in school it was never OK to hit, but in his neighborhood (which was known for having gang violence), his father said to give someone three chances and if they were still bothering you to hit them as hard as you can. It is not my place to judge this family's survival skills and message to his son. In fact, that message probably kept his son from getting involved in difficult situations. Instead, we could differentiate between school behaviors and neighborhood behaviors.

Once teams consider whether the student is having difficulty with a standard because of development or culture, the team can then discuss ways to offer reteaching and additional practice to certain students. SEL skills take practice—opportunities to be coached in the moment around when to use certain skills. Depending on the standard in question, teams may consider forming weekly lunch groups where students will practice using a targeted skill. At recess, teachers can devise a schedule and take shifts monitoring and supporting specific groups of students and providing additional coaching within each social skill. Being mindful of students who showed difficulty demonstrating the skill, teams may intentionally plan how to embed questioning or opportunities for these specific students to practice and demonstrate the skill within the daily lessons. Keep in mind that pulling students out of the classroom to teach social skills is not effective unless students practice those skills throughout the school day. The key to using SEL skills is for generalization to occur. Relying on small pull-out groups to teach skills often leads to students being able to perform the task within the small group but unable to use the skill outside the group (Swan, Carper, & Kendall, 2015). Teams should be mindful of this as they consider how best to address students who did not demonstrate the SEL skills on the common assessment.

Conclusion

Once teams are committed to collaboratively monitoring their students' social-emotional learning and development, we believe they will begin to see their students in a new light. Observing students' development and response to SEL lessons and supports will provide teams with insight that will support the students they teach that year as well as the next. The more teams learn to watch students with "SEL eyes," the more they will naturally make adaptations and differentiations to support these skills, particularly in the learning to strengthen those foundational building blocks.

Tips for Administrators, Teachers, and Support Staff

Figure 6.12 contains tips and reflection questions relating to the contents of this chapter. As you consider these questions and next steps, reflect on your current practices in your own classroom and school.

Administrators	Teachers	Support Staff
• As collaborative teams work on common formative assessments, ask them what they plan to do with the data. Are they taking data for data's sake, or do they understand the purpose of their work? • Consider if the adults in the school recognize how a child's culture impacts their social norms and behaviors throughout the school day. If not, how can you provide learning opportunities in this area where they are free to discuss these differences?	• When sitting down to make common assessments be sure to know the purpose of the assessment before moving forward. Avoid taking data for data's sake and be sure it's being used to support instruction. • Be intentional as you look for trends in your data. If students from a similar culture or developmental profile are showing difficulties with a skill consider whether it is an appropriate skill to assess. If not, how can your expectations change? What similar skill would be more appropriate?	• Become familiar with the goals of the interventions being used with students. Look for ways you can support these learning goals outside of interventions or lessons. Are you able to coach students in these skills on the playground, at recess, or while they are walking in line? • Ask classroom teachers to share birthdates and important information on students' cultural backgrounds so that you have an understanding of the developmental and cultural differences.

Figure 6.12: Tips for administrators, teachers, and support staff from chapter 6.

Appendix

The following figures show the integration of SEL frameworks within social-emotional building blocks and offer sample SEL transition activities, interactive whiteboard daily routines, and journal prompts.

SEL Building Blocks	Six Domains of SEL (EASEL Lab)	CASEL Core Competencies
Sense of Self: Who am I? Where do I belong? What do I like or dislike?	**Emotional Domain:** Emotional knowledge and expression **Identity Domain:** Self-knowledge, self-esteem, understanding of place in the world **Perspective Domain:** Optimism, enthusiasm/zest	**Self-Awareness:** Identifying one's emotions Developing a personal identity Identifying personal, cultural, and linguistic assets
Reciprocal Engagement: Do I relate and engage with others? Do I maintain two-way communication with others? Can I initiate engagement with others? Can I get my needs met? Do I recognize and understand social cues?	**Social Domain:** Understanding social cues, prosocial/cooperative behavior **Cognitive Domain:** Attention control (in relation to prolonged interactions with others) **Identity Domain:** Understands self and own needs in order to interact with others **Perspective Domain:** Openness to others **Values Domain:** Performance values, civic values	**Relationship Skills:** Developing positive relationships, communicating effectively, seeking or offering support and help when needed
Social Awareness: Do I understand I am separate from others? Do I understand I have different opinions, experiences, and perspectives? Do I recognize and understand prosocial behaviors?	**Emotional Domain:** Empathy, perspective taking **Social Domain:** Understanding social cues, prosocial and cooperative behavior **Perspective Domain:** Openness, gratitude **Values Domain:** Civic values, ethical values	**Self-Awareness:** Integrating personal and social identities, examining prejudices and biases, demonstrating honesty and integrity **Social Awareness:** Taking others' perspectives, recognizing strengths in others, demonstrating empathy and compassion, showing concern for others' feelings, understanding and expressing gratitude **Relationship Skills:** Demonstrating cultural competency **Responsible Decision Making:** Demonstrating curiosity and open-mindedness
Social-Emotional Regulation: How do I stay calm and regulated? How do I maintain attention on target goals? How do I set goals and create plans?	**Emotional Domain:** Emotion and behavior regulation **Cognitive Domain:** Attention control, inhibitory control, working memory **Identity Domain:** Self-efficacy, growth mindset	**Self-Awareness:** Having a growth mindset, experiencing self-efficacy **Self-Management:** Managing one's emotions, using stress management strategies, exhibiting self-discipline and self-motivation, setting personal and collective goals, demonstrating personal agency, showing courage to take initiative **Responsible Decision Making:** Anticipating and evaluating the consequences of one's actions

SEL Building Blocks	Six Domains of SEL (EASEL Lab)	CASEL Core Competencies
Logical Decision Making: Can I see the whole picture? Can I make logical connections between ideas? Can I see the outcomes of my actions and how they may affect others?	**Social Domain:** Conflict resolution, social problem solving **Cognitive Domain:** Planning skills, cognitive flexibility, and critical thinking **Values Domain:** Ethical values, performance values, civic values, and intellectual value **Identity Domain:** Sense of purpose in the world	**Self-Awareness:** Linking feelings, values, and thoughts Developing interests and a sense of purpose **Social Awareness:** Identifying diverse social norms including unjust ones, recognizing situational demands and opportunities, understanding the influences of organizations or systems on behavior **Relationship Skills:** Practice teamwork and collaborative problem solving, resolve conflicts constructively **Responsible Decision Making:** Identifying solutions for personal and social problems; learning to make a reasoned judgement after analyzing information, data, facts; recognizing how critical thinking skills are useful; reflecting on one's role to promote personal, family, and community well-being; evaluating personal, interpersonal, community, and institutional impacts **Self-Management:** Using planning and organizable skills

Source: Adapted from CASEL, n.d.e; EASEL Lab, n.d.; Jones et al., 2021.

Figure A.1: Integration of SEL frameworks within social-emotional building blocks.

SEL Transition Activities

Teachers can use the SEL transition cards with students during transitional periods throughout the day. They include a mixture of general short and quick activities targeted for either lower- or upper-elementary students or both. We recommend that you look at your grade-level standards and specifically use transitional activities that correlate with your grade-level SEL learning targets.

Figure A.2 (page 318) and figure A.3 (page 319) offer transitions used to ground or calm.

Blowing Out Candles

5, 4, 3, 2, 1, 0

Directions:

Students hold up one hand and count back from five. After they say the number, they use a long slow deep breath to blow out each candle and put the finger down. As the numbers decrease, their voice decreases until they get to zero.

My Five Senses

Directions:

There are two ways to play.

1. Think of five things you see, four things you hear, three things you can touch, two things you smell, and one thing you taste.

2. You can also separate each sense. For example, during one transition you can just think about five things you see and use your fingers to represent and keep track of all five things you see. Students hold up their five fingers to show when they have found all five things. You all can do this with each of the senses and with whatever number you choose.

Tracing Shapes by 3s With Deep Breathing

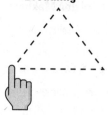

Directions:

Ask students to trace a shape in the air using their finger. As they trace the shape, they count and engage in deep breathing. (Note: Shapes should correlate with grade-level standards; for example, upper elementary students could trace an isosceles triangle, rhombus, trapezoid, or parallelogram.)

Example: Picture an imaginary triangle in front of you. What does it look like? How many sides does it have? You will count and engage in deep breathing as you trace each side. You may choose to close your eyes or keep them open during this exercise.

Letter Sound Look-Fors

"C" sound

Directions:

Show students a letter or tell them the letter. Ask them to find something that starts with that letter or make that letter sound.

Observations

Directions:

Find an object in the classroom. Use your inner thinking voice to describe the object in detail (its color, texture, shape, and so on).

Target Calm Counting

1, 2, 3... 12

Directions:

Show students a number or tell them the number. Ask the students to close their eyes and mentally count to that number using their "thinking voice." When they get to their target number, have them hold up their thumb to show the teacher they are finished counting. (Note: Students in upper elementary grades can skip-count forwards or backwards to target numbers. For example, if the target number is 107 and the student is counting by tens, have them start at 7 and count: 7, 17, 27, 37, and so on until 107.)

Figure A.2: Decrease energy transition activities: Transitions used to ground or calm.

Balloon Blowing	**Miming**	**Tracing Numbers or Words With Deep Breathing**

Directions: Students imagine themselves blowing up an imaginary balloon. They inhale and exhale for about five seconds, each time imagine themselves blowing up a balloon. To make this activity fun and something to do with a partner, have students each come up with an imaginary balloon shape (animal, fun object, and so on) and pretend to hand it to each other to blow up. When they engage in the balloon-blowing exercise, they can imagine that shape, animal, or fun object as they are blowing it up. When they finish, they can imaginatively hand it back to their partner.	Directions: There are two ways to play. 1. You and students get into a circle. You start off holding a pretend object and mime using the object. You pass the imaginary object to the student next to you and that student can mime the same object or change it to a new object. It moves around the circle until the "object" gets back to the teacher. For example, you use an imaginary brush to comb hair and pass the imaginary brush to the student next to you. That student changes the imaginary brush to a fishing pole and casts the line and reels. This student passes the fishing pole to the student next to them and then that student chooses a new object to mime. The students can always mime the same object passed to them. 2. Students can stay at their seats while you call out the word mime. At that moment, each student thinks of their own imaginary object to mime. After five seconds, you call out "Change," and at that moment the students change to a new item to mime. Repeat for several rounds.	Directions: There are two ways to play. 1. You ask students to think of a number between two intervals, or with varied conditions. When they have their number, they take a deep breath and trace it in the air, and when they are done tracing it they exhale. (Note: Upper-elementary students should work with higher numbers. Teacher: "Think of a number more than 130,000 and less than 195,000" or "Choose a four-digit number with the digit 8 in the hundreds place.") This could also be done with words. Teacher: "Trace a word that rhymes with mouse." (Inhale or exhale after tracing each letter.) 2. To make this a partner activity, students can choose a number between two designated intervals or with certain conditions, breathe, and trace the number. They can then share that number with their partner. The partner can use active listening skills during this time and determine if their partner chose a number that fits these criteria the teacher designated.

Figure A.3: Decrease energy transitions: Transitions used to ground or calm. continued →

Imaginary Canvas Painting

Directions:

Have students paint an imaginary canvas picture. Let them choose what they paint or give them a theme. If you do the latter, tell students they have to paint a picture of a beach. This can occur in two ways:

1. Students paint their picture and do not share aloud. This makes it a quick and quiet transition activity

2. Students share one to two details aloud with the whole group, or they find a partner and use as much detail as possible to describe their painting. Have the partner retell or paraphrase what their partner shared.

Imaginary Bubble Blowing

Directions:

Direct the students to use their finger as a bubble wand and use long slow breaths to blow bubbles. Give them several bubbles to blow out and ask them to quietly and calmly use the tip of their finger to imaginatively pop each bubble.

Rhyme Time

Directions:

Give the students a word and have them think of as many words as possible that rhyme with it. Have them use their fingers to signify how many words they came up with. Look for the student holding up the most fingers and have them share out with the group. Then follow up, asking if any other student has a word that was not mentioned.

Figure A.4 offers transitions to increase blood flow and oxygen to the brain.

Stretching or Yoga

Directions:

Have students do basic stretches, simple yoga poses, or exercises to increase blood flow to the brain.

These could include the following:

- Cross crawls
- Jumping jacks
- Toe touches
- Yoga positions

Dancing

Directions:

Play a song and incorporate dance moves to the music or allow students to have free dance where they make up their own moves.

- Floss dance
- Line dance
- Raise the roof
- Free dance

Number Actions

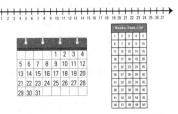

Directions:

A student picks a number on the classroom number line, calendar, or number chart and tells the class an "action" to do that many times. For example, a student chooses the number five and asks the class to do five jumping jacks.

Subitizing Exercises

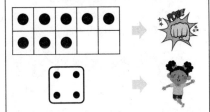

Directions:

First, you flash an image of a dice pattern, a ten-frame image, or their fingers for a few seconds. You then show the movement or exercise or call the name of the movement or exercise. Students complete the exercise move the number of times they saw on the finger image, dice, or ten frames.

Dance and Play Instrument

Directions:

You play a song with multiple instruments. The students listen for ten seconds and then select an "instrument" they want to pretend to play that they heard within the song. You call out, "Play your instrument." After pretend playing for ten seconds, the teacher calls "Switch," and the students change to a new instrument they hear. Repeat several times.

Letter Sound Exercises

Bb

Balance

Directions:

Correlate letters and letter sounds with various exercises. Create visuals and model exercise moves for students.

Figure A.4: Increase energy transitions: Transitions to increase blood flow and oxygen to the brain.

Figure A.5 offers sample transitions to support social-emotional learning with mixed-regulation activities.

Think of . . .	**Name . . .**	**This or That**

Think of . . .

Directions:

This activity fosters *sense of self*. Students can close their eyes as the teacher poses a situation. Students give a thumbs-up to show they have thought of something. You as teacher can choose to have students keep their thoughts to themselves or share aloud. Prompts:

- Say, "Think of a time when you were very excited, happy, sad, angry, worried, or silly;" or

- Ask, "What job might you enjoy when you grow up?"

Name . . .

Directions:

To foster a *sense of self*, you as the teacher give a prompt asking students to name some things. For example:

- Name your favorite things you like to do for fun; or

- Name the things you are great at

Students can close their eyes and think about the prompt. You ask them to use their fingers as tools to keep track of all the different answers to the prompt. For example, if a student thought of three things, then they would hold up three fingers. Have students share aloud their responses to the prompt.

This or That

Directions:

To foster *sense of self,* you ask students either-or questions. For example,

- Would you rather read a book alone or listen to a book read to you aloud?

- Would you rather climb a tree outside or watch a movie?

- Would you rather play an active sport outside with friends (basketball, soccer, or hopscotch), or play a board game inside with a friend?

You can have students keep the thought to themselves or interact with their peers. A possibility includes assigning a number to the activities or objects in the *this or that* questions posed. For example, if you choose to climb a tree outside you hold up one finger. If you choose to watch a movie you hold up two fingers. You can even have students pair up by finding a partner with the same or different preference and share their thoughts and ideas with each other.

Name and Describe

Directions:

This social-emotional activity asks students to name and describe:

- Three things that help them get calm
- Something creative they enjoy doing
- Three healthy foods they enjoy eating
- Personal traits of a character from their favorite book
- A time when they needed help with something

Students can close their eyes, think about the statement the teacher poses, and give a thumbs-up to show they have thought of something. The teacher can choose to have them share out to the whole group or with a partner.

Sentence Starters

Directions:

This social-emotional activity gives students the following sentence prompts.

- I made a good choice when . . .
- When I am frustrated or upset, I can . . .
- I am being a good friend when I . . .

Students can keep their thoughts to themselves or share out with the whole group or with a partner. They could also quickly jot their answers down on a sticky note and post them in the classroom so that students can view and gather ideas from their peers.

Big Problem, Little Problem

Directions:

This social-emotional activity calls you to pose a scenario, and the students have to identify if the problem is a big problem or a little problem using their thumb as an indicator (big = thumbs up and little = thumbs down). Next, students share out with the whole group or with a partner a self-regulation strategy that the person could use to help.

Scenario:

- A student is playing a game with a friend, and they are beginning to get frustrated
- A student fell at recess playing basketball and can't move their leg
- A student got ketchup on their shirt at lunch

Figure A.5: Mixed-energy transitions—Transitions to support social-emotional learning.

Figure A.6 offers sample transitions to support social-emotional learning using social awareness and reciprocal engagement activities.

Name and Describe

Directions:

In this social awareness activity, you as the teacher pose a question to students, such as:

- Why does the character in your favorite book feel the way they do?
- What are 1–2 positive traits in your friend or your sibling?
- What is personal space?

Students can close their eyes, think about the statement you pose, and give a thumbs-up to show they have thought of something. The teacher can choose to have them keep this thought to themselves or share aloud.

Sentence Starters

Directions:

In this social awareness activity, pose a situation to your students, such as:

- When someone is disappointed, I can . . .
- When I disagree with my partner, I can show respect by . . .

Students can keep their thoughts to themselves or share out with the whole group or with a partner. They can also quickly jot down their answers on a sticky note and post them in the classroom so that students can view and gather ideas from their peers.

Turn and Talk With a Friend

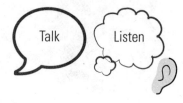

Directions:

This social awareness activity is a time for students to practice greeting a person and using active listening skills. Ask the students one of the following questions.

- How would someone feel if you broke their game on purpose?
- How can you tell if someone is lonely?

Model for students what "turn and talk" looks like and sounds like. You may want to have one partner share their ideas and the partner retell or paraphrase what their partner said.

Think of . . .	**Name . . .**	**Turn and Talk With a Friend**

Directions:	Directions:	Directions:
In this reciprocal engagement activity, pose a statement for students, such as the following.	In this reciprocal engagement activity, provide the students with a prompt, such as the following.	This reciprocal engagement activity is a time for students to practice greeting a person and using active listening skills. Pose a statement for students, such as:
• Think of three places you might meet a new friend.	• Name the many ways students can help each other in the classroom, at recess, or at home.	• Describe what good sharing looks like.
• Think of the things you can do if you want to play with a new friend on the playground.	• Name the many ways you might greet a friend, a peer you don't know, or an adult.	• Describe the physical things you notice your friend doing to show they are actively listening to you.
Students can close their eyes, think about the statement, and give a thumbs-up to show they have thought of something. You can choose to have them keep this thought to themselves or share aloud with a friend.	Students can close their eyes and think about the prompt. Teach them to use their fingers as tools to keep track of all the different answers to the prompt. For example, if a student thought of three ways, then they would hold up three fingers. Have students share aloud their responses to the prompt.	Model for students what "turn and talk" looks like and sounds like. You may want to have one partner share their ideas and the partner retell or paraphrase what their partner said.

Figure A.6: Mixed-energy transitions—Transitions to support social-emotional learning.

Figure A.7 offers sample transition activities using logical and responsible decision making.

Logical and Responsible Decision Making Transition Activity:	Logical and Responsible Decision Making Transition Activity:	Logical and Responsible Decision Making Transition Activity:
Thumbs-Up (Good Choice), Thumbs-Down (Poor Choice)	**Turn and Talk With a Friend**	**Sentence Starters**
Directions:	Directions:	Directions:
Pose a situation for students, such as,	This is a time for students to practice greeting a person and using active listening skills. Pose a situation for students, such as,	Provide students with a sentence starter, such as,
• Asking if it is okay before you take something. • Laughing at someone sitting alone on the playground. • Making a big mess and walking away. • Holding the door open for others.	• A person interrupts your friend when he is telling a story. Turn and talk with your partner about a better choice. • You and your friend want to play a game together but you each want to play a different game. What could you do?	• When I have an important decision to make, I have to . . . • I am responsible for . . . • When I meet a challenging situation, I can . . .
Students use their thumb to signal if they think it is a *good choice* or *poor choice*. You can ask follow-up questions like, "Why do you think it is a good choice?" If they think it is a poor choice, you can ask questions such as, "Can you think of a better choice for this situation?"	Model for students what "turn and talk" looks like and sounds like. You may want to have one partner share their ideas and the partner retell or paraphrase what their partner said.	Students can keep their thoughts to themselves or share out whole group or with a partner. They can also quickly jot down their answers on a sticky note and post them in the classroom so that students can view and gather ideas from their peers.
_____	_____	_____
Transition Activity:	Transition Activity:	Transition Activity:
Directions:	Directions:	Directions:

Figure A.7: Mixed-energy transitions—Transitions to support social-emotional learning.

Interactive Whiteboard Daily
Routine Examples

Figure A.8 (page 328) offers sample interactive whiteboard daily routines.

SEL Component	Interactive Whiteboard Slide Visuals	Interactive Whiteboard Questions or Prompts	Possible Routine Description
Sense of Self	What is your current energy level? Choose a color based on your current energy level and put that color dot in the Venn diagram. 	What is your current energy level? **High energy:** What does your body feel like when you have high energy? What can you do to decrease energy if necessary to stay focused and get started on a learning task? **Low energy:** What does your body feel like when it has low energy? What can you do to increase energy, so you are able to stay focused and take initiative to start on a learning task? **Mixed energy:** What does your body feel like when it has mixed energy? Can you tell if you are ready to learn when your energy feels balanced?	**Routine description:** Student self-monitors their current energy level and places a symbol, in this case a colored dot (green, yellow, or red), on the Venn diagram to represent their energy level at that moment. **Teacher-student discussion:** Discuss how your body feels with high energy, mixed energy, or low energy. The body feelings may differ from person to person. There is no "right" energy and no "right" feeling. How you feel is how you feel, and your energy level may vary based on everyday life situations. **Mathematics connection:** • What observations can you make from the Venn diagram? • How many more students are feeling low energy compared to high energy? • How many fewer students are feeling mixed energy than high energy, and so on?

SEL Component	Interactive Whiteboard Slide Visuals	Interactive Whiteboard Questions or Prompts	Possible Routine Description
Self-Regulation	What strategy best helps calm you down when you are frustrated or upset? Number of students	Self-regulation calming strategies When you are angry or frustrated, what strategy helps to calm you down: • Counting • Listening to music • Drawing • Breathing exercises • Other _____	**Routine description:** Which one of these strategies best helps to calm you when you are frustrated or upset? Place one picture of a calming strategy on the picture graph to represent your data. **Teacher-student discussion:** Ask students to share examples of when one of these strategies would not work or be available to them (for example, you can't draw when you are walking in the hallways). Ask students to share the "other" category and describe other strategies they can use to help self-calm. **Mathematics connection:** • What observations can you make from the picture graph? • How many students answer the question, and how do you know? • Which two categories have the same amount of data? • Which strategy do students use the least, and which do they use most? • How many more people use a drawing strategy than a deep breathing strategy?

continued →

Figure A.8: Sample SEL interactive whiteboard daily routines.

SEL Component	Interactive Whiteboard Slide Visuals	Interactive Whiteboard Questions or Prompts	Possible Routine Description
Social Awareness	Positive Personal Traits Positive Personal Trait / Negative Personal Trait Friendly, Kind, Showing off, Honest, Lies, Rude, Funny, Courageous, Bossy, Confident, Polite	Help sort positive versus negative personal traits into the table.	**Routine description:** Choose one personal trait and decide if you think it is a positive personal trait or a negative personal trait. Move the trait onto the table. **Teacher-student discussion:** • Think of a character you read about in a story that has this same trait. Can you think of another trait that is similar? • Why are positive personal traits important? • What personal traits do you look for in a friend? • Is there anything you disagree with on the table? **Language arts connections:** • Are these internal character traits or external traits? • What is the difference between a feeling and a trait? • Can you give specific examples of a person or character's actions to say they are honest, rude, or confident?

SEL Journal Prompts

Figure A.9 offers sample SEL journal prompts.

Teachers can use the following social-emotional journal prompts with students.	
Sense of Self	Prompts: • Think about the last time you were so happy that you could not stop laughing. What made you laugh? How did your body feel? What happened when you stopped laughing? • What makes you angry? Make a list of five things that make you upset and order from what upsets you a little to what makes you really angry. Choose what makes you the angriest and write about a time that has happened. What did you do when you were angry? • What are you the proudest of accomplishing so far in your life? What is the hardest you have worked on something?
Reciprocal Engagement	Prompts: • Write about a time you were talking with someone but they did not seem to understand what you were saying, even when you were speaking the same language. What happened? Why didn't they understand you? • How does it feel when you are talking with someone, and they check their smartphone? What do you think about when this happens? Why? • With a partner, write a story. Take turns writing each sentence. You cannot change the sentence your partner wrote, no matter how crazy it is. Add on to whatever they write.
Self-Regulation	Prompts: • Imagine you are angry with your family. What will you do to calm yourself down before you talk with them? What will you say when you talk to them? • List five calming strategies we have learned this year. Which ones work the best for you? Which ones do not work? Why? • What is a goal you have in your life? What are the steps you will take to achieve this goal? How will you know if or when you achieve it? • If your goal is to make a peanut butter and jelly sandwich, what are the steps you need to take to achieve your goal?
Social Awareness	Prompts: • Imagine that you see your friend is sad and not talking with you. What will you say or do to your friend to help them feel better? • You notice that a kindergartener on the bus is being picked on by older students. What can you do to help them? • What is an act of kindness someone has done for you? How can you do an act of kindness for someone else?

Figure A.9: SEL building block-focused journal prompts.   continued →

Logical and Responsible Decision Making	Prompts: • You are about to be late for school, but you notice a friend fell off his bike and cannot move. Will you stop and help them, or go to school and get an adult? Why do you make your decision? • In J.K. Rowling's *Harry Potter and the Chamber of Secrets*, Harry and Ron are late to school because they took Ron's father's car. Do you think they made the right decision? Why or why not? Should Ron's father punish them? • In Kwame Alexander's book *The Crossover*, the twins are not with their father when he dies. Would you have stayed with him, or gone to the game? Why or why not?

References and Resources

American Speech-Language-Hearing Association. (n.d.). *Classroom acoustics*. Accessed at www.asha.org/public/hearing/Classroom-Acoustics/ on August 9, 2021.

Ames, C., & Archer, J. (1988). Achievement goals in the classroom: Students learning strategies and motivation processes. *Journal of Educational Psychology, 80*(3), 260–267.

Anthes, E. (2009). Building around the mind: Brain research can help us craft spaces that relax, inspire, awaken, comfort, and heal. *Scientific American Mind*. Accessed at www.emilyanthes.com/data/uploads/neuroarchitecture.pdf on December 2, 2021.

Aspen Institute. (2018). *From a nation at risk to a nation of hope: Recommendations from the National Commission on Social, Emotional, and Academic Development*. Washington, DC: National Commission on Social, Emotional, and Academic Development. Accessed at http://nationathope.org/wp-content/uploads/2018_aspen_final-report _full_webversion.pdf on August 6, 2021.

Bacher-Hicks, A., Billings, S. B., & Deming, D. J. (2019, September). The school to prison pipeline: Long-run impacts of school suspensions on adult crime. *NBER Working Paper Series*. Accessed at www.nber.org/system/files/working_papers/w26257/w26257.pdf on September 14, 2021.

Bailey, B. (2015). *Conscious discipline: Building resilient classrooms*. Oviedo, FL: Loving Guidance.

Bandura, A. (2001). Social cognitive theory: An agentic perspective. *Annual Review of Psychology, 52*(1), 1–26.

Bandura, A., & Schunk, D. H. (1981). Cultivating competence, self-efficacy, and intrinsic interest through proximal self-motivation. *Journal of Personality and Social Psychology, 41*(3), 586–598.

Beachum, F. D., & Gullo, G. L. (2020). School leadership: Implicit bias and social justice. In R. Papa (Ed.), *Handbook on promoting social justice* (pp. 429–454). Switzerland: Springer Nature. Accessed at https://doi.org/10.1007/978-3-030-14625-2_66 on January 11, 2021.

Bechtel, L., Clayton, M., & Denton, P. (2003). *Responsive Classroom: Level 1 workbook*. Greenfield, MA: Northeast Foundation for Children.

Bellini, S. (2016). *Building social relationships 2: A systematic approach to teaching social interaction skills to children and adolescents on the autism spectrum.* Shawnee, Kansas: AAPC Publishing.

Benson, T., & Fiarman, S. (2020). *Unconscious bias in schools* (revised edition). Cambridge, MA: Harvard Education Press.

Berkowitz, R., Moore, H., Astor, R. A., & Benbenishty, R. (2016). A research synthesis of the associations between socioeconomic background, inequality, school climate, and academic achievement. *Review of Educational Research, 87*(2), 425–469. Accessed at https://doi.org/10.3102/0034654316669821 on May 20, 2021.

Blomeke, S., Olsen, R. V., & Suhl, U. (2016). Relation of student achievement to the quality of their teachers and instructional quality. In T. Nilsen & J. E. Gustafsson (Eds.), *Teacher quality, instructional quality and student outcomes: Relationships across countries, cohorts and time* (pp. 21–50). Switzerland: IEA Research for Education 2, Springer Open.

Boaler, J., & Staples, M. (2008). Creating mathematical futures through an equitable teaching approach: The case of Railside School. *The Teachers College Record, 110,* 608–645.

Boudreau, E. (2020, August 3). A leader's guide to talking about bias: How a binary view of racism can inhibit productive conversations about race in school settings [Blog post]. *Usable Knowledge.* Accessed at www.gse.harvard.edu/news/uk/20/08/leaders -guide-talking-about-bias on January 11, 2021.

Bridgeland, J., Bruce, M., & Hariharan, A. (2013). *The missing piece: A national survey on how social and emotional learning can empower children and transform schools.* Washington, DC: Civic Enterprises with Peter D. Hart Research Associates.

Brown, S. L. (2009). *Play: How it shapes the brain, opens the imagination, and invigorates the soul.* New York: Avery.

Buckley, K. (2020). *Integrating social and emotional learning throughout the school system: A compendium of resources for district leaders.* San Francisco, CA: Center to Improve Social and Emotional Learning and School Safety at WestEd. Accessed at https://selcenter.wested.org/wp-content/uploads/sites/3/2020/09/SELCenter _CompendiumofResources.pdf on August 6, 2021.

Buffum, A., Mattos, M., Weber, C., & Hierck, T. (2015). *Uniting academic and behavior interventions: Solving the skill or will dilemma.* Bloomington, IN: Solution Tree Press.

Bullard, J. (2017). *Creating environments for learning: Birth to age eight* (3rd ed.). Boston: Pearson.

Burt, J. L., & Whitney, T. (2018). From resource room to the real world: Facilitating generalization of intervention outcomes. *Teaching Exceptional Children, 50*(6), 364–372. Accessed at doi:10.1177/0040059918777246 on May 20, 2021.

Campbell, A., Hagan-Burke, S. & Burke, M. (2020). *Increasing the cultural relevance of interventions to reduce emotional and behavioral disorders among African American students.* Presented at Council for Exceptional Children International Conference, Portland, OR.

Cannon, L., Kenworthy, L., Alexander, K. C., Werner, M. A., & Anthony, L. G. (2014). *Unstuck and on target! An executive function curriculum to improve flexibility, planning, and organization* (2nd ed.). Baltimore, MD: Paul H. Brookes.

Castelli, G. (2017, May 18). Time-out: Early, often, and for everyone [Blog post]. *Responsive Classroom*. Accessed at www.responsiveclassroom.org/time-out-early-often-everyone on December 12, 2020.

Centers for Disease Control and Prevention. (n.d.). *Violence prevention: CDC-Kaiser ACE study*. Accessed at www.cdc.gov/violenceprevention/acestudy/about.html on May 20, 2021.

Centers for Disease Control and Prevention. (2009). *School connectedness: Strategies for increasing protective factors among youth*. Accessed at www.cdc.gov/healthyyouth/protective/pdf/connectedness.pdf on May 20, 2021.

Cipriano, C., Rappolt-Schlichtmann, G., & Brackett, M. (2020). *Supporting school community wellness with social and emotional learning (SEL) during and after a pandemic*. Accessed at www.conexionternura.com/media/documents/Supporting_School_Community_Wellness.pdf on May 20, 2021.

Circle of Security. (2020). *Circle of security in the classroom*. Accessed at www.circleofsecurityinternational.com/circle-of-security-model/cos-classroom-coaching on November 13, 2020.

Coelho, V., Cadima, J., Pinto, A. I., & Guimarães, C. (2018). Self-regulation, engagement, and developmental functioning in preschool-aged children. *Journal of Early Intervention, 41*(2), 105–124.

Collaborative for Academic, Social, and Emotional Learning. (n.d.a). *Indicators of schoolwide SEL*. Accessed at https://schoolguide.casel.org/what-is-sel/indicators-of-schoolwide-sel on October 2, 2020.

Collaborative for Academic, Social, and Emotional Learning. (n.d.b). *The CASEL guide to schoolwide social and emotional learning*. Accessed at https://schoolguide.casel.org on September 25, 2020.

Collaborative for Academic, Social, and Emotional Learning. (n.d.c). *The CASEL guide to schoolwide SEL leads school-based teams through a process for systemic SEL implementation*. Accessed at https://schoolguide.casel.org/how-it-works on October 24, 2020.

Collaborative for Academic, Social, and Emotional Learning. (n.d.d). *Adopt an evidence-based program for SEL*. Accessed at https://schoolguide.casel.org/focus-area-3/school/adopt-an-evidence-based-program-for-sel on January 13, 2021.

Collaborative for Academic, Social, and Emotional Learning. (n.d.e). *SEL: What are the core competence areas and where are they promoted?* Accessed at https://casel.org/sel-framework on December 2, 2020.

Collaborative for Academic, Social, and Emotional Learning. (n.d.f). *What is SEL?* Accessed at https://casel.org/what-is-sel on August 3, 2021.

Collaborative for Academic, Social, and Emotional Learning. (n.d.g). *SEL as a lever for equity*. Accessed at https://drc.casel.org/sel-as-a-lever-for-equity/ on August 5, 2021.

Collaborative for Academic, Social, and Emotional Learning. (2013). *CASEL guide: Effective social and emotional learning programs, preschool and elementary school edition*. Accessed at https://www.casel.org/wp-content/uploads/2016/01/2013-casel-guide-1.pdf on August 14, 2021.

Collaborative for Academic, Social, and Emotional Learning. (2017). *SEL discussion series for parents and caregivers: Supporting parents and caregivers through social and emotional learning*. Accessed at https://casel.org/wp-content/uploads/2017/11 /CASELCaregiverGuide_English.pdf on September 25, 2020.

Collaborative for Academic, Social, and Emotional Learning. (2020). *Evidence-based social and emotional learning programs: CASEL criteria updates and rationale.* Accessed at https://casel.org/wp-content/uploads/2021/01/11_CASEL-Program-Criteria-Rationale .pdf on August 19, 2021.

Collado, W., Hollie, S., Isiah, R., Jackson, Y., Muhammad, A., Reeves, D., & Williams, K. (2021). *Beyond conversations about race: A guide for discussions with students, teachers, and communities.* Bloomington, IN: Solution Tree Press.

Conscious Discipline. (n.d.). *Kindness tree structure plan.* Accessed at https:// consciousdiscipline.com/resources/kindness-tree-structure-plan on October 30, 2020.

Conzemius, A. E., & O'Neill, J. (2014). *The handbook for SMART school teams: Revitalizing best practices for collaboration* (2nd ed.). Bloomington, IN: Solution Tree Press.

Cooper, G., Hoffman, K., & Powell, B. (2017). Circle of security in child care: Putting attachment theory into practice in preschool classrooms. *Zero to Three Journal, 37*(3), 27–34.

Copeland, L. (2015). *Hunter and his amazing remote control.* Chapin, SC: Youthlight, Inc.

Council for Exceptional Children. (2017). News from CEC: High-leverage practices in special education. *Teaching Exceptional Children, 49*(5), 355–360. Accessed at https:// doi.org/10.1177/0040059917713206 on May 20, 2021.

Crowe, C. (2009). *Solving thorny behavior problems: How teachers and students can work together.* Turners Falls, MA: Northeast Foundation for Children.

da Cruz, A. D., Alves Silvério, K. C., Da Costa, A. R., Moret, A. L., Lauris, J. R., & de Souza Jacob, R. T. (2016). Evaluating effectiveness of dynamic soundfield system in the classroom. *Noise & Health, 18*(80), 42–49.

Dabbs, L. (2017). *How the morning meeting can transform classroom culture.* Accessed at www.edweek.org/education/opinion-how-the-morning-meeting-can-transform -classroom-culture/2017/12 on January 12, 2021.

Darling-Hammond, L., Zielezinski, M. B., & Goldman, S. (2014). *Using technology to support at-risk students' learning.* Accessed at https://mk0all4edorgjxiy8xf9.kinstacdn .com/wp-content/uploads/2014/09/UsingTechnology.pdf on May 20, 2021.

Davis, C., & Yang, A. (2005). *Parents & teachers working together.* Turners Falls, MA: Northeast Foundation for Children.

Decker, D. M., Dona, D. P., & Christenson, S. L. (2007). Behaviorally at-risk African American students: The importance of student-teacher relationships for student outcomes. *Journal of School Psychology, 45*(1), 83–109.

Delahooke, M. (2019). *Beyond behaviors: Using brain science and compassion to solve children's behavioral challenges.* Eau Claire, WI: PESI Publishers.

Denham, S. A. (2018). *Keeping SEL developmental: The importance of a developmental lens for fostering and assessing SEL competencies.* Accessed at https://casel.org/wp-content /uploads/2020/04/Keeping-SEL-Developmental.pdf on January 5, 2021.

Denton, P. (2007). *The power of our words: Teacher language that helps children learn.* Turners Falls, MA: Northeast Foundation for Children.

Department of Energy. (2007). *National best practices manual for building high-performance schools.* Accessed at https://doi.org/10.2172/15002037 on August 8, 2021.

Dexter, D. D., & Hughes, C. A. (2011). Graphic organizers and students with learning disabilities: A meta-analysis. *Learning Disability Quarterly, 34*(1), 51–72.

Downer, J., Rimm-Kaufman, S., & Pianta, R. (2007). How do classroom conditions and children's risk for school problems contribute to children's behavioral engagement in learning? *School Psychology Review, 36*(3), 413–432.

DuFour, R., DuFour, R., Eaker, R., & Many, T. (2010). *Learning by doing: A handbook for professional learning communities at work* (2nd ed.). Bloomington, IN: Solution Tree Press.

DuFour, R., DuFour, R., Eaker, R., Many, T. W., & Mattos, M. (2016). *Learning by doing: A handbook for professional learning communities at work* (3rd ed.). Bloomington, IN: Solution Tree Press.

Durlak, J. A., Weissberg, R. P., Dymnicki, A. B., Taylor, R. D., & Schellinger, K. (2011). The impact of enhancing students' social and emotional learning: A meta-analysis of school-based universal interventions. *Child Development, 82,* 405–432.

Dusenbury, L., Weissberg, R. P., Goren, P., & Domitrovich, C. (2014). *State standards to advance social and emotional learning: Findings from CASEL's state scan of social and emotional learning standards, preschool through high school, 2014.* Accessed at https://casel.org/wp-content/uploads/2016/06/casel-brief-on-state-standards-january-2014.pdf on May 20, 2021.

Dweck, C. S. (2006). *Mindset: The new psychology of success.* New York: Random House.

Eaker, R., & Marzano, R. J. (Eds.). (2020). *Professional learning communities at work® and high reliability schools: Cultures of continuous learning.* Bloomington, IN: Solution Tree Press.

EASEL Lab. (n.d.). *Harvard Graduate School of Education.* Accessed at https://easel.gse.harvard.edu/ on August 8, 2021.

EdTrust. (2020). *Social, emotional, and academic development through an equity lens.* Accessed at https://edtrust.org/wp-content/uploads/2014/09/Social-Emotional-and-Academic-Development-Through-an-Equity-Lens-August-6-2020.pdf on December 13, 2020.

Ferris, S. (2014). Revoicing: A tool to engage all learners in academic conversations. *The Reading Teacher, 67*(5), 353–357.

Finley, T. (2017). Mastering classroom transitions: Move students in and out of class and between activities smoothly to save valuable instruction time. *Edutopia Blog: Teaching Strategies* Accessed at www.edutopia.org/article/mastering-transitions-todd-finley on August 8, 2021.

Fosco, W. D., Hawk, L. W., Rosch, K. S., & Bubnik, M. G. (2015). Evaluating cognitive and motivational accounts of greater reinforcement effects among children with attention-deficit/hyperactivity disorder. *Behavioral and Brain Functions.* Accessed at https://doi.org/10.1186/s12993-015-0065-9 on May 20, 2021.

Fredricks, J. A. (2014). *Eight myths of student disengagement: Creating classrooms of deep learning.* Thousand Oaks, CA: Corwin Press. Accessed at doi: 10.4135/9781483394534 on May 20, 2021.

Fredricks, J. A., Blumenfeld, P. C., & Paris, A. H. (2004). School engagement: Potential of the concept, state of the evidence. *Review of Educational Research, 74*(1), 59–109. Accessed at https://sk.sagepub.com/books/eight-myths-of-student-disengagement on May 20, 2021.

Friend, M. (2007). The coteaching partnership. *Educational Leadership, 64*(5), 48–51.

Froh, J. J., & Bono, G. (2012). *How to foster gratitude in schools.* Accessed at https://greatergood.berkeley.edu/article/item/how_to_foster_gratitude_in_schools on October 29, 2020.

Gold, C. (2017). *The developmental science of early childhood: Clinical applications of infant mental health concepts from infancy through adolescence.* New York: Norton.

Greenberg, M. T., Brown, J. L., & Abenavoli, R. M. (2016). *Teacher stress and health effects on teachers, students, and schools.* University Park, PA: Edna Bennett Pierce Prevention Research Center, Pennsylvania State University. Accessed at www.prevention.psu.edu/uploads/files/rwjf430428.pdf on September 16, 2021.

Greenberg, M., Domitrovich, C., Weissberg, R., & Durlak, J. (2017). Social and emotional learning as a public health approach to education. *The Future of Children, 27*(1), 13–32.

Greene, R. W. (2008). *Lost at school: Why our kids with behavioral challenges are falling through the cracks and how we can help them.* New York: Scribner.

Greene, R. W. (2016a). *Lost and found: Helping behaviorally challenging students (and, while you're at it, all the others).* San Francisco: Jossey-Bass.

Greene, R. W. (2016b). *A more compassionate, productive, effective approach to understanding and helping behaviorally challenged kids.* Accessed at www.livesinthebalance.org/sites/default/files/FAQ%20020816.pdf on October 23, 2020.

Greenspan, S. I. (2006). *Engaging autism: Using the floortime approach to help children relate.* Cambridge, MA: Da Capo Lifelong Books.

Guardino, C. (2010). Changing behaviors by changing the environment: A case study of an inclusion classroom. *Teaching Exceptional Children, 42,* 8–13.

Hamilton, L. S., Doss, C. J., & Steiner, E. D. (2019). *Teacher and principal perspectives on social and emotional learning in America's schools: Findings from the American educator panels.* Accessed at www.rand.org/pubs/research_reports/RR2991.html on May 20, 2021.

Hamre, B. K., & Pianta, R. C. (2001). Early teacher-child relationships and the trajectory of children's school outcomes through eighth grade. *Child Development, 72*(2), 625–638.

Hannigan, J., Hannigan, J. D., Mattos, M., & Buffum, A. (2021). *Behavior solutions: Teaching academic and social skills through RTI at work.* Bloomington, IN: Solution Tree Press.

Hanover Research. (2019). *Best practices in social-emotional learning.* Prepared for WASA School Information and Research Service.

Hardiman, M. M. (2003). *Connecting brain research with effective teaching: The brain-targeted teaching model.* Lanham, MD: Scarecrow Press.

Harvard University Center on the Developing Child. (n.d.a). *Three principles to improve outcomes for children and families.* Accessed at https://developingchild.harvard.edu

/resources/three-early-childhood-development-principles-improve-child-family-outcomes on May 20, 2021.

Harvard University Center on the Developing Child. (n.d.b). *ACES and toxic stress: Frequently asked questions.* Accessed at https://developingchild.harvard.edu/resources/aces-and-toxic-stress-frequently-asked-questions on May 20, 2021.

Harvard University Center on the Developing Child. (n.d.c). *Serve and return.* Accessed at https://developingchild.harvard.edu/science/key-concepts/serve-and-return/ on August 6, 2021.

Harvard University Center on the Developing Child. (n.d.d). *What is executive function and how does it relate to child development?* Accessed at https://developingchild.harvard.edu/resources/what-is-executive-function-and-how-does-it-relate-to-child-development/ on August 6, 2021.

Harvard University Center on the Developing Child. (2012). *InBrief: Executive function.* Accessed at https://developingchild.harvard.edu/resources/inbrief-executive-function/#:~:text=Scientists %20refer%20to%20these%20capacities,the%20potential%20to%20develop%20them on January 12, 2020.

Hattie, J. (2009). *Visible learning: A synthesis of over 800 meta-analyses relating to achievement.* New York: Routledge.

Hattie, J., & Donoghue, G. (2016). Learning strategies: A synthesis and conceptual model. *npj Science of Learning, 1,* 16013.

Herman, B., & McKown, C. (n.d.). *I'm from the government and I'm here to help: The role of the state education agency in the assessment of social and emotional learning.* Accessed at https://casel.org/im-from-the-government-and-im-here-to-help-the-role-of-the-state-education-agency-in-the-assessment-of-social-and-emotional-learning on December 2, 2020.

Heschong Mahone Group. (1999). *Daylighting in schools: An investigation into the relationship between daylighting and human performance.* Accessed at http://h-m-g.com/downloads/Daylighting/schoolc.pdf on August 8, 2021.

Holland, B. (2017). *From "EduSpeak" to a language of pedagogy.* Accessed at www.edweek.org/leadership/opinion-from-eduspeak-to-a-language-of-pedagogy/2017/07 on December 17, 2020.

Huitt, W. (2007). *Maslow's hierarchy of needs.* Accessed at www.edpsycinteractive.org/topics/regsys/maslow.html on January 14, 2021.

Illinois Department of Education. (n.d.). *Social/emotional learning standards.* Accessed at www.isbe.net/Documents/descriptor_1-5.pdf on Dec 2, 2021.

Illinois Early Learning Project. (2013). *List of goals, standards, and benchmarks.* Accessed at https://illinoisearlylearning.org/ields/ields-benchmarks on February 26, 2020.

Illinois State Board of Education. (2020). *Illinois priority learning standards 2020–21.* Accessed at https://www.isbe.net/Documents/Illinois-Priority-Learning-Standards-2020-21.pdf on August 7, 2021.

Immordino-Yang, M. H., & Faeth, M. (2010). The role of emotion and skilled intuition in learning. In D. A. Sousa (Ed.), *Mind, brain, & education: Neuroscience implications for the classroom* (pp. 69–83). Bloomington, IN: Solution Tree Press.

Interdisciplinary Council on Development and Learning. (2020). *Functional emotional development*. Accessed at www.icdl.com/dir/fedcs/functional-emotional-developmental-levels-basic-chart on January 4, 2021.

IRIS Center. (2021). *Classroom diversity: An introduction to student differences*. Accessed at https://iris.peabody.vanderbilt.edu/module/div/#content on November 13, 2020.

Jennings, P. A. (2011). Promoting teachers' social and emotional competencies to support performance and reduce burnout. In A. Cohan & A. Honigsfeld (Eds.), *Breaking the mold of pre-service and in-service teacher education: Innovative and successful practices for the 21st century* (pp. 133–143). Lanham, MD: Rowman & Littlefield.

Jensen, E. (2005). *Teaching with the brain in mind* (2nd ed.). Alexandria, VA: Association for Supervision and Curriculum Development.

Jersild, T. (1955). *When teachers face themselves*. New York: Teachers College, Columbia University.

Johnston, P. (2004). *Choice words: How our language affects children's learning*. Portland, ME: Stenhouse Publishers.

Jones, B. F., Rasmussen, C. M., & Moffitt, M. C. (1997). *Real-life problem solving: A collaborative approach to interdisciplinary learning*. Washington, DC: American Psychological Association.

Jones, F. H. (2000). *Tools for teaching: Discipline, instruction, motivation*. Santa Cruz, CA: F. H. Jones & Associates.

Jones, S. M., Barnes, S. P., Bailey, R., & Doolittle, E. J. (2017). Promoting social and emotional competencies in elementary school. *Future of Children, 27*(1), 49–72.

Jones, S. M., & Bouffard, S. M. (2012). Social and emotional learning in schools: From programs to strategies. *Social Policy Report, 26*(4), 1–22.

Jones, S., Brush, K., Bailey, R., Brion-Meisels, G., McIntyre, J., Kahn, J., et al. (2017, 2021). *Navigating SEL from the inside out: Looking inside & across 25 leading SEL programs: A practical resource for schools and OST providers*. Accessed at www.wallacefoundation.org/knowledge-center/Documents/Navigating-Social-and-Emotional-Learning-from-the-Inside-Out.pdf on April 19, 2021.

Jones, S. M., Brush, K., Ramirez, T., Xinyi Mao, Z., Marenus, M., Wettje, S., Finney, K., Raisch, N., Podoloff, N., Kahn, J., Barnes, S., Stickle, L., Brion-Meisels, G., McIntyre, J., Cuartas, J., & Bailey, R. (2021). *Navigating SEL from the inside out: Looking inside & across 33 leading SEL programs: A practical resource for schools and OST providers*. The EASEL Lab at the Harvard School of Education. Accessed at www.wallacefoundation.org/knowledge-center/Documents/navigating-social-and-emotional-learning-from-the-inside-out-2ed.pdf on August 2, 2021.

Jones, S. M., & Kahn, J. (2017). *The evidence base for how we learn: Supporting students' social, emotional, and academic development*. Washington, DC: Aspen Institute. Accessed at www.aspeninstitute.org/wp-content/uploads/2017/09/SEAD-Research-Brief-9.12_updated-web.pdf on September 14, 2021.

Jordan, A., Fern, B., Morris, C., Cross, R., & Mathur, S. (2014). Critical thinking in the elementary classroom: Exploring student engagement in elementary science classrooms through a case-study approach. *Journal of Emerging Trends in Educational Research and Policy Studies, 5*(6), 673–678. Accessed at https://mmsdamps.files.wordpress.com/2017/03/critical-thinking.pdf on August 12, 2021.

Jung, L. A., & Smith, D. (2018). Tear down your behavior chart! *Educational Leadership*, *76*(1), 12–18.

Kane, E., Hoff, N., Cathcart, A., Heifner, A., Palmon, S., & Peterson, R. L. (2016). *School climate & culture: Strategy brief, February 2016*. Accessed at https://k12engagement .unl.edu/strategy-briefs/School%20Climate%20&%20Culture%202-206-16%20.pdf on January 12, 2021.

Kaufman, C. (2010). *Executive function in the classroom: Practical strategies for improving performance and enhancing skills for all students*. Baltimore, MD: Paul H. Brookes Publishing.

Kelly, B. (2020). How responsive classroom practices can act as the glue for a virtual classroom. *Responsive Classroom Blog*. Accessed at www.responsiveclassroom.org /how-responsive-classroom-practices-can-act-as-the-glue-for-a-virtual-classroom/ on August 19, 2021.

Kelly, S., & Turner, J. (2009). Rethinking the effects of classroom activity structure on the engagement of low-achieving students. *The Teachers College Record, 111*, 1665–1692.

Kerr, D., Hulen, T. A., Heller, J., & Butler, B. K. (2021). *What about us? The PLC at Work process for grades preK–2 teams*. Bloomington, IN: Solution Tree Press.

Klapp, A., Belfield, C., Bowden, B., Levin, H., Shand, R., & Zander, S. (2017). A benefit-cost analysis of a long-term intervention on social and emotional learning in compulsory school. *International Journal of Emotional Education, 9*(1), 3–19.

Kuhfeld, M. (2019). *Measuring social-emotional learning: The tradeoff between measuring narrower skills versus broad competencies*. Accessed at www.nwea.org/content/uploads /2020/03/researchbrief-measuring-social-emotional-learning-the-tradeoff-between -measuring-narrower-skills-versus-broad-competencies-2019.pdf on January 12, 2021.

Larkin, M. (2002). *Using scaffolded instruction to optimize learning*. Accessed at www.vtaide .com/png/ERIC/Scaffolding.htm on February 3, 2020.

Lee, J-S. & Bowen, N. K. (2006). Parent involvement, cultural capital, and the achievement gap among elementary school children. *American Educational Research Journal, 43*(2), 193–218.

Lesh, R., Post, T. R., & Behr, M. (1987). Representations and translations among representations in mathematics learning and problem solving. In C. Janiver (Ed.), *Problems of representation in the teaching and learning of mathematics* (pp. 33–40). Lawrence Erlbaum.

Levine, K., & Chedd, N. (2007). *Replays: Using play to enhance emotional and behavioral development for children with autism spectrum disorders*. Philadelphia, PA: Jessica Kingsley Publishers.

Lillas, C. (2014). The neurorelational framework in infant and early childhood mental health. In K. Brandt, B. Perry, S. Seligman, & E. Tronick, *Infant and early childhood mental health: Core concepts and clinical practice* (pp. 85–95). Arlington, VA: American Psychiatric Publishing.

Lillas, C., & Turnbull, J. (2009). *Infant/child mental health, early intervention, and relationship-based therapies: A neurological framework for interdisciplinary practice*. New York: Norton.

Little, S. D., & Tolbert, L. V. A. (2018). The problem with black boys: Race, gender, and discipline in Christina and private elementary schools. *Christian Education*

Journal: Research on Educational Ministry, 15(3), 408–421. Accessed at DOI: 10.1177/0739891318805760 on May 20, 2021.

Locke, E. A., & Latham, G. P. (2002). Building a practically useful theory of goal setting and task motivation: A 35-year odyssey. *American Psychologist, 57*(9), 705–717.

Locke, E. A., & Latham, G. P. (2006). New directions in goal-setting theory. *Current Directions in Psychological Science, 15*(5), 265–268. Accessed at doi: 10.1111/j.1467 -8721.2006.00449.x on May 20, 2021.

Ma, X., Yue, Z. Q., Gong, Z. Q., Zhang, H., Duan, N. Y., Shi, Y. T., et al. (2017). The effect of diaphragmatic breathing on attention, negative affect and stress in healthy adults. *Frontiers in Psychology, 8*, 874. Accessed at https://doi.org/10.3389/fpsyg.2017 .00874 on May 20, 2021.

Macklem, G. L. (2008). *Practitioner's guide to emotion regulation in school-aged children.* New York: Springer Science + Business Media, LLC.

Malik, R. (2017). *New data reveal 250 preschoolers are suspended or expelled every day.* Accessed at www.americanprogress.org/issues/early-childhood/news/2017/11/06 /442280/new-data-reveal-250-preschoolers-suspended-expelled-every-day on September 23, 2019.

Mantz, L., & Bear, G. (2020). *Student-student relationships.* University of Delaware and Delaware Positive Behavior Support Project—School Climate & Student Success.

Markham, T., Larmer, J., & Ravitz, J. (2003). *Project-based learning: A guide to standards-focused project based learning for middle and high school teachers* (2nd revised special ed.). Novato, CA: Buck Institute for Education.

Marzano, R. J., Marzano, J. S., & Pickering, D. (2003). *Classroom management that works: Research-based strategies for every teacher.* Alexandria, VA: Association for Supervision and Curriculum Development.

Matthews, G. (2015). *Goal-setting research.* Proceedings of the 9th Annual International Conference of the Psychology Research Unit of Athens Institute for Education and Research. Athens, Greece. Accessed at www.dominican.edu/dominicannews/study -highlights-strategies-for-achieving-goals on February 3, 2020.

Mattos, M. (2016, July). *When all means all.* Keynote at PLC at Work Institute, San Antonio, Texas.

McClelland, M., Tominey, S. L., Schmitt, S. A., & Duncan, R. (2017). SEL interventions in early childhood. *The Future of Children, 27*, 33–47.

McCloskey, G., Perkins, L. A., & Van Divner, B. (2009). *Assessment and intervention for executive functioning difficulties.* New York: Routledge Press: Taylor and Francis Group.

McIntosh, K., & MacKay, L. D. (2008). Enhancing generalization of social skills: Making social skills curricula effective after the lesson. *Beyond Behavior, 18*, 18–25.

Meece, J. L., Blumenfeld, P. C., & Hoyle, R. H. (1988). Students' goal orientations and cognitive engagement in classroom activities. *Journal of Educational Psychology, 80*(4), 514–523.

Michigan Department of Education. (2017). *Early childhood to grade 12 social and emotional learning (SEL) competencies and indicators.* Accessed at www.michigan.gov /documents/mde/SEL_Competencies-_ADA_Compliant_FINAL_605109_7.pdf on January 10, 2021.

Midwest Comprehensive Center. (2018). *Student goal setting: An evidence-based practice.* Accessed at www.air.org/sites/default/files/MWCC-Student-Goal-Setting-Evidence -Based-Practice-Resource-508.pdf on December 7, 2020.

MIT Teaching+Learning Lab. (n.d.). *Growth mindset.* Accessed at https://tll.mit.edu /teaching-resources/inclusive-classroom/growth-mindset on January 10, 2021.

Moore, S. (2016). *Transforming inclusive education* [Video file]. Accessed at https://youtu.be /RYtUlU8MjlY on November 13, 2020.

Morsy, L., & Rothstein, R. (2019). *Toxic stress and children's outcomes: African American children growing up poor are at greater risk of disrupted physiological functioning and depressed academic achievement.* Accessed at www.epi.org/publication/toxic-stress-and -childrens-outcomes-african-american-children-growing-up-poor-are-at-greater -risk-of-disrupted-physiological-functioning-and-depressed-academic-achievement on May 21, 2021.

Muhammad, A. (2009). *Transforming school culture: How to overcome staff division.* Bloomington, IN: Solution Tree Press.

Murayama, K., & Elliot, A. J. (2009). The joint influence of personal achievement goals and classroom goal structures on achievement-relevant outcomes. *Journal of Educational Psychology, 101*(2), 432–447.

Nasir, N. S., Jones, A., & McLaughlin, M. W. (2011). School connectedness for students in low-income urban high schools. *Teachers College Record, 113,* 1755–1793.

National Association of Elementary School Principals. (n.d.). *The principal's guide to building culturally responsive schools.* Accessed at www.naesp.org/sites/default/files /NAESP_Culturally_Responsive_Schools_Guide.pdf on November 6, 2020.

National School Climate Council. (2009). *National school climate standards: Benchmarks to promote effective teaching, learning and comprehensive school improvement.* Accessed at www.schoolclimate.org/themes/schoolclimate/assets/pdf/policy/school-climate -standards.pdf on January 12, 2021.

Nelson, B., Parker, S., & Siegel, D. (2014). Interpersonal neurobiology, mindsight, and integration: The mind, relationships, and the brain. In K. Brandt, B. Perry, S. Seligman, & E. Tronick (Eds.), *Infant and early childhood mental health: Core concepts and clinical practice* (pp. 129–143). Arlington, VA: American Psychiatric Publishing.

Nguyen, T. D., Cannata, M., & Miller, J. (2016). Understanding student behavioral engagement: Importance of student interaction with peers and teachers. *The Journal of Educational Research.* Accessed at http://dx.doi.org/10.1080/00220671.2016.1220359 on August 12, 2021.

Niehaus, K., Moritz Rudasill, K., & Rakes, C. (2012). A longitudinal study of school connectedness and academic outcomes across sixth grade. *Journal of School Psychology, 50*(4), 443–460.

Niemi, K. (2020). CASEL is updating the most widely recognized definition of social- emotional learning. Here's why. *The 74 Million Blog.* Accessed at www.the74million .org/article/niemi-casel-is-updating-the-most-widely-recognized-definition-of-social -emotional-learning-heres-why/ on August 5, 2021.

Oberle, E., Domitrovich, C. E., Meyers, D. C., & Weissberg, R. P. (2016). Establishing systemic social and emotional learning approaches in schools: A framework for schoolwide implementation. *Cambridge Journal of Education, 46*(3), 277–297. Accessed at http://dx.doi.org/10.1080/0305764X.2015.1125450 on May 21, 2021.

Osher, D., Cantor, P., Berg, J., Steyer, L., & Rose, T. (2020). Drivers of human development: How relationships and context shape learning and development. *Applied Developmental Science, 24*(1), 6–36.

Oxford, M., & Findlay, D. (2019). *NCAST caregiver/parent-child interaction: Teaching manual.* Seattle: Parent-Child Relationship Programs at the Barnard Center, University of Washington.

Pajares, F., Britner, S. L., & Valiante, G. (2000). Relation between achievement goals and self-beliefs in middle school students in writing and science. *Contemporary Educational Psychology, 25*(4), 406–422.

Park, D., Gunderson, E. A., Tsukayama, E., Levine, S. C., & Beilock, S. L. (2016). Young children's motivational frameworks and math achievement: Relation to teacher-reported instructional practices, but not teacher theory of intelligence. *Journal of Educational Psychology, 108*(3), 300–313. Accessed at http://doi.org/10.1037/edu0000064 on May 21, 2021.

Peeters, J., De Backer, F., Reina, V. R., Kindekens, A., Buffel, T., & Lombaerts, K. (2013). The role of teachers' self-regulatory capacities in the implementation of self-regulated learning practices. *Procedia—Social and Behavioral Sciences, 116.* Accessed at doi:10.1016/j.sbspro.2014.01.504 on May 21, 2021.

Perry, B. (n.d.). *NN Covid-19 stress, distress & trauma series.* Accessed at www.neurosequential.com/covid-19-resources on May 21, 2021.

Perry, B. (2014). The neurosequential model of therapeutics: Application of a developmentally sensitive and neurobiology-informed approach to clinical problem solving in maltreated children. In K. Brandt, B. Perry, S. Seligman, & E. Tronick (Eds.), *Infant and early childhood mental health: Core concepts and clinical practice* (pp. 21–32). Arlington, VA: American Psychiatric Publishing.

Perry, B. (2016). Creating an emotionally safe classroom. *Early Childhood Today Magazine. Scholastic.* Accessed at www.scholastic.com/teachers/articles/teaching-content/creaing-emotionally-safe-classroom/ on August 20, 2021.

Perry, B. (2020a). *Emotional contagion: Neurosequential network stress & trauma series* [Video file]. Accessed at www.youtube.com/watch?v=96evhMPcY2Y&feature=youtu.be on May 21, 2021.

Perry, B. (2020b). *Understanding regulation: Neurosequential network stress & trauma series* [Video file]. Accessed at https://youtu.be/L3qIYGwmHYY on September 11, 2020.

Peterson, K., & Deal, T. (1998, Sept.). How leaders influence the culture of schools. *Educational Leadership, 56*(1), 28–30.

Porges, S. W. (2004). Neuroception: A subconscious system for detecting threats and safety. *Zero to Three,* 19–24. Accessed at https://static1.squarespace.com/static/5c1d025fb27e390a78569537/t/5ccdff181905f41dbcb689e3/1557004058168/Neuroception.pdf on September 11, 2020.

Porges, S. W. (2017). *The pocket guide to the polyvagal theory: The transformative power of feeling safe* (1st ed.). New York: Norton.

Puteh, M., Che Ahmad, C. N., Mohamed Noh, N., Adnan, M., & Ibrahim, M. H. (2015). The classroom physical environment and its relation to teaching and learning comfort level. *International Journal of Social Science and Humanity, 5*(3), 237–240.

Quality Talk. (n.d.). *What is quality talk?* Accessed at www.qualitytalk.psu.edu/quality -talk on November 13, 2020.

Rattan, A., Good, C., & Dweck, C. S. (2012). "It's ok—Not everyone can be good at math": Instructors with an entity theory comfort (and demotivate) students. *Journal of Experimental Social Psychology, 48*(3), 731–737. Accessed at http://doi.org/10.1016/j .jesp.2011.12.012 on May 24, 2021.

Riddle, T., & Sinclair, S. (2019). Racial disparities in school-based disciplinary actions are associated with county-level rates of racial bias. *Proceedings of the National Academy of Sciences, 116*(17), 8255–8260. Accessed at https://doi.org/10.1073/pnas.1808307116 on May 24, 2021.

Rimm-Kaufman, S. E., & Chiu, Y. I. (2007). Promoting social and academic competence in the classroom: An intervention study examining the contribution of the Responsive Classroom approach. *Psychology in the Schools, 44*(4), 397–413. Accessed at https://doi .org/10.1002/pits.20231 on May 24, 2021.

Robert Wood Johnson Foundation. (n.d.). *Social and emotional learning: Establishing social and emotional skills that provide a foundation for success in school, work and life.* Accessed at www.rwjf.org/socialemotionallearning on December 11, 2019.

Roffey, T. (n.d.). *Why makerspace?* Accessed at www.makerspaceforeducation.com/why -makerspace.html on November 13, 2020.

Rogoff, B. (2003). *The cultural nature of human development.* Oxford: Oxford University Press.

Rosenberg, G. G., Blake-Rahter, P., Heavner, J., Allen, L., Redmond, B. M., Phillips, J., & Stigers, K. (1999). Improving classroom acoustics (ICA): A three-year FM sound field classroom amplification study. *Journal of Educational Audiology, 7,* 8–28.

Rucker, N. W. (2019). Getting started with culturally responsive teaching. *Edutopia.* Accessed at www.edutopia.org/article/getting-started-culturally-responsive-teaching on October 24, 2021.

Rudasill, K. M., Reio, T. G., Stipanovic, N., & Taylor, J. E. (2010). A longitudinal study of student–teacher relationship quality, difficult temperament, and risky behavior from childhood to early adolescence. *Journal of School Psychology, 48*(5), 389–412. Accessed at doi: 10.1016/j.jsp.2010.05.001 on May 24, 2021.

Schilling, D. L., & Schwartz, I. S. (2004). Alternative seating for young children with autism spectrum disorder: Effects on classroom behavior. *Journal of Autism and Developmental Disorders, 34*(4), 423–432. Accessed at https://pubmed.ncbi.nlm.nih. gov/15449517/ on May 24, 2021.

Schneider, M. (2002). *Do school facilities affect academic outcomes?* Accessed at https://files .eric.ed.gov/fulltext/ED470979.pdf on November 11, 2020.

Schueler, B. E., Capotosto, L., Bahena, S., McIntyre, J., & Gehlbach, H. (2014). Measuring parent perceptions of school climate. *Psychological Assessment, 26*(1), 314– 320. Accessed at doi:10.1037/a0034830 on May 24, 2021.

Schunk, D. H., & Rice, J. M. (1993). Strategy fading and progress feedback: Effects on self-efficacy and comprehension among students receiving remedial reading services. *Journal of Special Education, 27*(3), 257–276.

Shabiralyani, G., Hasan, K. S., Hamad, N., & Iqbal, N. (2015). Impact of visual aids in enhancing the learning process case research: District Dera Ghazi Khan. *Journal of Education and Practice, 6*(19), 226–233.

Shishegar, N., & Boubekri, M. (2016). *Natural light and productivity: Analyzing the impacts of daylighting on students' and workers' health and alertness* [Conference paper presentation]. International Conference on Health, Biological and Life Science, Istanbul, Turkey.

Shonkoff, J. P., & Phillips, D. A. (2000). *From neurons to neighborhoods: The science of early childhood development.* Washington, DC: National Academies Press. Accessed at www.ncbi.nlm.nih.gov/books/NBK225562 on May 24, 2021.

Simmons, D. (2019). Why we can't afford whitewashed social-emotional learning. *ASCD Education Update, 61*(4). Accessed at https://www.ascd.org/el/articles/why-we-cant-afford-whitewashed-social-emotional-learning on March 28, 2021.

Simmons, D. (2021). Why SEL alone isn't enough. *Educational Leadership, 78*(6), 30–34. Accessed at www.ascd.org/publications/educational-leadership/mar21/vol78/num06/Why-SEL-Alone-Isn%27t-Enough.aspx on April 6, 2021.

Skiba, R. J., Arredondo, M. I., & Williams, N. T. (2014). More than a metaphor: The contribution of exclusionary discipline to a school-to-prison pipeline. *Equity & Excellence in Education, 47*(4), 546–564.

Souto-Manning, M. (n.d.). Defining culturally responsive teaching. *Heinemann Blog.* Accessed at https://blog.heinemann.com/defining-culturally-responsive-teaching#:~:text=Adapted%20from%20No%20More%20Culturally%20Irrelevant%20Teaching%20GenevG,more%20relevant%20to%20and%20effective%20for%20them%22%20%2831%29 on October 24, 2021.

Strong-Wilson, T., & Ellis, J. (2007). Children and place: Reggio Emilia's environment as third teacher. *Theory Into Practice, 46*(1), 40–47.

Swan, A. J., Carper, M. M., & Kendall, P. C. (2015). In pursuit of generalization: An updated review. *Behavior Therapy, 47*(5). Accessed at https://doi.org/10.1016/j.beth.2015.11.006 on May 24, 2021.

Tatter, G. (2019). *Teaching social and emotional skills all day.* Accessed at www.gse.harvard.edu/news/uk/19/01/teaching-social-and-emotional-skills-all-day on May 24, 2021.

Taylor, R. D., Oberle, E., Durlak, J. A., & Weissberg, R. P. (2017). Promoting positive youth development through school-based social and emotional learning interventions: A meta-analysis of follow-up effects. *Child Development, 88*(4), 1156–1171.

Tervalon, M., & Murray-García, J. (1998). Cultural humility versus cultural competence: A critical distinction in defining physician training outcomes in multicultural education. *Journal of Health Care for the Poor and Underserved, 9*(2), 117–125.

Thomas, J. W. (2000). *A review of research on project-based learning.* Accessed at http://live-buckinstitute.pantheonsite.io/sites/default/files/2019-01/A_Review_of_Research_on_Project_Based_Learning.pdf on May 24, 2021.

Thomas, J. W., Mergendoller, J. R., & Michaelson, A. (1999). *Project-based learning: A handbook for middle and high school teachers.* Novato, CA: Buck Institute for Education.

Thompson, B. N. (2017, July 3). Theory of mind: Understanding others in a social world [Blog post]. *Psychology Today.* Accessed at www.psychologytoday.com/us/blog

/socioemotional-success/201707/theory-mind-understanding-others-in-social-world on February 3, 2020.

Tomasello, M. (2019). *Becoming human: A theory of ontogeny.* Cambridge, MA: Belknap Press of Harvard University Press.

Tomlinson, C. A., & Moon, T. R. (2013). *Assessment and student success in a differentiated classroom.* Alexandria, VA: Association for Supervision and Curriculum Development.

Toshalis, E., & Nakkula, M. J. (2012). *Motivation, engagement, and student voice.* Accessed at www.studentsatthecenter.org/topics/motivation-engagement-and-student-voice on May 24, 2021.

Toub, T. S., Rajan, V., Golinkoff, R. M., & Hirsh-Pasek, K. (2016). Guided play: A solution to the play versus discovery learning dichotomy. In D. C. Geary & D. B. Berch (Eds.), *Evolutionary perspectives on child development and education* (pp. 117–141). Accessed at https://doi.org/10.1007/978-3-319-29986-0_5 on May 24, 2021.

Trites, N. (2017). *What is co-teaching? An introduction to co-teaching and inclusion.* Accessed at http://castpublishing.org/introduction-co-teaching-inclusion on November 14, 2020.

Tronick, E. (2014). Typical and atypical development: Peek-a-boo and blind selection. In K. Brandt, B. Perry, S. Seligman, & E. Tronick (Eds.), *Infant and early childhood mental health: Core concepts and clinical practice* (pp. 55–70). Arlington, VA: American Psychiatric Publishing.

Tronick, E., & Gold, C. M. (2020). *The power of discord: Why the ups and downs of relationships are the secret to building intimacy, resilience, and trust.* New York: Little, Brown and Company.

van Druten-Frietman, L., Strating, H., Denessen, E., & Verhoeven, L. (2016). Interactive storybook-based intervention effects on kindergartners' language development. *Journal of Early Intervention, 38*(4), 212–229.

Van Heck, J. (2017). *The relationship between roles and responsibilities of co-teachers and co-teacher self-efficacy.* [Dissertation]. Accessed at https://digitalscholarship.unlv.edu/cgi/viewcontent.cgi?article=4181&context=thesesdissertations on November 14, 2020.

VDOE. (2015). *History and social science standards of learning for Virginia Public Schools—March 2015: Grade three.* Accessed at www.doe.virginia.gov/testing/sol/standards_docs/history_socialscience on January 14, 2021.

VDOE. (2019). *2018 Virginia science standards of learning curriculum framework.* Accessed at www.doe.virginia.gov/testing/sol/standards_docs/science/2018/frameworks/science3.pdf on April 21, 2021.

Volante, L., DeLuca, C., & Klinger, D. A. (2019). *Here's how teaching must adapt in the age of globalization.* Accessed at www.weforum.org/agenda/2019/02/culturally-responsive-teaching-in-a-globalized-world on December 2, 2020.

Wacker, C., & Olson, L. (2019). *Teacher mindsets: How educators' perspectives shape student success.* Accessed at www.future-ed.org/wp-content/uploads/2019/06/Final-report_Teacher-Mindsets.pdf on May 24, 2021.

Walker, C. O., & Greene, B. A. (2009). The relations between student motivational beliefs and cognitive engagement in high school. *The Journal of Educational Research, 102,* 463–472.

Walker, T. (2016). *The evidence is in: 'Happy' schools boost student achievement.* Accessed at www.nea.org/advocating-for-change/new-from-nea/evidence-happy-schools-boost-student-achievement on January 10, 2021.

Watanabe, M. (2008). Tracking in the era of high stakes state accountability reform: Case studies of classroom instruction in North Carolina. *Teachers College Record, 110,* 489–534.

Waterford.org. (2019). 51 mindful exercises for kids in the classroom. *Waterford Blog.* Accessed at www.waterford.org/resources/mindfulnes-activities-for-kids/ on August 21, 2021.

Willen, L. (2015). *"Edu-speak" is a disease that undermines efforts to improve U. S. schools.* Accessed at https://hechingerreport.org/edu-speak-is-a-disease-that-undermines-efforts-to-improve-u-s-schools on December 17, 2020.

Williams, A. M. (2011). *The use of morning meeting to develop social and emotional skills* [Thesis]. Accessed at https://fisherpub.sjfc.edu/cgi/viewcontent.cgi?article=1201&context=education_ETD_masters on January 14, 2021.

Willingham, D. T. (2009). *Why don't students like school?: A cognitive scientist answers questions about how the mind works and what it means for the classroom.* San Francisco, CA: Jossey-Bass.

Willis, J. (2010). The current impact of neuroscience on teaching and learning. In D. A. Sousa (Ed.), *Mind, brain, & education: Neuroscience implications for the classroom* (pp. 45–67). Bloomington, IN: Solution Tree Press.

Wills, T. (n.d.). *Collaborative games: Play TOGETHER. Interact with other players in real time.* Accessed at www.theresawills.com/games on April 19, 2021.

Wills, T. (2021). *Teaching math at a distance: A practical guide to rich remote instruction.* Thousand Oaks, CA: Corwin.

Winfrey, O. (2011). *The powerful lesson Maya Angelou taught Oprah.* Accessed at www.oprah.com/oprahs-lifeclass/the-powerful-lesson-maya-angelou-taught-oprah-video on August 6, 2021.

Wood, C. (2015). *Yardsticks: Children in the classroom ages 4–14* (3rd ed.). Turner Falls, MA: Center for Responsive Schools, Inc.

Woolner, P., Hall, E., Higgins, S., McCaughey, C., & Wall, K. (2007). A sound foundation? What we know about the impact of environments on learning and the implications for building schools for the future. *Oxford Review of Education, 33*(1), 47–70. Accessed at doi: 10.1080/03054980601094693 on May 24, 2021.

Yolen, J. (2014). *How do dinosaurs stay safe?* New York: Blue Sky Press.

Zenger, J., & Folkman, J. (2013). *The ideal praise-to-criticism ratio.* Accessed at https://hbr.org/2013/03/the-ideal-praise-to-criticism on October 23, 2020.

Index

Q

R

Y

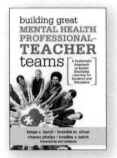
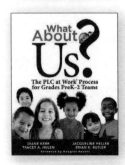

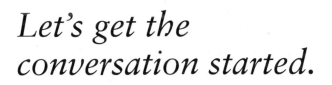